AUTOMATED ACCOUNTING 7.0

Windows® 3.1 • Windows® 95

Warren W. Allen, M.A.
Dale H. Klooster, Ed.D.

JOIN US ON THE INTERNET
WWW: http://www.thomson.com
EMAIL: findit@kiosk.thomson.com   A service of I(T)P®

South-Western Educational Publishing

an International Thomson Publishing company I

3 5100 00000049 4

Cincinnati • Albany, NY • Belmont, CA • Bonn • Boston • Detroit • Johannesburg • London • Madrid
Melbourne • Mexico City • New York • Paris • Singapore • Tokyo • Toronto • Washington

Team Leader: Eve Lewis

Editors: Mark Beck, Mark Cheatham, Janet Kinney, Carol Sturzenberger, Cassandra Washington

Internal Design: Graphica

Cover Design: Ann Small

Cover Illustration: Kenneth Spengler

Marketing Manager: Nancy Long

Marketing Coordinator: Tina Edmondson

ISBN: 0-538-66249-2

1 2 3 4 5 6 7 8 WCB 02 01 00 99 98 97

Printed in the United States of America

International Thomson Publishing

We are living in an era in which powerful, low-cost personal computers are meeting a wide variety of business record-keeping and accounting needs. During the past two decades we have seen, and will continue to see, expansion of personal computers that now use powerful graphical user interface operating systems such as Microsoft® Windows®[1] and OS/2 from IBM®[2]. The *Automated Accounting 7.0* software that accompanies this textbook enables students to learn how computers are used for accounting applications with today's powerful computer systems.

Major Features

The major feature of *Automated Accounting 7.0* is its seamless integration within the *Automated Accounting 7.0* software applications of general ledger, accounts payable, accounts receivable, bank reconciliation, plant assets, budgeting, payroll, inventory, and sales order processing. For example, as payroll transactions are entered, the resulting journal entry is immediately placed into the general ledger. In addition, menu options are available to generate periodic journal entries such as depreciation adjusting entries and employer's payroll taxes. The *Automated Accounting 7.0* software also offers integration with other applications such as spreadsheets and word processors via copy and paste capabilities.

Highlights of *Automated Accounting 7.0*

This version of *Automated Accounting 7.0* retains the features that made the previous Windows and DOS versions successful while taking full advantage of the innovations of the respective graphical user interface operating systems. It will run in the Windows 3.x, Windows NT, and Windows 95 environments. The design and development of the software follows the standard conventions of each of these graphical user interface operating systems. This standardization has been tremendously helpful to users. When you have learned to use one application, you have learned the essentials for using most other applications that run in the same environment. The authors have taken great care in the development of the software to follow the standard interface to ensure that operating procedures learned while running other applications are immediately transferable to *Automated Accounting 7.0*. Likewise, the operating procedures learned while running *Automated Accounting 7.0* are immediately transferable to other applications.

---

[1]Microsoft and Windows are registered trademarks of Microsoft Corporation. Any reference to Microsoft or Windows refers to this footnote.
[2]IBM is a registered trademark of International Business Machines Corporation. Any reference to IBM refers to this footnote.

The major features of this version of *Automated Accounting 7.0* include the following:

1. All of the frequently used options are accessible by clicking on a toolbar button which takes the user to a window with multiple tabs. The tabs access the various data entry screens, which are now grid-based so that multiple transactions can be entered into the grid rather than requiring a one-at-a-time approach—thereby making entering transactions much easier.

2. A tool tips feature allows the user to place the mouse pointer over a toolbar button and a "tool tip" will appear, indicating what that button will do. A menu item is available that allows the feature to be turned on and off.

3. A comprehensive setup/customization capability has been provided that permits customization to be collected in one place and contained in one window with six tabs.

4. A Features selection is provided that allows the user to select which systems are active. The accounting system is always active. Plant assets, payroll, inventory, and budgeting are optional. If a system is not selected, all traces of it disappear from the software. For example, if payroll is inactive, the employee maintenance and payroll transaction tabs disappear from the respective input windows, all menu options pertaining to payroll disappear, and all payroll reports disappear from the report selection.

5. The setup process is far more intuitive. For example, the classify accounts defaults to the most likely possibility so most often no keying is needed. The required accounts needed for system integration are automatically determined by examining account titles based upon the type of business and business organization.

6. A journal wizard is provided that allows users to create their own journal columns and to tailor journals to the many varieties of problems in the textbook.

7. A tax table is provided that allows the user to change federal and state tax tables, as well as tax rates and limits for Social Security, Medicare, unemployment, and city tax rates.

8. Five planning tools have been added to this version of the software for personal use as well as for problems in the textbook. The planning tools are the: (1) college planner, (2) savings planner, (3) retirement planner, (4) loan planner, and (5) notes and interest planner.

9. The software now generates the actual closing entries that look like those prepared manually. Journal entries are no longer purged during

the closing process; therefore, errors discovered after closing can be corrected easily.

10. A powerful application integration capability is available that permits all the accounting reports to be copied to the clipboard for pasting to a spreadsheet or word processor.

11. An optional check writing feature is available that will prepare checks when a cash payment transaction involving a vendor is posted.

12. A menu option to automatically generate the depreciation adjusting entries for plant assets is provided.

13. The payroll system has been substantially improved. Employee maintenance and transactions are entered in a grid so that multiple employee data can be viewed on the same screen.

14. Menu options are available that automatically generate the journal entry to record the payroll and the employer's payroll taxes.

15. An option to generate payroll checks is provided. When this option is used, a payroll check will be generated after each employee's payroll transaction data is entered.

16. The inventory system has been enhanced in that transactions are entered in a grid so that multiple transactions can be viewed on the same screen.

17. An order processing capability has been added to this version of the software, which provides the ability to process sales orders on the computer. As the invoice is processed, the system automatically generates a sales invoice and updates inventory, the sales journal, the customer account, and the general ledger accounts.

18. A budgeting system has been provided for income statement accounts. A budget report can be generated that shows an income statement with account balances, budgets, and variances.

19. Reports are displayed in a more attractive font than that used in the previous editions.

20. A printer setup option is available that utilizes the Windows common dialog for selecting the printer and printer options.

21. The software now has a user-selectable font, font size, etc., so that users can exploit their particular printer capabilities.

22. A graphing feature is provided that automatically generates a variety of different graphs from the following data: (1) income statement, (2) expense distribution, (3) actual vs. budgeted income statement, (4) balance sheet, and (5) sales.

23. Data files are upward compatible from the previous edition of Windows as well as DOS versions 4 and 5.

24. Run dates (which appear on all reports) are automatically determined by the software. When a report is selected, the default run date appears as editable text so it can be accepted or changed. All dates used by the computer can be changed by clicking on a calendar icon button and selecting the desired date, by striking the + and – keys, or by keying the desired date.

25. A more comprehensive, context-sensitive help system has been provided that offers a quick way to find information about operating the software.

Organizational Features

The textbook consists of thirteen chapters and three comprehensive problems. Each chapter begins with an introduction that describes the topics to be covered. The introduction is followed by the operating procedures with ample illustrations and notes required to process the accounting material presented, and a chapter summary. A computer tutorial problem follows that contains detailed step-by-step instructions for completing a problem that covers the material presented in the chapter. Following the tutorial problem is a student exercise, a computer practice problem, and a computer mastery problem. The computer practice and mastery problems have accompanying audit questions designed to interpret the computer-generated output. Also, each computer problem contains optional spreadsheet and word processing activities that utilize the information generated by the computer. These optional activities are not required to complete the problems; however, if access to a spreadsheet and/or word processor is available, it is highly recommended that they be completed.

Learning Objectives

This courseware package is intended for students who want to learn about computerized accounting principles. Therefore, the major objectives of this book and its associated software are: (1) to present and integrate accounting principles in such a way that no prior knowledge of computers or computerized accounting is required, (2) to provide a hands-on approach to learning how modern computerized automated accounting systems function, and (3) to provide knowledge and hands-on experience in integrating accounting with other business applications such as spreadsheets and word processors. Each chapter identifies the learning objectives to be mastered for that chapter.

Additional flexibility has been designed into the computer software to permit use with most traditional accounting textbooks. The computer may be used to solve manual accounting problems in these textbooks.

Message to the Student

The *Automated Accounting 7.0* software is designed so that computer-generated output and the accounting procedures are very similar to those currently used in business and industry. The significant difference between the software used in this package and an actual business system is the simplicity of computer operation.

When a business uses a computerized system to control such valuable assets as cash, inventory, and accounts receivable, very tight controls are maintained on security, data entry, and audit trail procedures. These controls often complicate the operation of a computerized system. Some of these restrictions have been intentionally omitted from this package to simplify the operations and provide a usable, relevant educational tool.

Message to the Instructor

This package has been designed so that the material and the computer problems presented in this textbook can be introduced gradually through the use of template (opening balances) files that permit the processing of ongoing accounting systems. In this way, students can concentrate on learning accounting topics while they gain experience with the various features of the software.

Each chapter contains a tutorial problem. Each chapter also contains a student exercise and two computer challenge problems (with audit questions) to ensure that the students comprehend the material presented. This approach permits the students to work independently and at their own speed.

An instructor's manual is provided to assist you while using *Automated Accounting 7.0*. In addition, a solution checker disk called The Electronic Auditor is available to automatically check your students' solutions against the solutions that are installed to your hard disk along with the Auditor software. These solution files contain the same data provided in print in the instructor's manual.

Required Hardware

The *Automated Accounting 7.0* package can be installed and executed on computers capable of running the Microsoft Windows 3.x, Windows NT, and Windows 95 operating systems. A minimum of 2 megabytes of memory is required. Approximately 2 megabytes of hard disk space are required. Access to a printer is optional but recommended.

Acknowledgments

We would like to express our appreciation to all who have provided helpful comments and suggestions. Many useful comments from instructors and students have resulted in significant improvements in the textbook and software. We would also like to acknowledge the excellent support received from the sales, editorial, and production staffs at South-Western Educational Publishing. Their expertise, professionalism, and commitment to quality have made our association with them a rewarding working experience.

Warren W. Allen
Dale H. Klooster

Brief Contents

Contents

CHAPTER 2   General Ledger—Service Business   41

CHAPTER 3   General Ledger—End-of-Fiscal-Period for a Service Business and Bank Reconciliation   69

CHAPTER

4   Purchases and Cash Payments   109

CHAPTER 13 | Accounting System Setup   439

JOIN US ON THE INTERNET VIA WWW, FTP, OR EMAIL:

WWW: http://www.swpco.com
FTP: ftp.thomson.com
EMAIL: findit@kiosk.thomson.com

Through *swpco.com,* Internet users can search catalogs, examine subject-specific resource centers, and subscribe to electronic discussion lists.
For technical support, you may email **hotline_education@kdc.com**
For more information about *Century 21 Accounting,* visit our Web site at **http://www.swpco.com/swpco/bus_ed/acctg_ed.html**

A service of I(T)P®

1 Introduction

Tooltip

Menu Bar

Title Bar

Toolbar

Point

Click

Drag

Point and Click

Double Click

Drop-Down Menu

Menu Title

Shortcut Key

Menu Item

Access Key

Select

Choose

Window

Focus

Text Box

Grid Cells

Selection List Box

Option Button

Check Box

Command Button

Tab Sequence

Clipboard

LEARNING OBJECTIVES

Upon completion of this chapter, you will be able to:

1. Describe the capabilities of *Automated Accounting 7.0* and perform *Automated Accounting* installation and start-up procedures.

2. Perform general operating procedures.

3. Perform operating procedures related to using menu bar and toolbar items.

INTRODUCTION

Professional business managers and accountants need to know how to use computers in order to be efficient in performing accounting tasks. This program will teach you computerized accounting and accounting spreadsheet applications using a hands-on approach. You will learn to enter realistic accounting transactions for a variety of business applications and generate financial statements and spreadsheet and other management information reports.

The *Automated Accounting 7.0* software makes use of a standard computer user interface (Windows) that utilizes drop-down menus, a toolbar, movable overlapping windows, mouse support, on-screen help, and other operational conventions. Because this software uses your operating system's standard user interface, visual and functional consistency is achieved within and across a wide array of different software applications. This consistency facilitates the learning process and greatly reduces the need to retrain for each new application you use in the future.

The Software

Automated Accounting 7.0 contains integrated software designed to handle general ledger, accounts payable, accounts receivable, financial statement analysis processing, bank reconciliation, plant assets, order processing, inventory, and payroll. In addition, data from the *Automated Accounting 7.0* software may be transferred into most modern spreadsheet programs (for example, Lotus 1-2-3, Quattro, Excel) for further analysis and processing. Report contents may be transferred into most word processing programs (for example, Word, Works, WordPerfect) for use in reporting activities or presentations. You are not

E T H I C S

Using a computer to access another computer user's data can actually be a criminal activity. This activity is commonly referred to as "hacking." The term hacking is often used by computer enthusiasts to describe the challenge of breaking codes or other protection schemes that prohibit unauthorized access. Hackers that break codes to access other users' confidential information, records, computer time, and so on are committing a crime.

a. Do you think that most hackers realize they are committing a criminal act?

b. What can be done to deter hacking?

c. A hacker gains unauthorized access to government records but leaves the information unharmed. Do you believe this behavior is ethical or unethical? Explain.

required to have access to spreadsheet or word processing software in order to use *Automated Accounting 7.0*. However, each of the end-of-chapter problems contains optional steps for spreadsheet and word processing analysis and reporting.

This Textbook

Each chapter begins with an introduction that describes the topics to be covered. The introduction is followed by the operating procedures required to process the accounting material presented. A computer tutorial problem follows the introductory section. The tutorial contains detailed step-by-step instructions for completing a problem that covers the material presented in the chapter. It is recommended that you read the material in the chapter prior to attempting to complete the tutorial problem unless you are experienced with the computer interface being used. Following the tutorial problem is a student exercise, an independent practice problem, and a mastery problem.

At any time while using the software, the Help system may be accessed for additional assistance.

This text will make learning the *Automated Accounting 7.0* software easy and will allow you to locate reference information quickly and easily. Some of the software and text features and benefits are

1. A context sensitive Help system unique to the user interface you are using allows you to receive on-line help during critical stages of problem solving.

2. Windows, drop-down menus, menu items, toolbar buttons, and other features used to control the operation of the software (such as buttons, check boxes, text boxes, lists, and so on) are shown and explained in detail throughout this textbook. This will allow you to master the operation of the software quickly.

3. Useful illustrations and notes are provided throughout the text to help you better understand *Automated Accounting* concepts.

4. Completed input forms are illustrated to lead you step by step through a problem.

5. Use of planning tools for common personal and business financial applications are explained so you may become familiar with common financial planning tools.

6. Detailed step-by-step operational procedures are provided throughout each chapter and in your computer's Help system that can be used as a reference to successfully complete the end-of-chapter problems.

Various screen illustrations may appear slightly different than on your computer's display screen, since *Automated Accounting 7.0* adheres to the standard user interface used by your computer. The location and names

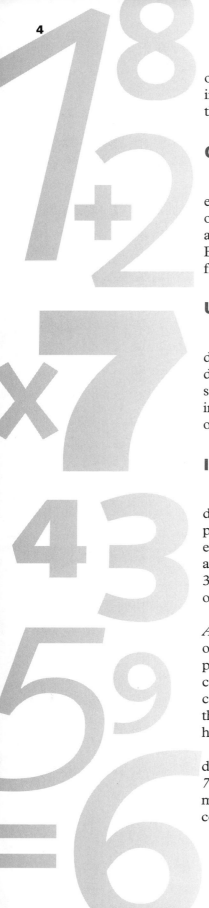

of buttons, options, text boxes, and so on may differ based upon the interface used (for example, Open and Save As dialog boxes). However, the functions that they perform are the same.

Opening Balance Data

The installation disks contain files that have opening balance data for each problem in the textbook. When *Automated Accounting 7.0* is installed on your hard disk drive or network server, the opening balance files will automatically be included in the same directory/folder as the software. Before a problem can be solved, the opening balances file must be loaded from this directory/folder.

User Data Files

Automated Accounting 7.0 permits you to store data on a separate data disk, hard disk, or network file server. This feature enables you to save data for future reference or completion. If you are using a floppy disk to save your data, make sure that it is properly formatted before use. For information on formatting a disk, refer to your computer system's operations manual.

Installation and Memory Requirements

Automated Accounting 7.0 comes complete on two 3½-inch high density disks. To use the software you need an IBM system 386 or higher processor (or 100% compatible computer) running in the Windows environment with a minimum of 2MB of available RAM memory. In addition, a hard disk drive with at least 2MB of available disk space and a 3½-inch high density disk drive for installation is required. A printer is optional but highly recommended.

The disks included in the software package contain compressed *Automated Accounting 7.0* programs, opening balance files, and the optional spreadsheet opening balance files required to complete all the problems in this textbook. During the installation process, all of these compressed files are expanded into an executable format onto your computer's hard disk. Detailed step-by-step instructions are provided on the installation disk labels. Your instructor or computer center technician has probably already completed this one-time installation procedure.

Important Note: It is possible, in rare cases, that the computer's default or user selected colors may conflict with *Automated Accounting 7.0*. If you experience any problems with colors, adjustments may be made through the control panel. It is recommended that the default colors for the operating system be used.

MOUSE	DESCRIPTION
Point	Moving the pointer (⇖) to a specific location on the screen.
Click	Quickly pressing and releasing the mouse button.
Drag	Pressing and holding down the mouse button and moving the mouse.
Point and Click	Pointing to an object on the screen and clicking on the mouse button. For example, if you are directed to "click on" Cancel, you should point to the Cancel button and click on the left mouse button.
Double-Click	Pointing to an object on the screen and clicking on the mouse button twice very rapidly, once to select the item (highlight the item) and once to choose it.

Table 1.1
Common Mouse Operations

Automated Accounting 7.0 System Start-Up

Table 1.1 describes the mouse terminology and common operations used in this textbook. Refer to this table as necessary during system start-up. Additional instructions and equivalent keyboard operations that accomplish many of the same tasks performed with the mouse will be discussed later in this chapter. The following steps will allow you to begin working with *Automated Accounting 7.0* (after the installation has been completed):

1: **Turn on your computer and find the *Automated Accounting 7.0* icon (if necessary, open the group window or folder that contains *Automated Accounting 7.0*).**

2: **Load *Automated Accounting 7.0* by double-clicking on the *Automated Accounting 7.0* icon.**

3: **After the software loads, copyright information will appear immediately underneath the application window toolbar shown in Figure 1.1. Click the mouse button, or press any keyboard key, to dismiss the copyright information.**

Automated Accounting 7.0 contains several components to perform accounting processing tasks. Review Figure 1.1 to acquaint yourself with terminology and location of the information provided. Notice the information message dialog "End Automated Accounting Program." This is called a Tooltip. A **tooltip** is an explanation of a toolbar icon that occurs when the mouse is dragged over an icon. As shown in Figure 1.1, the "End Automated Accounting Program" message appears when the pointer is positioned on the Exit toolbar button icon.

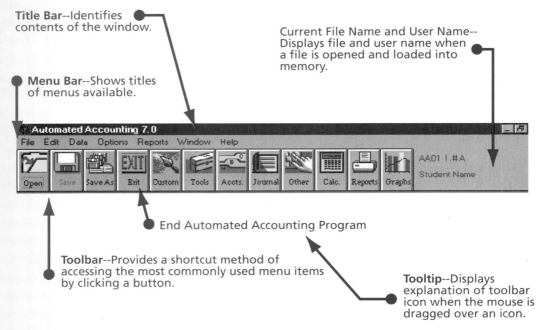

Title Bar--Identifies contents of the window.

Current File Name and User Name--Displays file and user name when a file is opened and loaded into memory.

Menu Bar--Shows titles of menus available.

End Automated Accounting Program

Toolbar--Provides a shortcut method of accessing the most commonly used menu items by clicking a button.

Tooltip--Displays explanation of toolbar icon when the mouse is dragged over an icon.

Figure 1.1
Automated Accounting 7.0 Application Window

OPERATING PROCEDURES—GENERAL

The following topics cover use of the menu bar, menu item selection, window controls, navigation, and other special features that have been provided to make the operation of the software easy to learn and efficient to use.

The Menu Bar

One of the ways to communicate with the computer is to use the menu bar. As shown in Figure 1.1, the menu bar used by *Automated Accounting 7.0* contains seven menu titles—File, Edit, Data, Options, Reports, Window, and Help. Each title contains menu items that instruct the computer to perform processing tasks. The type of menu used in *Automated Accounting 7.0* is called a **drop-down menu.** A drop-down menu is a list of menu items that displays immediately below the selected menu title. Figure 1.2 illustrates the parts of the *Automated Accounting 7.0* File drop-down menu.

You may use the mouse or keyboard to select drop-down menus and choose menu items. Table 1.2 describes keyboard keys that you will find useful when working with drop-down menus. If an item is "dimmed", it is not available.

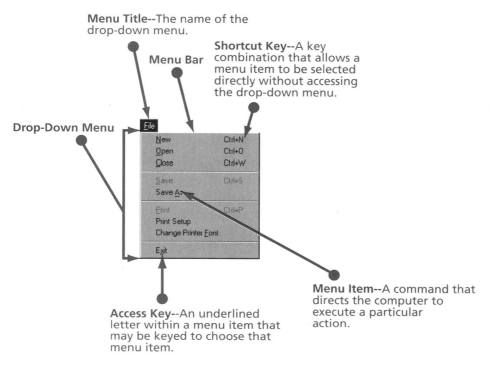

Menu Title--The name of the drop-down menu.

Shortcut Key--A key combination that allows a menu item to be selected directly without accessing the drop-down menu.

Menu Bar

Drop-Down Menu

Menu Item--A command that directs the computer to execute a particular action.

Access Key--An underlined letter within a menu item that may be keyed to choose that menu item.

Figure 1.2
Drop-Down Menu

KEYBOARD	DESCRIPTION
Alt/Option	Use this key to transfer control to the menu bar to select a drop-down menu.
Esc	Use this key to release control from the menu bar or to remove any drop-down menu.
Down Arrow	Use this key to drop down a menu. Each time this key is pressed while a menu is pulled down, the highlight bar will move down to the next menu item. If the highlight bar is on the last menu item, it will wrap around to the first menu item.
Up Arrow	Use this key to move the highlight bar up to the previous menu item within a drop-down menu.
Right Arrow	Use this key to select the next menu title.
Left Arrow	Use this key to select the previous menu title.
Enter/Return	Use this key to choose the currently highlighted menu title or menu item.

Table 1.2
Keyboard Operation used with Drop-Down Menus

Selecting and Choosing Menu Titles and Menu Items

In this text, the terms select and choose have different meanings. **Select** means to highlight a menu title on the menu bar or a menu item. **Choose** means to direct the software to take an appropriate action. A highlighted (or selected) menu title or item is *chosen* by clicking the OK button. An item may be selected and chosen simultaneously by double-clicking on an object. Dimmed items are not available for selection. You may need to select another item or perform a processing task before a dimmed item is activated.

1: Pull down the menu by pointing to the desired menu title on the menu bar and clicking on the left mouse button.
When using the keyboard, press the Alt/Option key. When the Alt/Option key is pressed, the first menu item on the menu bar is selected.

2: Point to the menu item and click on the left mouse button. As a shortcut, move directly to a menu item, point to the menu title, and drag the highlight bar down the menu until the desired item is highlighted; then release the mouse button.
When using the keyboard, press the left or right arrow key to select a menu title, then press Enter/Return to choose the selected menu title. If the menu item has an access key (underlined letter), you can choose it by typing the access key. For example, to choose Open, type O.

Window Controls

Interaction with *Automated Accounting 7.0* is accomplished through windows. A **window** is a rectangular area of the screen in which the software is communicating with the user. Often the display screen contains only one window. At times, two or more overlapping windows may appear on the screen. However, only one window is active at a time.

Automated Accounting uses several different windows to perform its accounting activities. For example, some windows consist of text boxes and grid cells used to enter data from the keyboard, some contain lists and reports, and others may display dialog messages and operational information. Regardless of the activity, the location within a window in which the software will receive the next piece of input is said to have the **focus.** For example, a data field that has the focus is identified by the insertion point (also referred to as the pipe character), which appears as a vertical bar (|). A decision or choice of several options that has the focus is identified by a dotted rectangular box.

Many of the windows that appear may be moved, resized, made inactive/active, and so on. Reference the Help system for specific information regarding moving a window, changing its size, or making it inactive/active for the user interface you are using. You will be shown how to use the Help system later in this chapter. You may also reference your computer's user interface operations manual.

It is important to understand how the operational controls in the windows enable you to enter and edit data, generate reports, select items from lists, and navigate the grids and controls. Refer to this section of the text for reference as you encounter these controls later in this textbook. The following paragraphs identify the controls used by this software and describe how to utilize these controls.

Tabs *Automated Accounting 7.0* has been designed to use the visual image of folders to clarify and simplify operation. Various menu items (or toolbar selections) contain windows that include multiple folders with identifying tabs. Tabs provide for additional entry of data, options, and processing. For example, the Account Maintenance folder that appears when the *Maintain Accounts* menu item is chosen from the Data menu (or the *Accts.* Toolbar button is clicked) is shown in Figure 1.3. Notice the window contains three different tabs: Accounts, Vendors, and Customers. The first tab (Accounts) appears as the active tab and is used to maintain accounts in the chart of accounts. To switch to another account maintenance item within the window, simply click on the desired tab. For example, to perform vendor maintenance click on the tab labeled Vendors.

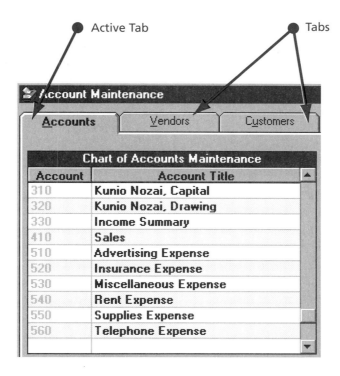

Figure 1.3
Tabs in the Account Maintenance Window

Text Boxes   A **text box** is a field into which the user keys information. An example of a text box is shown in Figure 1.4. The user can accept the current text, edit it, or delete it. When a text box receives the focus, existing text is selected and the insertion point appears to the right of the last character of text. Selected text is highlighted (indicated with light text on a dark background). An example of selected text is shown in Figure 1.5. If the insertion point is moved, the text is unselected. If the user keys data with text selected, the selected text is discarded and replaced with the newly keyed data.

Figure 1.4
Text Box

| Company Name | Nozai Travel Services |

Figure 1.5
Text Box with Selected Text

| Company Name | Nozai Travel Services |

Grid Cells   Most of the data you will enter into the Automated Accounting software will be entered into windows that contain grid cells. Like text boxes, **grid cells** are an arrangement of rows and columns that is used to enter, edit, or delete data and text. When a grid cell receives the focus, any existing data or text within it is selected (highlighted) and the insertion point appears to the right of the last character within the cell.

Figure 1.6 shows an example of how data appears when it has been entered into grid cells. Notice a $20.00 Debit, with a reference of C715, has been selected. If the insertion point is moved within the cell, the text is unselected and the contents may be edited. If the user keys data in a selected grid cell, the selected text within the cell is discarded and replaced with the newly keyed data. In the next chapter you will learn how to enter data into grid cells.

1: Move the pointer to the left of the text to be selected.
When using the keyboard, use the directional keys to place the insertion point to the left of the text to be selected.

2: Click and drag the insertion point over the text to be selected.
When using the keyboard, hold down the shift key and press the Right Arrow key.

Calendar Control   When you are required to enter dates, you'll access the calendar through the calendar icon shown at the top of Figure 1.7. A calendar's year, month, and date may be selected by pointing and clicking the mouse. The date text box which has the focus will receive the

Selected grid cell

Date	Refer.	Acct. No.	Debit	Credit
		110		80.00
10/08/--	M214	120	205.95	
		250		205.95
10/09/--	C715	530	20.00	
		110		20.00
10/10/--	C716	120	45.00	
		110		45.00
10/10/--	C717	130	285.00	
		110		285.00

Figure 1.6
Example of Grid Cells

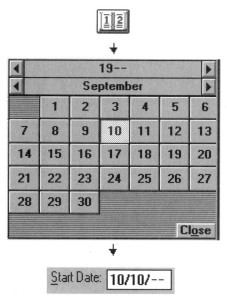

Figure 1.7
Calendar Control

date from the calendar. The calendar may be used to set starting and ending dates to control data printed in reports or to specify the date that is to appear on a report. The calendar shown in Figure 1.7 appears when the calendar icon is clicked.

Each time the right arrow of the year box on the calendar is clicked, the year will increase one. Each time the left arrow is clicked, the year will decrease by one. The desired month may be selected in a similar manner. Simply clicking on the desired day of the month will select that day of the month and year shown. As the date is being selected, it will appear in the corresponding text box in the mm/dd/yy format as shown in Figure 1.7.

1: **Click on the appropriate right arrow to increase the year or month.**

2: **Click on the appropriate left arrow to decrease the year or month.**

3: **Click the desired day of the month and year.**

4: **Click the *Close* command button to exit the calendar.**

Selection List Boxes   A **selection list box** is a list of choices associated with a text box from which the user may choose. A list box and a drop-down list are similar in that each allows the user to select a single entry from a list of items. They differ in appearance and in the way list items are selected.

List Box   Figure 1.8 shows a chart of accounts list box. A highlight bar (or underline) identifies the currently selected item. To choose an item, highlight the item by clicking on it, then click OK. As an alternative, double-click on the desired item. Both the mouse and keyboard can be used to scroll through the list and choose items from the list. Table 1.3 illustrates how items are scrolled using the mouse and keyboard.

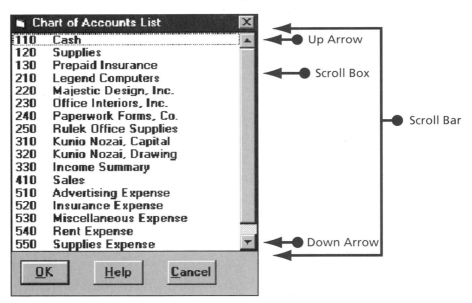

Figure 1.8
List Box

Drop-Down List   The drop-down list consists of a text box with a drop-down arrow button immediately to the right. The text must be selected from among the items present in the drop-down list. The drop-down list control does not allow the user to key new data that is not in the existing list into the text box. However, the user may key an item that is in the drop-down list into the text box. Upon keying the first one or more characters, the computer will search the list and place the first occurrence of the matching item from the list in the text box.

ACTION	MOUSE OPERATIONS
Scroll Up One Line	Click on the up arrow (⬆) located at the top of the scroll bar to scroll upward.
Scroll Down One Line	Click on the down arrow (⬇) located at the bottom of the scroll bar to scroll downward.
Scroll Up One Page	Click anywhere within the scroll bar between the up arrow and scroll box to scroll up one page.
Scroll Down One Page	Click anywhere within the scroll bar between the down arrow and scroll box to scroll down one page.
Scroll Anywhere	Click-and-drag the scroll box along the scroll bar to the relative vertical position of the report to scroll anywhere within a report. For example, to scroll to the middle of the report, click-and-drag the scroll box to the middle of the scroll bar.
ACTION	**KEYBOARD OPERATION**
Scroll Up One Line	Up Arrow key.
Scroll Down One Line	Down Arrow key.
Scroll Up One Page	Page Up.
Scroll Down One Page	Page Down. The first time this key is pressed, the highlight bar moves to the bottom of the first page. Each time thereafter, the list is paged down one full page.

Table 1.3
Mouse and Keyboard Operations to Scroll Items in a List Box

A drop-down list used to control the customizing of a report is shown in Figure 1.9 before it has been opened. The same drop-down list is shown in Figure 1.10 after it has been opened. If the drop-down list contains more items than will fit, a scroll bar will be included. To toggle a drop-down list between open and closed, click on the drop-down arrow or press Alt/Option+Down Arrow (while holding down the Alt/Option key, strike the Down Arrow key).

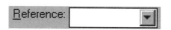

Figure 1.9
Drop-Down List (Closed)

1: **Click on the drop-down arrow to open the list. Click on the drop-down arrow a second time to close the list.**
When using the keyboard, while the drop-down list control has the focus, press Alt/Option+Down Arrow.

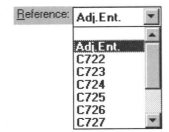

Figure 1.10
Drop-Down List
(Open)

2: **Click on the desired item.**
    When using the keyboard, use the arrow keys to select the
    desired item. Then press Enter/Return to choose the selected
    item.

    Important Note: While the drop-down list has the focus, an
    easy way to select an item from the list is to type the first
    character of the desired item. The first occurrence will appear
    in the text box. Succeeding occurrences of items starting with
    the same character can be accessed by subsequent striking of
    the key corresponding to the first character. As an alternative,
    you may use the up arrow and down arrow keys to scroll
    through the items until the desired item is displayed in the text
    box.

Option Buttons   An **option button,** also commonly referred to as a
radio button, is a selection method that represents a single choice within
a set of mutually exclusive choices. You can select only one button from
the choices provided. Option buttons are represented by circles. When an
option is selected, the circle is filled (⊙). When an option is not selected,
the circle is empty. (See Figure 1.11.)

• **Click on the desired option.**
    When using the keyboard, press the Tab key to navigate to the
    appropriate group of option buttons. Then use the directional
    arrow keys to select the option desired.

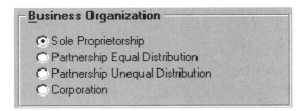

Figure 1.11
Option Buttons
within a Group
Box

Check Boxes   A **check box** is a box located to the left of each of several choices that contains either a blank or a check mark and permits the user to select or deselect the choices. When a task requiring multiple choices is selected, a group section will appear containing check boxes (□) to the left of each choice. The check boxes are turned On or Off in any combination. When a check box is selected, it contains a check mark (☑) or an X inside it. Figure 1.12 shows the check boxes that allow the user to select the Plant Assets and Inventory features of the software.

```
┌─Features────────────────────────────────┐
│  ┌──────────────────────────────────┐  │
│  │ ☑  Plant Assets                   │  │
│  │ ☐  Payroll                        │  │
│  │ ☑  Inventory                      │  │
│  │ ☐  Budgeting                      │  │
│  └──────────────────────────────────┘  │
└──────────────────────────────────────────┘
```

Figure 1.12
Check Boxes

- **To select a check box, click on the box or the label to toggle the check box On or Off.**
  When using the keyboard, use the directional keys to select the desired check box. Then press the Space Bar to toggle it On or Off.

Command Buttons   A **command button** is a rectangular shaped figure containing a label that specifies an immediate action or response that will be taken by the software when the command button is chosen. Figure 1.13 illustrates three command buttons.

Figure 1.13
Command Buttons

- **To choose a command button, click on the command button.**
  When using the keyboard, use the Tab key to navigate to the desired command button. Then, while the command button has the focus, press the Enter/Return key.

When a command button has a dotted line and/or shadow around the button (see the OK button in Figure 1.13), it is said to be the default button. The default command button can be chosen from anywhere in the window by pressing the Enter/Return key.

Navigation

Grid cells, text boxes, option buttons, check boxes, and command buttons should be keyed or selected in the normal tab sequence. The **tab sequence** is the logical order in which the program expects the user to proceed. The sequence is usually left to right and top to bottom. Table 1.4 describes keys that you will find useful when navigating within and among controls.

KEY	FUNCTION
Tab	Use this key to move the focus to the next control in the tab sequence.
Shift+Tab	Strike the Tab key while holding down the Shift key to move the focus back to the previous control in the tab sequence.
Enter/Return	Press the Enter/Return key to choose the action or response of the default command button or command button that currently has the focus.
Home	Use the Home key to move the insertion point to the first position within the current text box.
End	Use the End key to move the insertion point to the last position within the current text box.
Right/Down Arrow	Use the Right ($\rightarrow$) key to move the insertion point one position to the right within the text box. Also, use these arrow keys to select option buttons within an option group.
Left/Up Arrow	Use the Left ($\leftarrow$) key to move the insertion point one position to the left within the text box. Also, use these arrow keys to select option buttons within an option group.
Backspace	Use this key, within a text box, to erase the character immediately to the left of the insertion point.
Delete	Use the Del key, within a text box, to erase the character to the right of the insertion point.
Esc	Use the Esc key to choose Cancel or Close within the active window, tab, list, or dialog box.

Table 1.4
Keys Used to
Navigate, Enter,
and Edit Data

OPERATING PROCEDURES—USING MENU BAR AND TOOLBAR ITEMS

The following topics cover use of the File, Edit, Data, Options, Reports, Window, and Help menus. In addition, the operating procedures for using the on-screen calculator are covered.

File Menu

When File is selected from the menu bar, the menu shown in Figure 1.14 appears.

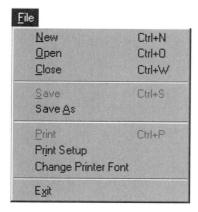

Figure 1.14
File Menu

New   New erases any existing data in the computer's memory and establishes an empty accounting system file. New does *not* remove any data from disk.

Open   Open will load the data file so the file may be used.

1: **Choose *Open* from the File menu or click on the Open toolbar button.**

2: **Choose the disk drive containing the file you wish to open.** The directories/folders on the selected drive will appear in the Directories/Folders list box.

3: **If the file you wish to load appears in the File Name list box, choose it by highlighting it and clicking the OK command button.**

4: **If the file you wish to load does not appear in the File Name list box, choose the directory/folder that contains the file and return to the previous instruction.**

If the file you have loaded is an opening balance file for one of the end-of-chapter problems, you will be prompted to enter your name into the user name dialog box shown in Figure 1.15.

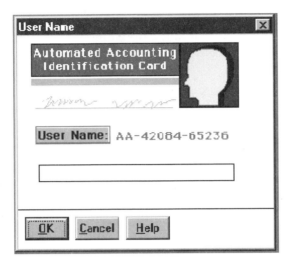

Figure 1.15
User Name
Dialog Box

Close   Close will close the current file displayed in the active window and remove the data from the computer's memory. The active window and all other windows containing data from the same file will be closed. Close does *not* remove any data from disk.

Save   Save will save your data to disk so that you can continue a problem in a later session. The data will be saved in the current path with the file name displayed near the upper right corner of the application window. If you wish to save your data with a path (disk drive and/or directory/folder) or file name different from the current path and file name, use Save As.

- **Choose Save from the File menu or click on the Save toolbar button.**

Before you use Save, check the current file name in the upper right corner of the window to make certain you want to save with this name. If not, use Save As to save with a different name.

Note that you *cannot* save a file to disk with the same file name as an opening balance file.

Save As   Save As is the same as Save except that the data can be saved with a path and/or file name different from the current path and file name. Save As is useful for making a backup or copy of a data file. For example, you may want to make a backup of your data file before keying adjusting entries or before performing period-end closing. To make a backup copy, open the data file you wish to back up and use Save As to save it under a different name.

1:   **Choose *Save As.***
     A Save As dialog will appear.

2:   **Choose the disk drive to which you wish to save your file.**

3:   **Choose the directory/folder into which you wish to save your file.**
     If you are using a floppy disk to save your work, make sure your formatted data disk is in the appropriate disk drive. If you are using the hard disk to store your work, it is recommended that you save your data files to your own directory/folder.

4:   **Key the file name under which you would like the data file saved.**

5:   **Click the OK command button.**

Print   Print will generate a hard copy of your data. The entire contents of the window will be printed when Print is chosen.

Print Setup   Print Setup provides choices about the printer(s) connected to your computer, the paper size, printing enhancements, and so on. *Automated Accounting 7.0* uses the current printer information specified in your computer's user interface when asked to print. Check with your instructor for the proper information before making changes.

Change Printer Font   Change Printer Font will allow you to change the printer font, style, and/or size to make reports more attractive or to make the size smaller if fields are overflowing or wrapping incorrectly. Also, changing the font to one that is native to the printer you are using (for example, Courier) will often increase the print speed.

1:   **Choose *Change Printer Font* from the File menu.**
     The Font dialog box appears.

2:   **Select the name of the font you want to use.**
     Or type the name of the font in the Font text box.

3:   **Select the font style (such as regular, bold).**

4: **Select a size for the font.**
    Or type the new size in the Size text box.

5: **Click *OK*.**

Exit   Exit will enable you to quit *Automated Accounting 7.0*. Exit is
the standard command for Windows users. When Exit is chosen, the
computer checks to see if the current data in its memory has been
saved. If not, a dialog box will appear asking if you wish to save your
data.

Edit Menu

The Edit menu (shown in Figure 1.16) contains several menu
items that can be used to remove and copy data from one location
within *Automated Accounting* as well as to/from other application
programs.

Figure 1.16
Edit Menu

Cut, Copy, and Paste   The Cut and Copy menu items may be used
to remove or copy then paste the current selection. (The current
selection is data that is highlighted in text or cell grid boxes.) The current
selection is moved or copied to the clipboard in preparation for being
pasted elsewhere. The **clipboard** is a temporary storage area where a
report may be copied then pasted into another software application such
as a spreadsheet or word processor. Cut erases the current selection;
Copy leaves the current selection intact. The clipboard command in
Automated Accounting 7.0 works the same as it does in other applications:

1: **Select the source you want to copy or cut.**

2: **Click *Copy* to copy the selected data to the clipboard, or *Cut* to
    copy and remove the data from its present location.**

3: **Select the destination. The destination can be a text or grid
    box or other data field.**

4: **Click *Paste* to paste the data from the clipboard into the destination.**
    Caution: If the destination already contains data, you'll overwrite it when you choose Paste. Be careful that you allow enough space for the complete source to be pasted.

Find and Find Next   Find and Find Next help you locate data. Both of these features will be discussed in detail as they are utilized throughout the text.

Data Menu

When the Data menu is chosen, the drop-down menu shown in Figure 1.17 will appear. These features will be discussed in detail as they are presented throughout the text. Discussion of the Planning Tools feature follows because each of the tool planners is included in selected end-of-chapter problems in this text.

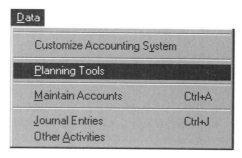

Figure 1.17
Data Menu

Planning Tools   Planning tools, as shown in Figure 1.18, are convenient, fast, easy-to-use ways of producing results for commonly used applications. These applications may be for your personal use and/or business use. Five different planners are available: college, savings, loan, retirement, and notes & interest. Each of these planners direct the computer to calculate different information. To use the planner, select the tab identifying the planner, enter the data required, and click the *Report* button to calculate the desired result(s) and display a report.

The College Planner is used to show you how to select calculation options, enter data, and generate a report(s) showing the results using

An accounting file does not have to be loaded into memory in order to use any of the planning tools.

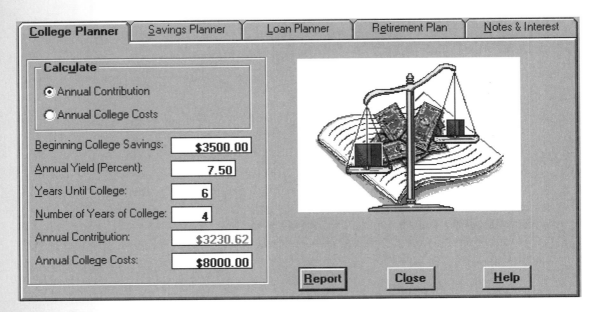

Figure 1.18
College Planner

any of the planning tools provided. The operational procedure of each of the planning tools is the same.

The College Planner is used to calculate the amount of an annual contribution required to reach a particular savings amount and calculate the amount saved for each year of college. A completed College Planner is illustrated in Figure 1.18. The Figure shows the Calculate option set to Annual Contribution and the data entered into the appropriate text boxes. The following steps illustrate how to select options, enter data, and display a report.

1: Choose *Planning Tools* from the Data menu or click the *Tools* toolbar button.

2: Select the desired planning tool by clicking the appropriate tab. In this example, the College Planner is the default and is already selected.

3: Select the desired Calculate option by using the arrow keys or mouse. In this example, the Annual Contribution option is selected.

4: Enter the data in the text boxes.
   Note: As data is entered, and the computer performs the calculations, the Annual Contribution text box will display the calculated result as a dimmed value indicating that this is a calculated amount that cannot be keyed.

5: Click on *Report* to produce a report.

6: **Click on *Close* to exit the report.**
Repeat the above steps with a different Calculate option and/or data if desired.

7: **Click on *Close* to exit Planning Tools.**

Options Menu

When the Options menu is chosen, a drop-down menu will appear. Each of these features will be discussed in detail as they are utilized throughout the text.

Reports Menu

When *Report Selection* is chosen from the Reports menu or the *Reports* toolbar button is chosen, the Report Selection dialog box shown in Figure 1.19 will appear. The Run Date text box that appears at the top right is the date that will appear on the report. This date may be changed by keying the new date or by clicking on the calendar icon and using the calendar as discussed earlier.

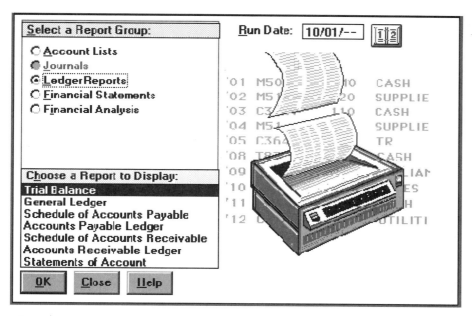

Figure 1.19
Report Selection Dialog

Option buttons are provided for various types of accounting system reports. A report is chosen by choosing the option button for the desired report. Based on the option button chosen, a list of all the reports within the chosen option will appear. Select the desired report and choose *OK*. If there is insufficient data to generate a particular report, that button will be dimmed to indicate that it is not active. The corresponding information that is displayed in the report window can be printed to an attached printer and/or copied for inclusion in another application (such as a spreadsheet or word processor).

After choosing OK, the report will appear in the scrollable report window shown in Figure 1.20. The report can be printed by choosing the Print command button that appears at the bottom of the report window.

Nozai Travel Services
Trial Balance
10/01/--

Acct. Number	Account Title	Debit	Credit
110	Cash	14089.95	
120	Supplies	891.83	
130	Prepaid Insurance	165.64	
220	Majestic Design, Inc.		248.21
230	Office Interiors, Inc.		281.58
240	Paperwork Forms, Co.		80.49
310	Kunio Nozai, Capital		14537.14
	Totals	15147.42	15147.42

Print   Help   Close   Copy

Figure 1.20
Trial Balance

Copying Report Contents to the Clipboard   At any time while a report is displayed in a report window, its entire contents can be copied to the temporary storage area known as the clipboard, replacing any previous contents. Once copied to the clipboard, the report may be pasted (copied) to another application that is running. For example, a trial balance report displayed in a report window can be copied to the clipboard then pasted into a spreadsheet or word processing document. This procedure is commonly referred to as copy and paste.

1: **While the report appears in the report window, click on the Copy command button located at the bottom of the report window.**

2: **When the Copy Report to Clipboard dialog appears (see Figure 1.21), select the desired option button for spreadsheet or word processor format.**
    The entire report will be copied to the clipboard.

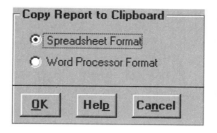

Figure 1.21
Copy Report to
Clipboard

Printing the Contents of a Report Window   At any time while
a report is displayed in a report window, it can be printed by choosing
the Print command button located at the bottom of the window.

Window Menu

As you work with *Automated Accounting 7.0,* you open windows
within the *Automated Accounting 7.0* application window. All of the open
windows are listed below the *Close All Windows* menu item. Figure 1.22
shows that the Account Maintenance, Journal Entries, and Report
Selection windows are currently open. Report Selection is the active
window as identified with a check mark to the left of its name.

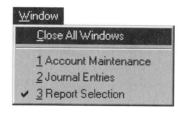

Figure 1.22
Window Menu

You can close all of the windows within the application window by
choosing Close All Windows. You can switch to any of the open windows
by choosing it from the Window menu.

Help Menu

The on-screen Help system for *Automated Accounting 7.0* offers a
quick way to find information about operating the software. If you are
unfamiliar with the Help system, choose *How to Use Help* to obtain
information on using the Help system.

To access Help you can (1) choose either the *Contents* or *Search for
Help On* menu item from the Help menu; (2) press the F1 function key
at any time; or (3) choose the Help command button that appears at the
bottom of various windows. In each case, a Help window will appear.

The topic that is displayed depends on which Help command you chose or which window you were using when you chose the Help button. Within a Help topic, there may be one or more *jumps,* which you can click (or select and press Enter) to display a new Help topic. The Help window illustrating the Save and Save As menu items is shown in Figure 1.23.

Choose
Contents
to see
list of
Help
topics.

Choose
Search to
get help on
a specific
topic.

Words with
underlines
are
definitions
or examples.
Click on the
word to see
the
definition
or example.

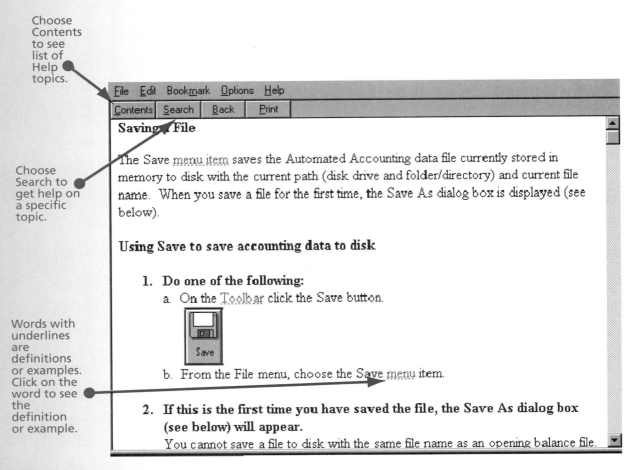

Figure 1.23
Help Window

You can use the Search window to find words or topics quickly by clicking on the Search command button. A Search window similar to that shown in Figure 1.24 will appear. The Search window shown in Figure 1.24 will also appear if you choose the Search for Help On menu item in the Help menu.

Search for a word
or phrase that you
wish to learn more
about, click the
entry you want,
then display your
selection.

You can scroll this
list to select the word
or phrase as
an alternative to
entering a word.

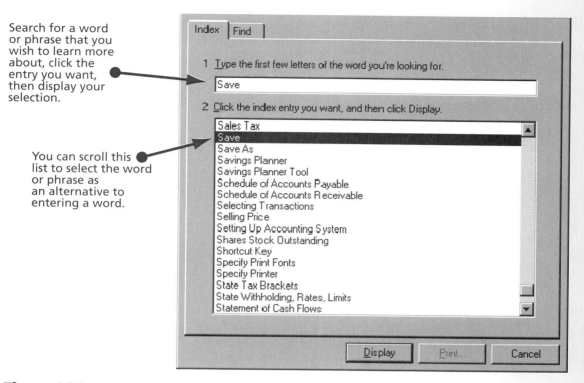

Figure 1.24
Help Search Window

You can browse through the Help system like you page through a
book. For a list of topics in *Automated Accounting 7.0,* choose the
Contents command button from any Help window or by choosing the
Contents menu item from the Help menu. The *Automated Accounting 7.0*
help contents window is shown in Figure 1.25. Notice that this window
consists of seven major topics. When one of these topics is chosen, a
detailed list of sub-topics will appear from which you may select the
desired help information. Figure 1.25 shows the sub-topics that appear
when the Common Tasks topic is selected.

Internet Relay Chats (IRCs) are live discussions
between participants in a "chat room." Chat
groups can be found all over the Internet.
Nearly every commercial service has a chat
group feature.

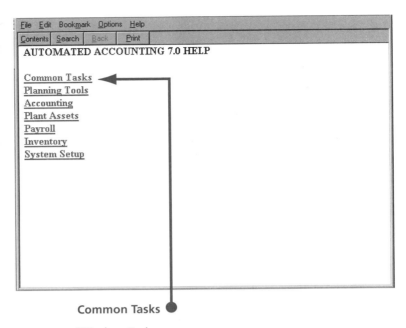

Figure 1.25
Help Contents
Window (with
Common Tasks
Sub-Window)

On-Screen Calculator

The on-screen calculator is operated like a hand-held calculator. The results can be pasted into the text box that has the focus. Once the Calculator appears, as shown in Figure 1.26, a Help menu is available from the calculator providing detailed explanation of the calculator operation.

1: **Choose the Calculator menu item from the Options menu or click on the Calculator toolbar button.**

2: **Enter the first number in the calculation. You can use the mouse or keyboard.**
    The number appears in the calculator's display.

3: **Choose the operator you want to use in the calculation.**

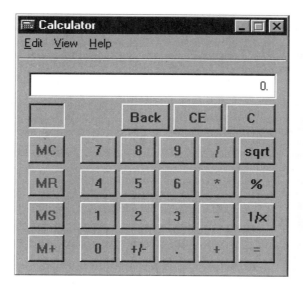

Figure 1.26
Example On-
Screen Calculator

4: **Enter the next number in the calculation.**

5: **Enter any remaining numbers and operations.**

6: **Click on the equal sign (=), or strike the = key from the keyboard.**

Chapter Review

1. *Automated Accounting 7.0* contains integrated features designed to handle general ledger, accounts payable, accounts receivable, financial statement analysis, bank reconciliation, fixed assets, order processing, inventory, and payroll. In addition, data may be transferred to spreadsheet and word processing applications for a variety of other accounting-related uses.

2. One of the ways you communicate with the computer is to use the menu bar. When a menu is chosen from the menu bar, a list of menu items that instruct the computer to perform its processing tasks displays immediately below the menu title. *Automated Accounting* uses several different windows to perform its accounting activities. At times, two or more overlapping windows may appear on the screen. However, only one window is active at a time. Some windows contain tabs consisting of text boxes and grid cells used to enter data from the keyboard, some contain lists and reports, and others may display dialog messages and operational information. Tab sequence is the logical order in which the program expects the

An Internet address is a set of numbers or words that identifies a unique user or computer. Every user and computer on the Internet must have a different address so that the system knows to send electronic mail and other data.

user to proceed. The sequence is usually left to right and top to bottom. The focus identifies the location within a window in which the computer will receive the next piece of input.

3. All accounting activities are performed by choosing a menu bar or toolbar item.

ACCOUNTING CAREERS IN DEPTH

And just what are the career options open to those students who specialize in accounting?

Accounting education provides many career paths. Some accounting careers are more challenging than others. It all depends on your interest, ambition, and perseverance. Ask yourself how you like spending your workday and what kind of life-style you want to have.

There are different levels of education and skill required of accountants. For example, you may want to become a Certified Public Accountant (C.P.A.). To accomplish this goal, you must receive your high school diploma. Next, you will need to get a college education and then pass the C.P.A. examination.

Every single type of business needs accountants. Therefore, students have a unique opportunity to combine other interests with accounting by finding employment in a business area most appealing to them.

Accounting Careers in Depth will present you with a view of different careers in accounting and various industries that would allow you to use your skills. It is important to remember that if college is not a choice for you, there are still many job opportunities available. In many cases, these accounting jobs provide career advancement and continuing education courses in areas related to your accounting position.

Accounting Careers in Depth may be your window to a future in accounting.

TUTORIAL   PROBLEM   1–T

In this tutorial problem, you will practice what you have learned in this chapter. Follow the step-by-step instructions. Each step lists a task to be completed at the computer. More detailed information on how to complete the task is provided immediately following the step. If you need additional operating instructions in order to complete the task, refer to the Operating Procedures section of the chapter. Before starting this problem, be sure you have a properly formatted data disk (or established hard disk directory/folder) for saving your data.

STEP 1:   **Start up *Automated Accounting 7.0.***
Click on the *Automated Accounting 7.0* icon.

STEP 2:   **Open the file named AA01–T.**
Choose *Open* from the File menu or click on the *Open* toolbar button. When the Open file dialog box appears, select the drive and directory/folder containing the opening balance files. Then choose file AA01–T from the File Name list box.

STEP 3:   **When the User Name dialog appears, enter your name in the User Name text box, and click *OK*.**
Check carefully that you have keyed your name correctly because you will not be able to change it for the duration of the problem.

STEP 4:   **Save the file. Enter a file name of XXX1–T where XXX are your initials.**
Choose *Save As* from the File menu or click the *Save As* toolbar button. Save the file to your disk and directory/folder as XXX1–T where XXX are your initials and 1–T represents Chapter 1 Tutorial Problem.

STEP 5:   **Experiment with using the How to Use Help information.**
Select How to Use Help from the Help menu.

STEP 6:   **Experiment using the Help system to obtain information about the Open menu item.**
Select *Open* from the File menu but do not release the mouse button. With *Open* still highlighted in the File menu, press the F1 function key. When the Help information appears, experiment clicking on the examples and related topics and the pop-up definitions. Choose Exit from the File menu when finished to dismiss the Help window and exit the Help system.

▶

TUTORIAL PROBLEM 1-T

STEP 7: **Experiment accessing the Search Help window to obtain information about the Save command.**
Choose *Search for Help On* from the Help menu. When the Search window appears, key *Save,* then click on the *Display/Show Topics* button. Click *Go To.* Close the Help report display window when finished.

STEP 8: **Experiment accessing Help information from the Contents window.**
Choose *Contents* from the Help menu. When the Contents window appears, experiment selecting Help information by clicking on various underlined topics. Click on the *Back* command to return to the Contents window. Close the Help document display window when finished.

STEP 9: **Use the on-screen calculator to multiply $2,892.50 times 2%.**
Choose *Calculator* from the Options menu or click the *Calculator* toolbar button. Make sure the calculator view is set to "standard." When the calculator appears, key the number *2892.50,* strike the asterisk key (* for multiply), key *2,* and then the % key. As an alternative, use the mouse to click on each of the appropriate keys to perform the calculation. The result should be 57.85. Close the calculator when finished.

STEP 10: **Calculate the annual contribution toward the cost of college using the College Planner.**

Choose *Planning Tools* from the Data menu or click the *Tools* toolbar button. When the Planning Tools window appears, click the College Planner tab if not already selected. Click the Annual Contribution option in the Calculate section, then enter the following information:

Beginning College Savings 3500.00
Annual Yield (Percent) 7.50
Years Until College   6
Number of Years of College   4
Annual College Costs 8000.00

After entering Annual College Costs, the calculated Annual Contribution will appear.

Click the Report button to display the report. The College Savings Plan Schedules for Annual Contribution is shown in Figure 1.27.

College Savings Plan
10/01/--

Schedule of College Savings

Year	Annual Contribution	Annual Yield	College Savings
(Beginning Balance)			3500.00
1	3230.62	262.50	6993.12
2	3230.62	524.48	10748.22
3	3230.62	806.12	14784.96
4	3230.62	1108.87	19124.45
5	3230.62	1434.33	23789.40
6	3230.62	1784.21	28804.23

Schedule of College Payments

College Year	Annual Payments	Annual Yield	Savings Balance
(College Savings)			28804.23
1	8000.00	1560.32	22364.55
2	8000.00	1077.34	15441.89
3	8000.00	558.14	8000.03
4	8000.03		.00

Figure 1.27
College Savings Plan Schedules for Annual Contribution

The report consists of two schedules based on the data in the college planner. The first schedule shows the annual contribution, annual yield, and the total amount saved each year until college. The second schedule shows the effect of the $8,000.00 per year payments. Note that the amount of savings continues to generate interest. The calculated annual contribution is $3,230.62. This is the annual amount of savings required to provide $8,000.00 per year for four years of college

T U T O R I A L   P R O B L E M   1 – T

expenses given the other data provided. When finished, close the report and planning tools windows.

STEP 11:   **Display the chart of accounts.**
Choose Report Selection from the Reports menu or click on the *Reports* toolbar button. When the Report Selection dialog appears, choose the Account Lists option. Make sure that the Chart of Accounts report is highlighted, then click on *OK*.

STEP 12:   **Print the chart of accounts.**
To print the report currently displayed, click the Print button at the bottom of the report window. Click the Close button to exit.

STEP 13:   **Display and print the trial balance.**
Choose the Ledger Reports option button. Make sure the Trial Balance report is highlighted, then click *OK*. When the report appears in the report window, click the Print command button.

STEP 14:   **Optional spreadsheet integration activity—copy and paste the trial balance into a spreadsheet:**
a.   If not already displayed, display the trial balance in the report window.
b.   Click on the *Copy* button and select the option to copy the report to the clipboard in spreadsheet format.
c.   Start up your spreadsheet application software.
d.   Open and load spreadsheet template file: SS01–T. While in the directory/folder containing the *Automated Accounting* opening balance files, look at *all* files to find file SS01–T. A message may display, stating that the file is read-only. Dismiss the message. You will be saving the changed file to a new name. Note: Column B has been formatted to accommodate the account title.
e.   Select cell A1 as the current cell if not already selected.
f.   Paste the trial balance (copied to the clipboard in step a) into the spreadsheet by choosing the Paste menu item from the Edit menu.
g.   Print the spreadsheet trial balance report (cells A1–D19). The completed trial balance report is shown in Figure 1.28.

▶

```
A                    B                    C         D
 1              Student Name
 2
 3              Nozai Travel Services
 4                Trial Balance
 5                As Of 10/01/--
 6
 7  Acct.    Account
 8  Number   Title                        Debit     Credit
 9
10    110    Cash                       14089.95
11    120    Supplies                     891.83
12    130    Prepaid Insurance            165.64
13    220    Majestic Design, Inc.                    248.21
14    230    Office Interiors, Inc.                   281.58
15    240    Paperwork Forms, Co.                      80.49
16    310    Kunio Nozai, Capital       ---------    14537.14
17
18             Totals                   15147.42    15147.42
19                                      =========    =========
```

Figure 1.28
Spreadsheet Trial Balance Report

Note: You may want to format your spreadsheet to look like Figure 1.28. For example, center align the headings. Additional formatting may be needed.

h. Save your spreadsheet with a file name of XXX1–T where XXX are your initials and 1–T identifies Tutorial Problem 1–T.

i. End your spreadsheet session and return to the *Automated Accounting* application.

STEP 15: **Save the data file.**
Click on the *Save* toolbar button. The file will be saved to disk with the current path and file name. Note the file name in the upper right corner of the *Automated Accounting* application window.

STEP 16: **End the *Automated Accounting 7.0* session.**
Click the *Exit/Quit* toolbar button.

Applying Your Information Skills

I. MATCHING

Directions: In the *Working Papers,* write the letter of the appropriate term next to each definition.

a. point	n. access key
b. click	o. select
c. drag	p. choose
d. point and click	q. window
e. double click	r. focus
f. title bar	s. text box
g. menu bar	t. grid cells
h. toolbar	u. selection list box
i. tooltip	v. option button
j. drop-down menu	w. check box
k. menu title	x. command button
l. shortcut key	y. tab sequence
m. menu item	z. clipboard

1. The name of the drop-down menu.

2. Quickly pressing and releasing the mouse button.

3. To direct the software to take an appropriate action.

4. The logical order in which the program expects the user to proceed.

5. Shows titles of menus available.

6. A list of items that displays immediately below the selected menu title.

7. A field into which the user keys information.

8. An underlined letter within a menu item that may be keyed to choose that menu item.

9. A key combination that allows a menu item to be selected directly without accessing the drop-down menu.

10. A rectangular area of the screen in which the software is communicating with the user.

11. A list of choices associated with a text box from which the user may choose.

12. A selection method that represents a single choice within a set of mutually exclusive choices.

13. A rectangular shaped figure containing a label that specifies an immediate action or response that will be taken by the software when the command button is chosen.

14. A box located to the left of each of several choices that contains either a blank or a ✓ and permits the user to select or deselect the choices.

15. Provides a shortcut method of accessing the most commonly used menu items by clicking a button.

16. An arrangement of rows and columns that is used to enter, edit, or delete data and text.

17. The location within a window in which the software will receive the next piece of input.

18. Moving the mouse pointer to a specific location on the screen.

19. Pressing and holding down the mouse button and moving the mouse.

20. Displays an explanation of the toolbar icon when the mouse is dragged over the icon.

21. A temporary storage area where a report may be copied then pasted into another software application such as a spreadsheet or word processor.

22. Pointing to an object on the screen and clicking on the mouse button.

23. To highlight a menu title on a menu bar or a menu item.

24. Identifies contents of the window.

25. A command that directs the computer to execute a particular action.

26. Pointing to an object on the screen and clicking on the mouse button twice very rapidly.

II. QUESTIONS

Directions: Write the answers to the following questions in the *Working Papers*.

1. Explain how the terms *select* and *choose* differ with regard to the way they are used in this text.

2. What is the purpose of the Alt/Option key?

3. What is contained on *Automated Accounting 7.0* installation disks?

4. How can you tell which command button is the default command button?

5. Briefly describe how menu items are chosen from a drop-down menu.

6. Explain how to switch from one tab to another within a window.

7. Explain the difference between the Save and Save As menu items.

8. How is the on-screen calculator accessed?

9. What is the significance of a "dimmed" menu item?

10. Briefly explain the procedure to obtain a printed copy of a report.

11. Explain the procedure to copy and paste the contents of a report into a spreadsheet application.

12. Identify the five planning tools provided in *Automated Accounting 7.0*.

Independent Practice Problem 1–P

In the following problem, you will practice what you have learned in this chapter. Practice problems are numbered with the current chapter number and a "P" (1–P for Chapter 1 Practice Problem).

STEP 1: Complete the Applying Your Technology Skills 1–P questions at the end of this section as you work through the following steps.

STEP 2: Start up *Automated Accounting 7.0*.

STEP 3: Open and load file AA01–P.

STEP 4: Enter your name in the User Name dialog.

STEP 5: Choose *Save As* and save the file with a file name of XXX1–P.

STEP 6: Access the Help system to obtain information about saving a file.

STEP 7: Use the on-screen calculator to multiply $5,165.50 times 2%.

STEP 8: Calculate the annual cost of college based upon savings using the College Planner. With the Annual College Costs option set on, enter the following data. Then display the schedule of college savings and payments reports.

```
Beginning College Savings . . . . . . . . . . . . . . .    3000.00
Annual Yield (Percent) . . . . . . . . . . . . . . . . . .     7.00
Years Until College . . . . . . . . . . . . . . . . . . . . .        8
Number of Years of College . . . . . . . . . . . . . .        4
Annual Contribution . . . . . . . . . . . . . . . . . . .   2400.00
```

STEP 9:   **Display the chart of accounts.**

STEP 10:   **Display the trial balance.**

STEP 11:   **Optional word processing integration activity—copy and paste the trial balance report into a blank word processor document:**
   a. Copy the trial balance to the clipboard in word processor format.
   b. Start up your word processing software and load template file WP01–P as a text file. While in the directory/folder containing the *Automated Accounting* opening balance files, look at *all* files to find file WP01–P.
   c. Replace FROM: Student Name with your name.
   d. Select the entire document and change it to a fixed font if necessary. Courier, type size 10, is preferred.
   e. Position the insertion point two lines after the last line in the document.
   f. Paste the trial balance from the clipboard into the document. The completed document is shown in Figure 1.29.
   Note: You may want to format your word processing document to look like Figure 1.29. For example, center align the Memorandum heading, trial balance report headings, and so on.
   g. Print the completed document.
   h. Save your document with a file name of XXX1–P where XXX are your initials.
   i. End your word processing session and return to the *Automated Accounting* application.

STEP 12:   **Click on the *Save* toolbar button to save the data file.**

STEP 13:   **End the *Automated Accounting* session.**

A host is a computer that is attached directly to the Internet and that provides services to users. Host computers are called *servers*.

```
                    INTEROFFICE MEMORANDUM

   TO:        Mrs. Davis, Controller

   FROM:      Student Name

   DATE:      October 1, 19--

   SUBJECT:   Trial Balance

   As per your request, the following trial balance
   reflects the account balances as of the end of the
   day, October 1:

                 Perez Employment Services
                      Trial Balance
                        10/01/--

   Acct.     Account
   Number    Title                    Debit        Credit

   110       Cash                    15425.49
   120       Supplies                  976.37
   130       Prepaid Insurance         181.34
   220       Becker Computer Center                   88.12
   230       Business Forms Plus                     271.74
   250       Office Mart Supply                      308.27
   310       Rosa Perez, Capital     ---------     15915.07

             Totals                  16583.20      16583.20
                                     =========     =========
```

Figure 1.29
Completed Word
Processing
Document

 Applying Your Technology Skills 1–P

Directions: Write the answers to the following questions in the *Working Papers* while completing Problem 1–P.

1. From the Save Help information, list the options in the Save As dialog box.

2. Using the calculator, what is 2 percent of $5,165.50?

3. From the college planner, what are the calculated annual college costs calculated in Step 8?

4. What account number is assigned to Sales?

5. What is the balance of the Cash account shown on the trial balance report?

6. What are the total debits and total credits shown on the trial balance report?

2
General Ledger— Service Business

LEARNING OBJECTIVES

Upon completion of this chapter, you will be able to:

1. Complete the general journal input form.

2. Enter chart of accounts maintenance data.

3. Enter and correct general journal transactions.

4. Display accounts, journal entries, graphs, and ledger reports.

INTRODUCTION

Many businesses that use computerized accounting systems enter data directly into the computer from source documents. **Input forms** are also used to organize and record accounting transaction data for entry.

In this chapter you will learn how to add, change, and delete accounts from a chart of accounts. You will learn how to record general journal entries onto an input form, enter and correct general journal entries, and generate corresponding reports and graphs. You will perform the accounting duties for Pittman Consulting. Pittman Consulting is organized as a **sole proprietorship.** A sole proprietorship is a business owned by one person.

CHART OF ACCOUNTS MAINTENANCE

The process of keeping a business's chart of accounts up to date by adding new accounts, changing titles of existing accounts, and deleting inactive accounts is called **account maintenance.** When the *Maintain Accounts* menu item is chosen from the Data menu, or the *Accts.* toolbar button is clicked on, the Account Maintenance window will appear. Click on the *Accounts* tab to display the Accounts window shown in Figure 2.1.

Adding a New Account

1:   **Enter the account number in the Account column at the end of the list then strike the Tab key.**

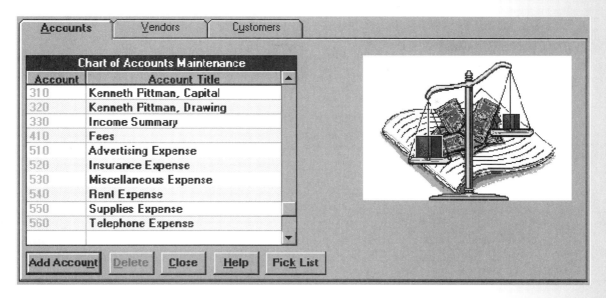

Figure 2.1
Accounts Maintenance

2: **Enter the title for the new account.**

3: **Click the *Add Account* button.**
    The new account will be inserted into the chart of accounts in account number sequence.

4: **Click the *Close* button to exit the Accounts window.**

Changing an Account Title

1: **Select the account title that you wish to change.**

2: **Enter the correct account title.**

3: **Click the *Change* button. When an account title is changed, the *Add Account* button becomes *Change.***
    Note: The account number cannot be changed. An account with an incorrect account number must be deleted then added as a new account with the correct number.

Deleting an Account

1: **Select the account that you wish to delete.**

2: **Click the *Delete* button.**
    Note: General ledger accounts cannot be deleted unless the account being deleted has a zero balance.

3: **Click the *OK* button of the confirmation dialog box.**

When the *Pick List* command button is clicked, a master chart of accounts list will appear. Chapter 13 will show you how to use this account list to help create a chart of accounts to set up a new automated accounting system.

GENERAL JOURNAL TRANSACTIONS

A **journal** is a record of the debit and credit parts of each transaction recorded in date sequence. A journal does not show the current account balance of individual accounts. Therefore, the journal entry information must be transferred to a ledger account. The process of updating the ledger accounts with all debits and credits affecting each account is called **posting.**

As transactions are entered into a journal and posted, the appropriate ledger account balance is updated. After all transactions have been entered and posted, the account information can be further processed (totals accumulated, and so on), displayed, or printed in various report formats. The data can also be stored to disk for recall at a later time.

General Journal Input Form

A General Journal is a journal with two amount columns in which all kinds of entries can be recorded. A **general journal input form,** which can be found in the *Working Papers,* is used for recording transactions in a general journal. Each debit part and credit part of a transaction is recorded on a separate line of the input form, as shown in the partially completed general journal input form in Figure 2.2.

General Journal Input Form

Date 10/10/--   Problem No. 2-T

Date	Reference	Account Number	Debit Amount	Credit Amount	Vendor/Customer
10/01/--	C711	540	950.00		
		110		950.00	
10/01/--	C712	560	263.45		
		110		263.45	
10/03/--	T256	110	1935.20		
		410		1935.20	
		Totals	3148.65	3148.65	

Figure 2.2
General Journal
Input Form

The bottom of the form contains totals for the Debit and Credit columns. To prove the equality of debits and credits, these totals must equal.

Oct. 01   Paid cash for office rent, $950.00. C711.
     01   Paid cash for telephone bill, $263.45. C712.
     03   Received cash from sales, $1,935.20. T256.

Each line represents one part of a transaction. Each column on the form matches one of the columns in the General Journal window in which the data will be keyed. (The Vendor/Customer column will be discussed in the next chapter.) Notice that the Date and Reference columns are completed only for the first line of each journal entry. The field names and a description of each column are illustrated in the General Journal window shown in Figure 2.3.

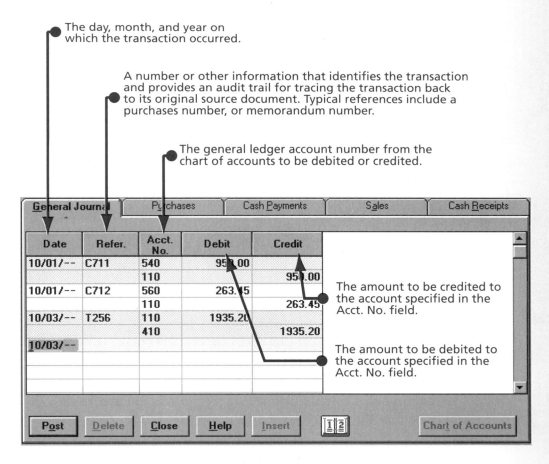

Figure 2.3
General Journal

General Journal Tab

The **General Journal tab** within the Journal Entries window is used to enter and post general journal entries and to make corrections to or delete existing journal entries. In chapters 4 and 5 you will learn how to use the other tabs in this window to enter purchases, cash payments, sales, and cash receipts journal transactions. When the *Journal Entries* menu item is chosen from the Data menu, or the *Journal* toolbar button is clicked on, the Journal Entries window shown in Figure 2.3 will appear.

When the *General Journal* tab is chosen, the general journal shown in Figure 2.3 appears. When the general journal first appears, the Date column will contain the date of the last transaction that was entered even if it was entered in an earlier session. The Reference column will contain the next number in sequence for the last transaction that was entered. If no transactions have been entered, the Date column will contain a default date and the Reference column will be blank. Figure 2.3 shows the journal entries previously entered from the general journal input form in Figure 2.2.

Entering a General Journal Entry

1: **Enter the date of the transaction, then press the Tab key.**
Strike the + key to increase the date, the − key to decrease the date, or key the date.

2: **Enter the Reference information, then press the Tab key.**
If the software has not correctly anticipated the next reference, key the correct reference.
Note: The Reference column will contain the next number in sequence for the last transaction that was entered. During keying of transactions, the computer will default to the correct reference even if different, multiple references have been entered.

3: **Enter the account number, then press the Tab key. The account title will be displayed at the bottom of the general journal just above the command buttons.**
While the Account Number text box has the focus, click the *Chart of Accounts* button to display the chart of accounts selection list. Select an account and click *OK*.

4: **Enter the debit or credit amount, then press the Tab key.**
Continue entering the account number and debit or credit amount for each part of the journal entry.

5: **When the journal entry is complete, click the *Post* button.**
Note: A general ledger account can be added, changed, or deleted while entering a journal entry. Choose the *Maintain*

As another alternative, you may click on the Calendar icon. When the calendar appears, select the desired date.

Use the Page Up and Page Down keys and/or click on the scroll bar arrows to scroll the report data.

Accounts menu item from the Data menu or click on the *Accts.* toolbar button. When the Account Maintenance window appears, click on the *Accounts* tab to display the Accounts window.

Changing or Deleting General Journal Transactions

1: **Select the transaction that you wish to change or delete.**

2: **Correct the transaction and click the *Post* button. If you wish to delete the transaction, click the *Delete* button.**

Inserting a Transaction Part

1: **Select the transaction to which you need to add a debit or credit part.**

2: **Click the *Insert* button.**
A blank line will be inserted at the end of the selected transaction.

3: **Enter the additional transaction debit or credit part and click the Post button.**
Note: If you accidentally insert a blank line, leave it. It will be removed when the journal is posted.

Finding a Journal Entry

1: **Choose the *Find* menu item from the Edit menu.**
The Find Journal Entry dialog box shown in Figure 2.4 will appear.

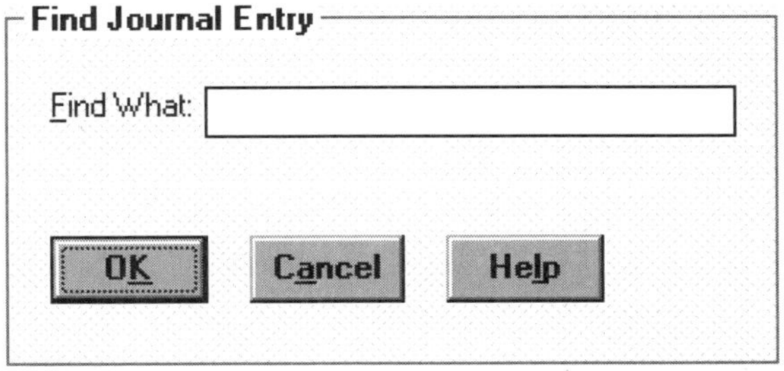

Figure 2.4
Find Journal
Entry Dialog Box

2: **Enter the date, reference, amount, or any other data of the transaction you want to find in the Find What text box, then click *OK.***

3: **If a matching transaction is found, it will be displayed so that it may be changed or deleted.**
Subsequent choosing of the *Find Next* item in the Edit menu will locate the next occurrence of the search item.

GENERAL JOURNAL REPORT

In Chapter 1 you learned how to choose the chart of accounts and trial balance reports from the Reports menu. In this chapter you will learn how to select journal reports and to specify which journal entries are to appear in the report. The **general journal report** is a display or printout of the general journal that is useful in detecting errors and verifying the equality of debits and credits. The totals of debits and credits on the general journal report must match the totals of debits and credits on the general journal input form. This report becomes a permanent accounting document and provides an audit trail so that transactions may be traced to their original source document.

1: **Choose the *Report Selection* menu item from the Reports menu or click the *Reports* toolbar button.**

2: **When the Report Selection window appears, choose the *Journals* option.**
A list of all the reports within the chosen Journals option will appear, as shown in Figure 2.5. The date that appears in the upper right corner will be used to date the selected report(s).

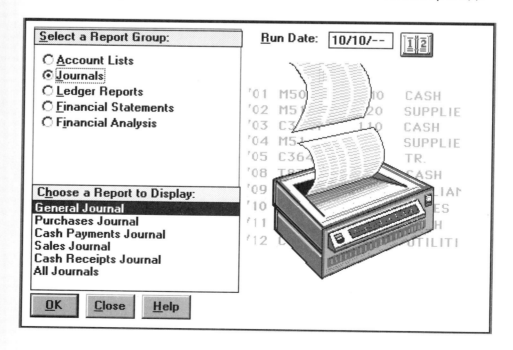

Figure 2.5
Report Selection
Dialog Box

To change this date, select the run date box. Enter the desired date, strike + to increase and – to decrease the date, or click on the calendar icon.

3: Select the *General Journal* report, then click the *OK* button.
The Journal Report Selection dialog box shown in Figure 2.6 will appear. You may display all general journal entries or customize your general journal report.

Figure 2.6
Journal Report Selection Dialog Box

4: Choose the *Customize Journal Report* option to control the data to be included on the report.
If you want to include all journal transactions on the report, choose the *Include All Journal Entries* option. When the *Customize Journal Report* option is chosen, the dialog box shown in Figure 2.7 will appear. Notice the calendar appears on the right side of the dialog box because the calendar icon, located next to the start and end dates, was clicked on.

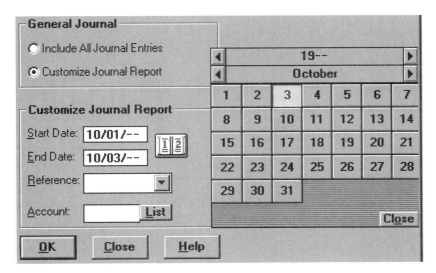

Figure 2.7
Customize Journal Report Dialog Box

5: **Set the range of dates to be included in the journal report in the Start Date and End Date text boxes.**
Enter the desired dates. As an alternative, select the Start or End date text box, then click on the calendar icon. When the calendar appears, as shown in Figure 2.7, select the desired date. Click on *Close* when finished with the calendar.

6: **Enter an identifying reference in the *Reference* text box if you wish to restrict the report to a particular reference. This can be done by clicking on the drop-down arrow to obtain a list of all the available references. For example, you might want to display only adjusting entries or only a certain invoice.**
As an alternative, you may key the first character of the reference in the text box. The first entry that begins with that character will be displayed in the text box. Use the Up and Down arrow keys to browse through the entries.

7: **Enter an account number in the *Account* text box if you wish to restrict the report to a particular account. This can be done by clicking the *List* button to obtain a chart of accounts selection list window to select an account number.**

8: **Click *OK*.**

To print the displayed report, click the *Print* button at the bottom of the display window. A printed general journal report listing the transactions entered in the general journal in Figure 2.3 is shown in Figure 2.8.

```
                          Pittman Consulting
                           General Journal
                              10/03/--

        ----------------------------------------------------------------
        Date    Refer.   Acct.   Title              Debit      Credit
        ----------------------------------------------------------------

        10/01   C711     540     Rent Expense       950.00
        10/01   C711     110     Cash                          950.00

        10/01   C712     560     Telephone Expense  263.45
        10/01   C712     110     Cash                          263.45

        10/03   T256     110     Cash               1935.20
        10/03   T256     410     Fees                          1935.20
                                                    --------   --------
                                 Totals             3148.65    3148.65
                                                    ========   ========
```

Figure 2.8
General Journal
Report

GRAPHING AND CHARTING

Many accounting software packages have the capability to produce graphs and charts of data contained within their files. The terms **chart** and **graph** refer to pictorial representations of data that can be produced by the computer and depicted on the screen and printer. Charts and graphs produced by the computer are used to clarify the meaning of the words and numbers that appear. Charts are commonly used to enhance presentations, track sales, monitor expenses, identify trends, and make forecasts.

Automated Accounting 7.0 can generate two- and three-dimensional pie and bar charts and line graphs from data used in the following reports: income statement, expense distribution, actual versus budget, balance sheet, and sales. Menu items will be unavailable for charts and graphs that are inappropriate for some reports.

1: **Choose the** *Graph Selection* **menu item from the Reports menu or click the** *Graphs* **toolbar button.**

2: **When the Graph Selection dialog box (Figure 2.9) appears, select an option from the Data to Graph list.**

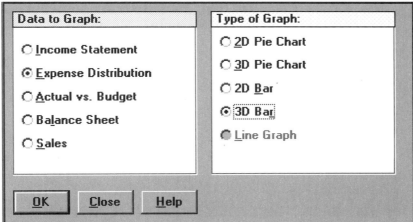

Figure 2.9
Graph Selection
Dialog Box

3: **Select an option from the Type of Graph list.**
   Note: Graph types that cannot be generated due to insufficient data will appear dimmed or a message window will appear informing you that there is insufficient data.

4: **Click the** *OK* **button.**
   A three-dimensional bar graph illustrating expense distribution is shown in Figure 2.10.

The bar graph shown in Figure 2.10 illustrates the relative account balances in each of the expense accounts. The graph clearly shows that rent expense is the larger expense followed by telephone expense.

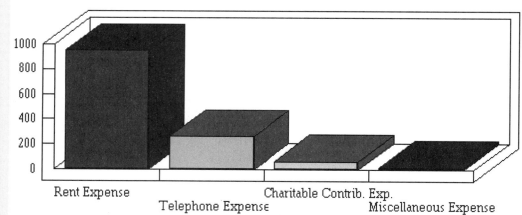

Expense Distribution

Figure 2.10
Three-Dimensional Expense Distribution Bar Graph

INTERNET

In certain browsers and other Internet programs, a bookmark or hotlist is a special file used to save addresses and locations. By saving and recalling addresses, it is easy for you to visit your favorite sites over and over.

Chapter Review

1. Input forms that correspond to the computer journal windows may save computer time and help you organize your data prior to commencing an automated accounting computer session.

2. To work the problems in this text, you can first complete the input forms in the *Working Papers* or enter transactions directly from the narrative provided. *Automated Accounting 7.0* has been specifically designed to facilitate either mode of entry.

3. The general journal input form is used for recording transactions in a general journal.

4. The Accounts tab within the Account Maintenance window is used to add new accounts to the chart of accounts, change account titles, and delete inactive accounts.

5. A journal is used to record the debit and credit parts of each transaction in date sequence.

6. Posting is the process of updating the ledger account balances with all debits and credits that affect each account.

7. As transactions are entered and posted into a computer's journal, the appropriate ledger account balance is updated.

8. The General Journal tab within the Journal Entries window is used to enter and post general journal entries and to make corrections to or delete existing journal entries.

9. The general journal report is a display or printout that is useful in detecting errors and verifying the equality of debits and credits.

10. Charts and graphs are pictorial representations of data produced by the computer that are used to clarify the meaning of the words and numbers, enhance presentations, track sales, monitor expenses, identify trends, and make forecasts.

ACCOUNTING   CAREERS   IN   DEPTH

Teller

A teller receives and pays out money, and keeps records of money and negotiable instruments involved in financial transactions. A teller performs the following duties:

- Receiving checks and cash for deposit, verifying amounts, and examining checks for endorsements.
- Cashing checks and paying out money after the verification of signatures and customer balances.
- Entering customers' transactions into a computer to record transactions, and issuing computer-generated receipts.
- Placing holds on accounts for uncollected funds.
- Ordering a daily supply of cash, and counting incoming cash.
- Balancing currency, coins, and checks in the cash drawer at the end of the shift, using a calculator, and comparing totaled amounts with data displayed on the computer screen.
- Explaining, promoting, or selling products or services, such as traveler's checks, savings bonds, money orders, and cashier's checks.

A teller may also do the following:

- Opening new accounts.

- Removing deposits from, and counting and balancing cash in, automated teller machines and the night depository.
- Accepting utility bill and loan payments.
- Using a computer, a typewriter, a photocopier, and a check protector to prepare checks and financial documents.

There is a great deal of customer contact in teller positions. Therefore, giving excellent customer service would be necessary when representing a financial institution. This involves clear communication and exhibiting a pleasant personality and a helpful attitude toward the customer.

Studying accounting in high school could be a good way to start out your career as a teller. The background knowledge gained in accounting would provide a job applicant with a competitive advantage. If you are interested in applying for positions at a higher level, there are always opportunities for advancement. Also, in financial institutions there are courses that are offered which can help new employees learn about the banking industry, securities industry, etc., and also prepare them for future assignments.

A career as a teller can open the door for many opportunities. It can be a great start, especially if you enjoy working with customers.

TUTORIAL PROBLEM 2-T

The general journal entries for Pittman Consulting are illustrated in Figure 2.11.

Date	Refer.	Acct. No.	Debit	Credit
10/01/--	C711	540	950.00	
		110		950.00
10/01/--	C712	560	263.45	
		110		263.45
10/03/--	T256	110	1935.20	
		410		1935.20
10/06/--	C713	512	65.00	
		110		65.00
10/07/--	C714	250	80.00	
		110		80.00
10/08/--	M214	120	205.95	
		250		205.95
10/09/--	C715	530	20.00	
		110		20.00
10/10/--	C716	120	45.00	
		110		45.00
10/10/--	C717	130	285.00	
		110		285.00

Figure 2.11
Completed General Journal Window

STEP 1:   **Start up *Automated Accounting 7.0*.**

STEP 2:   **Load the opening balances template file, AA02–T.**
Click the *Open* toolbar button, select the drive and directory/folder containing the opening balance files, then select file AA02–T from the File Name list box.

STEP 3:   **Enter your name in the User Name text box and click on *OK*.**

STEP 4:   **Save the file to your disk and directory/folder with a file name of XXX2–T, where XXX are your initials.**
Choose *Save As* from the File menu and save the file as XXX2–T where XXX are your initials and 2–T represents Chapter 2, Tutorial Problem.

STEP 5:   **Add Charitable Contrib. Exp. to the chart of accounts with an account number of 512 so that it will be positioned immediately following Advertising Expense.**
Click the *Accts.* toolbar button then click on the *Accounts* tab and add the Charitable Contrib. Exp. account.

▶

T U T O R I A L   P R O B L E M   2 – T

STEP 6: **Enter the general journal transactions shown in Figure 2.11.**
Click on the *Journal* toolbar button. When the Journal Entries window appears, click on the General Journal tab (if not already chosen) and enter the journal entries. The following transactions for Pittman Consulting occurred during the period of October 1 through October 10 of the current year. The transaction reference numbers are abbreviated as follows: Check no., C; Memorandum, M; Calculator tape, T.

Oct. 01 Paid cash for office rent, $950.00. C711.
    01 Paid cash for telephone bill, $263.45. C712.
    03 Received cash from sales, $1,935.20. T256. Note: Pittman Consulting records sales in the Fees account, account number 410.
    06 Paid cash for charitable contribution, $65.00. C713.
    07 Paid cash on account to Westcott Office Supply, $80.00. C714.
    08 Bought supplies on account from Westcott Office Supply, $205.95. M214.
    09 Paid cash for miscellaneous expense, $20.00. C715.
    10 Paid cash for supplies, $45.00. C716.
    10 Paid cash for insurance, $285.00. C717. Note: Insurance coverage is paid in advance and is considered an asset because it is something of value owned by Pittman Consulting. Therefore, the premium is recorded in the asset account Prepaid Insurance, account number 130.

STEP 7: **Display the chart of accounts.**
Click the *Reports* toolbar button. When the Report Selection window appears, choose the *Account Lists* option from Select a Report Group. Select the *Chart of Accounts* report from the Choose a Report to Display list (if not already highlighted), and click *OK*. Examine the report in Figure 2.12 and verify that the account you entered in Step 5 is correct.

To print the report currently displayed in the report window, click the *Print* button. To close the report window, click the *Close* button.

Pittman Consulting
Chart of Accounts
10/10/--

Assets

110 Cash
120 Supplies
130 Prepaid Insurance

Liabilities

210 Arnst Business Supplies
220 Baker Advertising, Inc.
230 Computer Center
240 Gregor Graphics, Inc.
250 Westcott Office Supply

Owner's Equity

310 Kenneth Pittman, Capital
320 Kenneth Pittman, Drawing
330 Income Summary

Revenue

410 Fees

Expenses

510 Advertising Expense
512 Charitable Contrib. Exp.
520 Insurance Expense
530 Miscellaneous Expense
540 Rent Expense
550 Supplies Expense
560 Telephone Expense

Figure 2.12
Chart of Accounts Report

Use the Page Up and Page Down keys and/or click on the scroll bar arrows to scroll the report data.

STEP 8:   **Display the general journal report.**
From the Report Selection window, select the *Journals* option and the *General Journal* report, then click *OK*. When the Journal Report Selection window appears, choose the *Customize Journal Report* option. Set the Start Date to 10/01/-- and the End Date to 10/10/-- (where -- is the current year), then click *OK*. The General Journal report is shown in Figure 2.13.

Pittman Consulting
General Journal
10/10/--

Date	Refer.	Acct.	Title	Debit	Credit
10/01	C711	540	Rent Expense	950.00	
10/01	C711	110	Cash		950.00
10/01	C712	560	Telephone Expense	263.45	
10/01	C712	110	Cash		263.45
10/03	T256	110	Cash	1935.20	
10/03	T256	410	Fees		1935.20
10/06	C713	512	Charitable Contrib. Exp.	65.00	
10/06	C713	110	Cash		65.00
10/07	C714	250	Westcott Office Supply	80.00	
10/07	C714	110	Cash		80.00
10/08	M214	120	Supplies	205.95	
10/08	M214	250	Westcott Office Supply		205.95
10/09	C715	530	Miscellaneous Expense	20.00	
10/09	C715	110	Cash		20.00
10/10	C716	120	Supplies	45.00	
10/10	C716	110	Cash		45.00
10/10	C717	130	Prepaid Insurance	285.00	
10/10	C717	110	Cash		285.00
			Totals	3849.60	3849.60

Figure 2.13
General Journal Entries Report

TUTORIAL PROBLEM 2-T

Note: If the transactions were entered correctly, the Start and End Dates in the Customize Journal Report box will be the default dates set automatically by the software. The software uses the first day of the month as the Start Date and the latest date of the general journal transactions as the End Date.

STEP 9: **Display a trial balance.**
Choose *Ledger Reports* in the Report Selection window, select the *Trial Balance* report, then click *OK*. The report appears in Figure 2.14.

Pittman Consulting
Trial Balance
10/10/--

Acct. Number	Account Title	Debit	Credit
110	Cash	14113.66	
120	Supplies	1100.04	
130	Prepaid Insurance	447.00	
220	Baker Advertising, Inc.		276.90
240	Gregor Graphics, Inc.		245.10
250	Westcott Office Supply		205.95
310	Kenneth Pittman, Capital		14296.00
410	Fees		1935.20
512	Charitable Contrib. Exp.	65.00	
530	Miscellaneous Expense	20.00	
540	Rent Expense	950.00	
560	Telephone Expense	263.45	
	Totals	16959.15	16959.15

Figure 2.14
Trial Balance Report

STEP 10: **Generate a 3D expense distribution bar graph.**
Click on the *Graphs* toolbar button. Choose the *Expense Distribution* option from the Data to Graph list, then select the *3D Bar* option from the Type of Graph list and click the *OK* button. The 3D expense distribution bar graph is shown in Figure 2.15.

▶

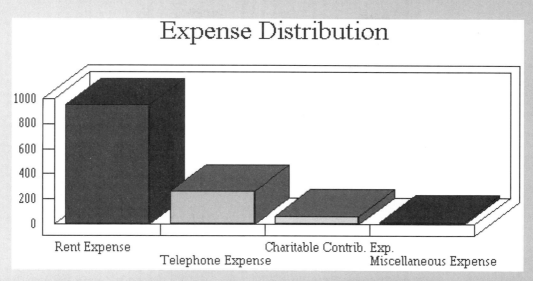

Figure 2.15
Expense Distribution Bar Graph

STEP 11:   **Save the data file.**
            Click on the *Save* toolbar button.

STEP 12:   **Optional spreadsheet activity:**
            You will create a spreadsheet report showing only the
            cash paid during the period October 1–10 from the
            accounting system data.
            a. Follow the procedure in Step 8 to display the
                general journal report for October 1–10. When the
                general journal report appears, click the *Copy*
                button and select the *Spreadsheet Format* option to
                copy the report to the clipboard.
            b. Start up your spreadsheet software.
            c. Open spreadsheet template file SS02–T.
            d. Select cell A1 as the current cell, if not already
                selected.
            e. Select *Paste* from the Edit menu and paste the
                general journal report (copied to the clipboard in
                step a) into the spreadsheet.
            f. Delete all rows of data that are not a cash payment
                transaction (all rows with a reference starting with
                something other than C). Leave one blank row
                between each journal entry.

T U T O R I A L   P R O B L E M   2 – T

   g. Change the title of the report from General Journal
       to Cash Paid.
   h. Replace the old totals with the Sum of the debit, for
       example, @SUM(F9..F28), and credit, for example,
       @SUM (G9..G28), columns.
   i. Format the spreadsheet to match the completed
       spreadsheet shown in Figure 2.16.

```
                          Student Name

                        Pittman Consulting
                            Cash Paid
                          As Of 10/10/--

----------------------------------------------------------------
Date     Refer.  Acct.  Title                 Debit      Credit
----------------------------------------------------------------

01-Oct   C711    540    Rent Expense          $950.00
01-Oct   C711    110    Cash                               $950.00

01-Oct   C712    560    Telephone Expense     $263.45
01-Oct   C712    110    Cash                               $263.45

06-Oct   C713    512    Charitable Contrib. Exp.  $65.00
06-Oct   C713    110    Cash                                $65.00

07-Oct   C714    250    Westcott Office Supply $80.00
07-Oct   C714    110    Cash                                $80.00

09-Oct   C715    530    Miscellaneous Expense  $20.00
09-Oct   C715    110    Cash                                $20.00

10-Oct   C716    120    Supplies               $45.00
10-Oct   C716    110    Cash                                $45.00

10-Oct   C717    130    Prepaid Insurance     $285.00
10-Oct   C717    110    Cash                               $285.00
                                              --------   --------
                        Totals              $1,708.45   $1,708.45
                                            ========    ========
```

Figure 2.16
Spreadsheet
Cash Paid
Report
(October 1–10)

   j. Print the completed cash payments report (cells
       A1–G31).
   k. Save your spreadsheet file with a file name of
       XXX2–T, where XXX are your initials and 2–T
       identifies tutorial problem 2–T.
   l. End your spreadsheet session and return to the
       Automated Accounting application.

STEP 13: **End your *Automated Accounting* session.**
          Click the *Exit/Quit* toolbar button.

Applying Your Information Skills

I. MATCHING

Directions: In the *Working Papers,* write the letter of the appropriate term next to each definition.

  a. input form(s)
  b. sole proprietorship
  c. account maintenance
  d. journal
  e. posting
  f. general journal input form
  g. general journal tab
  h. general journal report
  i. chart and graph

1. A pictorial representation of data that can be produced by the computer and depicted on the screen and printer.

2. A basic two column (debit and credit) form that is used for recording transactions in a general journal.

3. Forms used to organize and record accounting transactions for data entry.

4. A record of the debit and credit parts of each transaction recorded in date sequence.

5. Used to enter and post general journal entries and to make corrections to or delete existing journal entries.

6. The process of updating the ledger accounts with all debits and credits affecting each account.

7. A display or printout of the general journal that is useful in detecting errors and verifying the equality of debits and credits.

8. The process of keeping a business's chart of accounts up to date by adding new accounts, changing titles of existing accounts, and deleting inactive accounts.

9. A business owned by one person.

II. TRUE/FALSE

Directions: Write the answers to each of the following questions in the *Working Papers.*

1. An entry to add a new account is entered in the general journal window.

2. Only transactions that do not involve cash may be recorded in the general journal window.

3. General ledger accounts cannot be deleted unless the account balance is zero.

4. The *Find* menu item in the Edit menu could be used to find a transaction that contained a specified debit or credit amount.

5. The *Chart of Accounts* button in the general journal window displays a chart of accounts selection list.

6. A new general ledger account can be added or changed while entering a journal entry.

7. Instead of keying an account number in the General Journal, you may select the account from the Chart of Accounts selection list window.

III. QUESTIONS

Directions: Write the answers to each of the following questions in the *Working Papers*.

1. Describe the process for adding an account to the chart of accounts.

2. Describe the process for changing the title of an existing account in the chart of accounts.

3. Describe the process for deleting an account from the chart of accounts that has a zero balance.

4. What kind of transaction(s) may be entered in the general journal?

5. Describe the process for correcting a general journal entry.

6. Describe the process for deleting a general journal entry.

7. Explain how the *Chart of Accounts* button can be used while entering general journal transactions.

8. Complete the date range section of the Journal Report Selection window in Figure 2.17 to display all general journal entries from July 1 through July 31 of the current year.

9. Complete the Journal Report Selection window in Figure 2.17 to display all general journal entries from August 1 through August 10 of the current year with a reference of C412.

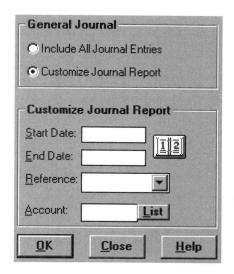

Figure 2.17
Journal Report Selection Window

Independent Practice Problem 2–P

P

In this problem, you will process any additions, changes, and deletions to the chart of accounts as well as the general journal entries for the period October 11 through October 20 of the current year.

STEP 1: **Start up *Automated Accounting 7.0.***

STEP 2: **Open the opening balances file named AA02–P.**

STEP 3: **Enter your name in the User Name text box.**

STEP 4: **Save the opening balances file with a file name of XXX2–P, where XXX are your initials.**

STEP 5: **Enter the following account maintenance and October 11–20 general journal transactions. The transaction reference numbers are abbreviated as follows: Check no., C; Memorandum, M; Calculator tape, T.**

Oct. 14 Received cash from sales, $2,785.50. T257.
Note: Delete Computer Center from the chart of accounts.

14 Bought a subscription on account from Barre Journals, Inc., $155.65. M215.
Note: Add Dues & Subscriptions Exp. to the chart of accounts with account number 515, and add Barre Journals, Inc. to the chart of accounts with account number 225.

15   Paid cash for miscellaneous expense, $90.00. C718.

15   Paid cash on account to Baker Advertising, Inc. $276.90. C719.

15   Received cash from sales, $2,995.00. T258.

16   Bought advertising on account from Baker Advertising, Inc., $595.00. M216.

17   Paid cash on account to Gregor Graphics & Design, $245.10. C720.
      Note: Change the account title of Gregor Graphics, Inc. to Gregor Graphics & Design.

20   Paid cash for travel expense, $173.73. C721.
      Note: Add Travel & Entertain. Exp. to the chart of accounts with account number 570.

STEP 6:   **Display a chart of accounts report.**

STEP 7:   **Display the general journal report for the period October 11 to October 20. Make corrections, if necessary.**

STEP 8:   **Display a trial balance.**

STEP 9:   **Generate a 3D expense distribution bar graph.**

STEP 10:   **Save your data to disk.**

STEP 11:   **Optional spreadsheet and word processing integration activity:**
Use a spreadsheet to create a report showing only the fees entered into the accounting system for the period October 11–20. Then prepare an interoffice memorandum that contains this information.

a. Display and copy the general journal report for October 11–20 to the clipboard in spreadsheet format.

b. Start up your spreadsheet software and load spreadsheet template file SS02–T.

c. Select cell A1 as the current cell and paste the general journal report into the spreadsheet.

d. Delete all rows of data that are not fee received transactions. Keep only those rows with a reference starting with T. Change the title of the report from General Journal to Fees, and replace the old totals with the sum of the debit and credit columns. Format the spreadsheet similar to Figure 2.16.

e. Print the completed fees received report.

f. Save your spreadsheet file with a file name of XXX2–P.

g. Select and copy the spreadsheet report to the clipboard.
h. End your spreadsheet application.
i. Start up your word processing application software and load template file WP02–P (load as a text file).
j. Replace FROM: Student Name with your name.
k. Position the insertion point one line after the last line in the document and paste the spreadsheet report. Format your document as necessary.
l. Print the completed document.
m. Save your document with a file name of XXX2–P.
n. End your word processing application and return to the *Automated Accounting* application.

STEP 12: End the session.

Applying Your Technology Skills 2–P

Directions: Write the answers to the following questions in the *Working Papers*.

1. Why do you think account number 515 was assigned to Dues & Subscriptions Exp.?

2. What is the amount of check number 719 shown on the general journal report?

3. What is the balance in the Rent Expense account?

4. What is the balance in the Dues & Subscriptions Expense account?

5. What are the debit and credit totals on the trial balance report?

6. From the Expense Distribution bar graph, what are the three highest expenses?

Cyberspace is the electronic world of the Internet that exists only on computers. Cyberspace is sometimes called *virtual reality.*

Mastery Problem 2–M

In this problem, you will process any additions, changes, and deletions to the chart of accounts as well as the general journal entries for the period October 21 through October 31 of the current year.

STEP 1:   **Load the opening balances file AA02–M.**

STEP 2:   **Enter the following account maintenance and October 21–31 general journal transactions.**

Oct. 21   Bought supplies on account from Westcott Office Supply, $218.10. M217.
Note: Delete Arnst Business Supplies from the chart of accounts.

   23   Paid cash for insurance, $325.00. C722.

   23   Received cash from sales, $2,500.00. T259.

   27   Paid cash on account to Westcott Office Supply, $205.95. C723.

   28   Bought supplies on account from Gregor Graphics & Design, $425.50. M218.

   29   Received cash from sales, $2,535.75. T260.

   30   Paid cash for electric bill, $493.34. C724.
Note: Add Utilities Expense to the chart of accounts with account number 580 so that it will be positioned immediately following Travel & Entertain. Exp.

   30   Paid cash for charitable contribution, $125.00. C725.

   31   Paid cash for miscellaneous expense, $175.00. C726.

   31   Paid cash to owner for personal use, $4,500.00. C727.

CHECK FIGURES:
Trial Balance debit and
credit totals =
$28,441.70

STEP 3:   **Display the following reports and graph: Chart of Accounts, General Journal Report (October 21–31), Trial Balance, 3D Expense Distribution Bar Chart.**

STEP 4:   **Save your data with a file name of XXX2–M.**

STEP 5:   **Display reports as necessary to answer the questions in the Applying Your Technology Skills 2–M.**

STEP 6:   **Optional spreadsheet activity:**
Create a spreadsheet report showing the cash that was paid for the period October 21–31 from the accounting system data:

a. Start up your spreadsheet software and load spreadsheet template file SS02–T.
b. Copy and paste the October 21–31 general journal report into the spreadsheet.
c. Delete all rows of data that are not cash paid transactions. Change the title of the report, replace the old totals with the sum of the debit and credit columns, and format the spreadsheet similar to Figure 2.16.
d. Print the completed report.
e. Save your spreadsheet file with a file name of XXX2–M.

Applying Your Technology Skills 2–M

Directions: Write the answers to the following questions in the *Working Papers*.

1. Why was account number 580 assigned to Utilities Expense?

2. What are the debit and credit totals on the general journal report?

3. What is the amount of check number 724 shown on the general journal report?

4. What is the balance in the Advertising Expense account?

5. What is the balance in the Miscellaneous Expense account?

6. From the expense distribution bar chart, what expense account has the smallest account balance?

A Uniform Resource Locator (URL) is an address code for finding hypertext or hypermedia documents on World Wide Web (WWW) servers around the world. URLs can be accessed by WWW browsers.

ACCOUNTING CAREERS IN DEPTH

Tax Accountant

A tax accountant's job duties include:

- Preparing federal, state, or local tax returns of an individual, a business establishment, or another organization.
- Examining accounts and records and computing taxes owed according to prescribed rates, laws, and regulations, using a computer.
- Advising management regarding the effects of business activities on taxes, and regarding strategies for minimizing tax liability.
- Ensuring that the business complies with periodic tax payment, information reporting, and other taxing authority requirements.
- Representing the business principal before taxing bodies.

Tax accountants also formulate tax strategies involving issues such as financial choice, how to best treat a merger or acquisition, deferral of taxes, and when it is best to expense items. This work requires a thorough understanding of economics and the tax code.

Preparation for a career as a tax accountant includes completing a four-year college degree in accounting and, ideally, a cooperative experience within a business practicing tax accounting. Increasingly, large corporations are looking for persons with both an accounting and a legal background in tax. For example, a person with a J.D. (law degree) and a C.P.A. designation (Certified Public Accountant) would be especially desirable to many accounting firms. Students who pursue this route are also able to later set up self-employment and provide tax services to the public for a fee.

A career choice as a self-employed tax accountant is ideal for those who prefer to work for themselves. This choice comes with great responsibility. Many who choose this career path prefer to be certified as a Certified Public Accountant in order to eliminate accountability to others and to experience more autonomy in their work.

The skills required in addition to a college education include: people skills, sales skills, communication skills, analytical skills, creative ability, initiative, computer skills, and a willingness to work 40–70 hours per week.

Tax accountants meet many people and can enjoy varied rewards when choosing to be self-employed. This form of work requires you to generate your own business, but has the benefits of offering close customer contact, a high degree of independence and, depending on how good you are, considerable financial compensation.

One of the major impediments to the development of true commerce on the Internet has been the problem of providing secure ways to shop using the Internet and the World Wide Web.

3
General Ledger— End-of-Fiscal- Period for a Service Business and Bank Reconciliation

LEARNING OBJECTIVES

Upon completion of this chapter, you will be able to:

1. Record and display adjusting entries.

2. Display financial statements.

3. Complete bank reconciliation procedures.

4. Perform period-end closing.

INTRODUCTION

In this chapter, you will learn how to complete the end-of-fiscal-period processing for a service business. In the previous chapter, you learned how to maintain the chart of accounts and process transactions. To complete the accounting cycle, adjusting entries are recorded on the general journal input form, entered into the computer, and verified for accuracy. The financial statements are then generated. Finally, closing journal entries are generated and posted by the software, and a post-closing trial balance is prepared. In this chapter you will also learn how to use the software to complete a bank reconciliation.

E T H I C S

Copyright is the right to prohibit other people from making copies. This is known as an exclusive right to reproduce the work. Copyright involves five exclusive rights: (1) the exclusive right to make copies; (2) the exclusive right to distribute copies to the public; (3) the exclusive right to prepare derivative works; (4) the exclusive right to perform the work in public (applies mainly to plays, dances, etc.); and (5) the exclusive right to display the work in public.

The Software Act of 1980 made programs copyrightable as long as there is even a minimal amount of creativity. As a matter of fact, a program is also copyrightable if it is stored in a computer's memory rather than on paper.

Ideas cannot be copyrighted. Copyright law protects only words, images, sounds, and so on, which an author uses to express ideas. Other authors are free to express the same ideas in their own way.

The Software Act of 1980 allows the person who purchases a software product to make a backup copy as long as it is for archival purposes only. The archive copy cannot be given to another person for his or her use. Only the original and backup (not subsequent sales or rental) can be given away, sold, lent, or rented to others as long as the original purchaser does not retain a copy.

Any program that comes into existence in a tangible medium (such as, source and object code, flowchart, stored on a disk, and so on) is copyright protected. Programs do not have to be legally registered to be copyright protected, although it is a good idea. The reason that programs are registered is for protection *before* infringements take place. The court can award up to $100,000 per infringed work, called statutory damages, and impose other actions to stop the illegal copyright activities.

a. How can the copyright owner of computer software prevent someone from making an unauthorized copy of the work?

b. Do you agree that software copyright should be enforced by law? Explain your position.

c. What is the major effect of the copyright law on (1) the person (or business) who sells a software product; and (2) the person who buys the software product?

ADJUSTING ENTRIES

Journal entries recorded to update general ledger accounts at the end of a fiscal period are called **adjusting entries.** Portions of assets, such as supplies and prepaid insurance, are consumed during the fiscal period and become expenses of the business. For example, the amount of supplies that has been consumed must be deducted from the asset account *Supplies* and recorded in the expense account *Supplies Expense*. The amount of prepaid insurance that has been consumed must be deducted from the asset account *Prepaid Insurance* and recorded in the expense account *Insurance Expense*.

Adjusting entries are not entered in the general journal until after all other transactions for the accounting period have been recorded, entered into the computer, and posted. The trial balance is then displayed or printed. This trial balance and the period-end adjustment data are the basis for the adjusting entries. The adjusting entries may then be recorded on the general journal input form, entered into the computer, and posted. A journal entries report is then displayed to prove the equality of the debits and credits.

All the adjusting entries are for the same date and use *Adj. Ent.* as the reference. The trial balance before adjustments is shown in Figure 3.1 on the next page. The following adjustment data is for Pittman Consulting. The adjusting entries have been entered into the general journal as shown in Figure 3.2.

Adjustment Data for Pittman Consulting:
Supplies inventory $1,191.12
Value of insurance policies on October 31 . . . .   525.00

The adjustment amounts are calculated as follows:

Supplies account balance, Oct. 31 (from trial balance) . . . $1,743.64
Less supplies inventory, Oct. 31 . . . .   1,191.12
Equals supplies used during October (adjusting entry) . . $ 552.52

Prepaid Insurance account balance, Oct. 31 (from trial
balance) $772.00
Less current value of insurance policies 525.00
Equals insurance used during October (adjusting entry). . $247.00

In a manual accounting system, a work sheet is used as a tool for analyzing the adjusting entries and preparing the financial statements. Since the computer generates the financial statements directly from the

general ledger data, a work sheet is not required for an automated accounting system. Therefore, once the adjusting entries have been entered, posted, and verified, the financial statements may be displayed.

```
                        Pittman Consulting
                          Trial Balance
                            10/31/--

---------------------------------------------------------------
Acct.        Account
Number       Title                     Debit        Credit
---------------------------------------------------------------

110          Cash                      18319.89
120          Supplies                   1743.64
130          Prepaid Insurance           772.00
220          Baker Advertising, Inc.                   595.00
225          Barre Journals, Inc.                      155.65
240          Gregor Graphics & Design                  425.50
250          Westcott Office Supply                    218.10
310          Kenneth Pittman, Capital                14296.00
320          Kenneth Pittman, Drawing   4500.00
410          Fees                                    12751.45
510          Advertising Expense         595.00
512          Charitable Contrib. Exp.    190.00
515          Dues & Subscriptions Exp.   155.65
530          Miscellaneous Expense       285.00
540          Rent Expense                950.00
560          Telephone Expense           263.45
570          Travel & Entertain. Exp.    173.73
580          Utilities Expense           493.34
                                       --------      --------
             Totals                    28441.70     28441.70
                                       ========      ========
```

Figure 3.1
Trial Balance (Before Adjusting Entries)

Date	Refer.	Acct. No.	Debit	Credit
10/31/--	Adj.Ent.	550	552.52	
		120		552.52
10/31/--	Adj.Ent.	520	247.00	
		130		247.00

Figure 3.2
Adjusting Entries Entered in the General Journal

FINANCIAL STATEMENTS

The financial statements available for a nondepartmentalized business organized as a sole proprietorship are the income statement, balance sheet, and statement of owner's equity. The performance report is available only if budgeting data is available. Use the following steps to display financial statements.

1:   **Choose the *Report Selection* menu item from the Reports menu or click on the *Reports* toolbar button.**

2:   **When the Report Selection dialog appears, choose the *Financial Statements* option button from the Select a Report Group list.**
     A list of all the reports within the Financial Statements option will appear, as shown in Figure 3.3.

The date that appears in the upper right corner of the Report Selection Dialog will be used to date the selected report(s). You can use the calendar icon to change the date.

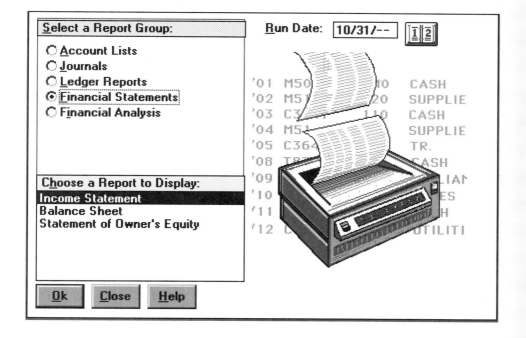

Figure 3.3
Report Selection (Financial Statements)

3:   **Choose the financial statement report you would like to display from the *Choose a Report to Display* list.**

4:   **Click the *OK* button.**

Income Statement

The **income statement** is a financial statement that provides information about the net income or net loss of a business over a specific period of time. The up-to-date account balances stored by the software are used to calculate and display the revenue earned and the expenses incurred during a fiscal period. Total revenue minus total expenses equals net income. If this difference is negative, it is the net loss.

Automated Accounting offers two formats of the income statement—Report by Month and Year and Report by Fiscal Period. This chapter uses the Report by Fiscal Period option in Figure 3.4. With this format, the profitability of the business is shown from the beginning of the fiscal period until the time when the income statement is displayed.

Also included for each amount is a component percentage. A **component percentage** shows the percentage relationship between one financial statement item and the total that includes that item. Component percentages calculated on an income statement show the relationship of items to total operating revenue or sales. The income statement that shows the profitability of the business for the current month as well as the profitability for the year to date is described and illustrated in later chapters.

Pittman Consulting Income Statement For Period Ended 10/31/--		
Operating Revenue		
Fees	12751.45	100.00
Total Operating Revenue	12751.45	100.00
Operating Expenses		
Advertising Expense	595.00	4.67
Charitable Contrib. Exp.	190.00	1.49
Dues & Subscriptions Exp.	155.65	1.22
Insurance Expense	247.00	1.94
Miscellaneous Expense	285.00	2.24
Rent Expense	950.00	7.45
Supplies Expense	552.52	4.33
Telephone Expense	263.45	2.07
Travel & Entertain. Exp.	173.73	1.36
Utilities Expense	493.34	3.87
Total Operating Expenses	3905.69	30.63
Net Income	8845.76	69.37

Figure 3.4
Income Statement by Fiscal Period

Balance Sheet

The **balance sheet** is a financial statement that reports assets, liabilities, and owner's equities on a specific date. The balance sheet can help financial statement users evaluate the overall financial strength of a business. Many factors determine the financial strength of a business, one factor being an adequate ratio of assets to liabilities.

While the balance sheet may be displayed at any time, it is typically displayed at the end of a fiscal period. The balance sheet is illustrated in Figure 3.5.

A branch or section of the Internet is called a *domain*. Domains can be assigned according to country, region, or state, or according to type of organization, such as education, commercial, government, or military.

```
                      Pittman Consulting
                       Balance Sheet
                          10/31/--

    Assets

    Cash                              18319.89
    Supplies                           1191.12
    Prepaid Insurance                   525.00
                                      --------
    Total Assets                                      20036.01
                                                      ========
    Liabilities

    Baker Advertising, Inc.             595.00
    Barre Journals, Inc.                155.65
    Gregor Graphics & Design            425.50
    Westcott Office Supply              218.10
                                      --------
    Total Liabilities                                  1394.25

    Owner's Equity

    Kenneth Pittman, Capital          14296.00
    Kenneth Pittman, Drawing          -4500.00
    Net Income                         8845.76
                                      --------
    Total Owner's Equity                              18641.76
                                                      --------
    Total Liabilities & Equity                        20036.01
                                                      ========
```

Figure 3.5
Balance Sheet

Statement of Owner's Equity

The **statement of owner's equity** is a financial statement that shows the changes to owner's equity during the fiscal period. The statement shows the capital at the beginning of the period, additions and subtractions to capital, and capital at the end of the fiscal period.

Business owners can review this report to determine if their equity is increasing or decreasing and what is causing the change. Changes to owner's equity are caused by additional investments, withdrawals, and net income or net loss. A sample owner's equity statement is shown in Figure 3.6.

Pittman Consulting
Statement of Owner's Equity
For Period Ended 10/31/--

Kenneth Pittman, Capital (Beg. Of Period)	14296.00
Kenneth Pittman, Drawing	−4500.00
Net Income	8845.76
Kenneth Pittman, Capital (End of Period)	18641.76

Figure 3.6
Owner's Equity Statement

BANK RECONCILIATION

A **bank reconciliation** is the process whereby the bank statement is reconciled to the checkbook balance every month. The bank reconciliation option is accessed via the Other Activities menu item in the Data menu or the Other toolbar button. Information maintained by the software, such as the checkbook balance and checks that were written during the period, will be automatically provided to make the reconciliation process simpler and more accurate.

1: **Choose the *Other Activities* menu item from the Data menu, or click on the *Other* toolbar button.**

2: **When the Reconciliation window appears, click on the *Clear* button.**
This will cause the computer to erase any previous reconciliation data and ready the system to perform a new reconciliation.

3: **Enter the bank credit, bank charge, bank statement balance, and outstanding deposit amounts. Figure 3.7 shows an incomplete Bank Reconciliation.**
Note: The Cash account balance automatically appears in the Checkbook Balance text box, and the checks written during the period are displayed in the Checks from the Journals list box. If necessary, you may key a different checkbook balance amount.

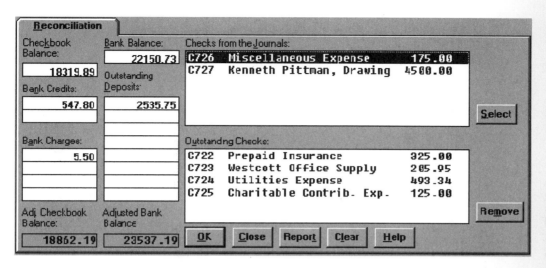

Figure 3.7
Bank
Reconciliation

4:   Select the outstanding checks.
Move the pointer to the Checks from the Journals list, select
the desired check (point and click to highlight), then click the
Select button (or double click on the desired check). The
selected check will appear in the Outstanding Checks list and
the Adjusted Bank Balance amount will automatically be
updated. Repeat this procedure for each outstanding check.
Notice Figure 3.7 shows all but two of the checks from the
journals have been selected as outstanding checks. Also, notice
that the bank reconciliation is out of balance (it will be in
balance when the remaining two checks from the journal are
selected).

5:   Click the *Report* command button.
The completed, reconciled, Bank Reconciliation report is shown
in Figure 3.8 on the next page. Notice that the Adjusted
Checkbook Balance is equal to the Adjusted Bank Balance.

6:   Click the *Close* command button to dismiss the report window.

**7:   When the Bank Reconciliation reappears, click the *OK*
command button to record your data and dismiss the Bank
Reconciliation.**

Click the *Clear* button if you want to erase all
the data that has been entered in the
Reconciliation window.

```
                        Pittman Consulting
                        Bank Reconciliation
                            10/31/--

Checkbook Balance                                          18319.89
Plus Bank Credits:                          547.80

                                                             547.80

Less Bank Charges                             5.50

                                                               5.50

Adjusted Checkbook Balance                                 18862.19

Bank Statement Balance                                     22150.73

Plus Outstanding Deposits:                  2535.75

                                                            2535.75

Less Outstanding Checks:
                            C722         325.00
                            C723         205.95
                            C724         493.34
                            C725         125.00
                            C726         175.00
                            C727        4500.00

                                                            5824.29

Adjusted Bank Balance                                      18862.19
```

Figure 3.8
Bank
Reconciliation
Report

PERIOD-END CLOSING

Period-end closing is the process of recording and posting closing entries to the general ledger to prepare temporary accounts for a new fiscal period. **Temporary accounts** are accounts that accumulate information until it is transferred to the owner's capital account. The **Income Summary account** is an account used to summarize the closing entries for the revenue and expense accounts.

In a manual accounting system, closing entries are recorded in the journal and posted to the general ledger to close all of the temporary income statement accounts to the income summary account, close the income summary account to the capital account, and close the drawing account to the capital account. In an automated accounting system, the software generates and records the closing journal entries in the general journal. When these closing entries are posted to the general ledger, the software updates the account balances and copies the current account balances and stores them as the last fiscal period's account balances for use with financial statement analysis.

In this system, the closing journal entries remain stored by the software after they are posted. This allows corrections to be made for the previous year if necessary.

After the period-end closing procedure is completed, a post-closing trial balance report is displayed. A **post-closing trial balance** is a trial balance that verifies debits equal credits in the general ledger accounts after closing entries are posted. The only difference between a regular trial balance and a post-closing trial balance is *when* it is displayed.

1: **Choose the *Generate Closing Journal Entries* menu item from the Options menu.**
The dialog box shown in Figure 3.9 will appear.

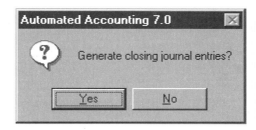

Figure 3.9
Generate Closing
Journal Entries

2: **Click the *Yes* command button to proceed.**
The closing entries shown in Figure 3.10 will appear.

Acct. #	Account Title	Debit	Credit
410	Fees	12751.45	
330	Income Summary		12751.45
330	Income Summary	3905.69	
510	Advertising Expense		595.00
512	Charitable Contrib. Exp.		190.00
515	Dues & Subscriptions Exp.		155.65
520	Insurance Expense		247.00
530	Miscellaneous Expense		285.00
540	Rent Expense		950.00
550	Supplies Expense		552.52
560	Telephone Expense		263.45
570	Travel & Entertain. Exp.		173.73
580	Utilities Expense		493.34
330	Income Summary	8845.76	
310	Kenneth Pittman, Capital		8845.76
310	Kenneth Pittman, Capital	4500.00	
320	Kenneth Pittman, Drawing		4500.00

Figure 3.10
Closing Entries

3: **Click the *Post* button to instruct the software to post the closing entries and store the last fiscal period's account balances for future use.**

4:   Display a post-closing trial balance report.
Click on the *Reports* toolbar button, select the *Ledger Reports*
option button from the Report Selection dialog box, then
choose the *Trial Balance* report.

The post-closing trial balance for Pittman Consulting is shown in
Figure 3.11.

Pittman Consulting
Trial Balance
10/31/--

Acct. Number	Account Title	Debit	Credit
110	Cash	18319.89	
120	Supplies	1191.12	
130	Prepaid Insurance	525.00	
220	Baker Advertising, Inc.		595.00
225	Barre Journals, Inc.		155.65
240	Gregor Graphics & Design		425.50
250	Westcott Office Supply		218.10
310	Kenneth Pittman, Capital		18641.76
	Totals	20036.01	20036.01

Figure 3.11
Post-Closing Trial Balance

If an error is detected after closing, (1) correct the journal entry in
error; (2) delete the closing entry; and (3) again generate, display, and
post the closing journal entries. If the closing entry is in error, correct the
entry and post. Be sure to print another post-closing trial balance.

Chapter Review

1.   Adjusting entries are not recorded in the general journal *until* all
other transactions for the accounting period have been entered into
the computer and posted. The trial balance is then displayed or
printed. This trial balance and the period-end adjustment data are
the basis for the adjusting entries.

2.   The income statement provides information about the net income
or net loss of a business over a specific period of time. Up-to-date

account balances stored by the computer are used to calculate and display the revenue earned and the expenses incurred during a fiscal period. Total revenue minus total expenses equals the net income or net loss. Included for each amount on the income statement is a component percentage, indicating each amount's percentage of total operating revenue.

3. The balance sheet reports assets, liabilities, and owner's equities on a specific date. The balance sheet can help financial statement users evaluate the overall financial strength of a business.

4. The statement of owner's equity shows the changes to owner's equity during the fiscal period. The statement shows the capital at the beginning of the period, additions and subtractions to capital, and capital at the end of the fiscal period.

5. Each month, after the bank statement is received, the bank statement is reconciled to the checkbook balance. The checkbook balance is the same as the Cash account balance in the general ledger.

6. Closing journal entries generated by the software close all of the temporary income statement accounts to the income summary account, close the income summary account to the capital account, and close the drawing account to the capital account. When the closing entries are posted to the general ledger, the software updates the account balances, copies the current account balances, and stores them as the last fiscal period's account balances for use with financial statement analysis.

7. A post-closing trial balance report is displayed to verify that debits equal credits in the general ledger accounts after closing entries are posted.

The World Wide Web is a sub-network of computers that displays multimedia information, including text, graphics, sound, and video clips. Web documents also contain special connections that allow users to switch to other documents that could be on computers anywhere in the world.

TUTORIAL PROBLEM 3 - T

In this tutorial problem, you will complete the end-of-fiscal-period processing for a service business, including reconciling a bank statement. You will also complete a spreadsheet activity (optional).

The adjusting entries for Pittman Consulting are for October of the current year and are illustrated in Figure 3.12.

STEP 1:   Start up *Automated Accounting 7.0*.

STEP 2:   Load the opening balances template file, AA03-T.
Click the *Open* toolbar button. Select the drive and directory/folder containing the opening balance files then select file AA03-T from the File list box.

STEP 3:   Enter your name in the User Name text box and click the *OK* button.

STEP 4:   Save the file to your disk and directory/folder with a file name of XXX3-T where XXX are your initials.
Click the *Save As* toolbar button and save the file as XXX3-T, where XXX are your initials.

STEP 5:   Enter the adjusting entries shown in Figure 3.12.
Click the *Journal* toolbar button, then click on the *General Journal* tab and enter the adjusting entries. The following adjustment data is for the month of October for Pittman Consulting:

Supplies inventory $1,191.12
Value of insurance policies on October 31 . . .   525.00

Date	Refer.	Acct. No.	Debit	Credit
10/31/--	Adj.Ent.	550	552.52	
		120		552.52
10/31/--	Adj.Ent.	520	247.00	
		130		247.00

Figure 3.12
General Journal (Adjusting Entries)

▶

T U T O R I A L   P R O B L E M   3 - T

STEP 6:   **Display the adjusting entries.**
Click the *Reports* toolbar button. When the Reports
Selection dialog box appears, select the *Journals* option
button. Choose the *General Journal* report and click the
OK button. When the Journal Report Selection dialog
appears (Figure 3.13), choose the *Customize Journal
Report* option and enter a reference restriction of
Adj.Ent. so that only the adjusting entries are reported.
The general journal report appears in Figure 3.14.

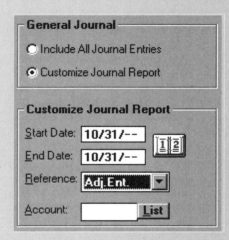

Figure 3.13
Journal
Report
Selection
Dialog

Pittman Consulting
General Journal
10/31/--

Date	Refer.	Acct.	Title	Debit	Credit
10/31	Adj.Ent.	550	Supplies Expense	552.52	
10/31	Adj.Ent.	120	Supplies		552.52
10/31	Adj.Ent.	520	Insurance Expense	247.00	
10/31	Adj.Ent.	130	Prepaid Insurance		247.00
			Totals	799.52	799.52

Figure 3.14
General
Journal Report
(Adjusting
Entries)

T U T O R I A L   P R O B L E M   3 – T

STEP 7:   **Display the income statement.**
Select the *Financial Statements* option button from the Report Selection dialog box, choose the *Income Statement* report, then click *OK*. The income statement is shown in Figure 3.15.

Pittman Consulting		
Income Statement		
For Period Ended 10/31/--		
Operating Revenue		
Fees	12751.45	100.00
Total Operating Revenue	12751.45	100.00
Operating Expenses		
Advertising Expense	595.00	4.67
Charitable Contrib. Exp.	190.00	1.49
Dues & Subscriptions Exp.	155.65	1.22
Insurance Expense	247.00	1.94
Miscellaneous Expense	285.00	2.24
Rent Expense	950.00	7.45
Supplies Expense	552.52	4.33
Telephone Expense	263.45	2.07
Travel & Entertain. Exp.	173.73	1.36
Utilities Expense	493.34	3.87
Total Operating Expenses	3905.69	30.63
Net Income	8845.76	69.37

Figure 3.15
Income Statement

STEP 8:   **Display the balance sheet.**
Choose the *Balance Sheet* report, then click the *OK* button. The balance sheet is shown in Figure 3.16.

STEP 9:   **Display the statement of owner's equity.**
Choose the *Statement of Owner's Equity* report, then click the *OK* button. The statement of owner's equity is shown in Figure 3.17.

TUTORIAL   PROBLEM   3 – T

```
                        Pittman Consulting
                         Balance Sheet
                            10/31/--

Assets

Cash                                18319.89
Supplies                             1191.12
Prepaid Insurance                     525.00
                                    --------
Total Assets                                        20036.01
                                                    ========
Liabilities

Baker Advertising, Inc.               595.00
Barre Journals, Inc.                  155.65
Gregor Graphics & Design              425.50
Westcott Office Supply                218.10
                                    --------
Total Liabilities                                    1394.25

Owner's Equity

Kenneth Pittman, Capital            14296.00
Kenneth Pittman, Drawing            -4500.00
Net Income                           8845.76
                                    --------
Total Owner's Equity                                18641.76
                                                    --------
Total Liabilities & Equity                          20036.01
                                                    ========
```

Figure 3.16
Balance Sheet

```
                        Pittman Consulting
                     Statement of Owner's Equity
                      For Period Ended 10/31/--

Kenneth Pittman, Capital (Beg. Of Period)           14296.00
Kenneth Pittman, Drawing                            -4500.00
Net Income                                           8845.76
                                                    --------
Kenneth Pittman, Capital (End of Period)            18641.76
                                                    ========
```

Figure 3.17
Statement of Owner's Equity

TUTORIAL PROBLEM 3-T

STEP 10: **Generate a 3D income statement bar chart.**
Click the *Graphs* toolbar button. When the Graph Selection dialog box appears, choose the *Income Statement* option button from the Data to Graph list, then select the *3D Bar* option from the Type of Graph list. Click on *OK*. The 3D income statement bar chart is illustrated in Figure 3.18.

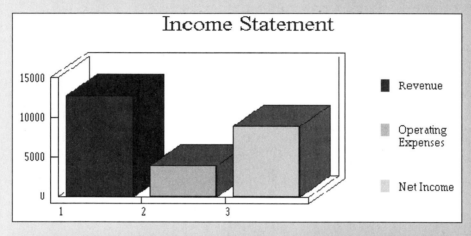

Figure 3.18
Income Statement Bar Chart

STEP 11: **Process the bank reconciliation data.**
Click the *Other* toolbar button. When the Reconciliation window appears, click the *Clear* button. Enter the bank credit, bank charge, balance shown on bank statement, and outstanding deposit amounts. The Checkbook balance will be provided by the software. To enter the outstanding checks, move the pointer to the Checks from the Journal list, choose the desired check (point and click to highlight), then click the *Select* button. The selected check will appear in the Outstanding Checks list and the Adjusted Bank Balance amount will automatically be updated. Repeat this procedure for each outstanding check.

Checkbook balance $18,319.89
Bank credit 547.80
Bank charge 5.50
Balance shown on bank statement 22,150.73
Outstanding deposit 2,535.75

Outstanding checks as follows:

Check No.	Amount
722	$325.00
723	$205.95
724	$493.34
725	$125.00
726	$175.00
727	$4,500.00

STEP 12: **Display the bank reconciliation report and record the reconciliation data.**
Click the *Report* button at the bottom of the Reconciliation window. Close the report window. When the Reconciliation window reappears, click the *OK* button to record your data and dismiss the Reconciliation window. The bank reconciliation is shown in Figure 3.19.

```
                      Pittman Consulting
                      Bank Reconciliation
                           10/31/--

Checkbook Balance                                    18319.89

Plus Bank Credits:                    547.80
                                      -------
                                                       547.80

Less Bank Charges:                      5.50
                                      -------
                                                         5.50
                                                     --------
Adjusted Checkbook Balance                           18862.19
                                                     ========
Bank Statement Balance                               22150.73

Plus Outstanding Deposits:           2535.75
                                     -------
                                                      2535.75

Less Outstanding Checks:
                             C722     325.00
                             C723     205.95
                             C724     493.34
                             C725     125.00
                             C726     175.00
                             C727    4500.00
                                     -------
                                                      5824.29
                                                      -------
Adjusted Bank Balance                                18862.19
                                                     ========
```

Figure 3.19
Bank Reconciliation Report

TUTORIAL PROBLEM 3-T

STEP 13: **Save your data file to disk with a file name of XXX3–TBC, where XXX are your initials.**
Click the *Save As* toolbar button and save your file as XXX3–TBC where XXX are your initials, 3–T is the problem number, and BC is "before closing."

STEP 14: **Optional spreadsheet integration activity:**
Use a spreadsheet to prepare a balance sheet for the month of October that shows the component percentage of total assets.

a. Display and copy the balance sheet to the clipboard in spreadsheet format.
b. Start up your spreadsheet software and load template file SS03–T.
c. Select cell A1 as the current cell (if not already selected).
d. Paste the balance sheet that was copied to the clipboard in step a into the spreadsheet. Select the *Paste* item from the Edit menu.
e. Enter the heading *Component %* in cell D8. Enter the formula to calculate the component percentage in cell D10. For example, @ABS(B10–C10)/+$C$14. Copy and paste the formula in cell D10 to cells D11, D12, D14, D19, D20, D21, D22, D24, D32, and D34.
f. Format the amounts in currency format ($X,XXX.XX) and the component calculations in percentage format (XXX.XX%) if necessary.
g. Print the spreadsheet (cells A1–D35). The completed spreadsheet report is shown in Figure 3.20.
h. Save your spreadsheet file with a file name of XXX3–T where XXX are your initials and 3–T identifies Tutorial Problem 3–T.
i. End your spreadsheet session.

STEP 15: **Optional word processing integration activity:**
You have been asked to provide Mr. Pittman, President of Pittman Consulting, with the income statement for the period ended October 31, 19--. Copy and paste the income statement from the accounting system into your word processor so you can enhance its appearance.

a. Display and copy the income statement to the clipboard in word processor format.

▶

TUTORIAL   PROBLEM   3 – T

```
Student Name

Pittman Consulting
Balance Sheet
As Of 10/31/--

----------------------------------------------------------
Assets                                        Component %
----------------------------------------------------------

Cash                         $18,319.89              91.43%
Supplies                      $1,191.12               5.94%
Prepaid Insurance               $525.00               2.62%
                             ----------
Total Assets                                 $20,036.01  100.00%
                                             ==========
Liabilities

Baker Advertising, Inc.         $595.00               2.97%
Barre Journals, Inc.            $155.65               0.78%
Gregor Graphics & Design        $425.50               2.12%
Westcott Office Supply          $218.10               1.09%
                             ----------
Total Liabilities                             $1,394.25   6.96%

Owner's Equity

Kenneth Pittman, Capital     $14,296.00
Kenneth Pittman, Drawing     ($4,500.00)
Net Income                    $8,845.76
                             ----------
Total Owner's Equity                         $18,641.76  93.04%

Total Liabilities & Equity                   $20,036.01  100.00%
                                             ==========
```

Figure 3.20
Balance Sheet Spreadsheet with Component Percentages

b. Start up your word processing software and create a new document.

c. Paste the income statement into your word processing document.

d. Format the income statement to enhance its appearance (the recommended font is Courier, size 10). Notice the completed document shown in Figure 3.21 has the main heading bold and centered and the classification headings also in bold. Experiment by adding further enhancements. For example, if your word processor has graphic capabilities, a company logo could be added.

e. Print your document.

T U T O R I A L   P R O B L E M   3 - T

    f. Save your document with a file name of XXX3–T.
    g. End your word processing application.

```
                    Pittman Consulting
                    Income Statement
               For Period Ended 10/31/--

Operating Revenue

Fees                              12751.45    100.00
                                  --------

Total Operating Revenue           12751.45    100.00

Operating Expenses

Advertising Expense                 595.00      4.67
Charitable Contrib. Exp.            190.00      1.49
Dues & Subscriptions Exp.           155.65      1.22
Insurance Expense                   247.00      1.94
Miscellaneous Expense               285.00      2.24
Rent Expense                        950.00      7.45
Supplies Expense                    552.52      4.33
Telephone Expense                   263.45      2.07
Travel & Entertain. Exp.            173.73      1.36
Utilities Expense                   493.34      3.87
                                   --------

Total Operating Expenses           3905.69     30.63
                                   --------

Net Income                         8845.76     69.37
                                  =========
```

Figure 3.21
Completed
Word
Processing
Integrated
Document

STEP 16: **Generate and post the closing journal entries.**
Choose the *Generate Closing Journal Entries* menu item from the Options menu. When the dialog box appears asking if you want to generate closing journal entries, click the *Yes* button. The closing journal entries automatically generated by the computer are shown in Figure 3.22. Click on *Post*.

STEP 17: **Display the closing entries.**
Click the *Reports* toolbar button. When the Reports Selection dialog box appears, choose the *Journals* option button, then select the *General Journal* report and click *OK*. When the Journal Report Selection dialog appears, choose the *Customize Journal Report* option and enter a Reference restriction of *Clo.Ent.* so that only the closing entries are reported. The report appears in Figure 3.23.

▷

TUTORIAL PROBLEM 3-T

Acct. #	Account Title	Debit	Credit
410	Fees	12751.45	
330	Income Summary		12751.45
330	Income Summary	3905.69	
510	Advertising Expense		595.00
512	Charitable Contrib. Exp.		190.00
515	Dues & Subscriptions Exp.		155.65
520	Insurance Expense		247.00
530	Miscellaneous Expense		285.00
540	Rent Expense		950.00
550	Supplies Expense		552.52
560	Telephone Expense		263.45
570	Travel & Entertain. Exp.		173.73
580	Utilities Expense		493.34
330	Income Summary	8845.76	
310	Kenneth Pittman, Capital		8845.76
310	Kenneth Pittman, Capital	4500.00	
320	Kenneth Pittman, Drawing		4500.00

Figure 3.22
Closing Journal Entries

```
                         Pittman Consulting
                          General Journal
                             10/31/--

--------------------------------------------------------------
   Date   Refer.   Acct.  Title                 Debit     Credit
--------------------------------------------------------------

  10/31  Clo.Ent.  410   Fees                 12751.45
  10/31  Clo.Ent.  330   Income Summary                 12751.45
  10/31  Clo.Ent.  330   Income Summary        3905.69
  10/31  Clo.Ent.  510   Advertising Expense              595.00
  10/31  Clo.Ent.  512   Charitable Contrib. Exp.         190.00
  10/31  Clo.Ent.  515   Dues & Subscriptions Exp.        155.65
  10/31  Clo.Ent.  520   Insurance Expense                247.00
  10/31  Clo.Ent.  530   Miscellaneous Expense            285.00
  10/31  Clo.Ent.  540   Rent Expense                     950.00
  10/31  Clo.Ent.  550   Supplies Expense                 552.52
  10/31  Clo.Ent.  560   Telephone Expense                263.45
  10/31  Clo.Ent.  570   Travel & Entertain. Exp.         173.73
  10/31  Clo.Ent.  580   Utilities Expense                493.34
  10/31  Clo.Ent.  330   Income Summary        8845.76
  10/31  Clo.Ent.  310   Kenneth Pittman, Capital        8845.76
  10/31  Clo.Ent.  310   Kenneth Pittman, Capital 4500.00
  10/31  Clo.Ent.  320   Kenneth Pittman, Drawing         4500.00
                                              -------  -------
                         Totals              30002.90 30002.90
                                              =======  =======
```

Figure 3.23
Closing Entries
Report

TUTORIAL PROBLEM 3 – T

STEP 18: **Display a post-closing trial balance.**
Choose the *Ledger Reports* option button, select the *Trial Balance* report, and click *OK*. The post-closing trial balance report appears in Figure 3.24.

Pittman Consulting
Trial Balance
10/31/--

Acct. Number	Account Title	Debit	Credit
110	Cash	18319.89	
120	Supplies	1191.12	
130	Prepaid Insurance	525.00	
220	Baker Advertising, Inc.		595.00
225	Barre Journals, Inc.		155.65
240	Gregor Graphics & Design		425.50
250	Westcott Office Supply		218.10
310	Kenneth Pittman, Capital		18641.76
	Totals	20036.01	20036.01

Figure 3.24
Post-Closing Trial Balance

STEP 19: **Use the Save As menu item to save your data with a file name of XXX3–TAC where XXX are your initials and AC is "after closing."**
Click the *Save As* toolbar button and save the data.

STEP 20: **End your *Automated Accounting* session.**
Click the *Exit/Quit* toolbar button.

Netiquette is an Internet phrase that refers to the rules of conduct and behavior on the Net. For example, don't send unwanted advertising, do keep your messages brief and to the point, and don't use ALL CAPS unless you mean to shout.

Applying Your Information Skills

I. MATCHING

Directions: In the *Working Papers* write the letter of the appropriate term next to each definition.

a. adjusting entries
b. income statement
c. component percentage
d. balance sheet
e. statement of owner's equity
f. bank reconciliation
g. period-end closing
h. temporary accounts
i. income summary account
j. post-closing trial balance

1. A financial statement that shows the changes to owner's equity during the fiscal period.

2. A financial statement that provides information on the net income or net loss of a business over a specific period of time.

3. A financial statement that reports assets, liabilities, and owner's equities on a specific date.

4. The process whereby the bank statement is reconciled to the checkbook balance every month.

5. The percentage relationship between one financial statement item and the total that includes that item.

6. Journal entries recorded to update general ledger accounts at the end of a fiscal period.

7. A trial balance that verifies that debits equal credits in the general ledger accounts after closing entries have been posted.

8. The process of recording and posting closing entries to the general ledger to prepare temporary accounts for a new fiscal period.

9. An account used to summarize the closing entries for the revenue and expense accounts.

10. Accounts that accumulate information until it is transferred to the owner's capital account.

II. QUESTIONS

Directions: Write the answers to the following questions in the *Working Papers.*

1. If the balance in the Supplies account after all transactions for the fiscal period have been processed and before adjusting entries is $1,500.00 and the current supplies inventory is $1,200.00, what is the amount of the supplies adjusting entry?

2. What financial statements are available for a nondepartmentalized business organized as a sole proprietorship?

3. How do you know when the bank statement reconciles to the checkbook on the bank reconciliation report?

4. Briefly describe the closing entries generated by the computer.

5. Describe the procedure to correct an error discovered after closing.

 # Independent Practice Problem 3–P

In Practice Problem 3–P, you will process any additions, changes, and deletions to the chart of accounts. You will also process the monthly transactions for November, complete the end of fiscal period processing, reconcile the bank statement, and complete a spreadsheet activity (optional).

STEP 1:   **Start up *Automated Accounting 7.0.***

STEP 2:   **Open and load the opening balances template file, AA03–P.**

STEP 3:   **Enter your name in the User Name text box.**

STEP 4:   **Use Save As to save the opening balances file with a file name of XXX3–P where XXX are your initials.**

STEP 5:   **Enter the following account maintenance and transactions for November.**

Nov. 03   Record the October bank service charge, $5.50. M219. Charge *Miscellaneous Expense.*

03   Record the October bank interest income, $84.23. M220.
Note: Add Interest Income (account number 710) to the chart of accounts.

03   Paid cash for rent, $950.00. C728.

04   Paid cash for telephone bill, $305.13. C729.

06   Bought repairs on account from Wilke Heating, $445.75. M221.

Note: Add Repair Expense (account number 545) and add Wilke Heating (account number 260) to the chart of accounts.

07   Paid cash for insurance, $110.50. C730.
10   Paid cash on account to Barre Journals, Inc., $155.65. C731.
14   Paid cash on account to Baker Advertising, Inc., $595.00. C732.
17   Received cash from fees, $3,221.88. T261.
18   Bought supplies on account from Gregor Graphics & Design, $225.00. M222.
19   Paid cash on account to Westcott Office Products, $218.10. C733.
      Note: Change the account title of Westcott Office Supply to Westcott Office Products in the chart of accounts.
20   Bought advertising on account from Baker Advertising, Inc., $275.98. M223.
21   Received cash from fees, $3,816.95. T262.
21   Paid cash for travel expense, $66.75. C734.
24   Paid cash on account to Gregor Graphics & Design, $425.50. C735.
25   Paid cash for electric bill, $437.20. C736.
26   Received cash from fees, $2,921.95. T263.
27   Paid cash to owner for personal use, $4,800.00. C737.
28   Paid cash for charitable contribution, $100.00. C738.
28   Paid cash for professional dues, $200.00. C739.

STEP 6:   **Display a chart of accounts report.**

STEP 7:   **Display the general journal report for the period November 1 through November 30 of the current year. Make corrections if necessary.**

CHECK FIGURES:
General journal debit and credit totals = $19,361.07

STEP 8:   **Display a trial balance report.**

STEP 9:   **Enter the November adjusting entries from the following data. Use the trial balance from Step 8 as the basis for making the adjusting entries. Use "Adj.Ent." as the reference.**

Supplies inventory on November 30 . . . . $670.00
Value of insurance policies on November 30 . .   263.45

STEP 10:   **Display the general journal report for the adjusting entries. Use a reference restriction of *Adj.Ent.* so that only adjusting entries will be included on the report.**

STEP 11: Display the financial statements.

STEP 12: Display a 3D balance sheet bar graph.

STEP 13: Process the bank reconciliation data based on the following information.

Checkbook balance	$19,995.57
Bank credit	717.00
Bank charge	5.50
Bank statement balance	23,965.92
Outstanding deposit	2,921.95

Outstanding checks:

Check No.	Amount
733	$218.10
735	$425.50
736	$437.20
737	$4,800.00
738	$100.00
739	$200.00

STEP 14: Display the bank reconciliation report.

STEP 15: Use the Save As menu item to save your data with a file name of XXX3–PBC.

STEP 16: Optional spreadsheet integration activity:
Prepare a balance sheet for the month of November that shows the component percentage of total assets.
- a. Display and copy the balance sheet to the clipboard in spreadsheet format.
- b. Start up your spreadsheet software and load template file SS03–T.
- c. Select cell A1 as the current cell (if not already selected) and paste the balance sheet into the spreadsheet.
- d. Enter the heading *Component* % in cell D8. Enter the formula to calculate the component percentage in cell D10, then copy and paste it into the appropriate cells using the format illustrated in Figure 3.20.
- e. Format the amounts in currency format ($X,XXX.XX) and the component calculations in percentage format (XXX.XX%) if necessary.
- f. Print the spreadsheet.
- g. Save your spreadsheet file with a file name of XXX3–P.
- h. End your spreadsheet session and return to *Automated Accounting*.

STEP 17: **Optional word processing integration activity:**
Copy and paste the income statement ended November 30, 19-- from the accounting system into your word processor and enhance its appearance.
  a. Display and copy the income statement to the clipboard in word processor format.
  b. Start up your word processing software application and create a new document.
  c. Paste the income statement into your word processing document.
  d. Format the income statement to enhance its appearance. The recommended font is Courier, size 10.
  e. Print your document.
  f. Save your document with a file name of XXX3–P.
  g. End your word processing application.

STEP 18: **Generate and post the closing journal entries.**

STEP 19: **Display the general journal report for Closing Entries.**
Use a reference restriction of Clo.Ent., so that only closing entries will be included on the report.

STEP 20: **Display a post-closing trial balance.**

STEP 21: **Save your data with a file name of XXX3–PAC where XXX are your initials and AC is "After Closing."**

STEP 22: **End your *Automated Accounting* session.**

Applying Your Technology Skills 3–P

Directions: Write the answers to the following questions in the *Working Papers*.

1. Based on the general journal report, what is the amount of check no. C737?

2. What is the balance in the cash account at the end of the month?

3. What are the totals of the Debit and Credit columns of the adjusting entries shown on the general journal report for adjusting entries?

4. What is the total operating revenue?

5. What are the total operating expenses?

6. What are the total operating expenses for the month as a percentage of total operating revenue?

7. What is the net income?

8. What is the net income for the month as a percentage of total operating revenue?

9. What are the total assets?

10. What are the total liabilities?

11. What is the owner's equity at the end of the fiscal period?

12. What is the adjusted bank balance amount on the bank reconciliation report?

 Mastery Problem 3–M

In this problem, you will process any additions, changes, and deletions to the chart of accounts. You will also process the monthly transactions for December, complete the end-of-fiscal-period processing, reconcile the bank statement, and complete a spreadsheet activity (optional).

STEP 1:   Open and load the opening balance file AA03–M.

STEP 2:   Enter your name in the User Name text box.

STEP 3:   Save the opening balances file with a file name of XXX3–M.

STEP 4:   Enter the following December accounts maintenance and general journal transactions.

Dec. 01   Record the November bank charges, $5.50. M224. Charge *Miscellaneous Expense*.
01   Record the November bank interest income, $87.46. M225.
02   Paid cash for rent, $950.00. C740.
03   Paid cash for telephone bill, $306.49. C741.
04   Bought supplies on account from Westcott Office Products, $376.64. M226.
05   Paid cash for travel expense, $52.88. C742.
08   Received cash from fees, $3,343.66. T264.
09   Paid cash on account to Gregor Graphics and Design, $225.00. C743.
10   Paid cash for charitable contribution, $155.00. C744.
11   Paid cash for a subscription, $202.30. C745. Note: Change the account Barre Journals, Inc. to Barre Periodicals.
15   Paid cash for insurance, $495.00. C746.
16   Paid cash on account to Wilke Heating, $445.75. C747.

17   Received cash from fees, $3,710.52. T265.
18   Bought advertising on account from Baker Advertising, Inc., $375.00. M227.
19   Paid cash on account to Baker Advertising, Inc., $275.98. C748.
22   Paid cash for miscellaneous expense, $84.56. C749.
26   Paid cash for electric bill, $417.30. C750.
26   Received cash from fees, $2,858.97. T266.
29   Bought repairs on account from Yates Plumbing, Inc., $274.43. M228.
      Note: Add Yates Plumbing, Inc. to the chart of accounts. Assign account number 270 so that it will be positioned immediately following Wilke Heating.
30   Paid cash to owner for personal use, $4,500.00. C751.

STEP 5:   Display a chart of accounts, general journal report of December transactions, and a trial balance.

STEP 6:   Enter the adjusting entries.

Supplies inventory on December 31 . . . . $560.00
Value of insurance policies on December 31 . .   175.68

STEP 7:   Display the adjusting entries.

STEP 8:   Display the financial statements.

STEP 9:   Display a 3D expense distribution pie chart.

STEP 10:   Process the bank reconciliation data.

Bank statement data:
Checkbook balance $21,880.42
Bank statement balance 25,835.80
Bank credit 822.01
Bank charge 5.50
Outstanding deposit 2,858.97

Outstanding checks:

Check No.	Amount
743	$225.00
746	$495.00
748	$275.98
749	$84.56
750	$417.30
751	$4,500.00

STEP 11:   Display a bank reconciliation report.

CHECK FIGURES:
General journal debit and credit totals = $19,142.44

STEP 12: **Optional spreadsheet integration activity:**
Prepare a balance sheet for the month of December that shows the component percentage of total assets.
  a. Display and copy the balance sheet to the clipboard in spreadsheet format.
  b. Start up your spreadsheet software and load template file SS03–T.
  c. Select cell A1 and paste the balance sheet into the spreadsheet.
  d. Enter the labels and formulas required to report and calculate the component percentage of total assets using the format illustrated in Figure 3.20.
  e. Print the spreadsheet.
  f. Save your spreadsheet file with a file name of XXX3–M.
  g. End your spreadsheet session and return to the Automated Accounting application.

STEP 13: **Save your data with a file name of XXX3–MBC.**

STEP 14: **Generate and post the closing entries.**

STEP 15: **Display the general journal report for Closing Entries.**

STEP 16: **Display a post-closing trial balance.**

STEP 17: **Save your data with a file name of XXX3–MAC.**

STEP 18: **End your *Automated Accounting* session.**

M Applying Your Technology Skills 3–M

Directions: Write the answers to the following questions in the *Working Papers.*

1. Based on the general journal report, what is the amount of check no. C748?

2. What is the balance in the cash account at the end of the month?

3. What are the totals of the Debit and Credit columns shown on the general journal report for adjusting entries?

4. What are the total fees for the period?

5. What is the total amount of telephone expense?

6. What are the total operating expenses for the month as a percentage of total operating revenue?

7. What is the net income?

8. What is the net income for the month as a percentage of total operating revenue?

9. What is the ending balance for supplies?

10. What are the total liabilities?

11. What is the owner's equity at the end of the fiscal period?

12. What is the total of outstanding checks on the bank reconciliation report?

Use your on-line Help options to learn more about your browser. The more features you learn and use, the more helpful your browser will be to you.

A modem is a hardware device that allows two computers to communicate over a telephone line. A modem turns internal computer information into sound, and reconverts sound into computer data.

R Reinforcement Activity R–1

A–1 Carpet Cleaning, Inc. is a small service business that cleans commercial and residential carpets. In Reinforcement Activity R–1, you will process the monthly transactions for April, complete the end-of-fiscal-period processing, reconcile the bank statement, and complete a spreadsheet activity (optional). Separate fee accounts are maintained for commercial and residential cleaning. As you are recording the fees received transactions, if the fee received is for commercial cleaning, record the account number for Fees—Commercial. If the fee received is for residential cleaning, record the account number for Fees—Residential.

STEP 1:   **Start up the *Automated Accounting 7.0* software.**

STEP 2:   **Open and load the opening balances template file, AAR–1.**

STEP 3:   **Enter your name in the User Name text box.**

STEP 4:   **Use the Save As menu item to save the opening balances file to your disk and directory/folder with a file name of XXXR–1, where XXX are your initials.**

STEP 5:   **Enter the following chart of accounts maintenance and general journal transactions.**

Apr. 01   Received bank statement showing March bank service charge, $5.75. Charge miscellaneous expense. M52.

01   Paid cash on account to Eubank Office Supplies, $442.54. C745.

01   Paid cash for rent, $1,200.00. C746.
     Note: Change the account Lemox Advertising Co. to Lemox Promotions.

02   Paid cash for water bill, $81.38. C747.

02   Received cash from commercial cleaning, $925.10. T232.

02   Received cash from residential cleaning, $506.52. T233.

05   Bought supplies on account from Pickard Supply Co., $478.45. M53.
     Note: Add Pickard Supply Co. to the chart of accounts. Assign account number 250 so that it will be positioned immediately following Lemox Promotions in the chart of accounts.

05   Paid cash to owner for personal use, $300.00. C748.

06 Bought advertising on account from Lemox Promotions, $350.00. M54.
Note: Add Advertising Expense to the chart of accounts. Assign account number 505 so that it will be positioned immediately following Fees—Residential in the chart of accounts.

06 Paid cash for miscellaneous expense, $74.29. C749.

07 Paid cash for repairs, $328.50. C750.
Note: Add Repairs Expense to the chart of accounts. Assign account number 535 so that it will be positioned immediately following Rent Expense in the chart of accounts.

07 Paid cash for telephone bill, $171.65. C751.

08 Paid cash for miscellaneous expense, $16.25. C752.

09 Received cash from commercial cleaning, $1,085.43. T234.

09 Received cash from residential cleaning, $513.50. T235.

12 Paid cash on account to Combs Supply Co., $792.99. C753.

12 Paid cash on account to Becker Chemicals, Inc., $1,003.07. C754.

12 Paid cash to owner for personal use, $300.00. C755.

13 Paid cash for electric bill, $358.16. C756.

13 Paid cash for miscellaneous expense, $30.00. C757.

14 Paid cash for repairs, $73.81. C758.

15 Bought supplies on account from Becker Chemicals, Inc., $414.05. M55.

15 Paid cash for advertising, $72.50. C759.

16 Received cash from commercial cleaning, $1,241.96. T236.

16 Received cash from residential cleaning, $657.82. T237.

19 Paid cash to owner for personal use, $300.00. C760.

19 Bought supplies on account from Eubank Office Supplies, $412.05. M56.

19 Paid cash for professional dues, $125.00. C761.
Note: Add Dues & Subscriptions Exp. to the chart of accounts. Assign account number 507 so that it will be positioned immediately following Advertising Expense in the chart of accounts.

20   Paid cash for insurance, $330.25. C762.

20   Paid cash for miscellaneous expense, $18.00. C763.

21   Paid cash on account to Lemox Promotions, $350.00. C764.

21   Bought supplies on account from Combs Supply Co., $214.30. M57.

21   Paid cash for advertising, $45.00. C765.

22   Paid cash on account to Pickard Supply Co., $478.45. C766.

23   Received cash from commercial cleaning, $1,036.54. T238.

23   Received cash from residential cleaning, $533.50. T239.

26   Paid cash to owner for personal use, $300.00. C767.

26   Paid cash for miscellaneous expense, $37.00. C768.

26   Bought supplies on account from Pickard Supply Co., $227.40. M58.

27   Paid cash on account to Combs Supply Co., $214.30. C769.

27   Paid cash for miscellaneous expense, $17.50. C770.

28   Paid cash for advertising, $195.00. C771.

28   Bought a subscription on account from Lemox Promotions, $80.00. M59.

28   Paid cash for repairs, $76.25. C772.

29   Paid cash for insurance, $175.33. C773.

29   Bought supplies on account from Schall Chemicals, Inc., $380.25. M60.

       Note: Add Schall Chemicals, Inc. to the chart of accounts. Assign account number 260 so that it will be positioned immediately following Pickard Supply Co. in the chart of accounts.

29   Paid cash on account to Becker Chemicals, Inc., $414.05. C774.

30   Received cash from commercial cleaning, $1,150.35. T240.

30   Received cash from residential cleaning, $790.75. T241.

30   Paid cash to replenish the petty cash fund, $96.25: miscellaneous expense, $56.00; repairs, $40.25. C775.

       Note: The two items (miscellaneous expense and repairs) are entered on separate lines in the general journal window.

> 30 Paid cash on account to Eubank Office Supplies, $412.05. C776.

STEP 6: Display a chart of accounts report.

STEP 7: Display the general journal report for the period April 1 through April 30 of the current year. Make corrections if errors are detected.

CHECK FIGURES:
General journal debit and credit totals = $19,833.29

STEP 8: Display a trial balance report.

STEP 9: Enter the adjusting entries for the month of April. The adjustment data are shown below. Use the trial balance printed in the previous step as the basis for making the adjusting entries. Record "Adj.Ent." as the reference.

Supplies inventory on April 30 . . . . $2,530.02
Value of insurance policies on April 30 . . . . . . 481.56

STEP 10: Display the general journal report for the adjusting entries. Use a reference restriction of *Adj.Ent.* so that only adjusting entries will be included on the report.

CHECK FIGURES:
Net income = $3,658.90
Total assets = $13,575.50

STEP 11: Display the financial statements.

STEP 12: Display a 3D income statement bar chart.

STEP 13: Process the bank reconciliation based on the information provided below.

Bank credit $318.07
Bank charge 5.75
Bank statement balance 8,902.83

Outstanding deposits are:
$1,036.54
$ 533.50
$1,150.35
$ 790.75

Outstanding checks are:

Check No.	Amount
768	$ 37.00
769	$214.30
770	$ 17.50
771	$195.00
772	$ 76.25
773	$175.33
774	$414.05
775	$ 96.25
776	$412.05

CHECK FIGURES:
Adjusted bank balance = $10,776.24

STEP 14: Display the bank reconciliation report.

STEP 15:   **Optional spreadsheet activity:**
Create a business summary report for the month of April that shows the cash balance, total liabilities, total fees, and total expenses:

   a.   Display and copy the trial balance to the clipboard in spreadsheet format.
   b.   Start-up your spreadsheet software and load template file SSR–1.
   c.   Select cell A1 as the current cell (if not already selected) and paste the trial balance into the spreadsheet. Center the contents of cell B–1 and the heading in cells B3 to B5. Center the column headings in rows 7 and 8.
   e.   Copy cell B3 to cell B34.
Enter *Business Summary Report* in cell B35.
Copy cell B5 to cell B36.
If necessary, center the contents of cells B34–B36.
Enter *Cash Balance* in cell B38, *Total Liabilities* in cell B39, *Total Fees* in cell B40, and *Total Expenses* in cell B41.
Copy cell C10 to cell C38.
Enter the formula to sum the total liabilities in cell C39 @SUM(D14..D16).
Enter the formula to sum the fees in cell C40 (+D19+D20).
Enter the formula to sum the total expenses in cell C41 @SUM(C21..C29)
Format columns: C and D in currency format if necessary.
   f.   Print the entire spreadsheet (cells A1–D41).
   g.   Save your spreadsheet file to your disk and directory/folder with a file name of XXXR–1 (where XXX are your initials and R–1 identifies Reinforcement Activity R–1).
   h.   End your spreadsheet session and return to the *Automated Accounting* application.

STEP 16:   Use the Save As menu item to save a backup copy of your data to disk with a file name of XXXR–1BC.

STEP 17:   Generate and post the closing journal entries.

STEP 18:   Display a post-closing trial balance.

STEP 19:   Save your data to disk with a file name of XXXR–1AC, where XXX are your initials.

STEP 20:   End the *Automated Accounting* session.

CHECK FIGURES:
Cash Balance = $10,463.92
Total Liabilities = $687.65
Total Fees = $8,441.47
Total Expenses = $4,782.57

Applying Your Technology Skills R–1

Directions: Write the answers to the following questions in the *Working Papers* or on a separate sheet of paper.

1. Based on the general journal report, what is the amount of check no. 774?

2. What are the totals of the debit and credit columns of the general journal report of the monthly transactions?

3. What is the balance in the cash account at the end of the month?

4. What are the totals of the Debit and Credit columns of the adjusting entries shown on the general journal report for adjusting entries?

5. What are the total fees for commercial?

6. What is the total operating revenue?

7. What are the total operating expenses?

8. What are the total operating expenses for the month as a percentage of total operating revenue?

9. What is the net income?

10. What is the net income for the month as a percentage of total operating revenue?

11. What are the total assets?

12. What are the total liabilities?

13. What is the owner's equity at the end of the fiscal period?

14. What is the adjusted bank balance amount on the bank reconciliation report?

ACCOUNTING CAREERS IN DEPTH

Payroll Clerk

A payroll clerk compiles payroll data; enters data or computes and posts wages; and reconciles errors, to maintain payroll records, using a computer or a calculator. A payroll clerk performs the following duties:

- Compiling payroll data, such as hours worked; sales or piecework; taxes, insurance, and union dues to be withheld; and employee identification numbers, from time sheets and other records.
- Preparing computer input forms, entering data into computer files or computing wages and deductions, using a calculator, and posting to payroll records.
- Reviewing wages computed and correcting errors to ensure the accuracy of the payroll.
- Recording changes affecting net wages, such as exemptions, insurance coverage, and loan payments for each employee to update the master payroll records.
- Recording data concerning the transfer of employees between departments.

The payroll clerk may also do the following:

- Prorating expenses to be debited or credited to each department for cost accounting.

- Preparing periodic reports of earnings, taxes, and deductions.
- Keeping records of leave pay and nontaxable wages.
- Preparing and issuing paychecks.

Attention to detail is very important for a payroll clerk. Entering incorrect information in computer systems or payroll documentation could directly affect an employee's paycheck. If you have ever experienced an error in your paycheck, you can understand how important it is to make as few errors as possible, if any at all.

A career as a payroll clerk can be very interesting. The data to be processed gives you the opportunity to see confidential information which would need to be handled very carefully. Also, you gain a better understanding of how employee and payroll figures are processed. The knowledge gained in accounting courses could provide a good background to a payroll clerk position and could give you a competitive edge when looking toward advancement opportunities.

The experience gained in a payroll clerk job is transferable in all industries because all companies have payroll departments. Therefore, if you are particularly interested in a specific industry, a career as a payroll clerk in that industry would be even more enjoyable.

The current worldwide telephone system is the backbone of the Internet. For the most part, the Internet uses the existing phone network to connect one computer or computer system to another.

4

Purchases and Cash Payments

Partnership

Merchandising Business

Merchandise

Merchandise Inventory

Purchases

Purchases Journal

Cash Payments Journal

Vendor

Purchase on Account

Purchases Journal Input Form

Cash Payment

Cash Payments Journal Input Form

Direct Payment

Cash Payments on Account

General Ledger Report

Schedule of Accounts Payable Report

Accounts Payable Ledger Report

LEARNING OBJECTIVES

Upon completion of this chapter, you will be able to:

1. Enter vendor maintenance data.

2. Enter purchases on account transactions.

3. Enter cash payments transactions.

4. Correct journal entries.

5. Generate journal reports.

6. Generate ledger reports.

INTRODUCTION

In previous chapters, you learned about accounting activities for a service business organized as a sole proprietorship. In this chapter, you will work with a merchandising business organized as a partnership as you learn to add, change, or delete vendors and to enter and correct purchases and cash payments journal entries. A **partnership** is a business that is owned by two or more persons. A **merchandising business** is a business that purchases and resells goods. The goods purchased for resale are called **merchandise.** An asset account titled Merchandise Inventory is included in the chart of accounts for a merchandising business. The **Merchandise Inventory** account shows the value of goods on hand for sale to customers. A merchandising business also has an account titled **Purchases.** The cost of the merchandise purchased for resale is recorded in the Purchases account.

A merchandising business has many frequently occurring transactions that affect single accounts. A number of these transactions would require many entries in the general journal's debit and credit columns. Therefore, special journals are used to simplify the record keeping process for these types of transactions. The special journal used to record the purchase of merchandise on account is called the **purchases journal.** The special journal used to record cash payments transactions is called the **cash payments journal.**

E T H I C S

The widespread use of CD-ROMs and online services such as CompuServe and America Online have made it very easy to obtain graphic images of almost any subject. With this easy access comes the temptation to use any graphic, regardless of its source and the intended use, for personal and commercial use.

To protect their rights, many photographers and artists copyright their images. Copyrighting makes it illegal to use an image without permission from the copyright owner. In addition, the ways in which copyrighted images can be used are strictly limited according to the wishes of the owner. Typically, a publisher will give permission to use the copyrighted image in newsletters and flyers but will place restrictions on selling the image in any form to others.

a. Suppose you created a masterpiece image using a drawing or painting program. After working on it for many hours, how would you react if someone else wanted to use the image? Explain.

b. How can photographers and artists protect their work from unauthorized copy or use?

c. How should violators of copyright laws be dealt with?

MAINTAIN VENDORS

A business from which merchandise is purchased or supplies and other assets are bought is called a **vendor.** Vendors may be added, changed, or deleted from the accounting system using a procedure similar to maintaining the chart of accounts, as shown in Figure 4.1.

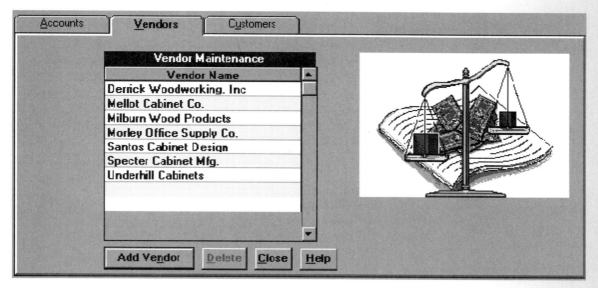

Figure 4.1
Vendor Maintenance

Adding a New Vendor

1: Click the *Accounts* toolbar button.

2: Click the *Vendors* tab.

3: Enter the vendor name.

4: Click the *Add Vendor* command button.

Changing a Vendor Name

1: Select (highlight) the vendor to change. The *Add Vendor* button will change to *Change Vendor.*

2: Enter the corrected vendor name.

3: Click the *Change Vendor* command button.

INTERNET

LISTSERV is a mailing list program designed to copy and distribute electronic mail to everyone who has subscribed to it.

Deleting a Vendor

1:   Select the vendor to delete.

2:   Click the *Delete* command button. A vendor cannot be deleted if it has a balance.

PURCHASES

A transaction in which merchandise that is purchased is paid for at a later date is called a **purchase on account.** Businesses that purchase merchandise on account from many vendors maintain a separate vendor file to avoid creating a bulky general ledger. The total owed to all vendors maintained in the vendor file is summarized in a single general ledger liability account titled Accounts Payable.

Purchases Journal Input Form

Purchases transactions may be entered directly into the computer from the transaction statement. Purchases of merchandise on account may also be recorded on the **purchases journal input form,** shown in Figure 4.2. They may then be entered into the computer from the data

PURCHASES JOURNAL INPUT FORM			
Date 02/10/--			Problem No. Example
Date	Refer.	Purch. Debit	Vendor
02/01/--	P220	1520.15	Specter Cabinet Mfg.
02/03/--	P221	657.70	Mellot Cabinet Co.

Figure 4.2
Purchases Journal
Input Form

recorded on the form. Each line on the input form is used to record a purchase invoice or one part of a purchase invoice that contains multiple purchases. When the debit portion of a purchase transaction is entered, the computer will automatically make the credit to accounts payable. Therefore, the credit to the Accounts Payable account need not be recorded on the input form. The field names and a description of each column of the input form are illustrated in the purchases journal shown in Figure 4.3.

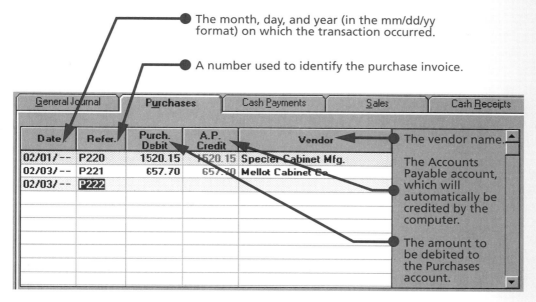

The month, day, and year (in the mm/dd/yy format) on which the transaction occurred.

A number used to identify the purchase invoice.

The vendor name.

The Accounts Payable account, which will automatically be credited by the computer.

The amount to be debited to the Purchases account.

Figure 4.3
Purchases Journal

S & W Custom Cabinets, a wholesale business, purchases merchandise directly from manufacturers, then sells merchandise wholesale to cabinet retailers.

The following transactions for S & W Custom Cabinets are recorded on the purchases journal input form shown in Figure 4.2. Each transaction is an example of a purchase of merchandise on account. Other purchases transactions on account and for cash (i.e., office supplies, rent, utilities, insurance, etc.) are entered in the general journal.

> Feb. 01 Purchased merchandise on account from Specter Cabinet Mfg., $1,520.15. P220.
> 03 Purchased merchandise on account from Mellot Cabinet Co., $657.70. P221.

Purchases Journal

The purchases journal, shown in Figure 4.3, is used for entering purchases transactions. Only merchandise that is purchased on account is recorded in this journal. Enter the date, invoice number, invoice amount in Purchases Debit (Purch. Debit), and vendor in the appropriate text boxes. The account debited reflects the merchandise that was purchased on account. The computer automatically calculates and displays the accounts payable credit amount after the Purchases Debit amount is entered.

It is not necessary to record the credit to the Accounts Payable account, since the computer makes this entry automatically.

1: **Click the *Journal* toolbar button.**
The Journal Entries window will appear.

2: **Click the *Purchases* tab.**
The Purchases journal will become the active tab.

3: **Enter the transaction date and press Tab.**
You can use the plus and minus keys to increase or decrease the date by one day.

4: **Enter the invoice number in the Refer. text box and press Tab.**
The computer will automatically increase the invoice number by one. Therefore, in most cases, the invoice number will be correct as displayed.

5: **Enter the amount of the invoice in the Purchases Debit (Purch. Debit) text box and press Tab.**
The Accounts Payable credit amount is calculated and displayed automatically by the computer.

6: **Choose a vendor name from the drop-down list.**
You can key the first letter of the vendor's name. The first vendor in the list beginning with that letter will appear in the text box. Or, use the Down Arrow key to scroll to the desired vendor name.

7: **Click the *Post* button.**

CASH PAYMENTS

Any type of transaction involving the payment of cash is called a **cash payment.** Cash payments transactions are recorded for expenses, cash purchases, payments to vendors, and payments not involving a check, such as a direct withdrawal from the bank for a service charge.

Cash Payments Journal Input Form

All cash payments may be recorded on the **cash payments journal input form,** shown in Figure 4.4. A description of each column of the input form is illustrated in the cash payments journal shown in Figure 4.5.

The following transactions are recorded on the cash payments journal input form. Each line on the form may be used to record a cash payment or one part of a cash payment. Additional examples of the various types of cash payments transactions that may be recorded on this form are illustrated in Tutorial Problem 4–T.

It is not necessary to record the credit to the Cash account, since the computer makes this entry automatically.

CASH PAYMENTS JOURNAL INPUT FORM

Date <u>02/10/--</u>   Problem No. <u>Example</u>

Date	Refer.	Acct. No.	Debit	Credit	A.P. Debit	Vendor
02/02/--	C136	1150	110.25			
02/03/--	C137	1160	175.65			
02/04/--	C138				1955.82	Santos Cabinet Design

Figure 4.4
Cash Payments Journal Input Form

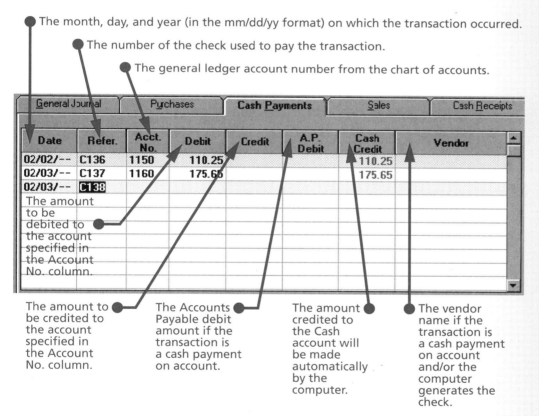

- The month, day, and year (in the mm/dd/yy format) on which the transaction occurred.
- The number of the check used to pay the transaction.
- The general ledger account number from the chart of accounts.

General Journal	Purchases	Cash Payments	Sales	Cash Receipts

Date	Refer.	Acct. No.	Debit	Credit	A.P. Debit	Cash Credit	Vendor
02/02/--	C136	1150	110.25			110.25	
02/03/--	C137	1160	175.65			175.65	
02/03/--	C138						

The amount to be debited to the account specified in the Account No. column.

The amount to be credited to the account specified in the Account No. column.

The Accounts Payable debit amount if the transaction is a cash payment on account.

The amount credited to the Cash account will be made automatically by the computer.

The vendor name if the transaction is a cash payment on account and/or the computer generates the check.

Figure 4.5
Cash Payments (Direct Payment)

Feb. 02   Paid cash for store supplies, $110.25. Check no. 136.
     03   Paid cash for insurance, $175.65. Check no. 137.
     04   Paid cash on account to Santos Cabinet Design, $1,955.82, covering P214. Check no. 138.

Cash Payments Transactions

The cash payments journal is used to enter all cash payments transactions. It is not necessary to enter the credit to cash because it is automatically calculated and displayed by the computer.

There are two types of cash payments: (1) direct payments and (2) cash payments on account. A **direct payment** is a cash disbursement that does *not* affect Accounts Payable. Examples of direct payments are checks written to pay expenses or buy assets. **Cash payments on account** are cash disbursements that do affect Accounts Payable.

Direct Payment   A cash payments journal with sample data for two direct cash payments is shown in Figure 4.5. Notice that the Vendor text box column is left blank. The vendor is needed only for transactions that affect accounts payable or if the computer is to generate the check as described in Chapter 9. The account debited reflects why the cash was disbursed, such as miscellaneous expense, rent, etc. The cash credit amount is automatically calculated and displayed by the computer.

1: **Choose the *Journal Entries* menu item from the Data menu or click the *Journal* toolbar button.**
   The Journal Entries window will appear.

2: **Click the *Cash Payments* tab.**
   The Cash Payments journal will become the active tab.

3: **Enter the transaction date and press Tab.**
   You can use the plus and minus keys to increase or decrease the date by one day.

4: **Enter the check number and press Tab.**
   The computer will automatically increase the check number by one.

5: **Enter the account numbers and amounts for each of the accounts to debit or credit and press Tab.**
   You can choose the *Chart of Accounts* command button and select an account from the Chart of Accounts list rather than key the account number. The cash credit amount is calculated and displayed automatically by the computer.

6: **If the transaction is correct, choose the *Post* button.**
   Leave the A.P. Debit and Vendor drop-down text boxes blank since they do not apply to a direct payment.

Cash Payments on Account   A cash payment on account is illustrated in Figure 4.6. A vendor is required because the Accounts Payable account is affected. The amount of the invoice is entered in the Accounts Payable Debit (A.P. Debit) text box column. The cash credit

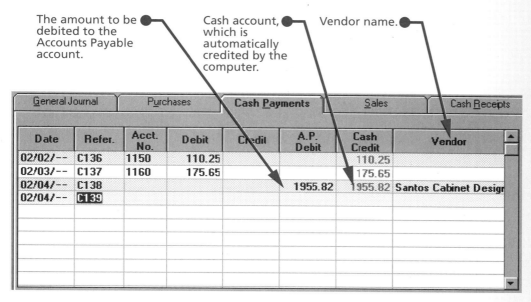

The amount to be debited to the Accounts Payable account.

Cash account, which is automatically credited by the computer.

Vendor name.

Date	Refer.	Acct. No.	Debit	Credit	A.P. Debit	Cash Credit	Vendor
02/02/--	C136	1150	110.25			110.25	
02/03/--	C137	1160	175.65			175.65	
02/04/--	C138				1955.82	1955.82	Santos Cabinet Design
02/04/--	C139						

General Journal | Purchases | Cash Payments | Sales | Cash Receipts

Figure 4.6
Cash Payments (Cash Payment on Account)

amount is automatically calculated and displayed by the computer. In a later chapter, you will learn how to use the Credit column to record purchases discounts.

1: **Choose the *Journal Entries* menu item from the Data menu, or click the *Journal* toolbar button.**

2: **Click the *Cash Payments* tab.**

3: **Enter the transaction date.**
You can also use the plus and minus keys to increase or decrease the date by one day.

4: **Enter the check number.**
The computer will automatically increase the check number by one.

5: **Enter the accounts payable debit amount.**
The cash credit amount is calculated and displayed automatically by the computer.

6: **Choose a vendor name from the drop-down list.**
You can also key the first letter of the vendor's name. The first vendor in the list beginning with that letter will appear in the text box. Use the Down Arrow key to scroll to the desired vendor name.

7: **If the transaction is correct, click the *Post* button.**

INTERNET

Many browser companies give their browser software away for free because they count on making money from services or transactions related to the browser.

CORRECTING JOURNAL ENTRIES

Sometimes it may be necessary to locate and correct journal entries after the entries have been posted. The procedures for locating and correcting journal entries are identical for all journals.

Finding a Journal Entry

1: Click the desired journal tab (*General, Purchases, Cash Payments*).

2: Choose the *Find* menu item from the Edit menu.
The Find dialog box in Figure 4.7 will appear.

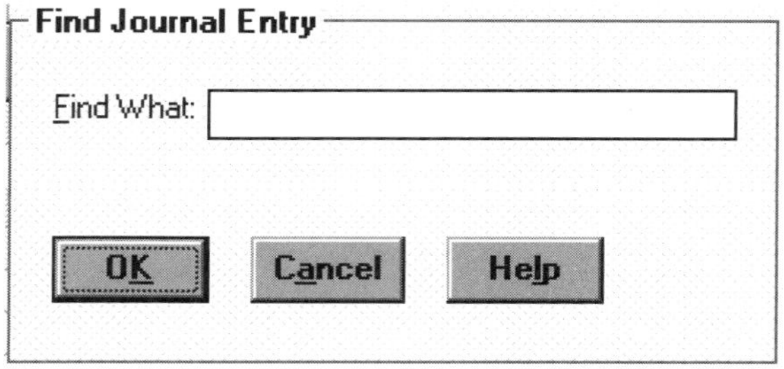

```
┌─ Find Journal Entry ──────────────────────────────┐
│                                                    │
│   Find What: [                              ]      │
│                                                    │
│                                                    │
│     ┌────────┐   ┌────────┐   ┌────────┐          │
│     │   OK   │   │ Cancel │   │  Help  │          │
│     └────────┘   └────────┘   └────────┘          │
│                                                    │
└────────────────────────────────────────────────────┘
```

Figure 4.7
Find Journal
Entry Dialog Box

3: Enter the date, reference, vendor name, or amount of the transaction you want to find in the Find What text box. Then click *OK*.
Information entered in the Find What text box is known as the search argument.

4: If a matching transaction is found, it will be displayed so that it may be changed or deleted.
Choose the *Find Next* command from the Edit menu to locate the next occurrence of the search argument.

Changing or Deleting Journal Transactions

1: Click the desired journal tab (*General, Purchases, Cash Payments*).

2: Select (highlight) the specific transaction text box that you wish to change.

3: Enter the correction and click the *Post* command button. Or if you wish to delete the entire transaction, choose the *Delete* command button.

JOURNAL REPORTS

Once the journal entries have been entered, the journal reports may be displayed.

1: Click the *Reports* toolbar button.

2: When the Report Selection dialog box appears, select the *Journals* option button from the Select a Report Group list.
A list of all the reports within the Journals option will appear, as shown in Figure 4.8.

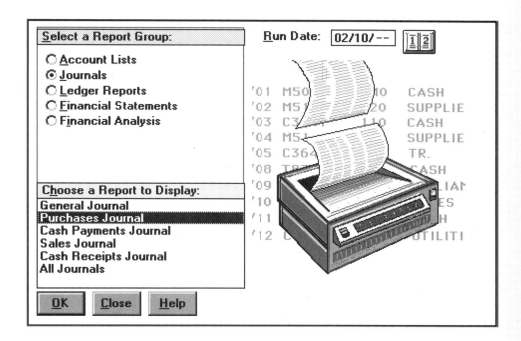

Figure 4.8
Report Selection
Dialog Box

3: Choose the desired Journal report from the Choose a Report to Display list. Then click *OK*.
The Journal Report Selection dialog shown in Figure 4.9 will appear, allowing you to display all the journal entries for the chosen journal or customize your journal report.

Figure 4.9
Journal Report
Selection Dialog

4: **Choose the *Customize Journal Report* option button to control the data to be included on the report.**
If you want to include *all* journal transactions on the report, choose the *Include All Journal Entries* option button. When the *Customize Journal Report* option is chosen, the dialog shown in Figure 4.10 will appear.

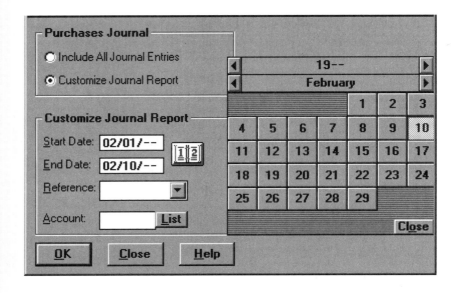

Figure 4.10
Customize
Journal Report
Dialog

5: **Set the range of dates to be included in the journal report in the Start Date and End Date text boxes.**
Enter the desired Start and End Dates by keying the actual dates, by using the + or – keys, or by using the Calendar icon.

6: **Enter an identifying reference in the Reference text box if you wish to restrict the report to a particular reference. Click the drop-down arrow to obtain a list of all the references available from which you may choose.**
As an alternative, you may key the first character of the reference in the text box. The first entry that begins with that character will be displayed in the text box. Use the Up and Down arrow keys to browse through the entries.

7: **Enter an account number in the Account text box if you wish to restrict the report to a particular account. Click the *List* command button to obtain a Chart of Accounts selection list. From the selection list you may choose the desired account number.**

8: **Click *OK*.**

A journal entries report is shown in Figure 4.11. To print the displayed report on an attached printer, click the *Print* command button or choose the *Print* menu item from the File menu.

```
                        S & W Custom Cabinets
                          Purchases Journal
                             02/10/--

------------------------------------------------------------------------
Date    Inv. No.  Acct.   Title                       Debit      Credit
------------------------------------------------------------------------

02/01   P220      5110    Purchases                  1520.15
02/01   P220      2110    AP/Specter Cabinet Mfg.                1520.15

02/03   P221      5110    Purchases                   657.70
02/03   P221      2110    AP/Mellot Cabinet Co.                   657.70

02/08   P222      5110    Purchases                   911.00
02/08   P222      2110    AP/Milburn Wood Products                911.00

02/09   P223      5110    Purchases                   895.75
02/09   P223      2110    AP/Underhill Cabinets                   895.75
                                                     -------     -------
                         Totals                      3984.60    3984.60
                                                     ======     ======
```

Figure 4.11
Purchases Journal Report

LEDGER REPORTS

Automated Accounting 7.0 uses three ledgers: (1) general ledger, (2) accounts payable ledger, and (3) accounts receivable ledger. There are two reports available for each. The general ledger reports are the trial balance and the general ledger. The two reports available for the accounts payable ledger are the schedule of accounts payable and the accounts payable ledger report. The accounts receivable ledger reports will be covered in Chapter 5.

1: Click the *Reports* toolbar button.

2: Select the *Ledger Reports* option button from the Select a Report Group list.
A list of all the ledger reports will appear, as shown in Figure 4.12.

3: Choose the report you would like to display.

4: Click *OK*.

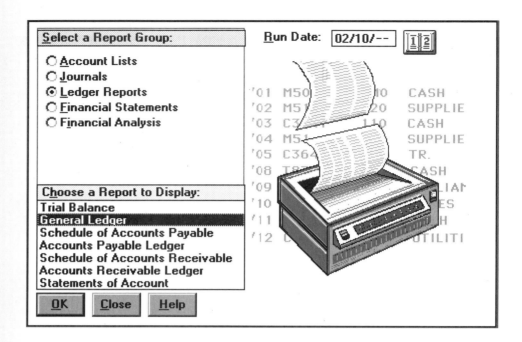

Figure 4.12
Report Selection
Dialog Box

General Ledger Report

The **general ledger report** shows detailed journal entry activity by account. Any range of accounts may be displayed, from one account to all accounts. If you have determined that a particular account balance is incorrect, displaying all journal activity for that account can be very useful in locating the error.

1: **When the *General Ledger* report is chosen, the Account Range selection dialog box shown in Figure 4.13 will appear. Enter the range of accounts to be included in the general ledger report.** Choose the *From:* and *To:* buttons and select the account numbers range from the Chart of Accounts list.

If only one account is to be displayed, the From: and To: text boxes can be the same. In the above example, account number 1110 is for the Cash account. Since the account number range is from 1110 to 1110, only activity for the Cash account will be displayed.

Figure 4.13
Account Range
Selection Dialog
Box

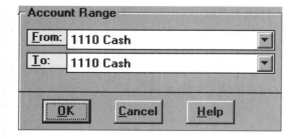

2: **Click the *OK* button.**
The general ledger report is shown in Figure 4.14.

```
                        S & W Custom Cabinets
                            General Ledger
                              02/10/--

Account        Journal          Date     Refer.    Debit      Credit      Balance

1110-Cash
               Balance Forward                                            37370.82Dr
               Cash Payment      02/01    C135                  5.50      37365.32Dr
               Cash Payment      02/02    C136                110.25      37255.07Dr
               Cash Payment      02/03    C137                175.65      37079.42Dr
               Cash Payment      02/04    C138               1955.82      35123.60Dr
               Cash Payment      02/05    C139                785.00      34338.60Dr
               Cash Payment      02/08    C140               1022.57      33316.03Dr
               Cash Payment      02/09    C141               1389.41      31926.62Dr
               Cash Payment      02/10    C142                147.08      31779.54Dr
               Cash Payment      02/10    C143                545.00      31234.54Dr
```

Figure 4.14
General Ledger Report for Cash Account

Schedule of Accounts Payable

The **schedule of accounts payable report** lists each vendor account balance and total balance due all vendors. The total due all vendors must equal the balance in the Accounts Payable account in the general ledger. A sample report is shown in Figure 4.15.

```
                  S & W Custom Cabinets
                Schedule of Accounts Payable
                        02/10/--

Name                                    Balance

Derrick Woodworking, Inc.               1636.50
Mellot Cabinet Co.                       657.70
Milburn Wood Products                   2085.40
Morley Office Supply Co.                 940.06
Specter Cabinet Mfg.                    1520.15
Underhill Cabinets                       895.75

Total                                   7735.56
                                        =======
```

Figure 4.15
Schedule of Accounts Payable

Accounts Payable Ledger Report

The **accounts payable ledger report** shows detailed journal entry activity by vendor. All the journal entries for the current fiscal period that affect each vendor are listed. This information is useful in locating errors within a single account, in obtaining status information about a specific vendor's activity, or in identifying transactions posted to the wrong vendor.

1: **When the *Accounts Payable Ledger* report is chosen, the Vendor Range dialog box shown in Figure 4.16 will appear. Select the range of vendors you wish to appear on the report.**

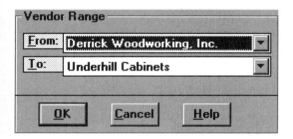

Figure 4.16
Vendor Range
Dialog Box

If only one vendor is to be displayed, the From: and To: portions of the vendor number range should be the same.

2: **Click *OK.***
The accounts payable ledger report for the range of vendors selected in Figure 4.16 is shown in Figure 4.17.

Chapter Review

1. Vendors may be added, changed, or deleted from the accounting system using a procedure similar to maintaining the chart of accounts.

2. The cost of the merchandise purchased for resale is recorded in the Purchases account. Purchases on account transactions may be entered directly into the computer. However, purchases transactions may be recorded on an input form before entering them into the computer.

3. Only purchases of merchandise on account are entered into the purchases journal.

S & W Custom Cabinets
Accounts Payable Ledger
02/10/--

Account	Journal	Date	Refer.	Debit	Credit	Balance
Derrick Woodworking, Inc.						
	Balance Forward					1636.50Cr
Mellot Cabinet Co.						
	Balance Forward					1022.57Cr
	Purchases	02/03	P221		657.70	1680.27Cr
	Cash Payment	02/08	C140	1022.57		657.70Cr
Milburn Wood Products						
	Balance Forward					1174.40Cr
	Purchases	02/08	P222		911.00	2085.40Cr
Morley Office Supply Co.						
	Balance Forward					471.60Cr
	General	02/03	M47		125.00	596.60Cr
	General	02/10	M50		343.46	940.06Cr
Santos Cabinet Design						
	Balance Forward					1955.82Cr
	Cash Payment	02/04	C138	1955.82		.00
Specter Cabinet Mfg.						
	Balance Forward					1389.41Cr
	Purchases	02/01	P220		1520.15	2909.56Cr
	Cash Payment	02/09	C141	1389.41		1520.15Cr
Underhill Cabinets						
	Purchases	02/09	P223		895.75	895.75Cr

Figure 4.17
Accounts Payable Ledger Report

4. Cash payments transactions are recorded for expenses, cash purchases, payments to vendors, and payments not involving a check, such as a direct withdrawal from the bank for a service charge.

5. There are two types of cash payments: (1) direct payments and (2) cash payments on account. A direct payment is a cash disbursement that does *not* affect accounts payable. Cash payments on account are cash disbursements that *do* affect accounts payable.

6. Journal entries may be corrected by finding the entry in the appropriate journal, highlighting the entry, keying the correct information, and posting the correct information.

7. *Automated Accounting 7.0* generates general ledger reports, schedule of accounts payable reports, and accounts payable ledger reports to obtain detailed information.

The Internet is not a single network but rather a super network made up of thousands of smaller subnetworks. The Internet is often referred to as the network of networks.

ACCOUNTING CAREERS IN DEPTH

Self-Employed C.P.A.

A C.P.A. is a Certified Public Accountant. Establishing a business as a C.P.A. would be a good career choice for those accountants who prefer to work for themselves. The services that can be provided include tax services, accounting services, auditing services, and investment services. A C.P.A.'s preparation of corporate and personal income tax statements helps provide suggestions and formulate tax strategies to assist a client in saving money.

For a self-employed C.P.A. there are many types of services to provide to the public—individuals as well as corporations. Though it is a big responsibility to work for yourself, it can be very rewarding. Some persons feel confined working a standard eight-hour day, but when you are self-employed you can schedule your own hours. However, you may have to work more hours in a day when you work for yourself. Although you must generate your own business, the work offers close customer contact, a high degree of independence, and potential financial rewards.

It is very important for an accountant to have a positive image with the public. This is especially important when you work for yourself because your name and the services you provide are what will bring you new clients.

The preparation for becoming a C.P.A. involves completing a four-year college degree in accounting, passing the C.P.A. exam, and gaining acceptable work experience. For a C.P.A., it is necessary to complete continuing education in order to keep one's certification. This could be done by participating in workshops, seminars, and short courses of study. Continuing education is required because of changes in laws that affect how companies can operate.

Those who choose to become self-employed C.P.A.s will enjoy a rewarding experience, will work hard, and most likely will become an integral part of the community where they have set up their business.

TUTORIAL PROBLEM 4 – T

In this tutorial problem you will maintain vendor accounts, enter purchases and cash payments journal entries, and display the related reports. You will enter purchases and cash payments transactions for S & W Custom Cabinets.

The general, purchases, and cash payments journal entries are illustrated in Figures 4.18 through 4.20.

Date	Refer.	Acct. No.	Debit	Credit	Vendor/Customer
02/03/--	M47	1145	125.00		
		2110		125.00	Morley Office Supply Co.
02/04/--	M48	3120	241.45		
		5110		241.45	
02/05/--	M49	1145	85.00		
		5110		85.00	
02/10/--	M50	1150	343.46		
		2110		343.46	Morley Office Supply Co.

Figure 4.18
General Journal (February 1–10)

Date	Refer.	Purch. Debit	A.P. Credit	Vendor
02/01/--	P220	1520.15	1520.15	Specter Cabinet Mfg.
02/03/--	P221	657.70	657.70	Mellot Cabinet Co.
02/08/--	P222	911.00	911.00	Milburn Wood Products
02/09/--	P223	895.75	895.75	Underhill Cabinets

Figure 4.19
Purchases Journal (February 1–10)

Date	Refer.	Acct. No.	Debit	Credit	A.P. Debit	Cash Credit	Vendor
02/01/--	C135	6120	5.50			5.50	
02/02/--	C136	1150	110.25			110.25	
02/03/--	C137	1160	175.65			175.65	
02/04/--	C138				1955.82	1955.82	Santos Cabinet Design.
02/05/--	C139	3140	785.00			785.00	
02/08/--	C140				1022.57	1022.57	Mellot Cabinet Co.
02/09/--	C141				1389.41	1389.41	Specter Cabinet Mfg.
02/10/--	C142	1145	147.08			147.08	
02/10/--	C143	3120	545.00			545.00	

Figure 4.20
Cash Payments Journal (February 1–10)

TUTORIAL PROBLEM 4-T

STEP 1:   **Start up *Automated Accounting 7.0.***

STEP 2:   **Open and load the opening balances template file, AA04–T.**
Click the *Open* toolbar button. When the Open file dialog box appears, choose file AA04–T from the File list box.

STEP 3:   **Enter your name in the User Name text box and click *OK.***

STEP 4:   **Save the file with a file name of XXX4–T.**
Click the *Save As* toolbar button, and save the file as XXX4–T where XXX are your initials.

STEP 5:   **Add Underhill Cabinets to the vendor list.**
Click the *Accts.* toolbar button, then choose the *Vendors* tab. Enter Underhill Cabinets and click the *Add Vendor* button.

STEP 6:   **Enter the journal entries from the general, purchases, and cash payments journals shown in Figures 4.18 through 4.20.**
Key the following information from the transaction statements or refer to Figures 4.18 through 4.20 for input data. The reference numbers have been abbreviated as follows: Check, C; Purchase invoice, P; Memorandum, M.

Feb. 01   Paid cash for miscellaneous expense, $5.50. C135.

01   Purchased merchandise on account from Specter Cabinet Mfg., $1,520.15. P220.

02   Paid cash for store supplies, $110.25. C136.

03   Purchased merchandise on account from Mellot Cabinet Co., $657.70. P221.

03   Bought office supplies on account from Morley Office Supply Co., $125.00. M47.

03   Paid cash for insurance, $175.65. C137.

04   Wayne Duncan, partner, withdrew merchandise for personal use, $241.45. M48. Record this transaction in the general journal.

04   Paid cash on account to Santos Cabinet Design, $1,955.82, covering P214, C138.

▶

05   Discovered that a transaction for office supplies bought for cash in January was journalized and posted in error as a debit to Purchases instead of Supplies—Office, $85.00. M49. Record this transaction in the general journal.

05   Scott Klare, partner, withdrew cash for personal use, $785.00. C139.

08   Purchased merchandise on account from Milburn Wood Products, $911.00. P222.

08   Paid cash on account to Mellot Cabinet Co., $1,022.57, covering P215. C140.

09   Purchased merchandise on account from Underhill Cabinets, $895.75. P223.

09   Paid cash on account to Specter Cabinet Mfg., $1,389.41, covering P216. C141.

10   Paid cash for office supplies, $147.08. C142.

10   Wayne Duncan, partner, withdrew cash for personal use, $545.00. C143.

10   Bought store supplies on account from Morley Office Supply Co., $343.46. M50.

STEP 7:   **Display the vendor list.**
Click the *Reports* toolbar button. Select the *Account Lists* option button and choose *Vendor List.* Click *OK.* Examine the vendor report in Figure 4.21 and verify that the vendor you keyed in Step 5 is correct.

S & W Custom Cabinets
Vendor List
02/10/--

Vendor Name

Derrick Woodworking, Inc.
Mellot Cabinet Co.
Milburn Wood Products
Morley Office Supply Co.
Santos Cabinet Design
Specter Cabinet Mfg.
Underhill Cabinets

Figure 4.21
Vendor List

TUTORIAL PROBLEM 4-T

STEP 8:   **Display the general journal, purchases journal, and cash payments journal reports.**
Select *Journals* from the Select a Report Group list. Choose the desired journal report and click *OK*. When the Journal Report Selection dialog appears, click *OK* to select Include All Journal Entries. The general journal, purchases journal, and cash payments journal reports appear in Figures 4.22 through 4.24.

S & W Custom Cabinets
General Journal
02/10/--

Date	Refer.	Acct.	Title	Debit	Credit
02/03	M47	1145	Supplies—Office	125.00	
02/03	M47	2110	AP/Morley Office Supply Co.		125.00
02/04	M48	3120	Wayne Duncan, Drawing	241.45	
02/04	M48	5110	Purchases		241.45
02/05	M49	1145	Supplies—Office	85.00	
02/05	M49	5110	Purchases		85.00
02/10	M50	1150	Supplies—Store	343.46	
02/10	M50	2110	AP/Morley Office Supply Co.		343.46
			Totals	794.91	794.91

Figure 4.22
General Journal Report

S & W Custom Cabinets
Purchases Journal
02/10/--

Date	Inv. No.	Acct.	Title	Debit	Credit
02/01	P220	5110	Purchases	1520.15	
02/01	P220	2110	AP/Specter Cabinet Mfg.		1520.15
02/03	P221	5110	Purchases	657.70	
02/03	P221	2110	AP/Mellot Cabinet Co.		657.70
02/08	P222	5110	Purchases	911.00	
02/08	P222	2110	AP/Milburn Wood Products		911.00
02/09	P223	5110	Purchases	895.75	
02/09	P223	2110	AP/Underhill Cabinets		895.75
			Totals	3984.60	3984.60

Figure 4.23
Purchases Journal Report

S & W Custom Cabinets
Cash Payments Journal
02/10/--

Date	Ck. No.	Acct.	Title	Debit	Credit
02/01	C135	6120	Miscellaneous Expense	5.50	
02/01	C135	1110	Cash		5.50
02/02	C136	1150	Supplies—Store	110.25	
02/02	C136	1110	Cash		110.25
02/03	C137	1160	Prepaid Insurance	175.65	
02/03	C137	1110	Cash		175.65
02/04	C138	2110	AP/Santos Cabinet Design	1955.82	
02/04	C138	1110	Cash		1955.82
02/05	C139	3140	Scott Klare, Drawing	785.00	
02/05	C139	1110	Cash		785.00
02/08	C140	2110	AP/Mellot Cabinet Co.	1022.57	
02/08	C140	1110	Cash		1022.57
02/09	C141	2110	AP/Specter Cabinet Mfg.	1389.41	
02/09	C141	1110	Cash		1389.41
02/10	C142	1145	Supplies—Office	147.08	
02/10	C142	1110	Cash		147.08
02/10	C143	3120	Wayne Duncan, Drawing	545.00	
02/10	C143	1110	Cash		545.00
			Totals	6136.28	6136.28

Figure 4.24
Cash Payments Journal Report

STEP 9:   Display a trial balance, a general ledger report for the
accounts payable account, a schedule of accounts
payable, and an accounts payable ledger report for all
vendors.
Select *Ledger Reports,* choose the desired ledger report,
then click the *OK* button. When displaying the general
ledger report, be sure to enter the Accounts Payable
account (2110) number in both the From: and To: text
boxes in the Account Range dialog box. When

▶

T U T O R I A L   P R O B L E M   4 – T

displaying the accounts payable ledger report, make sure the first vendor appears in the From: text box and the last vendor appears in the To: text box in the Vendor Range dialog box. The reports appear in Figures 4.25 through 4.28.

S & W Custom Cabinets
Trial Balance
02/10/--

Acct. Number	Account Title	Debit	Credit
1110	Cash	31234.54	
1120	Petty Cash	100.00	
1130	Accounts Receivable	1598.80	
1140	Merchandise Inventory	131278.14	
1145	Supplies—Office	918.97	
1150	Supplies—Store	907.98	
1160	Prepaid Insurance	1117.69	
2110	Accounts Payable		7735.56
2120	Sales Tax Payable		1051.06
3110	Wayne Duncan, Capital		81802.30
3120	Wayne Duncan, Drawing	786.45	
3130	Scott Klare, Capital		81802.30
3140	Scott Klare, Drawing	785.00	
5110	Purchases	3658.15	
6120	Miscellaneous Expense	5.50	
	Totals	172391.22	172391.22

Figure 4.25
Trial Balance

FTP stands for File Transfer Protocol. FTP software transfers files of data from one computer to another.

▶

T U T O R I A L   P R O B L E M   4 – T

S & W Custom Cabinets
General Ledger
02/10/--

Account	Journal	Date	Refer.	Debit	Credit	Balance
2110-Accounts Payable						
	Balance Forward					7650.30Cr
	Purchases	02/01	P220		1520.15	9170.45Cr
	General	02/03	M47		125.00	9295.45Cr
	Purchases	02/03	P221		657.70	9953.15Cr
	Cash Payments	02/04	C138	1955.82		7997.33Cr
	Purchases	02/08	P222		911.00	8908.33Cr
	Cash Payments	02/08	C140	1022.57		7885.76Cr
	Purchases	02/09	P223		895.75	8781.51Cr
	Cash Payments	02/09	C141	1389.41		7392.10Cr
	General	02/10	M50		343.46	7735.56Cr

Figure 4.26
General Ledger Report

S & W Custom Cabinets
Schedule of Accounts Payable
02/10/--

Name	Balance
Derrick Woodworking, Inc.	1636.50
Mellot Cabinet Co.	657.70
Milburn Wood Products	2085.40
Morley Office Supply Co.	940.06
Specter Cabinet Mfg.	1520.15
Underhill Cabinets	895.75
Total	7735.56

Figure 4.27
Schedule of Accounts Payable

S & W Custom Cabinets
Accounts Payable Ledger
02/10/--

Account	Journal	Date	Refer.	Debit	Credit	Balance
Derrick Woodworking, Inc.						
	Balance Forward					1636.50Cr
Mellot Cabinet Co.						
	Balance Forward					1022.57Cr
	Purchases	02/03	P221		657.70	1680.27Cr
	Cash Payments	02/08	C140	1022.57		657.70Cr
Milburn Wood Products						
	Balance Forward					1174.40Cr
	Purchases	02/08	P222		911.00	2085.40Cr
Morley Office Supply Co.						
	Balance Forward					471.60Cr
	General	02/03	M47		125.00	596.60Cr
	General	02/10	M50		343.46	940.06Cr
Santos Cabinet Design						
	Balance Forward					1955.82Cr
	Cash Payments	02/04	C138	1955.82		.00
Specter Cabinet Mfg.						
	Balance Forward					1389.41Cr
	Purchases	02/01	P220		1520.15	2909.56Cr
	Cash Payments	02/09	C141	1389.41		1520.15Cr
Underhill Cabinets						
	Purchases	02/09	P223		895.75	895.75Cr

Figure 4.28
Accounts Payable Ledger

STEP 10: **Save your data.**
Click the *Save* toolbar button.

STEP 11: **Optional spreadsheet activity:**
S & W Custom Cabinets has asked you to use a
spreadsheet to calculate the component percentage
owed each vendor as of February 10. Prepare a report

▶

TUTORIAL   PROBLEM   4 – T

showing this information and generate a pie chart depicting the same data.

a. Display and copy the schedule of accounts payable report to the clipboard in spreadsheet format.

b. Start up your spreadsheet software and load template file SS04–T. A blank, formatted worksheet will appear.

c. Select cell B1 as the current cell, if not already selected.

d. Paste the schedule of accounts payable report (copied to the clipboard in step 11a) into the spreadsheet.

e. Enter the word *Percent* in cell D7.
Enter the formula to calculate the component percentage in cell D9. For example, (+C9/+$C$16). Copy and paste the formula in cell D9 to cells D10, D11, D12, D13, and D14.

f. Format the amounts in currency format and the calculated percentages in percentage format if necessary.

g. Generate a pie chart.
Select the range of cells B9 through C14, then choose the Chart or Graph menu item from the spreadsheet program you are using. If the program asks for a graph name, etc., enter **Vendors** in the graph name text box. Choose Pie Chart if the graph that appears is not a pie chart. Finally, if the spreadsheet you are using permits copying and pasting the graph into the worksheet, copy and paste the graph into cells A22 through E40.

h. Print the spreadsheet and pie chart. The completed spreadsheet and pie chart are shown in Figure 4.29.

i. Save your spreadsheet data with a file name of XXX4–T.

j. What if Milburn Wood Products' balance amount is now $3,587.95? Enter this change and the formula to compute the total. Notice the effects of the change on the component percentages and pie chart.

k. End your spreadsheet session without saving your changes made in step 12j.

TUTORIAL PROBLEM 4 - T

```
Student Name

              S & W Custom Cabinets
            Schedule of Accounts Payable
                 As Of 02/10/19--

-----------------------------------------------------
Name                      Balance           Percent
-----------------------------------------------------

Derrick Woodworking, Inc.  $1,636.50         21.16%
Mellot Cabinet Co.           $657.70          8.50%
Milburn Wood Products      $2,085.40         26.96%
Morley Office Supply Co.     $940.06         12.15%
Specter Cabinet Mfg.       $1,520.15         19.65%
Underhill Cabinets           $895.75         11.58%
                           ----------
Total                      $7,735.56
                           ==========
```

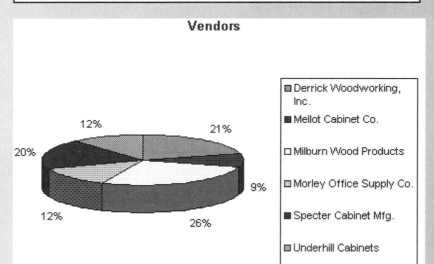

Figure 4.29
Vendor
Component
Percentage
Report and Pie
Chart

STEP 12:   Optional word processing integration activity:
S & W Custom Cabinets consults with Hicks Wolf &
Associates, a local accounting firm, for financial advice.
As part of the information needed, Mary Hicks, owner
and CPA of the accounting firm, has asked that you fax
her a list of the vendors and their account balances at
the end of each week. You are to use the word
processing fax template used by S & W Custom Cabinets
for most of its facsimile transmittals to prepare this

TUTORIAL PROBLEM 4-T

document for the week ended February 10 of the current year.

a. Display and copy the schedule of accounts payable report to the clipboard in word processing format.

b. Start up your word processing application software and load template file WP04–T as a text file.

c. Enter your name in the FROM field and complete the remainder of the top portion of the facsimile as shown in Figure 4.30.

```
                 S & W Custom Cabinets
                 9205 Creek View Drive
                Columbus, OH 43205-4530
                    (614) 555-4581


                       FACSIMILE

          TO:  Mary Hicks, CPA

     COMPANY:  Hicks Wolf & Associates

        DATE:  February 10, 19--

PHONE NUMBER:  (614) 555-7230

  FAX NUMBER:  (614) 555-7279

        FROM:  Your Name

     SUBJECT:  END OF THE WEEK VENDOR ACCOUNT
               BALANCES

Notes/Comments:

As per your request, our vendors and their account
balances as of February 10 are:

  Derrick Woodworking, Inc.    $1,636.50
  Mellot Cabinet Co.              657.70
  Milburn Wood Products         2,085.40
  Morley Office Supply Co.        940.06
  Specter Cabinet Mfg.          1,520.15
  Underhill Cabinets              895.75
```

Figure 4.30
Completed Facsimile

d. Position the insertion point one line after the text in the Notes/Comments section and paste the report. Delete report headings, totals, etc., and format the document to match Figure 4.30. Experiment adding further enhancement to the appearance of the fax.

e. Print the completed document. Many computers have the capability to fax documents electronically directly from the word processor so that a hard copy may not be necessary.

f. Save the document with a file name of XXX4–T.

g. End your word processing session.

STEP 13: **End your *Automated Accounting* session.** Click the *Exit/Quit* toolbar button.

Applying Your Information Skills

I. MATCHING

Directions: In the *Working Papers*, write the letter of the appropriate term next to each definition.

   a. partnership
   b. merchandising business
   c. merchandise
   d. merchandise inventory
   e. purchases
   f. purchases journal
   g. cash payments journal
   h. vendor
   i. purchase on account
   j. purchases journal input form
   k. cash payment
   l. cash payments journal input form
  m. direct payment
   n. cash payments on account
   o. general ledger report
   p. schedule of accounts payable report
   q. accounts payable ledger report

1. A report that shows detailed journal entry activity by vendor.

2. A business that purchases and resells goods.

3. A special journal used to record the purchase of merchandise on account.

4. A special journal used to record cash payments transactions.

5. An account that shows the value of goods on hand for sale to customers.

6. An account in which merchandise purchased for resale is recorded.

7. A cash disbursement that does *not* affect accounts payable.

8. Cash disbursements that *do* affect accounts payable.

9. A report that lists each vendor account balance and total balance due all vendors.

10. Goods purchased for resale.

11. A report that shows detailed journal entry activity by account.

12. Business from which merchandise is purchased or supplies and other assets are bought.

13. A transaction in which merchandise purchased is paid for at a later date.

14. A transaction involving the payment of cash.

15. An input form on which all purchases of merchandise on account may be recorded.

16. An input form on which all payments of cash may be recorded.

17. A business that is owned by two or more persons.

II. QUESTIONS

Directions: Write the answers to each of the following questions in the *Working Papers*.

1. How are vendors added to the accounting system?

2. What type of transaction is recorded in the purchases journal?

3. What are the two types of cash payments?

4. Why might it be necessary to locate journal entries after they have already been posted?

5. What are three journal reports that can be displayed once the journal entries have been entered?

6. What are the reports available for the general ledger and the accounts payable ledger?

Independent Practice Problem 4–P

In this problem you will process any additions, changes, or deletions to vendors. You will also process purchases and cash payments transactions for the period February 11 through February 20 of the current year.

STEP 1: **Start up *Automated Accounting 7.0.***

STEP 2: **Open and load the opening balances template file, AA04–P.**

STEP 3: **Enter your name in the User Name text box.**

STEP 4: **Save as XXX4–P, where XXX are your initials.**

STEP 5: **Enter the following transactions.**

Feb. 11   Paid cash for rent, $2,600.00. C144.
    11   Paid cash on account to Derrick Woodworking, Inc., $1,636.50, covering P217. C145.
    11   Paid cash for store supplies, $266.78. C146.
    12   Scott Klare, partner, withdrew merchandise for personal use, $383.90. M51. Record this transaction in the general journal.
    12   Purchased merchandise on account from Santos Cabinet Design, $2,206.53. P224.
    12   Paid cash for miscellaneous expense, $101.12. C147.
    15   Paid cash on account to Milburn Wood Products, $1,174.40, covering P218. C148.
    15   Paid cash for office supplies, $137.87. C149.
    15   Scott Klare, partner, withdrew cash for personal use, $785.00. C150.
    16   Discovered that a transaction for office supplies bought for cash in January was journalized and posted in error as a debit to Prepaid Insurance instead of Supplies—Office, $148.25. M52.
    16   Bought store supplies on account from Morley Office Supply Co., $242.66. M53.
    17   Paid cash on account to Morley Office Supply Co., $471.60, covering M45. C151.
    17   Purchased merchandise on account from Specter Cabinet Mfg., $2,076.85. P225.
    17   Purchased merchandise on account from Derrick Woodworking, Inc., $1,780.27. P226.

18   Paid cash on account to Mellot Cabinet Co.,
$657.70, covering P221. C152.

18   Purchased merchandise for cash, $2,628.82.
C153.

18   Paid cash for miscellaneous expense, $15.75.
C154.

18   Paid cash for insurance, $550.00. C155.

19   Paid cash for electric bill, $282.69. C156.

19   Paid cash on account to Specter Cabinet Mfg.,
$1,520.15, covering P220. C157.

19   Paid cash on account to Morley Office Supply
Co., $125.00, covering M47. C158.

19   Bought store supplies on account from
Superior Supply Co., $659.44. M54.
Note: Add Superior Supply Co. to the vendor
list.

19   Purchased merchandise on account from
Mellot Cabinet Co., $341.67. P227.

STEP 6:   **Display the following journal reports: general journal,
purchases journal, and cash payments journal for the
period February 11 through February 20 of the current
year. If errors are detected, make corrections.**

STEP 7:   **Display the following ledger reports: trial balance,
general ledger report for the cash account, schedule of
accounts payable, accounts payable ledger (all vendors).**

STEP 8:   **Save your data.**

STEP 9:   **Optional spreadsheet integration activity:**
S & W Custom Cabinets has asked you to use a
spreadsheet to calculate the component percentage
owed each vendor as of February 20. Prepare a report
showing this information and generate a pie chart
depicting the same data.
a. Display and copy the schedule of accounts payable
report to the clipboard in spreadsheet format.
b. Start up your spreadsheet software and load
template file SS04–T. A blank, formatted worksheet
will appear.
c. Select cell B1 as the current cell (if not already
selected) and paste the schedule of accounts payable
report into the spreadsheet.
d. Enter the word *Percent* in cell D7.
Enter the formula to calculate the component
percentage in cell D9. Copy and paste the formula in
cell D9 to the appropriate cells.

> **CHECK FIGURES:**
> Purchases journal debit
> and credit totals =
> $6,405.32
> Cash payments journal
> debit and credit totals
> = $12,953.38

e. Format the amounts in currency format and the calculated percentages in percentage format if necessary.

f. Generate a pie chart depicting the data in the report. Use **Vendors** as the title.

g. Print the spreadsheet and pie chart.

h. Save your spreadsheet data with a file name of XXX4–P.

i. What if Mellot Cabinet Co.'s balance is now $695.00 and Santos Cabinet Design's balance is now $3,136.90? Enter these changes and the formula to compute the total. Notice the effects of the changes on the component percentages and pie chart.

j. End your spreadsheet session without saving your changes from step 9i and return to *Automated Accounting.*

STEP 10:   **Optional word processing integration activity:**
You are to use the company's word processing fax template to prepare the vendor account balance information for the accounting firm the week ended February 20.

a. Display and copy the schedule of accounts payable report to the clipboard in word processing format.

b. Start up your word processing application software and load template file WP04–T as a text file.
Note: As an alternative, load the solution word processing file from Tutorial Problem 4–T and modify it as necessary to complete this activity.

c. Enter your name in the FROM field and complete the remainder of the top portion of the facsimile as shown in Figure 4.30.

d. Paste the report, delete report headings, totals, etc., and format the document to match Figure 4.30.

e. Print the completed document.

f. Save the document with a file name of XXX4–P.

g. End your word processing session.

STEP 11:   **End your *Automated Accounting* session.**

A "hit" is recorded every time someone connects to an Internet home page. A popular home page can take many hits. When traffic is too great on the Internet, you may not be able to reach a favorite site.

Applying Your Technology Skills 4–P

Directions: Using Independent Practice Problem 4–P, write the answers to the following questions in the *Working Papers*.

1. What are the totals of the debit and credit columns in the general journal report?

2. From the purchases journal report, what is the amount of invoice no. 225?

3. What is the amount of check no. 151 to Morley Office Supply Co.?

4. What is the current balance in Accounts Receivable?

5. What is the current balance in the Office Supplies account?

6. What was the balance at the beginning of the period in the Cash account?

7. What is the current balance owed to Specter Cabinet Mfg.?

8. What is the total owed to all vendors on February 20?

9. What was the balance owed to Mellot Cabinet Co. at the beginning of the period?

10. What is the total amount purchased from Mellot Cabinet Co. during February?

Mastery Problem 4–M

In this problem you will process any additions, changes, or deletions to vendors. You will also process purchases and cash payments transactions for the period February 21 through February 28 of the current year.

STEP 1:   **Open and load the opening balances file: AA04–M.**

STEP 2:   **Enter your name in the User Name text box.**

STEP 3:   **Save the opening balance data as XXX4–M.**

STEP 4:   **Enter the following transactions.**

Feb. 22   Purchased merchandise for cash, $590.05. C159.

22   Paid cash on account to Milburn Wood Products, $911.00, covering P222. C160.

22 Paid cash for miscellaneous expense, $22.00. C161.
23 Paid cash for store supplies, $103.81. C162.
23 Purchased merchandise on account from Santos Cabinet Design, $655.75. P228.
23 Paid cash on account to Underhill Cabinets, $895.75, covering P223. C163.
24 Paid cash for insurance, $134.73. C164.
24 Discovered that a payment for a miscellaneous expense was journalized and posted in error as a debit to Rent Expense instead of Miscellaneous Expense, $27.25. M55.
24 Purchased merchandise for cash, $303.81. C165.
24 Paid cash for office supplies, $142.91. C166.
24 Bought office supplies on account from Superior Supply Co., $157.90. M56.
25 Paid cash on account to Morley Office Supply Co., Inc., $343.46, covering M50. C167.
25 Purchased merchandise on account from Ashland Interiors, $800.28. P229.
    Note: Add Ashland Interiors to the vendor list.
25 Wayne Duncan, partner, withdrew cash for personal use, $835.00. C168.
25 Purchased merchandise on account from Milburn Wood Products, $631.87. P230.
26 Paid cash to replenish the petty cash fund, $100.00: miscellaneous expense, $48.00; office supplies, $15.00; store supplies, $37.00. C169.
    Note: Each of the items (miscellaneous expense, office supplies, etc.) is entered on separate lines in the cash payments journal.
26 Purchased merchandise on account from Mellot Cabinet Co., $349.80. P231.

CHECK FIGURES:
General journal debit and credit totals = $185.15
Purchases journal debit and credit totals = $2,437.70
Cash payments journal debit and credit totals = $4,382.52

STEP 5: Display the following reports: journal reports, trial balance, general ledger report for office and store supply accounts, schedule of accounts payable, accounts payable ledger (all vendors) for the period February 21 through February 28 of the current year.

STEP 6: Save your data.

STEP 7: Optional spreadsheet integration activity:
Prepare a report showing the component percentage

owed each vendor and generate a pie chart depicting
this data as of February 28.
a. Display and copy the schedule of accounts payable
    report to the clipboard in spreadsheet format.
b. Start up your spreadsheet software and load
    template file SS04–T.
c. Select cell B1 as the current cell and paste the
    schedule of accounts payable report into the
    spreadsheet.
d. Enter the labels and formulas required to report and
    compute the component percentages using the
    format illustrated in Figure 4.29.
e. Generate a pie chart depicting the data in the
    report.
f. Print the spreadsheet and pie chart.
g. Save your spreadsheet data with a file name of
    XXX4–M.
h. What if Ashland Interiors' balance is now $615.00
    and Specter Cabinet Mfg. is now $1,144.00? Enter
    these changes and the formula to compute the total.
    Notice the effects of the changes on the component
    percentages and pie chart.
i. End your spreadsheet session without saving your
    changes from step 7h.

STEP 8:   **Optional word processing integration activity:**
a. Display and copy the schedule of accounts payable
    report to the clipboard in word processing format.
b. Start up your word processing application software
    and load template file WP04–T as a text file.
    Note: As an alternative, and if completed, load your
    word processing solution file from either Tutorial
    Problem 4–T or Problem 4–P and modify it as
    necessary to complete this activity.
c. Enter your name in the FROM field and complete the
    remainder of the top portion of the facsimile as
    shown in Figure 4.30. Paste the report, delete report
    headings, totals, etc., and format the document as
    necessary.
d. Print the completed document.
e. Save the document with a file name of XXX4–M.
f. End your word processing session.

STEP 9:   **End your *Automated Accounting* session.**

M Applying Your Technology Skills 4–M

Directions: Using Mastery Problem 4–M, write the answers to the following questions in the *Working Papers*.

1. On the purchases journal report, what is the amount credited to Milburn Wood Products for invoice no. 230?

2. What is the amount of check no. 161 in the cash payments journal?

3. What is the balance in Scott Klare's Drawing account?

4. What is the balance in the Miscellaneous Expense account?

5. From the general ledger report, what is the amount of office supplies bought on memorandum no. 56?

6. From the general ledger report, was the amount of the office supply bought on memorandum no. 56 mentioned in Question 6 debited or credited to office supplies?

7. What is the balance owed to Ashland Interiors on February 28?

8. What is the total amount owed to all vendors as of February 28?

9. From the accounts payable ledger report, what is the amount of the cash payment to Morley Office Supply Co. on Feb. 25, check no. C167?

10. From the accounts payable ledger report, what is the amount for memorandum no. 56 to Superior Supply Co.?

INTERNET

The most important person on a network is the network administrator. The administrator manages all the hardware and software issues on a network and keeps things running.

5
Sales and Cash Receipts

LEARNING OBJECTIVES

Upon completion of this chapter, you will be able to:

1. Enter customer maintenance data.

2. Enter sales transactions.

3. Enter cash receipts transactions.

4. Display reports that summarize activities for the time period.

INTRODUCTION

In this chapter you will again work with S & W Custom Cabinets as you learn to add, change, and delete customers and to enter and correct sales and cash receipts journal entries. S & W Custom Cabinets is a wholesale merchandising business. This company sells merchandise on account to retail stores at wholesale prices. Retailers do not pay sales tax, since sales of merchandise for resale are not subject to sales tax. Occasionally, S & W Custom Cabinets sells on account to individuals. Sales on account to individuals are subject to sales tax. The company also sells merchandise at retail prices to individuals for cash. The cash sales to individuals are also subject to sales tax.

MAINTAIN CUSTOMERS

A business or individual to whom merchandise or services are sold is called a **customer.** Businesses that sell merchandise on account maintain

E T H I C S

One of the tasks that can be performed by computers is the coding and decoding of sensitive information. The coding of data is known as *encryption.* The reverse procedure—decoding—is known as *decryption.* In the encryption phase, readable data is turned into unreadable code. "Hello" might become "&W$Qd." Readable data means that it is readable to the computer, not necessarily to a human. In the decryption phase, unreadable code is turned back into readable data. In the coding and decoding of data, an element known as an *encryption key* is used. The key is composed of alphabetic characters and/or numeric values that are used by a mathematic formula that does all the work of encryption and decryption.

Coded data has played a major role in the military for many years. The outcome of wars has been determined by successfully breaking codes, and military advantage has been maintained by keeping secret codes secret. In fact, much of the research that has contributed to today's sophisticated encryption

techniques has come from the military. Coding is not limited to only the military. Encryption is a technique used frequently by businesses. Much data, especially that in transit electronically from one location to another, is subject to piracy by electronic interception. By preventing unauthorized eyes from spying on this information, companies can maintain confidentiality and a competitive edge.

a. Do you believe that breaking an encryption code and using (or selling) the information is ethical or unethical? Is it a violation of law? Explain.

b. Identify at least two reasons why businesses may want to use encryption when transmitting financial information from one location to another.

c. In general, do you think that the use of encryption is ethical or unethical? Explain.

a separate file for each customer. The total owed by all customers in the customer file is summarized in a single general ledger asset account titled Accounts Receivable.

Customers may be added, changed, or deleted from the accounting system using a procedure similar to maintaining the chart of accounts and vendor lists. When the *Maintain Accounts* menu item is chosen from the Data menu, or the *Accts.* toolbar button is clicked, the Account Maintenance window will appear. Choose the *Customers* tab to display the Customer Maintenance window shown in Figure 5.1.

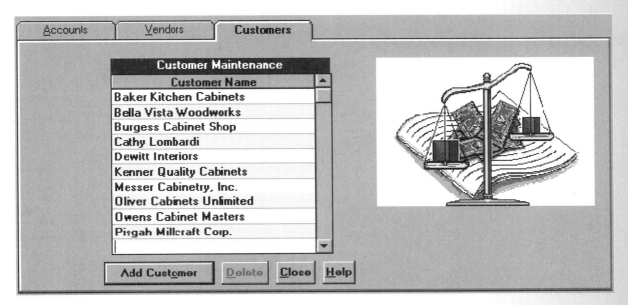

Figure 5.1
Customer Maintenance Window

Adding a New Customer

1: Enter the customer name.

2: Click *Add Customer.*

Changing a Customer Name

1: Select the customer to change. The *Add Customer* button will change to *Change Customer.*

2: Enter the corrected customer name.

3: Click *Change Customer.*

Customer accounts cannot be deleted unless the account being deleted has a zero balance.

Deleting a Customer

1:   Select the customer to delete.

2:   Click *Delete.*

SALES

A transaction in which merchandise is sold in exchange for another asset, usually money, is called a **sales transaction.** A sales transaction of merchandise may be (1) on account or (2) for cash.

Sales Journal Input Form

The **sales journal** is used to enter sales on account transactions. Sales on account may be entered directly into the computer from the transaction statement. Sales on account transactions may also be recorded on the **sales journal input form** and then entered into the computer. A sales journal input form is shown in Figure 5.2. Each line of the input form may be used to record a sales invoice or one part of a sales invoice that is charged to multiple revenue accounts.

**SALES JOURNAL
INPUT FORM**

Date 02/10/--   Problem No. Example

Date	Refer.	Sales Credit	Sales Tax Credit	Customer
02/02/--	S622	1561.95		Baker Kitchen Cabinets
02/10/--	S629	428.75	25.73	Cathy Lombardi

Figure 5.2
Sales Journal
Input Form

A **sales invoice** is a form used to describe the goods sold, the quantity, and the price. It is used as the source document for recording sales on account transactions. When the credit portion of a sales transaction is entered, the computer automatically calculates and displays the debit to the Accounts Receivable account. Therefore, the debit amount to the Accounts Receivable account need not be recorded on the input form. The field names and a description of each column of the input form are illustrated in the sales journal shown in Figure 5.3.

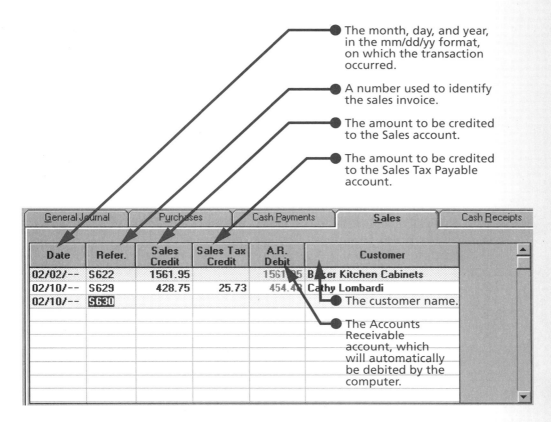

The month, day, and year, in the mm/dd/yy format, on which the transaction occurred.

A number used to identify the sales invoice.

The amount to be credited to the Sales account.

The amount to be credited to the Sales Tax Payable account.

The customer name.

The Accounts Receivable account, which will automatically be debited by the computer.

Figure 5.3
Sales Journal

Transactions are recorded on the sales journal input form illustrated in Figure 5.2. The first transaction is a sale of merchandise to a wholesale company that does *not* involve sales tax. The second transaction is a sale of merchandise to an individual that *does* involve sales tax.

Feb. 02   Sold merchandise on account to Baker Kitchen Cabinets, $1,561.95. Sales invoice no. S622.
10   Sold merchandise on account to Cathy Lombardi, $428.75; plus sales tax, $25.73; total, $454.48. Sales invoice no. S629.

Sales Journal

The sales journal is shown in Figure 5.3. Only sales on account transactions are entered into the sales journal. Enter the date, reference number, invoice amount in the Sales Credit field, sales tax in the Sales Tax Credit field (if necessary), and customer name. The computer automatically calculates and displays the Accounts Receivable Debit amount.

1:   **Click the *Journal* toolbar button.**
The Journal Entries window will appear.

2: Click the *Sales* tab.
The Sales journal will become the active tab.

3: Enter the transaction date and press Tab.
You can also use the plus and minus keys to increase or decrease the date by one day.

4: Enter the invoice number in the Refer. text box and press Tab.
The computer will automatically increase the invoice number by one.

5: Enter the amount of the invoice in the Sales Credit text box and press Tab.
The Accounts Receivable Debit amount is calculated and displayed automatically by the computer.

6: If the transaction involves sales tax, enter the amount of the sales tax in the Sales Tax Credit text box and press Tab, or press Tab to bypass this text box.
The Accounts Receivable Debit amount is again calculated and displayed automatically by the computer to reflect the sales tax.

7: Choose a customer name from the drop-down list.
You can also key the first letter of the customer's name. The first customer in the list beginning with that letter will appear in the text box. Use the Down Arrow key to scroll to the desired customer name.

8: Click *Post.*

CASH RECEIPTS

Any type of transaction involving the receipt of cash is called a **cash receipt.** Cash receipts transactions must be entered and posted for cash that is received on account (affects Accounts Receivable) and for direct receipts (do *not* affect Accounts Receivable).

Cash Receipts Journal Input Form

The **cash receipts journal** is used to enter all cash receipts transactions. Cash receipts may be entered directly into the computer from the transaction statement. Cash receipts transactions may also be recorded on the **cash receipts journal input form.** They may then be entered into the computer from the data recorded on the form. Figure 5.4 illustrates a completed cash receipts journal input form. Each line of the form may be used to record a cash receipts transaction or one part of a

CASH RECEIPTS JOURNAL INPUT FORM						
Date 02/10/--					Problem No. Example	
Date	Refer.	Acct. No.	Debit	Credit	A.R. Credit	Customer
02/01/--	R756				461.08	Bella Vista Woodworks
02/01/--	T5	4110		3499.77		
		2120		209.99		

Figure 5.4
Cash Receipts Journal Input Form

cash receipts transaction involving multiple parts. When the credit portion of a cash receipts transaction is entered, the computer automatically calculates and displays the debit to the Cash account. Therefore, the debit amount to the Cash account need not be recorded on the input form. The field names and a description of each field in the input form are illustrated in the cash receipts journal shown in Figure 5.5.

The following transactions are recorded on the cash receipts journal input form. Additional examples of the various types of cash receipts transactions that may be recorded on this form are illustrated in Tutorial Problem 5-T. The first transaction is an example of a cash receipt on account that does involve Accounts Receivable. The second transaction is an example of a direct receipt that does *not* involve Accounts Receivable.

INTERNET

Since the Internet contains opinions as well as facts, don't be too quick to believe everything you read.

> Feb. 01   Received cash on account from Bella Vista Woodworks, $461.08, covering sales invoice no. S617. Cash receipt no. 756.
>
> 01   Recorded cash and credit card sales, $3,499.77, plus sales tax, $209.99; total, $3,709.76. Calculator tape no. 5.

Cash Receipts Transactions

The cash receipts journal is shown in Figure 5.5. As the data is entered, the computer automatically calculates and displays the debit to Cash.

As you have already learned, there are two types of cash receipts: (1) direct receipts and (2) receipts on account. A **direct receipt** is a cash receipt that does *not* affect Accounts Receivable. Examples of direct receipts are cash sales, cash received from the sale of an asset, or cash received from money borrowed. A **cash receipt on account** involves a receipt of cash from a customer on account and *does* affect Accounts Receivable.

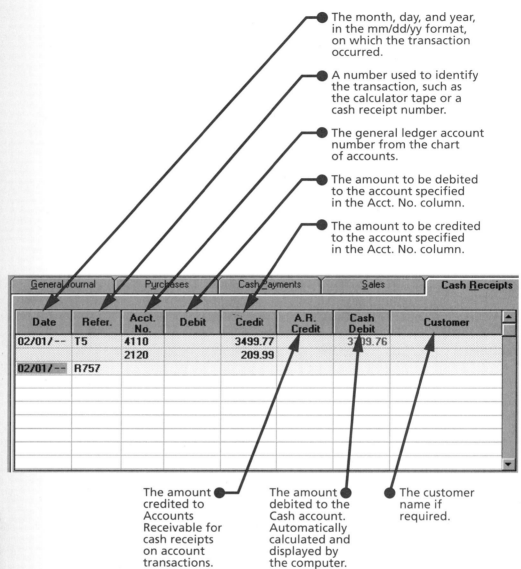

The month, day, and year, in the mm/dd/yy format, on which the transaction occurred.

A number used to identify the transaction, such as the calculator tape or a cash receipt number.

The general ledger account number from the chart of accounts.

The amount to be debited to the account specified in the Acct. No. column.

The amount to be credited to the account specified in the Acct. No. column.

Date	Refer.	Acct. No.	Debit	Credit	A.R. Credit	Cash Debit	Customer
02/01/--	T5	4110		3499.77		3709.76	
		2120		209.99			
02/01/--	R757						

The amount credited to Accounts Receivable for cash receipts on account transactions.

The amount debited to the Cash account. Automatically calculated and displayed by the computer.

The customer name if required.

Figure 5.5
Cash Receipts Journal (Direct Receipt)

Direct Receipt   A cash receipts journal with sample data for a direct cash receipt is shown in Figure 5.5. Notice that the Customer text box column is left blank. A customer name is needed only for transactions that affect Accounts Receivable. The Cash Debit amount is automatically calculated and displayed by the computer. The account(s) credited will vary depending on why the cash was received. A typical transaction is shown in Figure 5.5, with credits to Sales and Sales Tax Payable.

1:   **Click the *Journal* toolbar button.**

2:   **Click the *Cash Receipts* tab.**

3:   **Enter the transaction date and press Tab.**

4: Enter the reference and press Tab.

5: Enter the account number and press Tab.
You can choose the *Chart of Accounts* list command button
and select an account from the Chart of Accounts list rather
than key the account number.

6: Enter the amounts for each account as a debit or credit.
The Cash Debit amount is automatically calculated and
displayed by the computer. Leave the Accounts Receivable
Credit and Customer drop-down text boxes blank, since they
do not apply to a direct receipt.

7: Click *Post.*

Cash Receipt on Account   A cash receipt on account is illustrated
in Figure 5.6. A customer name is required because the Accounts
Receivable account is affected. The accounts receivable amount is
entered in the Accounts Receivable Credit (A.R. Credit) text box
column. The Cash Debit amount is automatically calculated and
displayed by the computer.

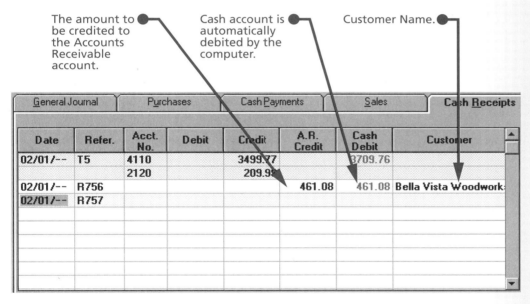

Figure 5.6
Cash Receipts Journal (Receipt on Account)

1: Click the *Journal* toolbar button.
The Journal Entries window will appear.

2: Click the *Cash Receipts* tab.
The Cash Receipts journal will become the active tab.

3: **Enter the transaction date.**

4: **Enter the transaction reference.**

5: **Press Tab repeatedly to bypass the Acct. No., Debit, and Credit text boxes.**

6: **Enter the Accounts Receivable Credit amount.**
   The Cash Debit amount is automatically calculated and displayed by the computer.

7: **Choose a customer name from the drop-down list.**
   You can also key the first letter of the customer's name. The first customer in the list beginning with that letter will appear in the text box. Use the Down Arrow key to scroll to the desired customer name.

8: **Click *Post*.**

REPORTS

After transactions have been entered, various reports may be generated that summarize activity for the time period.

Journal Reports

After all the journal entries have been entered, various journal reports may be displayed.

1: **Click the *Reports* toolbar button.**

2: **When the Report Selection dialog box appears, select *Journals* from the Select a Report Group list.**
   A list of all the reports within the Journals option will appear, as shown in Figure 5.7.

3: **Choose the desired journal report from the Choose a Report to Display list. Click *OK*.**
   The Journal Report Selection dialog shown in Figure 5.8 will appear, allowing you to display all the journal entries for the chosen journal or customize your journal report.

4: **Choose *Customize Journal Report* to control the data to be included on the report.**
   If you want to include *all* journal transactions on the report, choose *Include All Journal Entries.* When *Customize Journal Report* is chosen, the dialog box shown in Figure 5.9 will appear.

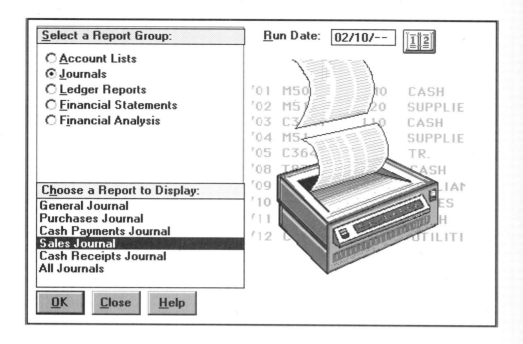

Figure 5.7
Report Selection
Dialog Box

Figure 5.8
Journal Report
Selection Dialog

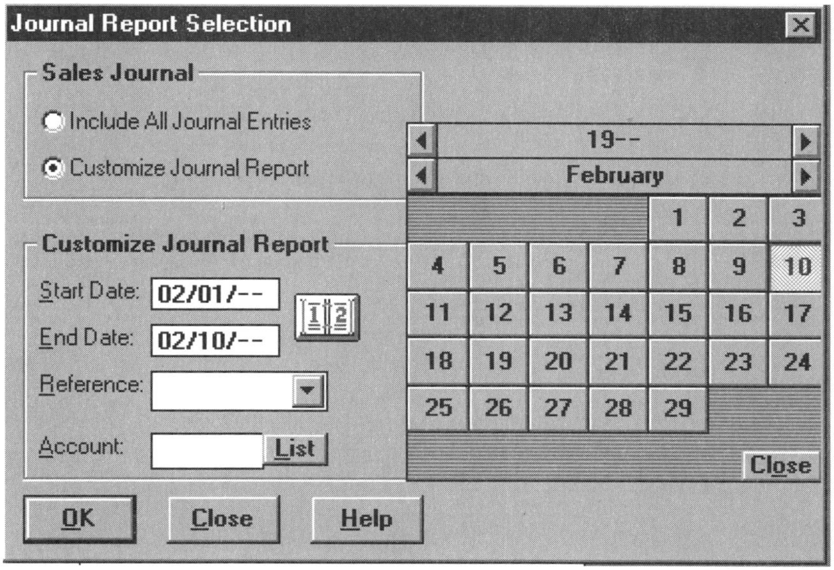

Figure 5.9
Customize
Journal Report
Dialog Box

INTERNET

Telnet is a computer program that permits you to connect to another computer system.

5: **Set the range of dates to be included in the journal report in the Start Date and End Date text boxes.**
Select the Start Date or End Date text box. Strike the + or − keys to increase or decrease the day of the month. As an alternative, click the Calendar icon. When the calendar appears, as shown in Figure 5.9, select the desired date and click *Close.*

6: **Enter an identifying reference in the Reference text box if you wish to restrict the report to a particular reference. Click the drop-down arrow to obtain a list of all the references available from which you may choose.**

7: **Enter an account number in the Account text box if you wish to restrict the report to a particular account.**

8: **Click *OK.***

A sales journal report is shown in Figure 5.10. To print the displayed report, click *Print* or choose *Print* from the File menu.

S & W Custom Cabinets
Sales Journal
02/10/--

Date	Inv. No.	Acct.	Title	Debit	Credit
02/01	S621	1130	AR/Kenner Quality Cabinets	406.60	
02/01	S621	4110	Sales		406.60
02/02	S622	1130	AR/Baker Kitchen Cabinets	1561.95	
02/02	S622	4110	Sales		1561.95
02/03	S623	1130	AR/Bella Vista Woodworks	1979.31	
02/03	S623	4110	Sales		1979.31
02/03	S624	1130	AR/Burgess Cabinet Shop	682.34	
02/03	S624	4110	Sales		682.34
02/04	S625	1130	AR/Owens Cabinet Masters	624.46	
02/04	S625	4110	Sales		624.46
02/05	S626	1130	AR/Messer Cabinetry, Inc.	1744.28	
02/05	S626	4110	Sales		1744.28
02/10	S627	1130	AR/Dewitt Interiors	1313.90	
02/10	S627	4110	Sales		1313.90
02/10	S628	1130	AR/Owens Cabinet Masters	1210.54	
02/10	S628	4110	Sales		1210.54
02/10	S629	1130	AR/Cathy Lombardi	454.48	
02/10	S629	4110	Sales		428.75
02/10	S629	2120	Sales Tax Payable		25.73
			Totals	9977.86	9977.86

Figure 5.10
Sales Journal
Report

Accounts Receivable Ledger Reports

Two ledger reports for accounts receivable are (1) the schedule of accounts receivable and (2) the accounts receivable ledger. The **schedule of accounts receivable report** lists each customer account balance and total amount due from all customers. The **accounts receivable ledger report** shows detailed journal entry activity by customer.

1: Click the *Reports* toolbar button.

2: When the Report Selection dialog box appears, select *Ledger Reports* from the Select a Report Group list.
   A list of all the ledger reports will appear, as shown in Figure 5.11.

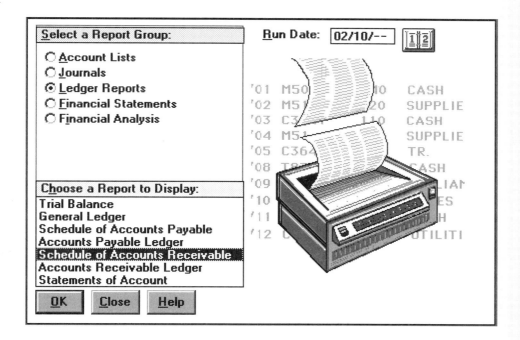

Figure 5.11
Report Selection
Dialog Box

3: Choose the report you would like to display.

4: Click *OK.*
   The schedule of accounts receivable report is illustrated in Figure 5.12.

5: When the *Accounts Receivable* ledger report is selected, the Customer Range dialog box shown in Figure 5.13 will appear. Select the range of customers you wish to appear on the report.

```
                    S & W Custom Cabinets
                Schedule of Accounts Receivable
                          02/10/--

    ------------------------------------------------------------
    Name                                              Balance
    ------------------------------------------------------------

    Bella Vista Woodworks                             1979.31
    Burgess Cabinet Shop                               682.34
    Cathy Lombardi                                     454.48
    Dewitt Interiors                                  1313.90
    Messer Cabinetry, Inc.                            1744.28
    Owens Cabinet Masters                             1835.00
                                                      -------

    Total                                             8009.31
                                                      =======
```

Figure 5.12
Schedule of Accounts Receivable

Figure 5.13
Customer Range Dialog Box

If only one customer is to be displayed, the From: and To: portions of the customer range can be the same.

6:   **Click** *OK.*
The accounts receivable ledger report displaying customers Baker Kitchen Cabinets through Cathy Lombardi is shown in Figure 5.14.

Remember that e-mail can be traced to the source, so whatever you write in an e-mail message should be considered seriously. Inappropriate activities can and will be pursued by legal authorities.

```
                              S & W Custom Cabinets
                             Accounts Receivable Ledger
                                     02/10/--
```

Account	Journal	Date	Refer.	Debit	Credit	Balance
Baker Kitchen Cabinets						
	Balance Forward					340.63Dr
	Sales	02/02	S622	1561.95		1902.58Dr
	Cash Receipts	02/04	R760		340.63	1561.95Dr
	Cash Receipts	02/09	R762		1561.95	.00
Bella Vista Woodworks						
	Balance Forward					461.08Dr
	Cash Receipts	02/01	R756		461.08	.00
	Sales	02/03	S623	1979.31		1979.31Dr
Burgess Cabinet Shop						
	Sales	02/03	S624	682.34		682.34Dr
Cathy Lombardi						
	Sales	02/10	S629	454.48		454.48Dr

Figure 5.14
Accounts Receivable Ledger Report

Statements of Account

A report that shows the customer name and date, description and amount of each sales invoice, payments on account, and total amount due for that customer is called a **statement of account.** Statements of account are mailed to the customer to solicit payment.

1: Click the *Reports* toolbar button.

2: When the Report Selection dialog box shown in Figure 5.11 appears, select *Ledger Reports* from the Select a Report Group list.

3: Choose the *Statements of Account* report from Choose a Report to Display.

4: Click *OK*.
The first statement of account will appear, as illustrated in Figure 5.15. Click *Print* to obtain a printed copy of the statement.

5: Click the << and >> command buttons to scroll through the statements.
The << and >> buttons will be dimmed when scrolling has reached the beginning and end of the statements respectively.

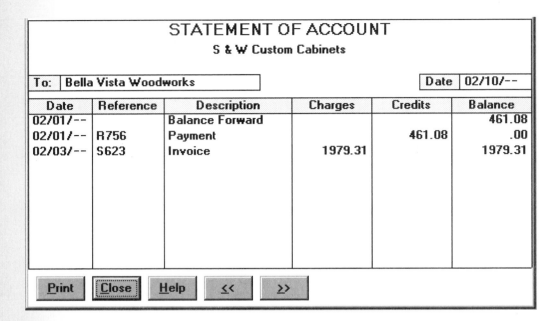

Figure 5.15
Statement of
Account

Chapter Review

1. Businesses or individuals to whom merchandise or services are sold
   are called customers. Customers must be added, changed, and
   deleted as necessary to maintain an up-to-date customer file.

2. Sales transactions may be for cash or on account. Sales on account
   transactions may be recorded on the sales journal input form or
   entered directly into the sales journal from the transaction.

3. A direct receipt transaction does not affect Accounts Receivable.
   A cash receipt on account transaction does affect Accounts
   Receivable. Both direct receipts and cash receipts on account may
   be recorded on the cash receipts journal input form or entered
   directly into the cash receipts journal from the transaction.

4. Once all journal entries have been entered, the journal reports may
   be displayed. Sales and cash receipts journal reports may be
   customized by date, a reference, or account number restriction.

5. The schedule of accounts receivable report lists each customer account
   balance and total due from all customers. The accounts receivable
   ledger report shows detailed journal entry activity by customer.

6. Periodically, customer statements are mailed to customers with a
   balance to solicit payment. These statements of account show the
   customer name and date, description and amount of each sales
   invoice, payments on account, and total due for each customer.

TUTORIAL PROBLEM 5-T

In this tutorial you will maintain customer accounts, enter sales and cash receipts journal entries, and display reports and graphs. You will enter sales and cash receipts transactions that occurred for S & W Custom Cabinets during the period February 1 through 10 of the current year. These journal entries are illustrated in Figures 5.16 and 5.17. Any additions, changes, or deletions to customers have been provided.

Date	Refer.	Sales Credit	Sales Tax Credit	A.R. Debit	Customer
02/01/--	S621	406.60		406.60	Kenner Quality Cabinets
02/02/--	S622	1561.95		1561.95	Baker Kitchen Cabinets
02/03/--	S623	1979.31		1979.31	Bella Vista Woodworks
02/03/--	S624	682.34		682.34	Burgess Cabinet Shop
02/04/--	S625	624.46		624.46	Owens Cabinet Masters
02/05/--	S626	1744.28		1744.28	Messer Cabinetry, Inc.
02/10/--	S627	1313.90		1313.90	Dewitt Interiors
02/10/--	S628	1210.54		1210.54	Owens Cabinet Masters
02/10/--	S629	428.75	25.73	454.48	Cathy Lombardi

Figure 5.16
Sales Journal

Date	Refer.	Acct. No.	Debit	Credit	A.R. Credit	Cash Debit	Customer
02/01/--	R756				461.08	461.08	Bella Vista Woodworks
02/01/--	T5	4110		3499.77		3709.76	
		2120		209.99			
02/02/--	R757				302.96	302.96	Owens Cabinet Masters
02/03/--	R758				183.58	183.58	Kenner Quality Cabinets
02/03/--	R759				310.55	310.55	Messer Cabinetry, Inc.
02/04/--	R760				340.63	340.63	Baker Kitchen Cabinets
02/08/--	T13	4110		2976.47		3155.06	
		2120		178.59			
02/08/--	R761				406.60	406.60	Kenner Quality Cabinets
02/09/--	R762				1561.95	1561.95	Baker Kitchen Cabinets

Figure 5.17
Cash Receipts Journal

T U T O R I A L   P R O B L E M   5 – T

STEP 1:   **Start up _Automated Accounting 7.0._**

STEP 2:   **Load the opening balances template file, AA05–T.**
Click the _Open_ toolbar button. Choose file AA05–T from
the File list box.

STEP 3:   **Enter your name in the User Name text box and click _OK._**

STEP 4:   **Save the file as XXX5–T.**
Click _Save As_ and save the file as XXX5–T where XXX
are your initials.

STEP 5:   **Add Burgess Cabinet Shop and Dewitt Interiors to the
customer list. Change the name of the customer Messer
Wood Products to Messer Cabinetry, Inc., and delete
J & L Fine Cabinetry from the customer list.**
Click the _Accts._ toolbar icon and then click the
Customers tab. Enter the customer maintenance data.

STEP 6:   **Enter the journal entries from the sales and cash
receipts journals shown in Figures 5.16 and 5.17.**

Key the following information from the transaction statements or
refer to Figures 5.16 and 5.17 for input data. The reference numbers
have been abbreviated as follows: Sales invoice, S; Cash receipt, R;
Calculator tape, T.

Some companies handwrite their calculator
tape numbers, while other registers assign the
numbers sequentially. In this chapter's
problems, "missing" tape numbers have been
assigned for other purposes.

Feb. 01   Sold merchandise on account to Kenner
Quality Cabinets, $406.60. S621.
  01   Received cash on account from Bella Vista
Woodworks, $461.08, covering S617. R756.

01   Recorded cash and credit card sales, $3,499.77, plus sales tax, $209.99 total, $3,709.76. T5.
02   Sold merchandise on account to Baker Kitchen Cabinets, $1,561.95. S622.
02   Received cash on account from Owens Cabinet Masters, $302.96, covering S620. R757.
03   Received cash on account from Kenner Quality Cabinets, $183.58, covering S616. R758.
03   Received cash on account from Messer Cabinetry, Inc., $310.55, covering S618. R759.
03   Sold merchandise on account to Bella Vista Woodworks, $1,979.31. S623.
03   Sold merchandise on account to Burgess Cabinet Shop, $682.34. S624.
04   Received cash on account from Baker Kitchen Cabinets, $340.63, covering S617. R760.
04   Sold merchandise on account to Owens Cabinet Masters, $624.46. S625.
05   Sold merchandise on account to Messer Cabinetry, Inc., $1,744.28. S626.
08   Recorded cash and credit card sales, $2,976.47, plus sales tax, $178.59; total, $3,155.06. T13.
08   Received cash on account from Kenner Quality Cabinets, $406.60, covering S621. R761.
09   Received cash on account from Baker Kitchen Cabinets, $1,561.95, covering S622. R762.
10   Sold merchandise on account to Dewitt Interiors, $1,313.90. S627.
10   Sold merchandise on account to Owens Cabinet Masters, $1,210.54. S628.
10   Sold merchandise on account to Cathy Lombardi, $428.75, plus sales tax, $25.73; total, $454.48. S629.

STEP 7:   **Display the customer list.**
Click the *Reports* toolbar button. Select the *Account Lists* option button and choose *Customer List.* Click *OK.* Examine the customer report in Figure 5.18 and verify that the maintenance data you keyed in Step 5 is correct.

S & W Custom Cabinets
Customer List
02/10/--

Customer Name

Baker Kitchen Cabinets
Bella Vista Woodworks
Burgess Cabinet Shop
Cathy Lombardi
Dewitt Interiors
Kenner Quality Cabinets
Messer Cabinetry, Inc.
Oliver Cabinets Unlimited
Owens Cabinet Masters
Pisgah Millcraft Corp.

Figure 5.18
Customer List

STEP 8:   **Display the sales journal and cash receipts journal
          reports.**
          Select *Journals* from the Select a Report Group list.
          Choose the desired journal report from the Choose a
          Report to Display list and then click *OK.* Click *OK* to
          select *Include All Journal Entries.* The reports appear in
          Figures 5.19 and 5.20.

Java is a programming language for use on the
Internet. Java programs can run in any
computer platform and are written to perform
specific tasks associated with World Wide Web
pages.

S & W Custom Cabinets
Sales Journal
02/10/--

Date	Inv. No.	Acct.	Title	Debit	Credit
02/01	S621	1130	AR/Kenner Quality Cabinets	406.60	
02/01	S621	4110	Sales		406.60
02/02	S622	1130	AR/Baker Kitchen Cabinets	1561.95	
02/02	S622	4110	Sales		1561.95
02/03	S623	1130	AR/Bella Vista Woodworks	1979.31	
02/03	S623	4110	Sales		1979.31
02/03	S624	1130	AR/Burgess Cabinet Shop	682.34	
02/03	S624	4110	Sales		682.34
02/04	S625	1130	AR/Owens Cabinet Masters	624.46	
02/04	S625	4110	Sales		624.46
02/05	S626	1130	AR/Messer Cabinetry, Inc.	1744.28	
02/05	S626	4110	Sales		1744.28
02/10	S627	1130	AR/Dewitt Interiors	1313.90	
02/10	S627	4110	Sales		1313.90
02/10	S628	1130	AR/Owens Cabinet Masters	1210.54	
02/10	S628	4110	Sales		1210.54
02/10	S629	1130	AR/Cathy Lombardi	454.48	
02/10	S629	4110	Sales		428.75
02/10	S629	2120	Sales Tax Payable		25.73
			Totals	9977.86	9977.86

Figure 5.19
Sales Journal Report

Use caution on the Internet! Think carefully before ever giving out your password, name, personal address, phone number, or credit card numbers.

TUTORIAL PROBLEM 5-T

S & W Custom Cabinets
Cash Receipts Journal
02/10/--

Date	Refer.	Acct.	Title	Debit	Credit
02/01	R756	1110	Cash	461.08	
02/01	R756	1130	AR/Bella Vista Woodworks		461.08
02/01	T5	1110	Cash	3709.76	
02/01	T5	4110	Sales		3499.77
02/01	T5	2120	Sales Tax Payable		209.99
02/02	R757	1110	Cash	302.96	
02/02	R757	1130	AR/Owens Cabinet Masters		302.96
02/03	R758	1110	Cash	183.58	
02/03	R758	1130	AR/Kenner Quality Cabinets		183.58
02/03	R759	1110	Cash	310.55	
02/03	R759	1130	AR/Messer Cabinetry, Inc.		310.55
02/04	R760	1110	Cash	340.63	
02/04	R760	1130	AR/Baker Kitchen Cabinets		340.63
02/08	T13	1110	Cash	3155.06	
02/08	T13	4110	Sales		2976.47
02/08	T13	2120	Sales Tax Payable		178.59
02/08	R761	1110	Cash	406.60	
02/08	R761	1130	AR/Kenner Quality Cabinets		406.60
02/09	R762	1110	Cash	1561.95	
02/09	R762	1130	AR/Baker Kitchen Cabinets		1561.95
			Totals	10432.17	10432.17

Figure 5.20
Cash Receipts Journal Report

STEP 9:　Display a trial balance, a schedule of accounts
receivable, an accounts receivable ledger report for all
customers, and a statement of account for Bella Vista
Woodworks.

Select *Ledger Reports* from the Select a Report Group
list. Choose the desired ledger report and then click *OK*.
When displaying the accounts receivable ledger report,

TUTORIAL PROBLEM 5 – T

select the first customer in the From: text box and the last customer in the To: text box in the Customer Range dialog box. The reports appear in Figures 5.21 through 5.24.

S & W Custom Cabinets
Trial Balance
02/10/--

Acct. Number	Account Title	Debit	Credit
1110	Cash	24330.81	
1120	Petty Cash	100.00	
1130	Accounts Receivable	8009.31	
1140	Merchandise Inventory	131278.14	
1145	Supplies—Office	1520.90	
1150	Supplies—Store	2217.67	
1160	Prepaid Insurance	1654.17	
2110	Accounts Payable		9903.02
2120	Sales Tax Payable		1465.37
3110	Wayne Duncan, Capital		81802.30
3120	Wayne Duncan, Drawing	1621.45	
3130	Scott Klare, Capital		81802.30
3140	Scott Klare, Drawing	1953.90	
4110	Sales		16428.37
5110	Purchases	15639.95	
6120	Miscellaneous Expense	219.62	
6130	Rent Expense	2572.75	
6160	Utilities Expense	282.69	
	Totals	191401.36	191401.36

Figure 5.21
Trial Balance Report

S & W Custom Cabinets
Schedule of Accounts Receivable
02/10/--

Name	Balance
Bella Vista Woodworks	1979.31
Burgess Cabinet Shop	682.34
Cathy Lombardi	454.48
Dewitt Interiors	1313.90
Messer Cabinetry, Inc.	1744.28
Owens Cabinet Masters	1835.00
Total	8009.31

Figure 5.22
Schedule of Accounts Receivable ▶

TUTORIAL PROBLEM 5-T

S & W Custom Cabinets
Accounts Receivable Ledger
02/10/--

Account	Journal	Date	Refer.	Debit	Credit	Balance
Baker Kitchen Cabinets						
	Balance Forward					340.63Dr
	Sales	02/02	S622	1561.95		1902.58Dr
	Cash Receipts	02/04	R760		340.63	1561.95Dr
	Cash Receipts	02/09	R762		1561.95	.00
Bella Vista Woodworks						
	Balance Forward					461.08Dr
	Cash Receipts	02/01	R756		461.08	.00
	Sales	02/03	S623	1979.31		1979.31Dr
Burgess Cabinet Shop						
	Sales	02/03	S624	682.34		682.34Dr
Cathy Lombardi						
	Sales	02/10	S629	454.48		454.48Dr
Dewitt Interiors						
	Sales	02/10	S627	1313.90		1313.90Dr
Kenner Quality Cabinets						
	Balance Forward					183.58Dr
	Sales	02/01	S621	406.60		590.18Dr
	Cash Receipts	02/03	R758		183.58	406.60Dr
	Cash Receipts	02/08	R761		406.60	.00
Messer Cabinetry, Inc.						
	Balance Forward					310.55Dr
	Cash Receipts	02/03	R759		310.55	.00
	Sales	02/05	S626	1744.28		1744.28Dr
Oliver Cabinets Unlimited						
	No Activity					.00
Owens Cabinet Masters						
	Balance Forward					302.96Dr
	Cash Receipts	02/02	R757		302.96	.00
	Sales	02/04	S625	624.46		624.46Dr
	Sales	02/10	S628	1210.54		1835.00Dr
Pisgah Millcraft Corp.						
	No Activity					.00

Figure 5.23
Accounts Receivable Ledger Report

TUTORIAL PROBLEM 5 – T

STATEMENT OF ACCOUNT
S & W Custom Cabinets

| To: | Bella Vista Woodworks | | | Date | 02/10/-- |

Date	Reference	Description	Charges	Credits	Balance
02/01/--		Balance Forward			461.08
02/01/--	R756	Payment		461.08	.00
02/03/--	S623	Invoice	1979.31		1979.31

[Print] [Close] [Help] [<<] [>>]

Figure 5.24
Statement of Account—Bella Vista Woodworks

STEP 10: **Generate a 3D sales bar graph.**
Click the *Graphs* toolbar button. Choose the *Sales* option and then select the *3D Bar* option and click *OK*. The 3D sales bar graph illustrating the daily sales for February 1 through February 10 is shown in Figure 5.25.

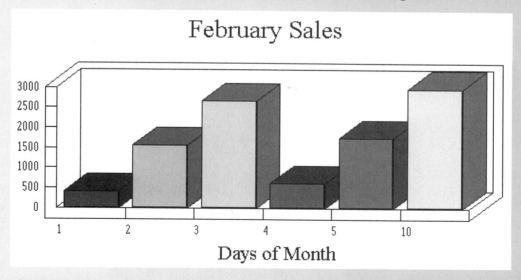

Figure 5.25
Sales Bar Graph

TUTORIAL   PROBLEM   5 - T

STEP 11:   **Save your data file.**
Click the *Save* toolbar button.

STEP 12:   **Optional spreadsheet integration activity:**
S & W Custom Cabinets has asked you to use a spreadsheet to calculate the component percentage owed by each customer as of February 10. Prepare a report showing this information and generate a pie chart depicting the same data.
a.   Display and copy the schedule of accounts receivable report to the clipboard in spreadsheet format.
b.   Start up your spreadsheet software and load template file SS05–T. A blank, formatted worksheet will appear.
c.   Select cell B1 as the current cell, if not already selected.
d.   Paste the schedule of accounts receivable report (copied to the clipboard in step 12a) into the spreadsheet.
e.   Enter the word *Percent* in cell D7. Enter the formula to calculate the component percentage in cell D9. For example, (+C9/+$C$16). Copy and paste the formula in cell D9 to cells D10, D11, D12, D13, and D14.
f.   Format the amounts in currency format and the calculated percentages in percentage format if necessary.
g.   Generate a pie chart. Select the range of cells B9 through C14, then choose the Chart or Graph menu item from the spreadsheet program you are using. If the computer asks for a graph name, etc., enter **Customers** in the graph name text box. Choose Pie Chart if the graph that appears is not a pie chart. Finally, if the spreadsheet you are using permits copying and pasting the graph into the worksheet, copy and paste the graph into cells A22 through E40.
h.   Print the spreadsheet and pie chart. The completed spreadsheet and pie chart are shown in Figure 5.26.
i.   Save your spreadsheet data with a file name of XXX5–T.

▶

T U T O R I A L   P R O B L E M   5 - T

```
Student Name

              S & W Custom Cabinets
          Schedule of Accounts Receivable
                 As Of 02/10/19--

--------------------------------------------------------
Name                        Balance          Percent
--------------------------------------------------------

Bella Vista Woodworks       $1,979.31         24.71%
Burgess Cabinet Shop          $682.34          8.52%
Cathy Lombardi                $454.48          5.67%
Dewitt Interiors            $1,313.90         16.40%
Messer Cabinetry, Inc.      $1,744.28         21.78%
Owens Cabinet Masters       $1,835.00         22.91%

Total                       $8,009.31
```

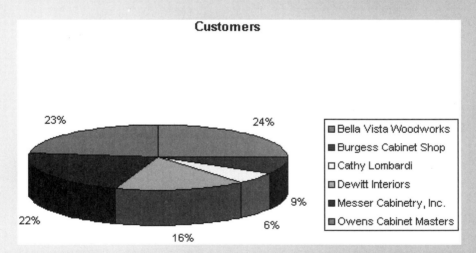

Figure 5.26
Customer Component Percentage Report and Pie Chart

j.   What if Burgess Cabinet Shop's balance is $1,050.00 and Messer Cabinetry, Inc.'s balance is now $2,897.48? Enter these changes and the formula to compute a new total. Observe the effect of the changes on the component percentages and pie chart.

k.   End your spreadsheet session without saving your changes made in step 12j.

T U T O R I A L   P R O B L E M   5 - T

STEP 13: **Optional word processing integration activity:**
S & W Custom Cabinets consults with Hicks Wolf & Associates, a local accounting firm, for financial advice. As part of the information needed, Mary Hicks, owner and CPA of the accounting firm, has asked that you fax her a list of the customers with their account balances at the end of each week. You are to use the word processing fax template used by S & W Custom Cabinets to prepare this document for the week ended February 10.

a. Display and copy the schedule of accounts receivable report to the clipboard in word processing format.

b. Start up your word processing application software and load template file WP05–T as a text file.

c. Enter your name in the FROM field and complete the remainder of the top portion of the facsimile as shown in Figure 5.27.

```
                    S & W Custom Cabinets
                     9205 Creek View Drive
                    Columbus, OH 43205-4530
                       (614) 555-4581

                          FACSIMILE

              TO:   Mary Hicks, CPA

         COMPANY:   Hicks Wolf & Associates

            DATE:   February 10, 19--

   PHONE NUMBER:    (614) 555-7230

    FAX NUMBER:     (614) 555-7279

           FROM:    Student Name

        SUBJECT:    END OF THE WEEK CUSTOMER ACCOUNT
                    BALANCES

Notes/Comments:

As per your request, our customers and their
account balances as of February 10 are:

   Bella Vista Woodworks       $ 1,979.31
   Burgess Cabinet Shop             682.34
   Cathy Lombardi                   454.48
   Dewitt Interiors               1,313.90
   Messer Cabinetry, Inc.         1,744.28
   Owens Cabinet Masters          1,835.00
```

Figure 5.27
Completed Facsimile

▶

    d. Position the insertion point two lines after the text in the Notes/Comments section and paste the report. Delete report headings, totals, etc., and format the document to match Figure 5.27. Experiment adding further enhancement to the appearance of the fax.

    e. Print the completed document.

    f. Save the document with a file name of XXX5–T.

    g. End your word processing session.

STEP 14: **End your *Automated Accounting* session.** Click the *Exit/Quit* toolbar button.

Applying Your Information Skills

I. MATCHING

Directions: In the *Working Papers*, write the letter of the appropriate term next to each definition.

    a. customer
    b. sales transaction
    c. sales journal
    d. sales journal input form
    e. sales invoice
    f. cash receipt
    g. cash receipts journal
    h. cash receipts journal input form
    i. direct receipt
    j. cash receipt on account
    k. schedule of accounts receivable report
    l. accounts receivable ledger report
   m. statement of account

1. A transaction in which merchandise is sold in exchange for another asset, usually money.

2. An input form used to record sales on account transactions.

3. A report that shows the customer name and date, description and amount of each sales invoice, payments on account, and total amount due for each customer.

4. A report that shows detailed journal entry activity by customer.

5. An input form used to record cash receipts transactions.

6. Any type of transaction involving the receipt of cash.

7. A cash receipt that does *not* affect Accounts Receivable.

8. A cash receipt from a customer that *does* affect Accounts Receivable.

9. A business or individual to whom merchandise or services are sold.

10. A report that lists each customer account balance and total due from all customers.

11. A journal used to enter sales on account transactions.

12. A journal used to enter all cash receipts transactions.

13. A form used to describe the goods sold, the quantity, and the price.

II. QUESTIONS

Directions: Write the answer to each of the following questions in the *Working Papers*.

1. How are customers added to the accounting system?

2. List the two types of sales transactions.

3. List the two types of cash receipts.

4. List the two accounts receivable ledger reports.

5. Why are statements of account generated?

P   Independent Practice Problem 5–P

In this problem you will process any additions, changes, or deletions to customers. You will also process sales and cash receipts transactions for the period February 11 through February 20 of the current year.

STEP 1:   **Start up *Automated Accounting 7.0.***

STEP 2:   **Load file AA05–P.**

STEP 3:   **Enter your name in the User Name text box.**

STEP 4:   **Use Save As to save the file as XXX5–P.**

STEP 5:   **Enter the following transactions.**

Feb. 11 Received cash on account from Owens Cabinet Masters, $624.46, covering S625. R763.

11 Sold merchandise on account to Riley Cabinet Company, $551.41. S630. Add Riley Cabinet Company to the customer list. Delete customer Pisgah Millcraft Corp.

12 Sold merchandise on account to Baker Kitchen Cabinets, $345.53. S631.

12 Sold merchandise on account to Messer Cabinetry, Inc., $912.48. S632.

15 Recorded cash and credit card sales, $2,672.42, plus sales tax, $160.35; total, $2,832.77. T20.

15 Received cash on account from Messer Cabinetry, Inc., $1,744.28, covering S626. R764.

15 Received cash on account from Burgess Cabinet Co., $682.34, covering S624. R765. Change the customer name of Burgess Cabinet Shop to Burgess Cabinet Co.

16 Sold merchandise on account to Kenner Quality Cabinets, $523.34. S633.

16 Sold merchandise on account to Bella Vista Woodworks, $499.06. S634.

16 Received cash on account from Owens Cabinet Masters, $1,210.54, covering S628. R766.

17 Sold merchandise on account to Dewitt Interiors, $657.53. S635.

17 Sold merchandise on account to Burgess Cabinet Co., $547.00. S636.

18 Recorded cash and credit card sales, $2,220.23, plus sales tax, $133.21; total, $2,353.44. T23.

18 Sold merchandise on account to Owens Cabinet Masters, $313.84. S637.

18 Sold merchandise on account to Cathy Lombardi, $221.12, plus sales tax, $13.27; total, $234.39. S638.

19 Received cash on account from Dewitt Interiors, $1,313.90, covering S628. R767.

19 Received cash on account from Riley Cabinet Company, $551.41, covering S630. R768.

19 Sold merchandise on account to Marcus Cabinet Works, $487.55. S639. Add Marcus Cabinet Works to the customer list.

19 Received cash on account from Cathy Lombardi, $454.48, covering S629. R769.

STEP 6:   **Display a customer list.**

STEP 7: Display the sales and cash receipts journal reports for the period February 11 through February 20 of the current year. If errors are detected, make corrections.

STEP 8: Display the following ledger reports: trial balance, schedule of accounts receivable, accounts receivable ledger (all customers), statement of account (first customer).

STEP 9: Generate a sales line graph.

STEP 10: Save your data file.

STEP 11: Optional spreadsheet integration activity:
S & W Custom Cabinets has asked you to use a spreadsheet to calculate the component percentage owed by each customer as of February 20. Prepare a report showing this information and generate a pie chart depicting the same data.

a. Display and copy the schedule of accounts receivable report to the clipboard in spreadsheet format.

b. Start up your spreadsheet software and load template file SS05–T.

c. Select cell B1 as the current cell and paste the schedule of accounts receivable report into the spreadsheet.

d. Enter the word *Percent* in cell D7. Enter the formula to calculate the percentage owed in cell D9. Copy and paste the formula in cell D9 to the appropriate cells.

e. Format the amounts in currency format and the calculated percentages in percentage format if necessary.

f. Generate a pie chart depicting the data in the report.

g. Print the spreadsheet and pie chart.

h. Save your spreadsheet data with a file name of XXX5–P.

i. What if Baker Kitchen Cabinets' balance is $975.25 and Messer Cabinetry, Inc.'s balance is now $1,349.95? Enter these changes and the formula to compute a new total. Observe the effect of the changes on the component percentages and pie chart.

j. End your spreadsheet session without saving your changes made in step 11i, and return to the *Automated Accounting application.*

STEP 12:   **Optional word processing integration activity:**
You are to use the company's word processing fax template to prepare the customer account balance information for the accounting firm the week ended February 20.
  a. Display and copy the schedule of accounts receivable report to the clipboard in word processing format.
  b. Start up your word processing application software and load template file WP05–T as a text file.
     Note: As an alternative, and if completed, load the solution word processing file from Tutorial Problem 5–T and modify it as necessary to complete this activity.
  c. Enter your name in the FROM field and complete the remainder of the top portion of the facsimile as shown in Figure 5.27.
  d. Paste the report, delete report headings, totals, etc., and format the document to match Figure 5.27.
  e. Print the completed document.
  f. Save the document with a file name of XXX5–P.
  g. End your word processing session.

STEP 13:   **End your *Automated Accounting* session.**

Applying Your Technology Skills 5–P

Directions: Using Independent Practice Problem 5–P, write the answers to the following questions in the *Working Papers*.

1. What are the totals of the debit and credit columns in the sales journal report?

2. From the sales journal report, what is the amount of invoice no. 635?

3. What is the amount of cash received from Riley Cabinet Company on cash receipt no. 768?

4. What is the current balance in Accounts Receivable?

5. What is the current balance in the Sales Tax Payable account?

6. What is the current balance for Owens Cabinet Masters?

7. What is the total due from customers as of February 20?

8. List the amounts of the cash receipts transactions for Owens Cabinet Masters for the period February 11 through February 20.

9. How many sales were made to Messer Cabinetry, Inc. during the period February 11 through February 20?

 Mastery Problem 5–M

In this problem you will process any additions, changes, or deletions to customers. You will also process sales and cash receipts transactions for the period February 21 through February 28 of the current year.

STEP 1:   **Start up *Automated Accounting 7.0* and load file AA05–M.**

STEP 2:   **Enter your name in the User Name text box.**

STEP 3:   **Save the file as XXX5–M.**

STEP 4:   **Enter the customer maintenance and transactions.**

Feb. 22   Sold merchandise on account to Baker Kitchen Cabinets, $321.04. S640.

22   Sold merchandise on account to Riley Cabinet Company, $425.11. S641.

23   Received cash on account from Bella Vista Woodworks, $1,979.31, covering S623. R770.

23   Sold merchandise on account to Messer Cabinetry, Inc., $352.95. S642.

23   Recorded cash and credit card sales, $1,849.23, plus sales tax, $110.95; total, $1,960.18. T28.

24   Sold merchandise on account to Burgess Cabinet Co., $508.73. S643.

24   Sold merchandise on account to Cathy Lombardi, $120.88, plus sales tax, $7.25; total, $128.13. S644.

24   Received cash on account from Baker Kitchen Cabinets, $345.53, covering S631. R771.

25   Received cash on account from Messer Cabinetry, Inc., $912.48, covering S632. R772.

25   Received cash on account from Dewitt Interiors, $657.53, covering S635. R773.

25   Sold merchandise on account to Sloan Finished Cabinets, $323.43. S645. Add Sloan Finished Cabinets to the customer list. Delete customer Oliver Cabinets Unlimited.

25   Sold merchandise on account to Dewitt Interiors, $95.87. S646.

26   Recorded cash and credit card sales, $1,570.76, plus sales tax, $94.25; total, $1,665.01. T31.

26   Received cash on account from Bella Vista Woodworks, $499.06, covering S634. R774.

26   Received cash on account from Burgess Cabinet Co., $547.00, covering S636. R775.

26   Sold merchandise on account to Kenner Quality Cabinets, $63.36. S647.

26   Received cash on account from Owens Cabinet Masters, $313.84, covering S637. R776.

26   Sold merchandise on account to Marcus Millcraft, Inc., $332.50. S648. Change the customer name of Marcus Cabinet Works to Marcus Millcraft, Inc.

STEP 5:   **Display the following reports for the period February 21 through February 28 of the current year: customer list, sales and cash receipts journal reports, trial balance, schedule of accounts receivable, accounts receivable ledger (all customers), statement of account (first customer).**

CHECK FIGURES:
Sales journal debit and credit totals = $2,551.12
Cash receipts journal debit and credit totals = $8,879.94

STEP 6:   **Generate a 3D sales bar graph.**

STEP 7:   **Save your data.**

STEP 8:   **Optional spreadsheet integration activity:**
Prepare a report showing the component percentage owed by each customer and generate a pie chart depicting this data as of February 28.

a.   Display and copy the schedule of accounts receivable report to the clipboard in spreadsheet format.

b.   Start up your spreadsheet software and load template file SS05–T.

c.   Select cell B1 as the current cell and paste the schedule of accounts receivable report into the spreadsheet.

d.   Enter the labels and formulas required to report and compute the customer component percentages using the format illustrated in Figure 5.26.

e.   Generate a pie chart depicting the data in the report.

f.   Print the spreadsheet and pie chart.

g.   Save your spreadsheet data with a file name of XXX5–M.

h.   What if Dewitt Interiors' balance is $267.45 and Riley Cabinet Company's balance is now $1,681.17? Enter these changes and the formula to compute a new total. Observe the effect of the changes on the component percentages and pie chart.

    i. End your spreadsheet session without saving your
        changes from step 8h, and return to the *Automated
        Accounting* application.

STEP 9:   **Optional word processing integration activity:**
    a. Display and copy the schedule of accounts receivable
        report to the clipboard in word processing format.
    b. Start up your word processing application software
        and load template file WP05–T as a text file.
        Note: As an alternative, and if completed, load your
        solution word processing file from either Tutorial
        Problem 5–T or Independent Practice Problem 5–P
        and modify it as necessary to complete this activity.
    c. Enter your name in the FROM field and complete the
        remainder of the top portion of the facsimile as
        shown in Figure 5.27. Be sure to change the date to
        February 28. Paste the report, delete report headings,
        totals, etc., and format the document as necessary.
    d. Print the completed document.
    e. Save the document with a file name of XXX5–M.
    f. End your word processing session.

STEP 10:   **End your *Automated Accounting* session.**

 Applying Your Technology Skills 5–M

Directions: Using Mastery Problem 5–M, write the answers to the
following questions in the *Working Papers*.

1. In the sales journal report, what is the amount debited to Sloan
   Finished Cabinets for invoice no. 645?

2. In the sales journal report, what is the amount of sales tax for invoice
   no. 644 to Cathy Lombardi?

3. What is the total of the debit column in the cash receipts journal?

4. What is the balance in the Sales Tax Payable account?

5. What is the balance in the Sales account?

6. What is the balance due from Burgess Cabinet Co. on February 28?

7. What is the total amount due from all customers as of February 28?

8. From the trial balance, what is the balance in the Accounts
   Receivable account?

9. From the accounts receivable ledger report, what is the amount of
   sales invoice no. 647 to Kenner Quality Cabinets?

6

End of Fiscal Period for a Partnership (Merchandising Business)

LEARNING OBJECTIVES

Upon completion of this chapter, you will be able to:

1. Process the adjusting entries for a merchandising business.

2. Generate the financial statements for a merchandising business organized as a partnership.

3. Complete the period-end closing process for a partnership.

INTRODUCTION

In previous chapters you performed computerized accounting activities for businesses that were organized as sole proprietorships. In this chapter you will learn how to complete the end-of-fiscal-period processing for a merchandising business that is organized as a partnership. A partnership is a business that is owned by two or more persons. Many small businesses are organized as partnerships in an effort to take advantage of the combined capital, managerial experience, and expertise of two or more individuals.

To complete the accounting cycle for a partnership, adjusting entries may be recorded on the general journal input form, entered into the computer, and verified for accuracy. Financial statements are then generated. After the financial statements have been produced, period-end closing may be completed.

ADJUSTING ENTRIES

Adjusting entries are entered after all other transactions for the accounting period have been processed and posted. A trial balance and the period-end adjustment data are the basis for the adjusting entries.

E T H I C S

Although the term "ethics" may seem theoretical or abstract, sometimes employees must make decisions about ethics in the workplace.

Consider the following case: An executive responsible for a business's finances gives a computer programmer in the company some detailed formulas to develop a program that will produce a report for investors showing the business's financial condition. While writing the program, the programmer discovers that the financial reports that will be generated by the new program will incorrectly show that the finances of the company are better than they really are. When the programmer tells the executive of this

discovery, the programmer is told to follow the specifications or be fired.

a. What would you do if you were the programmer?

b. Do you think that what the programmer was asked to do was ethical or unethical?

c. Could the programmer be considered to have committed a computer crime if he/she knowingly participated in producing a report that deceived investors? Explain your response.

A trial balance for S & W Custom Cabinets is shown in Figure 6.1. The
period-end adjustment data for S & W Custom Cabinets are as follows:

Merchandise inventory $124,024.00
Office supplies inventory $550.00
Store supplies inventory $835.00
Value of insurance policies on February 28 .... $472.05

```
                    S & W Custom Cabinets
                         Trial Balance
                           02/28/--

---------------------------------------------------------------
Acct.        Account
Number       Title                    Debit          Credit
---------------------------------------------------------------

1110         Cash                     44978.37
1120         Petty Cash                 100.00
1130         Accounts Receivable       3796.40
1140         Merchandise Inventory   131278.14
1145         Supplies—Office           1520.90
1150         Supplies—Store            2217.67
1160         Prepaid Insurance         1654.17
2110         Accounts Payable                         9903.02
2120         Sales Tax Payable                        1984.65
3110         Wayne Duncan, Capital                   81802.30
3120         Wayne Duncan, Drawing     1621.45
3130         Scott Klare, Capital                    81802.30
3140         Scott Klare, Drawing      1953.90
4110         Sales                                   32343.74
5110         Purchases                15639.95
6120         Miscellaneous Expense      219.62
6130         Rent Expense              2572.75
6160         Utilities Expense          282.69
                                     ---------      ---------
             Totals                  207836.01      207836.01
                                     =========      =========
```

Figure 6.1
Trial Balance Before Adjusting Entries

The adjusting entries are entered into the general journal. All
adjusting entries occur on the same date and have the same reference
(Adj.Ent.). Each adjusting entry should be entered and posted separately.
The adjusting entries shown in the general journal illustrated in Figure 6.2
were derived from the trial balance and period-end adjustment data
shown in Figure 6.1.

Similar to a manual accounting system, the changes in inventory
resulting from purchases and sales transactions are not reflected in the
Merchandise Inventory account of the automated accounting system.
Therefore, the Merchandise Inventory account balance must be adjusted
to reflect the changes resulting from purchases and sales during the fiscal

Date	Refer.	Acct. No.	Debit	Credit	Vendor/Customer
02/28/--	Adj.Ent.	3150	7254.14		
		1140		7254.14	
02/28/--	Adj.Ent.	6140	970.90		
		1145		970.90	
02/28/--	Adj.Ent.	6150	1382.67		
		1150		1382.67	
02/28/--	Adj.Ent.	6110	1182.12		
		1160		1182.12	

Figure 6.2
General Journal (Adjusting Entries)

period. Two accounts are used to adjust the merchandise inventory: Merchandise Inventory and Income Summary.

Notice in Figure 6.1 that before the adjustment, the Merchandise Inventory account has a debit balance of $131,278.14. The actual count of merchandise on February 28 shows that the inventory is valued at $124,024.00. The first adjusting entry in Figure 6.2 shows that Merchandise Inventory, account number 1140, is credited for $7,254.14, which is the difference between the current account balance of $131,278.14 and actual inventory on hand of $124,024.00. Income Summary, account number 3150, is debited for $7,254.14. If the current account balance of merchandise inventory is less than the actual amount of merchandise on hand, opposite entries would be made— Merchandise Inventory would be debited and Income Summary would be credited.

Adjustments that are made to Office Supplies, Store Supplies, and Insurance use their related temporary account. For example, in the second adjusting entry in Figure 6.2, when Supplies—Office, account number 1145, is adjusted, Supplies Expense—Office, account number 6140, is the related temporary account that is used.

See Chapter 3 for a full description of these financial statements.

FINANCIAL STATEMENTS

The financial statements generated by *Automated Accounting 7.0* for a nondepartmentalized business organized as a partnership are the income statement and the balance sheet. The Report Selection dialog box is illustrated in Figure 6.3. For businesses that account for budget data, a performance report will be available. Performance reports will be discussed in a later chapter.

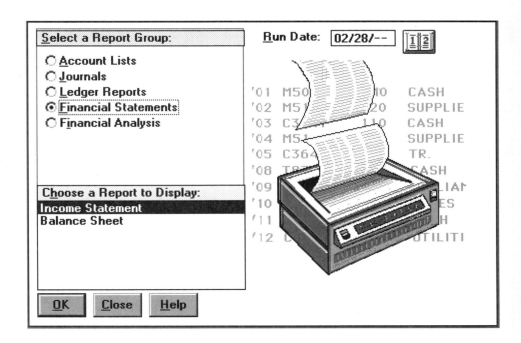

Figure 6.3
Report Selection
Dialog Box

PERIOD-END CLOSING FOR A PARTNERSHIP

At the end of the fiscal period in a manual accounting system, closing entries are recorded in the journal and posted to the general ledger. In an automated accounting system, the software generates and posts the entries to close the temporary accounts to the Income Summary account. An Income Summary account is used to summarize the closing entries for the revenue and expense accounts.

Partnerships have many different methods of distributing income, including allocating income on the basis of service rendered and on the basis of capital invested. The software automatically closes net income to the partners' capital accounts when income or loss is to be distributed equally among all partners. For a partnership with equal distribution of income or loss, the software generates and posts the entries to close out the revenue and expense accounts in the Income Summary account, distribute the balance in the Income Summary account to the partners' capital accounts, and close the partners' drawing accounts. Also, during the posting process, the software copies the current account balances and stores them as last fiscal period's account balances.

If the partnership has an unequal distribution of income or loss, closing entries will be generated and posted that will close out the revenue and expense accounts to the Income Summary account. The difference between revenue and expenses will be the partnership's net income or loss. Journal entries must then be made to distribute the net income or loss from the Income Summary account to the partners'

Temporary accounts are accounts that accumulate information until they are transferred to the owner's capital account.

capital accounts and to close the partners' drawing accounts to their respective capital accounts.

When the *Generate Closing Journal Entries* menu item is chosen from the Options menu, a dialog box will appear, asking if you want to generate closing journal entries. Click the *Yes* command button to proceed. A second dialog box showing the closing journal entries generated by the software will appear as illustrated in Figure 6.4. Click the *Post* command button to proceed with the closing.

Acct. #	Account Title	Debit	Credit
4110	Sales	32343.74	
3150	Income Summary		32343.74
3150	Income Summary	22250.70	
5110	Purchases		15639.95
6110	Insurance Expense		1182.12
6120	Miscellaneous Expense		219.62
6130	Rent Expense		2572.75
6140	Supplies Expense--Office		970.90
6150	Supplies Expense--Store		1382.67
6160	Utilities Expense		282.69
3150	Income Summary	2838.90	
3110	Wayne Duncan, Capital		1419.45
3130	Scott Klare, Capital		1419.45
3110	Wayne Duncan, Capital	1621.45	
3120	Wayne Duncan, Drawing		1621.45
3130	Scott Klare, Capital	1953.90	
3140	Scott Klare, Drawing		1953.90

Figure 6.4
Closing Journal Entries Dialog Box

As the last step of the accounting cycle for a merchandising business organized as a partnership, a post-closing trial balance is generated. A post-closing trial balance is displayed to verify that debits equal credits in the general ledger accounts after closing entries are posted.

Chapter Review

1. To complete the accounting cycle for a partnership, adjusting entries may be recorded on the general journal input form, entered into the computer, and verified for accuracy. The financial statements are then generated. After the financial statements have been generated, the period-end closing is performed.

2. A trial balance and the period-end adjustment data are the basis for the adjusting entries. The changes in inventory resulting from purchases and sales transactions are not reflected in the

Merchandise Inventory account. Therefore, the Merchandise Inventory account balance must be adjusted to reflect the changes resulting from purchases and sales during the fiscal period.

3. The income statement, balance sheet, and performance report (which is not discussed in this chapter) are available for a nondepartmentalized business organized as a partnership.

4. The software generates and posts all the journal entries to close all of the temporary accounts to the Income Summary account. For a partnership with equal distribution of income or loss, the software generates and posts the entries to close out the revenue and expense accounts in the Income Summary account, distribute the balance in the Income Summary account to the partners' capital accounts, and close the partners' drawing accounts. If the distribution is unequal, entries will be generated and posted that will close the net income or loss to the Income Summary account. Journal entries must then be made to distribute the income or loss from the Income Summary account to the partners' capital accounts and to close the partners' drawing accounts to their respective capital accounts. After posting the closing entries, a post-closing trial balance is generated to prove the equality of debits and credits.

Although senior citizens are far from being the dominant group among computer users, their numbers are growing and are bound to increase as the baby boomers get older. Many seniors find the Internet a rich source of friends, support, and information.

A search engine is a software program available on the Internet that allows users to find and retrieve specific information based on selected keywords.

TUTORIAL PROBLEM 6-T

In this tutorial problem, you will complete the end-of-fiscal-period processing for a merchandising business organized as a partnership. You will enter the adjusting entries, display the financial statements, generate and post closing journal entries, and use the Savings Planner tool. Since the partnership consists of two partners with an equal distribution of income or loss, the software will generate the entries to distribute the income or loss to the partners' capital accounts during the closing process.

STEP 1:   **Start up *Automated Accounting 7.0*.**

STEP 2:   **Load the opening balances file, AA06–T.**
Click the *Open* toolbar button. Select file AA06–T from the File list box.

STEP 3:   **Enter your name in the User Name text box and click the *OK* button.**

STEP 4:   **Save with a file name of XXX6–T.**
Click the *Save As* toolbar button and save the file as XXX6–T where XXX are your initials.

STEP 5:   **Enter the adjusting entries in the general journal as shown in Figure 6.5.**
These adjusting entries were derived from the period-end adjustment data and trial balance shown in Figure 6.1.

Date	Refer.	Acct. No.	Debit	Credit	Vendor/Customer
02/28/--	Adj.Ent.	3150	7254.14		
		1140		7254.14	
02/28/--	Adj.Ent.	6140	970.90		
		1145		970.90	
02/28/--	Adj.Ent.	6150	1382.67		
		1150		1382.67	
02/28/--	Adj.Ent.	6110	1182.12		
		1160		1182.12	

Figure 6.5
General Journal (Adjusting Entries)

STEP 6:   **Display the adjusting entries.**
Click the *Reports* toolbar button and choose *Journals* from the Select a Report Group list. Select the *General*

Journal report. Select *Include All Journal Entries* and click *OK*. The report appears in Figure 6.6.

S & W Custom Cabinets
General Journal
02/28/--

Date	Refer.	Acct.	Title	Debit	Credit
02/28	Adj.Ent.	3150	Income Summary	7254.14	
02/28	Adj.Ent.	1140	Merchandise Inventory		7254.14
02/28	Adj.Ent.	6140	Supplies Expense—Office	970.90	
02/28	Adj.Ent.	1145	Supplies—Office		970.90
02/28	Adj.Ent.	6150	Supplies Expense—Store	1382.67	
02/28	Adj.Ent.	1150	Supplies—Store		1382.67
02/28	Adj.Ent.	6110	Insurance Expense	1182.12	
02/28	Adj.Ent.	1160	Prepaid Insurance		1182.12
			Totals	10789.83	10789.83

Figure 6.6
General Journal Report (Adjusting Entries)

STEP 7:   **Display the financial statements.**
Choose *Financial Statements* and select the desired financial statement report. Click *OK*. The income statement and balance sheet are shown in Figures 6.7 and 6.8, respectively.

A collection of World Wide Web documents featuring commercial products and services is called a mall. Malls are often created by one particular Internet access provider.

TUTORIAL PROBLEM 6 – T

S & W Custom Cabinets
Income Statement
For Period Ended 02/28/--

Operating Revenue		
Sales	32343.74	100.00
Total Operating Revenue	32343.74	100.00
Cost of Merchandise Sold		
Beginning Inventory	131278.14	405.88
Purchases	15639.95	48.36
Merchandise Available for Sale	146918.09	454.24
Less Ending Inventory	−124024.00	−383.46
Cost of Merchandise Sold	22894.09	70.78
Gross Profit	9449.65	29.22
Operating Expenses		
Insurance Expense	1182.12	3.65
Miscellaneous Expense	219.62	0.68
Rent Expense	2572.75	7.95
Supplies Expense—Office	970.90	3.00
Supplies Expense—Store	1382.67	4.27
Utilities Expense	282.69	0.87
Total Operating Expenses	6610.75	20.44
Net Income	2838.90	8.78

Figure 6.7
Income
Statement

Special software is available that allows Internet "newbies" to create Web pages without mastering HTML. The packages contain Web page templates to make it easier for beginners.

S & W Custom Cabinets
Balance Sheet
02/28/--

A s s e t s

Cash	44978.37
Petty Cash	100.00
Accounts Receivable	3796.40
Merchandise Inventory	124024.00
Supplies—Office	550.00
Supplies—Store	835.00
Prepaid Insurance	472.05

Total Assets   174755.82

L i a b i l i t i e s

Accounts Payable	9903.02
Sales Tax Payable	1984.65

Total Liabilities   11887.67

O w n e r s '   E q u i t y

Wayne Duncan, Capital	81802.30
Wayne Duncan, Drawing	−1621.45
Scott Klare, Capital	81802.30
Scott Klare, Drawing	−1953.90
Net Income	2838.90

Total Owners' Equity   162868.15

Total Liabilities & Equity   174755.82

Figure 6.8
Balance Sheet

STEP 8:   **Generate an income statement 3D bar graph.**
Click the *Graphs* toolbar button. Choose *Income Statement* and *3D Bar*. Click *OK*. The income statement bar graph is illustrated in Figure 6.9.

TUTORIAL   PROBLEM   6 – T

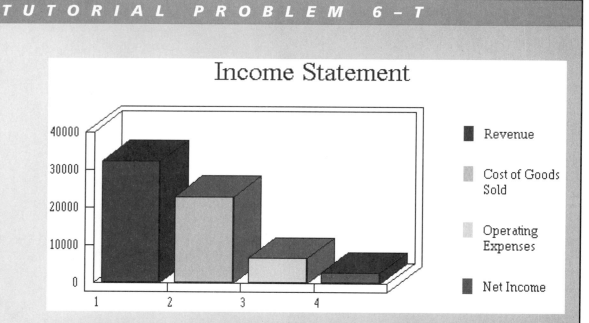

Figure 6.9
Income Statement Bar Graph

STEP 9:   **Save your data file as XXX6–TBC.**
Click *Save As.* Save your file as XXX6–TBC, where XXX are your initials, 6–T is the problem number, and BC is "Before Closing."

STEP 10:   **Optional spreadsheet integration activity:**
S & W Custom Cabinets has asked you to use a spreadsheet to prepare a Distribution of Net Income Statement for the period ended 2/28. A spreadsheet template file has partially been completed.
     a.   Display and copy the income statement to the clipboard in spreadsheet format.
     b.   Start up your spreadsheet software and load template file SS06–T.
     c.   Select cell A1 as the current cell, and paste the income statement into the spreadsheet.
     d.   Enter the formula to calculate the distribution of net income for each partner and the formula to obtain a sum of the two partners' distribution.
     e.   Format the amounts in currency format, if necessary. Format the percentage amounts in number format with two decimal places.
     f.   Print the spreadsheet. The completed spreadsheet is shown in Figure 6.10.

TUTORIAL PROBLEM 6-T

```
Student Name

                    S & W Custom Cabinets
                      Income Statement
                   For Period Ended 02/28/--

Operating Revenue

Sales                                  $32,343.74    100.00

Total Operating Revenue                $32,343.74    100.00

Cost of Merchandise Sold

Beginning Inventory                   $131,278.14    405.88
Purchases                              $15,639.95     48.36

Merchandise Available for Sale        $146,918.09    454.24
Less Ending Inventory                -$124,024.00   -383.46

Cost of Merchandise Sold               $22,894.09     70.78

Gross Profit                            $9,449.65     29.22

Operating Expenses

Insurance Expense                       $1,182.12      3.65
Miscellaneous Expense                     $219.62      0.68
Rent Expense                            $2,572.75      7.95
Supplies Expense—Office                   $970.90      3.00
Supplies Expense—Store                  $1,382.67      4.27
Utilities Expense                         $282.69      0.87

Total Operating Expenses                $6,610.75     20.44

Net Income                              $2,838.90      8.78


                    S & W Custom Cabinets
               Distribution of Net Income Statement
                   For Period Ended 02/28/--

Wayne Duncan
   50.0% of Net Income                  $1,419.45
Scott Klare
   50.0% of Net Income                  $1,419.45

Net Income                              $2,838.90
```

Figure 6.10
Distribution of Net Income Statement Spreadsheet

T U T O R I A L   P R O B L E M   6 - T

    g. Save your spreadsheet data with a file name of XXX6–T.

    h. What if the distribution of net income were changed as follows: Wayne Duncan, 70%; Scott Klare, 30%. Change the Distribution of Net Income Statement to reflect this change.

    i. End your spreadsheet session without saving your changes made in Step 10h.

STEP 11: Optional word processing integration activity:
You have been asked to prepare a memo addressed to each partner of S & W Custom Cabinets showing their distribution of net income for the period ended February 28.

    a. Start up your word processing software application and create a new document.

    b. Enter the memo to Wayne Duncan and Scott Klare shown in Figure 6.11. If you completed the optional spreadsheet activity in Step 10 above, copy and paste the Distribution of Net Income Statement from your spreadsheet into your document.

```
                       MEMORANDUM

      TO:   Wayne Duncan, Partner
            Scott Klare, Partner

    DATE:   February 28, 19--

    FROM:   Student Name

 SUBJECT:   Distribution of Net Income

For your information, the distribution of net
income for the period ended February 28, 19-- is
as follows:

   Wayne Duncan
      50.0% of Net Income      $1,419.45
   Scott Klare
      50.0% of Net Income      $1,419.45
                               ---------
   Net Income                  $2,838.90
                               =========
```

Figure 6.11
Completed Distribution of Net Income Document

TUTORIAL PROBLEM 6-T

    c. Print the memo.
    d. Save the memo with a file name of XXX6–T.
    e. End your word processing session.

STEP 12: Generate and post the closing journal entries.
Choose *Generate Closing Journal Entries* from the Options menu. When the dialog box appears asking if you want to generate closing journal entries, click the *Yes* button. When the closing entries have been generated, the Closing Entries dialog box shown in Figure 6.12 will appear. Click the *Post* button.

Acct. #	Account Title	Debit	Credit
4110	Sales	32343.74	
3150	Income Summary		32343.74
3150	Income Summary	22250.70	
5110	Purchases		15639.95
6110	Insurance Expense		1182.12
6120	Miscellaneous Expense		219.62
6130	Rent Expense		2572.75
6140	Supplies Expense--Office		970.90
6150	Supplies Expense--Store		1382.67
6160	Utilities Expense		282.69
3150	Income Summary	2838.90	
3110	Wayne Duncan, Capital		1419.45
3130	Scott Klare, Capital		1419.45
3110	Wayne Duncan, Capital	1621.45	
3120	Wayne Duncan, Drawing		1621.45
3130	Scott Klare, Capital	1953.90	
3140	Scott Klare, Drawing		1953.90

Figure 6.12
Closing Entries Dialog Box

STEP 13: Display the closing entries.
Click the *Reports* toolbar button and choose *Journals* from the Select a Report Group list. Select the *General Journal* report. Select *Customize Journal Report,* and then choose *Clo. Ent.* from the Reference drop-down list, and click *OK.* The report appears in Figure 6.13.

T U T O R I A L   P R O B L E M   6 – T

```
                    S & W Custom Cabinets
                       General Journal
                         02/28/--

Date   Refer.   Acct.  Title              Debit      Credit

02/28  Clo.Ent.  4110  Sales             32343.74
02/28  Clo.Ent.  3150  Income Summary                32343.74
02/28  Clo.Ent.  3150  Income Summary    22250.70
02/28  Clo.Ent.  5110  Purchases                     15639.95
02/28  Clo.Ent.  6110  Insurance Expense              1182.12
02/28  Clo.Ent.  6120  Miscellaneous Expense           219.62
02/28  Clo.Ent.  6130  Rent Expense                   2572.75
02/28  Clo.Ent.  6140  Supplies Expense—Office         970.90
02/28  Clo.Ent.  6150  Supplies Expense—Store         1382.67
02/28  Clo.Ent.  6160  Utilities Expense               282.69
02/28  Clo.Ent.  3150  Income Summary     2838.90
02/28  Clo.Ent.  3110  Wayne Duncan, Capital          1419.45
02/28  Clo.Ent.  3130  Scott Klare, Capital           1419.45
02/28  Clo.Ent.  3110  Wayne Duncan, Capital  1621.45
02/28  Clo.Ent.  3120  Wayne Duncan, Drawing          1621.45
02/28  Clo.Ent.  3130  Scott Klare, Capital   1953.90
02/28  Clo.Ent.  3140  Scott Klare, Drawing           1953.90

                       Totals            61008.69   61008.69
```

Figure 6.13
Closing Entries

STEP 14:   Display a post-closing trial balance.
Click the *Reports* toolbar button and choose *Ledger Reports;* then select *Trial Balance* and click *OK*. The post-closing trial balance report appears in Figure 6.14.

```
                    S & W Custom Cabinets
                        Trial Balance
                         02/28/--

Acct.      Account
Number     Title                  Debit       Credit

1110       Cash                  44978.37
1120       Petty Cash              100.00
1130       Accounts Receivable    3796.40
1140       Merchandise Inventory 124024.00
1145       Supplies—Office         550.00
1150       Supplies—Store          835.00
1160       Prepaid Insurance       472.05
2110       Accounts Payable                   9903.02
2120       Sales Tax Payable                  1984.65
3110       Wayne Duncan, Capital             81600.30
3130       Scott Klare, Capital              81267.85

           Totals               174755.82  174755.82
```

Figure 6.14
Post-Closing
Trial Balance

TUTORIAL PROBLEM 6–T

STEP 15:   **Save your data file as XXX6–TAC.**
Click *Save As.* Save your file as XXX6–TAC, where XXX are your initials, 6–T is the problem number, and AC is "After Closing."

STEP 16:   **Calculate the amount of savings over a given period of time using the Savings Planner.**
S & W Custom Cabinets' partners Wayne Duncan and Scott Klare are considering purchasing land and a building. Based upon their financial condition, they can transfer $5,000 from their checking account to a savings account and contribute $1,200 into the account monthly. This investment will earn interest of 8.5% over the next 5 years.

Click the *Tools* toolbar button. When the Planning Tools window appears, click the *Savings Planner* tab. With the Ending Savings Balance option in the Calculate grouping selected, enter the following savings information and generate the Savings Planner Schedule shown in Figure 6.15.

```
                          Savings Plan
                            02/28/--
Savings Planner Schedule
-----------------------------------------------------------------
Month              Monthly         Monthly      Cumulative
Number             Contribution    Yield        Total
-----------------------------------------------------------------

(Beginning Balance)                               5000.00
1                  1200.00          35.42         6235.42
2                  1200.00          44.17         7479.59
3                  1200.00          52.98         8732.57
4                  1200.00          61.86         9994.43
5                  1200.00          70.79        11265.22
6                  1200.00          79.80        12545.02
7                  1200.00          88.86        13833.88
8                  1200.00          97.99        15131.87
9                  1200.00         107.18        16439.05
10                 1200.00         116.44        17755.49
11                 1200.00         125.77        19081.26
12                 1200.00         135.16        20416.42
/\/\/\/\/\/\/\/\/\/\/\/\/\/\/\/\/\/\/\/\/\/\/\/\/\/\/\/\/\/\
55                 1200.00         608.61        87730.37
56                 1200.00         621.42        89551.79
57                 1200.00         634.33        91386.12
58                 1200.00         647.32        93233.44
59                 1200.00         660.40        95093.84
60                 1200.00         673.59        96967.43
```

Figure 6.15
Savings Planner Schedule Report

Beginning Savings $5,000.00
Annual Yield (Percent) 8.50
Number of Months   60
Monthly Contribution $1,200.00

STEP 17: **End the *Automated Accounting* session.**
Click the *Exit/Quit* toolbar button.

Applying Your Information Skills

I. QUESTIONS

Directions: Write the answers to the following questions in the *Working Papers.*

1. What is the amount of the office supplies adjusting entry if the current account balance shown in the trial balance is $1,685.50 and the actual amount is $736.25?

2. What is the amount of the prepaid insurance adjusting entry if the current account balance shown in the trial balance is $1,895.00 and the actual amount is $645.00?

3. List three reasons why small businesses are sometimes organized as partnerships.

4. Explain how the partners' capital accounts are affected by the period-end closing process for a partnership with a 50/50 split of net income or loss.

5. List four things that happen during the posting of closing journal entries.

P Independent Practice Problem 6–P

In this problem, you will process the monthly transactions for the month of March and complete the end-of-fiscal-period processing for S & W Custom Cabinets. In this partnership, the net income or loss is divided equally among partners.

STEP 1:   Start up *Automated Accounting 7.0.*

STEP 2:   Load the opening balance file, AA06–P.

STEP 3:   Enter your name in the User Name text box.

STEP 4:   Click *Save As* and save the opening balances file with a file name of XXX6–P.

STEP 5:   Enter the March transactions.

Mar. 01	Sold merchandise on account to Bella Vista Woodworks, $4,743.98. S649.
	03	Sold merchandise on account to Owens Cabinet Masters, $5,056.31. S650.
	04	Purchased merchandise for cash, $163.85. C170.
	05	Purchased merchandise on account from Underhill Cabinets, $5,154.77. P232
	05	Paid cash for miscellaneous expense, $58.20. C171.
	08	Purchased merchandise on account from Milburn Wood Products, $4,200.00. P233.
	09	Paid cash on account to Santos Cabinet Design, $2,206.53, covering P224. C172.
	10	Paid cash on account to Superior Supply Co., $659.44, covering M54. C173.
	11	Paid cash for rent, $2,600.00. C174.
	11	Received cash on account from Kenner Quality Cabinets, $523.34, covering S633. R777.
	12	Received cash on account from Cathy Lombardi, $234.39, covering S638. R778.
	15	Add Riverside Cabinetry to the customer list. Sold merchandise on account to Riverside Cabinetry, $4,442.00. S651.
	16	Bought store supplies on account from Morley Office Supply Co., $346.80. M57.
	17	Paid cash for insurance, $818.15. C175.
	18	Sold merchandise on account to Baker Kitchen Cabinets, $5,155.62. S652.
	19	Paid cash for electric bill, $372.92. C176.
	23	Bought office supplies on account from Superior Supply Co., $102.65. M58.
	24	Received cash on account from Messer Cabinetry, Inc., $352.95, covering S642. R779.
	25	Wayne Duncan, partner, withdrew merchandise for personal use, $123.75. M59. Record this transaction in the general journal.

26   Purchased merchandise on account from Specter Cabinet Mfg., $5,244.21. P234.

29   Discovered that a transaction for store supplies bought for cash in January was journalized and posted in error as a debit to Purchases instead of Supplies—Store, $140.77. M60. Record this transaction in the General Journal.

29   Paid cash on account to Derrick Woodworking, Inc., $1,780.27, covering P226. C177.

30   Paid cash on account to Ashland Interiors, $800.28, covering P229. C178.

31   Recorded cash and credit card sales, $5,161.64, plus sales tax, $309.70; total, $5,471.34. T36.

31   Scott Klare, partner, withdrew cash for personal use, $1,050.00. C179.

31   Wayne Duncan, partner, withdrew cash for personal use, $865.00. C180.

31   Paid cash to replenish the petty cash fund, $88.00: office supplies, $37.10; store supplies, $50.90. C181.

STEP 6: Display the general, purchases, cash payments, sales, and cash receipts journal reports for the period March 1 through March 31 of the current year. If errors are detected, make corrections.

CHECK FIGURE:
Trial balance debit and credit totals = $209,226.98

STEP 7: Display a trial balance, schedule of accounts payable, and schedule of accounts receivable.

STEP 8: Enter the adjusting entries using the following adjustment data. Use the trial balance generated in step 7 as the basis for making the adjusting entries. Use Adj.Ent. as the reference.

Merchandise inventory on March 31 . . . . . . $118,950.00
Office supplies inventory $342.00
Store supplies inventory $940.00
Value of insurance policies $1,000.00

CHECK FIGURE:
General journal (adjusting entries) debit and credit totals = $6,145.42

STEP 9: Display the general journal report for the adjusting entries. Use a reference restriction of Adj.Ent. so that only adjusting entries will be included on the report.

STEP 10: Display the income statement and balance sheet.

STEP 11: Generate an income statement 3D bar graph.

STEP 12: Use the Save As menu command to save your data with a file name of XXX6–PBC, where XXX are your initials, 6–P is the problem number, and BC is "Before Closing."

STEP 13: **Optional spreadsheet and word processing integration activity:**
S & W Custom Cabinets has asked you to use a spreadsheet to prepare an Owners' Equity Statement for the period ended March 31. Next, prepare a memo addressed to each partner of S & W Custom Cabinets, containing their statement of Owners' Equity.

Spreadsheet Activity:
a. Display and copy the trial balance to the clipboard in spreadsheet format.
b. Start up your spreadsheet software and load template file SS06–P.
c. Select cell A1 as the current cell and paste the trial balance into the spreadsheet.
d. Enter the respective partner's capital and drawing accounts cell references from the trial balance to the Owners' Equity Statement. Enter the no. 442.35 in cells C43 and C51. This is each partner's share of net income. Enter the formulas where indicated in the Owners' Equity Statement.
e. Format the amounts in currency format if necessary.
f. Print the entire spreadsheet, including the Trial Balance and Owners' Equity Statement.
g. Save your spreadsheet data with a file name of XXX6–P.

Word Processing Activity:
a. Start up your word processing software application and create a new document. If you completed the optional word processing activity in Tutorial Problem 6–T, load and use that memo template.
b. Enter the necessary memo information. Use the memo format shown in Figure 6.11. Two lines below the subject line, key "For your information, the statement of owner's equity for the period ended March 31, 19-- is as follows:". Copy and paste the body of the Owners' Equity Statement from your spreadsheet into your memo.
c. Print the memo.
d. Save the document with a file name of XXX6–P.
e. End your spreadsheet and word processing sessions.

STEP 14: **Generate and post the closing general journal entries.**

STEP 15: **Display the closing entries. Use a reference restriction of Clo.Ent. so that only closing entries will be included on the report.**

STEP 16:   **Display a post-closing trial balance.**

STEP 17:   **Use Save As to save your data as XXX6–PAC.**

STEP 18:   **Calculate the monthly savings contribution over a given period of time using the Savings Planner. S & W Custom Cabinets wants to save $100,000.00 over the next five years toward the purchase of land and a building.**
Note: Select the *Monthly Contribution* option in the Calculate grouping, then enter the following savings information:

Beginning Savings	$5,000.00
Annual Yield (Percent)	8.5
Number of Months	60
Ending Savings Balance	$100,000.00

STEP 19:   **End the *Automated Accounting* session.**

Applying Your Technology Skills 6–P

Directions: Using Independent Practice Problem 6–P, write the answers to the following questions in the *Working Papers*.

1. From the purchases journal report, what is the amount of the credit to Specter Cabinet Mfg.?

2. In the cash payments journal report, what are the total debits and total credits?

3. From the sales journal report, what is the amount of sales invoice no. 651?

4. From the cash receipts journal, what is the amount of cash received from Cathy Lombardi for cash receipt no. 778?

5. From the schedule of accounts payable, what is the amount currently owed to Milburn Wood Products?

6. From the schedule of accounts receivable, what is the amount currently due from Riverside Cabinetry?

7. What is the gross profit for the period?

8. What are the total operating expenses?

9. What is the net income?

10. What are the total assets?

11. How much must S & W Custom Cabinets contribute to savings each month over the next five years to accumulate $100,000.00 toward the purchase of land and a building?

Mastery Problem 6–M

In this problem, you will process the monthly transactions for the month of April and complete the end-of-fiscal-period processing for S & W Custom Cabinets. In this partnership, the net income or loss is divided equally among partners.

STEP 1:   **Load the file AA06–M.**

STEP 2:   **Enter your name in the User Name text box.**

STEP 3:   **Save the opening balances file as XXX6–M.**

STEP 4:   **Enter the April maintenance and transactions.**

Apr. 03   Paid cash for quarterly sales tax, $2,294.35. C182.

03   Sold merchandise on account to Riley Cabinet Company, $4,528.46. S653.

04   Sold merchandise on account to Burgess Cabinet Co., $4,071.13. S654.

05   Purchased merchandise on account from Mellot Cabinet Co., $5,244.00. P235.

06   Purchased merchandise for cash, $657.35. C183.

06   Paid cash for office supplies, $83.61. C184.

07   Purchased merchandise on account from Santos Cabinet Design, $3,824.71. P236.

07   Paid cash for miscellaneous expense, $37.42. C185.

07   Paid cash on account to Morley Office Supply Co., $589.46, covering M53 and M57. C186.

10   Paid cash on account to Mellot Cabinet Co., $691.47, covering P227 and P231. C187.

10   Paid cash for rent, $2,600.00. C188.

10   Received cash on account from Marcus Millcraft, Inc., $820.05, covering S639 and S648. R780.

11   Received cash on account from Burgess Cabinet Co., $508.73, covering S643. R781.

11   Add Sabin Fine Millwork to the vendor list. Purchased merchandise on account from Sabin Fine Millwork, $2,453.42. P237.

12   Bought office supplies on account from Superior Supply Co., $93.04. M61.

13   Sold merchandise on account to Messer Cabinetry, Inc., $3,799.10. S655.

13   Paid cash for electric bill, $407.28. C189.

14   Paid cash for insurance, $627.30. C190.

15   Sold merchandise on account to Dewitt Interiors, $4,779.83. S656.

15   Received cash on account from Kenner Quality Cabinets, $63.36, covering S647. R782.

16   Received cash on account from Baker Kitchen Cabinets, $321.04, covering S640. R783.

17   Scott Klare, partner, withdrew merchandise for personal use, $344.42. M62. Record this transaction in the general journal.

24   Purchased merchandise on account from Derrick Woodworking, Inc., $3,880.95. P238.

25   Discovered that a withdrawal of cash by Wayne Duncan, partner, was journalized and posted in error as a credit to Purchases instead of Cash, $525.00. M63. Record this transaction in the General Journal.

26   Paid cash on account to Specter Cabinet Mfg., $4,178.52, covering P225 and P234. C191.

27   Paid cash on account to Milburn Wood Products, $1,689.58, covering P230 and P233. C192.

28   Recorded cash and credit card sales, $5,790.50, plus sales tax, $347.43; total, $6,137.93. T37.

28   Scott Klare, partner, withdrew cash for personal use, $1,250.00. C193.

28   Wayne Duncan, partner, withdrew cash for personal use, $1,575.00. C194.

28   Paid cash to replenish the petty cash fund, $97.65: office supplies, $10.54; store supplies, $19.38; Scott Klare, partner, $26.00; miscellaneous expense, $41.73. C195.

STEP 5:   Display the journal reports.

CHECK FIGURE:
Trial balance debit and credit totals =
$212,882.57

STEP 6:   Display a trial balance, schedule of accounts payable, and schedule of accounts receivable.

STEP 7:   Enter the adjusting entries.

Merchandise inventory on April 30 . . . . $117,200.00
Office supplies inventory $420.00
Store supplies inventory $680.00
Value of insurance policies $1,300.00

STEP 8:   Display the adjusting entries.

STEP 9: **Display the financial statements.**

STEP 10: **Generate a sales line graph.**

STEP 11: **Save your data with a file name of XXX6–MBC.**

STEP 12: **Optional spreadsheet and word processing integration activity:**
Prepare an Owners' Equity Statement for the period ended April 30. Next, prepare a memo addressed to each partner of S & W Custom Cabinets showing their Owners' Equity.

CHECK FIGURE:
General journal (adjusting entries) debit and credit totals = $2,465.87

Spreadsheet Activity:
a. Display and copy the trial balance to the clipboard in spreadsheet format.
b. Start up your spreadsheet software and load template file SS06–M.
c. Select cell A1 as the current cell and paste the trial balance into the spreadsheet.
d. Enter the respective partner's capital and drawing accounts cell references from the trial balance into the proper cells in the Owners' Equity Statement. Enter the amount of each partner's net income into the proper cells: Wayne Duncan, $587.85; Scott Klare, $587.86. Enter the formulas where indicated in the Owners' Equity Statement.
e. Format the amounts in currency format if necessary.
f. Print the entire spreadsheet including the Trial Balance and Owners' Equity Statement.
g. Save your spreadsheet data with a file name of XXX6–M.

Word Processing Activity:
a. Start up your word processing software application and create a new document. If you completed the optional word processing activity in either Tutorial Problem 6–T or Independent Practice Problem 6–P, load and use that memo template.
b. Enter the necessary memo information. Use the memo format shown in Figure 6.11. Two lines below the subject line, key "For your information, the statement of owners' equity for the period ended April 30, 19-- is as follows:". Copy and paste the body of the Owners' Equity Statement into your memo.
c. Print the memo.
d. Save the document with a file name of XXX6–M.
e. End your spreadsheet and word processing sessions.

STEP 13:   **Generate and post the closing journal entries.**

STEP 14:   **Display the closing entries.**

STEP 15:   **Display a post-closing trial balance.**

STEP 16:   **Save your data with a file name of XXX6–MAC.**

STEP 17:   **Use the Savings Planner to calculate the number of months needed to accumulate $100,000 given the following information:**

Beginning Savings $10,000.00
Annual Yield (Percent) 8.75
Monthly Contribution $1,200.00
Ending Savings Balance $100,000.00

STEP 18:   **End the *Automated Accounting* session.**

 # Applying Your Technology Skills 6–M

Directions: Using Mastery Problem 6–M, write the answers to the following questions in the *Working Papers*.

1. From the purchases journal report, what is the amount purchased from Santos Cabinet Design?

2. In the cash payments journal report, what are the total debits and total credits?

3. From the sales journal report, what is the amount of sales invoice no. 655?

4. From the cash receipts journal, what is the amount of cash received from Marcus Millcraft, Inc. for cash receipt no. 780?

5. From the schedule of accounts payable, what is the amount currently owed to all vendors?

6. From the schedule of accounts receivable, what is the amount currently due from Riley Cabinet Company?

7. What is the gross profit for the period?

8. What are the total operating expenses?

9. What is the net income?

10. What are the total assets?

11. From the Savings Planner, how many months will it take S & W Custom Cabinets to save $100,000 based on the data provided?

Reinforcement Activity R–2

ACM Video & Electronics sells TVs, stereos, and VCRs to retail stores. In Reinforcement Activity R–2, you will process the monthly transactions for February and complete the end-of-fiscal-period processing for this business.

STEP 1: **Start up *Automated Accounting 7.0.***

STEP 2: **Load the opening balances file, AAR–2.**

STEP 3: **Enter your name in the User Name text box.**

STEP 4: **Click *Save As* and save the opening balances file with a file name of XXXR–2, where XXX are your initials.**

STEP 5: **Add Vogel Video Mfg. to the vendor list. Delete Setter Electronics Co. and Mathis Stereo Corp. from the vendor list.**

STEP 6: **Add Sandra Nichols and Laura Jarrett to the customer list. Delete Pauley Audio-Video Center from the customer list.**

STEP 7: **Enter the February transaction data. Abbreviate the reference numbers on the input forms as follows: Check No., C; Memorandums, M; Cash Receipts Tape, T; Cash Receipt No., R; Sales Invoice No., S; Purchase Invoice No., P.**

Feb. 01 Paid cash for sales tax, $1,397.11. C511.
    01 Sold merchandise on account to Munafo Television, $1,646.96. S904.
    01 Sold merchandise on account to Bartels TV & VCR Repairs, $2,206.90. S905.
    02 Sold merchandise on account to Clare Sound Systems, $1,780.80. S906.
    02 Paid cash for rent, $2,750.00. C512.
    02 Paid cash for electric bill, $492.20. C513.
    03 Bought store supplies on account from Vaught Office Supply Co., $121.17. M232.
    03 Received cash on account from Alice Timmons, $441.05, covering S895. R756.
    03 Purchased merchandise on account from Roland VCR Products, $1,496.95. P416.
    04 Purchased merchandise for cash, $795.76. C514.
    04 Paid cash for miscellaneous expense, $308.76. C515.
    05 Bought office supplies on account from Vaught Office Supply Co., $426.99. M233.

05   Sold merchandise on account to Munafo Television, $1,578.90. S907.

06   Sold merchandise on account to Morris Video & Service, $1,971.63. S908.

06   Sold merchandise on account to Tillis Video Products, $1,774.13. S909.

06   Paid cash for insurance, $1,391.13. C516.

06   Recorded cash and credit card sales, $2,131.53, plus sales tax, $127.89; total, $2,259.42. T5.

06   Discovered that a purchase of merchandise for cash was journalized and posted in error as a debit to Supplies—Office instead of Purchases, $346.75. M234. Record this transaction in the General Journal.

08   Purchased merchandise on account from Cooper Video Products, $1,154.21. P417.

08   Purchased merchandise on account from Dupont Electronics Inc., $1,545.95. P418.

09   Paid cash on account to Siemer Video Systems, $1,465.88, covering P400. C517.

09   Received cash on account from Slater Entertainment, $2,627.93, covering S896. R757.

10   Received cash on account from Setzer TV Satellite Co., $1,158.26, covering S897. R758.

10   Purchased merchandise on account from Sontag TV & Radio, $1,363.80. P419.

10   Paid cash for utilities expense, $418.05. C518.

11   Received cash on account from Clare Sound Systems, $3,025.55, covering S898. R759.

12   Sold merchandise on account to Sandra Nichols, $195.00, plus sales tax, $11.70; total, $206.70. S910.

12   Paid cash on account to Roland VCR Products, $3,492.85, covering P415 and P416. C519.

13   Paid cash on account to Vaught Office Supply Co., $472.08, covering M231. C520.

13   Paid cash on account to Sontag TV & Radio, $1,456.25, covering P414. C521.

13   Purchased merchandise on account from Vogel Video Mfg., $1,054.72. P420.

13   Recorded cash and credit card sales, $1,755.00, plus sales tax, $105.30; total, $1,860.30. T12.

15   Discovered that a payment for rent was journalized and posted in error as a debit to Purchases instead of Rent Expense, $2,750.00. M235. Record this transaction in the General Journal.

15 Bought store supplies on account from Vaught Office Supply Co., $92.40. M236.

16 Received cash on account from Bartels TV & VCR Repairs, $3,616.72, covering S899 and S905. R760.

16 Received cash on account from Tillis Video Products, $1,757.95, covering S902. R761.

16 Purchased merchandise for cash, $953.11. C522.

17 Ginger Rojas, partner, withdrew merchandise for personal use, $235.93. M237. Record this transaction in the General Journal.

17 Sold merchandise on account to Setzer TV Satellite Co., $1,053.23. S911.

18 Purchased merchandise on account from Craig TransVideo Co., $975.00. P421.

18 Purchased merchandise on account from Sontag TV & Radio, $1,463.50. P422.

19 Bought office supplies on account from Vaught Office Supply Co., $337.78. M238.

20 Discovered that a withdrawal of merchandise by Ginger Rojas for personal use was journalized and posted in error as a debit to Victor Rojas, Drawing instead of Ginger Rojas, Drawing, $525.00. M239. Record this transaction in the General Journal.

20 Purchased merchandise for cash, $681.16. C523.

20 Paid cash for miscellaneous expense, $240.19. C524.

20 Victor Rojas, partner, withdrew merchandise for personal use, $500.00. M240. Record this transaction in the General Journal.

20 Paid cash for store supplies, $52.58. C525.

20 Recorded cash and credit card sales, $2,452.07, plus sales tax, $147.12; total, $2,599.19. T19.

22 Received cash on account from Munafo Television, $1,646.96, covering S904. R762.

22 Received cash on account from Morris Video & Service, $1,977.70, covering S903. R763.

23 Sold merchandise on account to Laura Jarrett, $514.60, plus sales tax, $30.88; total, $545.48. S912.

23 Sold merchandise on account to Slater Entertainment, $2,252.60. S913.

24 Paid cash for office supplies, $106.32. C526.

24 Discovered that a payment for a miscellaneous expense was journalized and posted in error as a debit to Rent Expense instead of Miscellaneous Expense, $95.00. M241. Record this transaction in the General Journal.

25   Received cash on account from Munafo Television, $1,578.90, covering S907. R764.

25   Received cash on account from Sandra Nichols, $206.70, covering S910. R765.

26   Sold merchandise on account to Bartels TV & VCR Repairs, $2,090.21. S914.

26   Sold merchandise on account to Morris Video & Service, $1,782.33. S915.

26   Purchased merchandise on account from Dupont Electronics Inc., $1,156.41. P423.

26   Received cash on account from Bolin TV & Stereos, $685.41, covering S900. R766.

27   Paid cash on account to Vaught Office Supply Co., $978.34, covering M232, M233, M236, and M238. C527.

27   Ginger Rojas, partner, withdrew cash for personal use, $2,900.00. C528.

27   Victor Rojas, partner, withdrew cash for personal use, $2,900.00. C529.

27   Paid cash to replenish the petty cash fund, $97.00: office supplies, $16.00; store supplies, $36.50; Ginger Rojas, partner, $31.00; miscellaneous expense, $13.50. C530.

27   Recorded cash and credit card sales, $1,614.59, plus sales tax, $96.88; total, $1,711.47. T26.

STEP 8: Display the journal reports (general, purchases, cash payments, sales, and cash receipts) for the period February 1 through February 28 of the current year. If errors are detected, make corrections.

CHECK FIGURES:
Trial balance debit and credit totals = $166,384.61

STEP 9: Display a trial balance, schedule of accounts payable, and schedule of accounts receivable.

STEP 10: Enter the adjusting entries using the following adjustment data. Use the trial balance generated in Step 9 as the basis for making the adjusting entries. Use Adj.Ent. as the reference.

Merchandise inventory on February 28 . . . . . $87,200.00
Office supplies inventory $750.00
Store supplies inventory $620.00
Value of insurance policies $2,300.00

CHECK FIGURES:
General journal (adjusting entries) debit and credit totals = $5,801.28

STEP 11: Display the general journal report for the adjusting entries. Use a reference restriction of Adj.Ent. so that only adjusting entries will be included on the report.

STEP 12: Display the income statement and balance sheet.

STEP 13: **Generate income statement and balance sheet 3D bar graphs.**

STEP 14: **Use the Save As menu command to save your data with a file name of XXXR–2BC, where XXX are your initials, R–2 is the problem number, and BC is "Before Closing."**

STEP 15: **Optional spreadsheet and word processing integration activity:**
ACM Video & Electronics has asked you to use a spreadsheet to prepare an Owners' Equity Statement for the period ended February 28. Next, prepare a memo addressed to each partner, containing their owners' equity information.

Spreadsheet Activity:
a. Display and copy the trial balance to the clipboard in spreadsheet format.
b. Start up your spreadsheet software and load template file SSR–2.
c. Select cell A1 as the current cell and paste the income statement into the spreadsheet.
d. Enter the cell references from the trial balance of the respective partner's capital and drawing accounts. Enter 2262.55 in cell C43 and 2262.56 in cell C51. This is the share of net income from the Distribution of Net Income Statement. Enter the formulas where indicated in the Owners' Equity Statement.
e. Format the amounts in currency format if necessary.
f. Print the entire spreadsheet, including the Trial Balance and the Owners' Equity Statement.
g. Save your spreadsheet data with a file name of XXXR–2.

Word Processing Activity:
a. Start up your word processing software application and create a new document.
b. Enter a memo to Ginger and Victor Rojas. Copy and paste the owners' equity statement from your spreadsheet into the memo.
c. Print the memo.
d. Save the document with a file name of XXXR–2.
e. End your spreadsheet and word processing sessions.

STEP 16: **Generate and post the closing general journal entries.**

STEP 17: **Display a post-closing trial balance.**

STEP 18: Use Save As to save your data as XXXR–2AC, where
XXX are your initials and AC indicates "After Closing."

STEP 19: End the *Automated Accounting* session.

R Applying Your Technology Skills R–2

Directions: Using Reinforcement Activity R–2, write the answers to the following questions in the *Working Papers*.

Journals:

1. From the general journal, what is the total of the credit column?

2. From the purchases journal report, what is the amount of the credit to Cooper Video Products?

3. On the cash payments journal report, what are the total debits and total credits?

4. From the sales journal report, what is the amount of Sales Invoice No. 906?

5. From the cash receipts journal, what is the amount of cash received from Setzer TV Satellite Co. for Cash Receipt No. 758?

Ledgers:

6. From the schedule of accounts payable, what is the amount currently owed to all vendors?

7. From the schedule of accounts receivable, what is the amount currently due from Morris Video & Service?

Financial Statements:

8. What is the gross profit for the period?

9. What are the total operating expenses?

10. What is the net income?

11. What are the total liabilities?

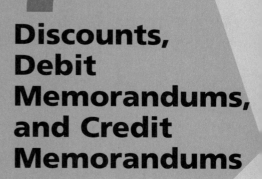

KEY TERMS

Purchases Discount

Sales Discount

Debit Memorandum

Credit Memorandum

Discount Period

7 Discounts, Debit Memorandums, and Credit Memorandums

LEARNING OBJECTIVES

Upon completion of this chapter, you will be able to:

1. Process purchases discounts.

2. Process sales discounts.

3. Process debit memorandums.

4. Process credit memorandums.

INTRODUCTION

In this chapter you will learn how to process purchases discounts, sales discounts, debit memorandums, and credit memorandums. You will learn how to analyze, enter, and post these transactions at the computer. As an alternative, you may record the transactions on input forms before entering and posting the transactions at the computer.

Buyers are often given a deduction on the sales invoice amount in order to encourage early payment. From the buyer's point of view, a deduction for early payment of an invoice is called a **purchases discount.** From the seller's point of view, a deduction for early payment of an invoice is referred to as a **sales discount.** If the invoice amount is paid within the time period specified on the invoice, the discount may be deducted from the payment.

Buyers are sometimes granted credit for returned or damaged merchandise. Credit given for damaged goods not returned is known as an allowance. From the buyer's point of view, returns and allowances

E T H I C S

The method of communication that conveys the most information is talking face to face with another person. Spoken words convey meaning, but meaning is also conveyed through voice inflection, posture, gestures, eye contact, and general demeanor. And all those elements can say as much—if not more—than words.

When communication is via e-mail (electronic mail), the words still have meaning; however, the meaning conveyed through other methods is lost. E-mail offers some advantages over letters and memos in that it is easy to compose and the message is delivered almost instantaneously to its recipients. But those advantages can lead to problems if e-mail is misused.

With e-mail, it is just as easy to send a message to a huge group of people as to one person. This capability leads some persons to use e-mail for non-business purposes, thus wasting the time required to screen "garbage" messages before deleting them.

A potentially more costly problem could be called "quick to anger." If an e-mail (or network) user gets mad at someone, it is tempting to immediately compose a nasty message and share it with everyone. Before e-mail, when thoughts had to be put on paper for delivery, at least there was an automatic "cooling-off period" enforced by the process itself. There is particular danger when supervisors transmit messages that have accusations that violate legal standards and open up potential employee lawsuits. Likewise, angry messages from employees can contain comments that lead to firing. A word of good advice is to never send an e-mail message that you would not want anyone else to see and to do unto others as you would like them to do unto you.

a. Do you think that e-mail should be used for private, confidential communication? Justify your belief.

b. Who, besides the sender and intended receiver, do you think can access e-mail communication?

c. Identify several policies that you think a company's employees should follow when using e-mail.

result in a debit to the vendor's account. The form prepared by the customer showing the price deduction for returns and allowances is called a **debit memorandum.** From the seller's point of view, returns and allowances result in a credit to the customer's account. The form prepared by the vendor showing the amount deducted for returns and allowances is called a **credit memorandum.**

PURCHASES DISCOUNTS

A purchases discount is an incentive offered by the vendor to pay the invoice before the due date. If the invoice is paid within the specified time period, a discount amount may be deducted from the invoice amount. The time period during which a deduction of the invoice amount may be taken is called the **discount period.** The discount amount is usually based on a percentage of the invoice amount and is shown on the invoice. For example, 1/10, n/30 means that 1% of the invoice amount may be deducted if the invoice is paid within 10 days of the invoice date and that the total invoice amount must be paid within 30 days.

Purchases discounts are entered into the computer at the time the invoice is paid. The sample transaction shown below has been entered in the cash payments journal in Figure 7.1.

> **FYI**
>
> 1/10, n/30 is read as *one ten, net thirty.*

> Feb. 01   Paid cash on account to Billingsley, Inc., $4,136.45, covering P300 for $4,178.23, less 1% discount, $41.78. C626.

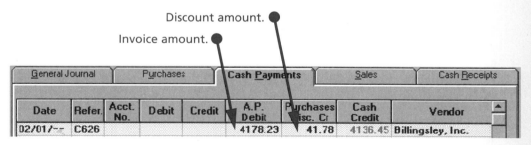

Figure 7.1
Cash Payments Journal (Purchases Discount)

1: Click the *Journal* toolbar button.

2: Click the *Cash Payments* tab.

3: Enter the transaction date (02/01/--).

4: Enter the check number (C626).

5: **Enter the amount of the invoice in the A.P. Debit cell (4178.23).** The amount of the invoice is automatically entered in the Cash Credit amount cell (4178.23).

6: **Enter the discount amount in the Purchases Disc. Cr cell (41.78).** The Cash Credit amount is calculated and displayed automatically by the software (4136.45).

7: **Choose a vendor name from the drop-down list (Billingsley, Inc.).**

8: **If the transaction is correct, click *Post*.**

SALES DISCOUNTS

In this accounting system, sales discounts are recorded in the cash receipts journal at the time the cash is received on account. The first sample transaction shown in Figure 7.2 is an example of a cash receipt on account with a sales discount. The second sample transaction is provided to show how cash and credit card sales are entered into the expanded cash receipts journal.

Feb. 02   Received cash on account from Blair Lighting Co., $5,356.12, covering S448 for $5,410.22, less 1% discount, $54.10. R217.

Feb. 10   Recorded cash and credit card sales, $3,675.94, plus sales tax, $257.32; total, $3,933.26. T17.

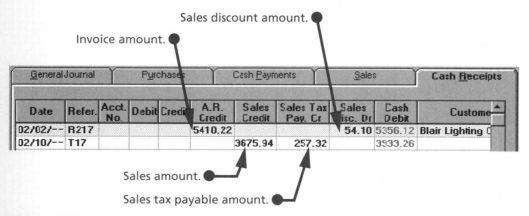

Figure 7.2
Cash Receipts Journal (Sales Discount and Cash Sales)

Entering a Cash Receipt with a Sales Discount

1:   Click the *Journal* toolbar button.

2:   Click the *Cash Receipts* tab.

3:   Enter the transaction date (02/02/--).

4:   Enter the reference (R217).

5:   Enter the amount of the invoice in the A.R. Credit cell (5410.22).
     The invoice amount is automatically entered into the Cash Debit cell by the computer (5410.22).

6:   Enter the discount amount in the Sales Disc. Dr cell (54.10).
     The Cash Debit amount is automatically calculated and displayed (5356.12).

7:   Choose a customer name from the drop-down list (Blair Lighting Co.).

8:   If the transaction is correct, click *Post*.

Entering Cash Sales

1:   Enter the transaction date (02/10/--).

2:   Enter the reference (T17).

3:   Enter the amount of cash sales in the Sales Credit cell (3675.94).
     The invoice amount is automatically entered into the Cash Debit cell by the computer (3675.94).

4:   Enter the amount of sales tax payable in the Sales Tax Pay [check tab here] cell (257.32).
     The Cash Debit amount is automatically recalculated and displayed (3933.26).

5:   If the transaction is correct, click *Post*.

DEBIT MEMORANDUMS

A debit memorandum results when a buyer receives credit from a vendor for merchandise returned or receives an allowance for inferior or damaged merchandise. Debit memorandums are recorded in the general journal. A sample transaction involving a debit memorandum is listed on the next page and shown entered into the general journal in Figure 7.3.

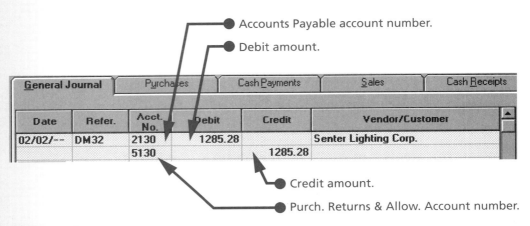

Figure 7.3
General Journal (Debit Memorandum)

Feb. 02   Returned merchandise to Senter Lighting Corp., $1,285.28, against P298. DM32.

1: Click the *Journal* toolbar button.

2: Click the *General Journal* tab.

3: Enter the date of the transaction (02/02/--).

4: Enter the reference (DM32).

5: Enter the account number for Accounts Payable (2130) and the debit amount (1285.28).

6: Choose the vendor name from the Vendor/Customer drop-down list (Senter Lighting Corp.).

7: Enter the account number for Purch. Returns & Allow. (5130) and the credit amount (1285.28).

8: Click *Post*.

CREDIT MEMORANDUMS

A credit memorandum results when a seller grants credit to a customer for merchandise returned or grants an allowance for inferior or damaged merchandise. Credit memorandums are recorded in the general journal. A sample transaction involving a credit memorandum is listed below and shown entered into the general journal in Figure 7.4.

Feb. 04   Granted credit to Webster Lite Shoppe for merchandise returned, $392.24, against S451. CM52.

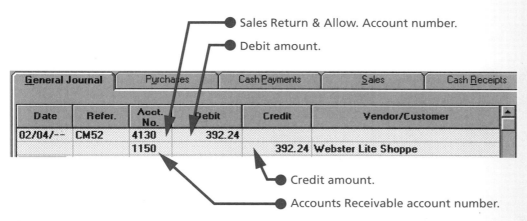

Figure 7.4
General Journal (Credit Memorandum)

1:   Click the *Journal* toolbar button.

2:   Click the *General Journal* tab.

3:   Enter the date of the transaction (02/04/--).

4:   Enter the reference (CM52).

5:   Enter the account number for Sales Return & Allow. (4130) and the debit amount (392.24).

6:   Enter the account number for Accounts Receivable (1150) and the credit amount (392.24).

7:   Choose the customer name from the Vendor/Customer drop-down list (Webster Lite Shoppe).

8:   Click *Post.*

Chapter Review

1.   A purchases discount is a deduction on the invoice amount of the purchase that is given a buyer in order to encourage early payment. Purchases discounts are recorded in the cash payments journal. A time period during which a deduction of the invoice amount may be taken is known as the discount period.

2.   A sales discount is a deduction on the invoice amount of the sale that is given by the seller to a buyer in order to encourage early payment. Sales discounts are recorded in the cash receipts journal.

3. A debit memorandum is the form prepared by the customer showing the price deduction for returns and allowances.

4. A credit memorandum is the form prepared by the vendor showing the amount deducted for returned or damaged merchandise. Both credit and debit memorandums are recorded in the general journal.

In the history of computing, few computer languages and operating systems have had as much impact and been as reliable as UNIX. This powerful operating system, developed in the 1960s, became a favorite of businesses and universities.

ACCOUNTING CAREERS IN DEPTH

Accounting Clerk

An accounting clerk performs any combination of the following duties:

- Calculating, posting, and verifying to obtain financial data for use in maintaining accounting records.
- Compiling and sorting documents such as invoices and checks to substantiate business transactions.
- Verifying and posting details of business transactions, such as funds received and disbursed, and totaling accounts, using a calculator or a computer.
- Computing and recording charges, refunds, cost of lost or damaged goods, freight charges, rentals, and similar items.

An accounting clerk may also do the following:

- Typing vouchers, invoices, check account statements, reports, and other records, using a typewriter or a computer.
- Reconciling bank statements.

The accounting clerk job is an entry-level position in most businesses. There are usually many opportunities for advancement if you are successful in your work. Taking accounting courses prior to working in this type of position is usually a requirement. In some companies, you are required to pass a test in order to be considered for the position. This should not be difficult if you have already studied accounting.

Accounting clerk positions can be found in most companies. Sometimes a different title may be used, but the work responsibilities are the same. An accounting clerk may be designated according to the type of accounting performed, such as Accounts-Payable Clerk and Accounts-Receivable Clerk.

There are usually many opportunities to be found in this career choice. Depending on your drive and plans for the future, a position as an accounting clerk can open doors to professional advancement.

TUTORIAL   PROBLEM   7 – T

In this tutorial problem, you will enter the journal entries for transactions involving sales discounts, purchases discounts, sales returns and allowances, and purchases returns and allowances. In addition, you will generate journal entries reports, a trial balance, and schedules of accounts payable and accounts receivable.

The journals in Figures 7.5 through 7.9 show the transaction statements already entered. The reference numbers have been abbreviated as follows: Purchase invoice no., P; Check no., C; Sales invoice no., S; Cash receipt no., R; Cash register tape, T; Memorandum, M; Credit memorandum, CM; Debit memorandum, DM.

Feb. 01 Paid cash on account to Billingsley, Inc., $4,136.45, covering P300 for $4,178.23, less 1% discount, $41.78. C626.

01 Purchased merchandise on account from Wyler Electric Light Co., $3,013.98. P303.

02 Received cash on account from Blair Lighting Co., $5,356.12, covering S448 for $5,410.22, less 1% discount, $54.10. R217.

02 Sold merchandise on account to Arnold's Lite-House, $4,859.31. S454.

02 Returned merchandise to Senter Lighting Corp., $1,285.28, against P298. DM32.

03 Received cash on account from Olinger Electric Supply, $4,304.56, covering S449, no discount. R218.

03 Sold merchandise on account to Rillo Lighting Systems, $6,008.22. S455.

04 Granted credit to Webster Lite Shoppe for merchandise returned, $392.24, against S451. CM52.

05 Sold merchandise on account to Milan Lighting Outlet, $4,486.17. S456.

05 Paid cash on account to Wyler Electric Light Co., $2,705.60, covering P296, no discount. C627.

06 Purchased merchandise on account from Dillon Lighting, Inc., $3,477.60. P304.

06 Paid cash on account to Southern Supplies, Inc., $514.25, covering M24 for $519.44, less 1% discount, $5.19. C628.

TUTORIAL PROBLEM 7-T

06 Received cash on account from Milan Lighting Outlet, $5,160.45, covering S452 for $5,212.58, less 1% discount, $52.13. R219.

08 Returned merchandise to Stacy Light Fixture Co., $1,054.92, against P302. DM33.

08 Paid cash on account to Senter Lighting Corp., $2,088.12, covering P298 less DM32, no discount. C629.

09 Received cash on account from Webster Lite Shoppe, $4,332.46, covering S451 less CM52, no discount. R220.

10 Granted credit to Rillo Lighting Systems for merchandise returned, $960.18, against S455. CM53.

10 Recorded cash and credit card sales, $3,675.94, plus sales tax, $257.32; total, $3,933.26. T17.

STEP 1: **Start up *Automated Accounting 7.0.***

STEP 2: **Load file AA07–T.**
Click the *Open* toolbar button. Select file AA07–T from the File list box.

STEP 3: **Enter your name in the User Name text box and click *OK*.**

STEP 4: **Save the file as XXX7–T.**
Click the *Save As* toolbar button and save the file as XXX7–T.

STEP 5: **Enter the data from the general journal shown in Figure 7.5.**
Click the *Journal* toolbar button. Click the *General Journal* tab and enter the journal entries.

Date	Refer.	Acct. No.	Debit	Credit	Vendor/Customer
02/02/--	DM32	2130	1285.28		Senter Lighting Corp.
		5130		1285.28	
02/04/--	CM52	4130	392.24		
		1150		392.24	Webster Lite Shoppe
02/08/--	DM33	2130	1054.92		Stacy Light Fixture Co.
		5130		1054.92	
02/10/--	CM53	4130	960.18		
		1150		960.18	Rillo Lighting Systems

Figure 7.5
General Journal

STEP 6:   Enter the data from the purchases journal shown in Figure 7.6.
Click the *Purchases* tab and enter the journal entries.

Date	Refer.	Purch. Debit	A.P. Credit	Vendor
02/01/--	P303	3013.98	3013.98	Wyler Electric Light Co.
02/06/--	P304	3477.60	3477.60	Dillon Lighting, Inc.

Figure 7.6
Purchases Journal

STEP 7:   Enter the data from the cash payments journal shown in Figure 7.7.
Click the *Cash Payments* tab and enter the journal entries.

Date	Refer.	Acct. No.	Debit	Credit	A.P. Debit	Purchases Disc. Cr	Cash Credit	Vendor
02/01/--	C626				4178.23	41.78	4136.45	Billingsley, Inc.
02/05/--	C627				2705.60		2705.60	Wyler Electric Light Co.
02/06/--	C628				519.44	5.19	514.25	Southern Supplies, Inc.
02/08/--	C629				2088.12		2088.12	Senter Lighting Corp.

Figure 7.7
Cash Payments Journal

STEP 8:   Enter the data from the sales journal shown in Figure 7.8.
Click the *Sales* tab and enter the journal entries.

Date	Refer.	Sales Credit	Sales Tax Credit	A.R. Debit	Customer
02/02/--	S454	4859.31		4859.31	Arnold's Lite-House
02/03/--	S455	6008.22		6008.22	Rillo Lighting Systems
02/05/--	S456	4486.17		4486.17	Milan Lighting Outlet

Figure 7.8
Sales Journal

T U T O R I A L   P R O B L E M   7 - T

STEP 9:   **Enter the data from the cash receipts journal shown in Figure 7.9.**
Click the *Cash Receipts* tab and enter the journal entries.

Date	Refer.	Acct. No.	Debit	Credit	A.R. Credit	Sales Credit	Sales Tax Pay. Cr	Sales Disc. Dr	Cash Debit	Customer
02/02/--	R217				5410.22			54.10	5356.12	Blair Lighting C
02/03/--	R218				4304.56				4304.56	Olinger Electric
02/06/--	R219				5212.58			52.13	5160.45	Milan Lighting
02/09/--	R220				4332.46				4332.46	Webster Lite S
02/10/--	T17					3675.94	257.32		3933.26	

Figure 7.9
Cash Receipts Journal

STEP 10:   **Display the journal reports.**
Click the *Reports* toolbar icon. Choose the *Journals* option button. Select the desired journal report, and then click OK. When the Journal Report Selection window appears, choose the *Customize Journal Report* option and click *OK*. Set the Start and End Dates to February 1 and February 10 of the current year and click *OK*. The reports appear in Figures 7.10 through 7.14.

```
                    Decor Light Fixture Corp.
                        General Journal
                          02/10/--

   -----------------------------------------------------------
   Date    Refer.   Acct.   Title              Debit      Credit
   -----------------------------------------------------------
   02/02   DM32     2130    AP/Senter Lighting Corp.  1285.28
   02/02   DM32     5130    Purch. Returns & Allow.            1285.28

   02/04   CM52     4130    Sales Returns & Allow.     392.24
   02/04   CM52     1150    AR/Webster Lite Shoppe              392.24

   02/08   DM33     2130    AP/Stacy Light Fixture Co. 1054.92
   02/08   DM33     5130    Purch. Returns & Allow.            1054.92

   02/10   CM53     4130    Sales Returns & Allow.     960.18
   02/10   CM53     1150    AR/Rillo Lighting Systems           960.18
                                                      ------     ------
                            Totals              3692.62    3692.62
                                                ======     ======
```

Figure 7.10
General Journal Report

TUTORIAL PROBLEM 7–T

```
                    Decor Light Fixture Corp.
                       Purchases Journal
                          02/10/--

--------------------------------------------------------------
Date    Inv. No.   Acct.   Title               Debit     Credit
--------------------------------------------------------------
02/01   P303       5110    Purchases           3013.98
02/01   P303       2130    AP/Wyler Electric Light Co.     3013.98

02/06   P304       5110    Purchases           3477.60
02/06   P304       2130    AP/Dillon Lighting, Inc.        3477.60
                                               -------   -------
                          Totals               6491.58   6491.58
                                               =======   =======
```

Figure 7.11
Purchases Journal Report

```
                    Decor Light Fixture Corp.
                     Cash Payments Journal
                          02/10/--

--------------------------------------------------------------
Date    Ck. No.    Acct.   Title               Debit     Credit
--------------------------------------------------------------
02/01   C626       2130    AP/Billingsley, Inc.  4178.23
02/01   C626       1110    Cash                            4136.45
02/01   C626       5120    Purchases Discount                41.78

02/05   C627       2130    AP/Wyler Electric Light Co.  2705.60
02/05   C627       1110    Cash                            2705.60

02/06   C628       2130    AP/Southern Supplies, Inc.   519.44
02/06   C628       1110    Cash                            514.25
02/06   C628       5120    Purchases Discount                5.19

02/08   C629       2130    AP/Senter Lighting Corp.  2088.12
02/08   C629       1110    Cash                            2088.12
                                               -------   -------
                          Totals               9491.39   9491.39
                                               =======   =======
```

Figure 7.12
Cash Payments Journal Report

Humor on the Internet is one of its most popular features. However, the freedom to post any type of humor can result in material that people might find not funny or even offensive.

T U T O R I A L   P R O B L E M   7 – T

Decor Light Fixture Corp.
Sales Journal
02/10/--

Date	Inv. No.	Acct.	Title	Debit	Credit
02/02	S454	1150	AR/Arnold's Lite-House	4859.31	
02/02	S454	4110	Sales		4859.31
02/03	S455	1150	AR/Rillo Lighting Systems	6008.22	
02/03	S455	4110	Sales		6008.22
02/05	S456	1150	AR/Milan Lighting Outlet	4486.17	
02/05	S456	4110	Sales		4486.17
			Totals	15353.70	15353.70

Figure 7.13
Sales Journal
Report

Decor Light Fixture Corp.
Cash Receipts Journal
02/10/--

Date	Refer.	Acct.	Title	Debit	Credit
02/02	R217	1110	Cash	5356.12	
02/02	R217	4120	Sales Discount	54.10	
02/02	R217	1150	AR/Blair Lighting Co.		5410.22
02/03	R218	1110	Cash	4304.56	
02/03	R218	1150	AR/Olinger Electric Supply		4304.56
02/06	R219	1110	Cash	5160.45	
02/06	R219	4120	Sales Discount	52.13	
02/06	R219	1150	AR/Milan Lighting Outlet		5212.58
02/09	R220	1110	Cash	4332.46	
02/09	R220	1150	AR/Webster Lite Shoppe		4332.46
02/10	T17	1110	Cash	3933.26	
02/10	T17	4110	Sales		3675.94
02/10	T17	2150	Sales Tax Payable		257.32
			Totals	23193.08	23193.08

Figure 7.14
Cash Receipts
Report

STEP 11: **Display a trial balance, a schedule of accounts payable, and a schedule of accounts receivable.**
Choose *Ledger Reports.* Select the desired ledger report and click *OK.* The reports are shown in Figures 7.15 through 7.17.

▶

TUTORIAL PROBLEM 7-T

Decor Light Fixture Corp.
Trial Balance
02/10/--

Acct. Number	Account Title	Debit	Credit
1110	Cash	24638.52	
1120	Petty Cash	200.00	
1130	Notes Receivable	7800.00	
1150	Accounts Receivable	26537.46	
1160	Merchandise Inventory	79633.79	
1170	Supplies—Office	470.00	
1180	Supplies—Store	885.00	
1190	Prepaid Insurance	800.00	
1510	Office Equipment	13085.00	
1520	Accum. Depr.—Ofc. Eqpt.		3492.38
1530	Store Equipment	10295.00	
1540	Accum. Depr.—Store Eqpt.		2350.00
2110	Notes Payable		10500.00
2130	Accounts Payable		17577.07
2150	Sales Tax Payable		1313.14
3110	Capital Stock		99000.00
3120	Retained Earnings		16645.60
4110	Sales		19029.64
4120	Sales Discount	106.23	
4130	Sales Returns & Allow.	1352.42	
5110	Purchases	6491.58	
5120	Purchases Discount		46.97
5130	Purch. Returns & Allow.		2340.20
	Totals	172295.00	172295.00

Figure 7.15
Trial Balance

Decor Light Fixture Corp.
Schedule of Accounts Payable
02/10/--

Name	Balance
Dillon Lighting, Inc.	7299.46
Foster Manufacturing	4043.00
Stacy Light Fixture Co.	3220.63
Wyler Electric Light Co.	3013.98
Total	17577.07

Figure 7.16
Schedule of Accounts Payable

TUTORIAL PROBLEM 7-T

```
                    Decor Light Fixture Corp.
                  Schedule of Accounts Receivable
                           02/10/--

----------------------------------------------------------
Name                                              Balance
----------------------------------------------------------

Arnold's Lite-House                             10407.26
Milan Lighting Outlet                            4486.17
Rillo Lighting Systems                          11644.03
                                                ----------
Total                                           26537.46
                                                ==========
```

Figure 7.17
Schedule of Accounts Receivable

STEP 12:   **Generate a sales line graph.**
                · Click the *Graphs* toolbar button. Choose the *Sales*
                graph, and then select the *Line* graph. Click *OK*. The
                sales line graph is shown in Figure 7.18.

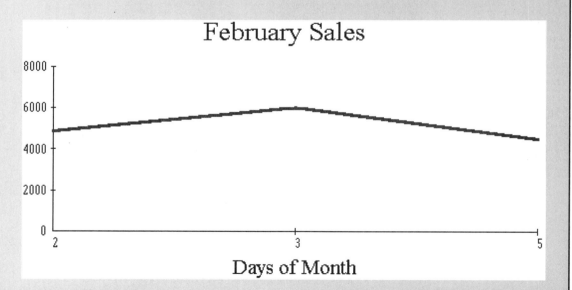

Figure 7.18
Sales Line Graph

T U T O R I A L   P R O B L E M   7 - T

STEP 13: **Calculate a loan payment amount using the Loan Planner.**
The management of Decor Light Fixture Corp. is
considering acquiring a loan to purchase a conveyer
system for its warehouse. Management has narrowed
its choices to two local banks and has asked you to use
the loan planner to furnish loan payment information
based upon the data provided from each bank.
Click the *Tools* toolbar button. When the Planning Tools
window appears, click the *Loan Planner* tab, enter the
Bank 1 data, and display a loan amortization schedule.
Repeat the procedure for Bank 2. The loan amortization
schedule shown in Figure 7.19 is for Bank 1. The loan
amortization schedule for Bank 2 will show a monthly
payment amount of $712.03.

```
******** Bank 1 ********     ******** Bank 2 ********
Loan Amount    $78000.00     Loan Amount    $78000.00
Annual Interest       7.75   Annual Interest       7.25
Number of Payments   360     Number of Payments   180
```

Loan Amortization Schedule
02/10/--

Payment Number	Payment Amount	Principal	Interest	Loan Balance
(Loan Amount)				78000.00
1	558.80	55.05	503.75	77944.95
2	558.80	55.41	503.39	77889.54
3	558.80	55.76	503.04	77833.78
4	558.80	56.12	502.68	77777.66
5	558.80	56.49	502.31	77721.17
6	558.80	56.85	501.95	77664.32
7	558.80	57.22	501.58	77607.10
8	558.80	57.59	501.21	77549.51
9	558.80	57.96	500.84	77491.55
10	558.80	58.33	500.47	77433.22
11	558.80	58.71	500.09	77374.51
12	558.80	59.09	499.71	77315.42
355	558.80	537.61	21.19	2743.07
356	558.80	541.08	17.72	2201.99
357	558.80	544.58	14.22	1657.41
358	558.80	548.10	10.70	1109.31
359	558.80	551.64	7.16	557.67
360	561.27	557.67	3.60	.00

Figure 7.19
Loan
Amortization
Schedule for
Bank 1

TUTORIAL PROBLEM 7–T

STEP 14: **Optional spreadsheet and word processing integration activity:**

Use a spreadsheet to create a business summary report. Then use a word processor to format and enhance the appearance of the report for management. The report should contain the account balances for cash, accounts receivable, accounts payable, net sales (sales minus sales discounts and sales returns and allowances), and net purchases (purchases minus purchases discounts and purchases returns and allowances) from the current trial balance.

Spreadsheet:

a. Display and copy the trial balance to the clipboard in spreadsheet format.

b. Start up your spreadsheet software and load template file SS07–T.

c. Select cell A1 as the current cell; then paste the trial balance (copied to the clipboard in step a) into the spreadsheet.

d. Enter the following label, cell references, and formulas in the cells indicated:

	B	C
38	+B3	
39	Summary Report	
40	+B5	
41		
42	+B10	+C10
43	+B13	+C13
44	+B23	+D23
45	Net Sales	+D27–(C28+C29)
46	Net Purchases	+C30–(D31+D32)

e. Print the summary report (cells B38–C46). The completed summary report for February 10 is shown in Figure 7.20.

f. Save the completed spreadsheet with a file name of XXX7–T. Subsequent trial balance reports for Decor Light Fixture Corp. that are saved in spreadsheet format may be merged into this template file whenever management requires an updated summary report.

▶

TUTORIAL PROBLEM 7-T

```
                    Decor Light Fixture Corp.
                         Summary Report
                         As Of 02/10/--

Cash                                              24638.52
Accounts Receivable                               26537.46
Accounts Payable                                  17577.07
Net Sales                                         17570.99
Net Purchases                                      4104.41
```

Figure 7.20
Spreadsheet Summary Report

Word Processing:
a. Start up your word processing software and create a new document. Use a fixed font such as Courier.
b. Copy and paste the spreadsheet summary report into the new document.
c. Format and enhance the report's appearance.
d. Print the report. The completed summary report is shown in Figure 7.21.
e. Save the document with a file name of XXX7–T.
f. End your spreadsheet and word processing sessions.

```
                 Decor Light Fixture Corp.
                      Summary Report
                      As Of 02/10/--

Cash                                         $ 24,638.52
Accounts Receivable                            26,537.46
Accounts Payable                               17,577.07
Net Sales                                      17,570.99
Net Purchases                                   4,104.41
```

Figure 7.21
Word Processed Summary Report

STEP 15: Save your data as XXX7–T.
Choose *Save* from the File menu and save the data.

STEP 16: End the Automated Accounting session.
Click the *Exit/Quit* toolbar button.

Applying Your Information Skills

I. MATCHING

Directions: In the *Working Papers*, write the letter of the appropriate term next to each definition.

    a. purchases discount
    b. sales discount
    c. debit memorandum
    d. credit memorandum
    e. discount period

1. The form prepared by the customer showing the price deduction for returns and allowances. From the buyer's point of view, returns and allowances result in a debit to the vendor's account.

2. From the seller's point of view, a deduction for early payment of an invoice.

3. From the buyer's point of view, a deduction for early payment of an invoice.

4. The specified time period within which an invoice must be paid in order to receive the discount.

5. The form prepared by the vendor showing the amount deducted for returns and allowances. From the seller's point of view, returns result in a credit to the customer's account.

II. QUESTIONS

Directions: Write the answers to each of the following questions in the *Working Papers*.

1. Which journal is used to enter a transaction involving a purchases discount?

2. When a transaction involving a purchases discount is entered, is the Purchases Discounts account debited or credited?

3. Which journal is used to enter a transaction involving a sales discount?

4. When a transaction involving a sales discount is entered, is the Sales Discounts account debited or credited?

5. In which journal is a debit memorandum entered?

6. Does a debit memorandum affect a vendor's account or a customer's account?

7. When a debit memorandum is entered, which general ledger account is credited?

8. When a credit memorandum is entered, which general ledger account is debited?

Independent Practice Problem 7–P   P

In this problem you will process selected transactions involving purchases discounts, sales discounts, debit memorandums, and credit memorandums for the period February 11 through February 20 of the current year.

STEP 1:   **Start up *Automated Accounting 7.0.***

STEP 2:   **Load the opening balances file AA07–P.**

STEP 3:   **Enter your name in the User Name text box.**

STEP 4:   **Use *Save As* to save the opening balances file as XXX7–P.**

STEP 5:   **Enter the transaction data.**

Feb. 11   Returned merchandise to Wyler Electric Light Co., $314.00, against P303. DM34.

11   Sold merchandise on account to Olinger Electric Supply, $2,450.81. S457.

11   Purchased merchandise on account from Foster Manufacturing, $4,243.60. P305.

12   Paid cash on account to Stacy Light Fixture Co., $3,220.63, covering P302 less DM33, no discount. C630.

12   Received cash on account from Arnold's Lite-House, $5,547.95, covering S450, no discount. R221.

12   Received cash on account from Arnold's Lite-House, $4,810.72, covering S454 for $4,859.31, less 1% discount, $48.59. R222.

13   Paid cash on account to Foster Manufacturing, $4,043.00, covering P299, no discount. C631.

13   Paid cash on account to Dillon Lighting, Inc., $3,821.86, covering P297, no discount. C632.

13   Bought office supplies on account from Southern Supplies, Inc., $821.50. M25.

15   Sold merchandise on account to Webster Lite Shoppe, $5,219.26. S458.

15   Sold merchandise on account to Blair Lighting Co., $4,206.00. S459.

15   Received cash on account from Milan Lighting Outlet, $4,441.31, covering S456 for $4,486.17 less 1% discount, $44.86. R223.

16   Received cash on account from Rillo Lighting Systems, $6,595.99, covering S453, no discount. R224.

16   Paid cash on account to Dillon Lighting, Inc., $3,442.82, covering P304 for $3,477.60, less 1% discount, $34.78. C633.

16   Granted credit to Olinger Electric Supply for merchandise returned, $480.77, against S457. CM54.

17   Purchased merchandise on account from Senter Lighting Corp., $3,446.78. P306.

18   Sold merchandise on account to Arnold's Lite-House, $1,746.76. S460.

19   Returned merchandise to Wyler Electric Light Co., $58.90, against P303. DM35.

19   Paid cash on account to Foster Manufacturing, $4,201.16, covering P305 for $4,243.60, less 1% discount, $42.44. C634.

19   Purchased merchandise on account from Stacy Light Fixture Co., $3,176.26. P307.

20   Purchased merchandise on account from Billingsley, Inc., $3,702.18. P308.

20   Granted credit to Arnold's Lite-House for merchandise returned, $130.98, against S460. CM55.

20   Recorded cash and credit card sales, $3,242.33, plus sales tax, $226.96; total, $3,469.29. T30.

STEP 6:   Display the general, purchases, cash payments, sales, and cash receipts journal reports for the period February 11 through February 20. If errors are detected, make corrections.

CHECK FIGURE:
Trial balance debit and credit totals = $186,047.97

STEP 7:   Display a trial balance, schedule of accounts payable, and schedule of accounts receivable.

STEP 8:   Generate a 3D sales bar graph.

STEP 9:   Save your data.

STEP 10: Calculate a loan amount using the Loan Planner. Decor Light Fixture Corp. believes it can comfortably afford a loan payment of $1,200.00 per month over the next 7 years for a conveyer system for its warehouse. You have been asked to use the loan planner to find the

loan amount, given the following information provided by two local banks.
Select the *Loan Amount* option in the Calculate grouping, and then enter the loan information provided below:

```
******** Bank 1 *********        ********* Bank 2 ********
Annual Interest        7.75      Annual Interest        7.25
Number of Payments      84       Number of Payments      84
Payment Amount  $1200.00         Payment Amount  $1200.00
```

STEP 11:   **Optional spreadsheet and word processing integration activity:**
Use a spreadsheet to create a business summary report. Then use a word processor to format and enhance the appearance of the report for management. The report should contain the cash balance, accounts receivable balance, accounts payable balance, net sales (sales minus sales discounts and sales returns and allowances), and net purchases (purchases minus purchases discounts and purchases returns and allowances) from the February 20 trial balance.

Spreadsheet:
a. Display and copy the trial balance to the clipboard in spreadsheet format.
b. Start up your spreadsheet software and load template file SS07–T. If you completed the optional spreadsheet activity in Tutorial Problem 7–T, load your solution file and skip step d.
c. Select cell A1 as the current cell, then paste the trial balance (copied to the clipboard in step a) into the spreadsheet.
d. Enter the appropriate label(s), cell references, and formulas (see Figure 7.20).
e. Print the summary report.
f. Save the completed spreadsheet with a file name of XXX7–P.

Word Processing:
a. Start up your word processing software and create a new document. Use a fixed font such as Courier.
b. Copy and paste the spreadsheet summary report into the new document.
c. Format and enhance the report's appearance similar to Figure 7.21.
d. Print the report.

e. Save the document with a file name of XXX7–P.

f. End your spreadsheet and word processing sessions.

STEP 12:   End the *Automated Accounting* session.

 Applying Your Technology Skills 7–P

Directions: Using Independent Practice Problem 7–P, write the answers to the following questions in the *Working Papers*.

Journals:

1. What is the amount of debit memorandum no. 34 for Wyler Electric Light Co.?

2. What is the amount of credit memorandum no. 55 for Arnold's Lite-House?

3. What is the amount of purchase invoice no. 305 for Foster Manufacturing?

4. What are the total debits and total credits in the purchases journal report?

5. What is the amount of check no. 630 for Stacy Light Fixture Co.?

6. What are the total debits and total credits in the cash payments journal?

7. What is the amount of sales invoice no. 460 for Arnold's Lite-House?

8. What are the total debits and total credits in the cash receipts journal?

Trial Balance:

9. What is the balance in the Cash account?

10. What is the balance in the Accounts Payable account?

Schedules of Accounts Payable and Accounts Receivable:

11. What is the current balance due to the vendor Southern Supplies, Inc.?

12. What is the total amount owed to all vendors?

13. What is the amount due from the customer Arnold's Lite-House?

14. What is the total amount due from all customers?

Loan Planner:

15. What is the calculated loan amount for Bank 1?

16. What is the calculated loan amount for Bank 2?

Mastery Problem 7–M

In this problem, you will process selected transactions involving purchases discounts, sales discounts, debit memorandums, and credit memorandums for the period February 21 through February 28 of the current year.

STEP 1:   **Start up *Automated Accounting 7.0.***

STEP 2:   **Load file AA07–M.**

STEP 3:   **Enter your name in the User Name text box.**

STEP 4:   **Save the opening balances file as XXX7–M.**

STEP 5:   **Enter the transactions.**

Feb. 22   Paid cash on account to Southern Supplies, Inc., $813.28, covering M25 for $821.50, less 1% discount, $8.22. C635.

22   Received cash on account from Webster Lite Shoppe, $5,167.07, covering S458 for $5,219.26, less 1% discount, $52.19. R225.

22   Received cash on account from Blair Lighting Co., $4,163.94, covering S459 for $4,206.00, less 1% discount, $42.06. R226.

22   Sold merchandise on account to Milan Lighting Outlet, $5,343.59. S461.

22   Sold merchandise on account to Blair Lighting Co., $3,235.37. S462.

23   Purchased merchandise on account from Foster Manufacturing, $2,997.84. P309.

23   Purchased merchandise on account from Dillon Lighting, Inc., $1,986.78. P310.

24   Received cash on account from Olinger Electric Supply, $1,970.04, covering S457 less CM54, no discount. R227.

24   Paid cash on account to Billingsley, Inc., $3,665.16, covering P308 for $3,702.18, less 1% discount, $37.02. C636.

24   Purchased merchandise on account from Stacy Light Fixture Co., $3,019.23. P311.

24   Paid cash on account to Wyler Electric Light Co., $2,641.08, covering P303 less DM34 and DM35, no discount. C637.

25   Sold merchandise on account to Webster Lite Shoppe, $4,992.52. S463.

25   Received cash on account from Arnold's Lite-House, $1,615.78, covering S460 less CM55, no discount. R228.

25   Paid cash on account to Senter Lighting Corp., $3,412.31, covering P306 for $3,446.78, less 1% discount, $34.47. C638.

26   Sold merchandise on account to Olinger Electric Supply, $5,278.67. S464.

26   Received cash on account from Rillo Lighting Systems, $5,048.04, covering S455 less CM53, no discount. R229.

26   Returned merchandise to Foster Manufacturing, $121.11, against P309. DM36.

26   Granted credit to Milan Lighting Outlet for merchandise returned, $245.44, against S461. CM56.

26   Sold merchandise on account to Rillo Lighting Systems, $2,316.52. S465.

27   Returned merchandise to Dillon Lighting, Inc., $102.24, against P310. DM37.

27   Granted credit to Blair Lighting Co. for merchandise returned, $122.20, against S462. CM57.

27   Purchased merchandise on account from Wyler Electric Light Co., $1,577.43. P312.

27   Paid cash on account to Stacy Light Fixture Co., $3,144.50, covering P307 for $3,176.26, less 1% discount, $31.76. C639.

27   Recorded cash and credit card sales, $2,936.13, plus sales tax, $205.53; total, $3,141.66. T37.

STEP 6:   **Display the journal reports.**

STEP 7:   **Display the trial balance, schedule of accounts payable, and schedule of accounts receivable.**

CHECK FIGURE:
Trial balance debit and credit totals = $206,261.25

STEP 8:   **Generate a sales 3D bar graph.**

STEP 9:   **Save your data with a file name of XXX7–M.**

STEP 10:   **Use the Loan Planner to calculate the number of payments, given the following information:**

********* Bank 1 ********		********* Bank 2 ********	
Loan Amount	$95000.00	Loan Amount	$95000.00
Annual Interest	7.25	Annual Interest	6.75
Payment Amount	$1500.00	Payment Amount	$2000.00

STEP 11:   **Optional spreadsheet and word processing integration activity:**
Create a spreadsheet business summary report. Then use a word processor to format and enhance the appearance of the report for management. The report should contain the cash balance, accounts receivable balance, accounts payable balance, net sales (sales minus sales discounts and sales returns and allowances), and net purchases (purchases minus purchases discounts and purchases returns and allowances) from the February 28 trial balance.

Spreadsheet:
a. Display and copy the trial balance to the clipboard in spreadsheet format.
b. Start up your spreadsheet software and load file SS07–T. If you completed Tutorial Problem 7–T or Independent Practice Problem 7–P, load your solution file.
c. Select cell A1, then copy and paste the February 28 trial balance into the spreadsheet.
d. Enter the appropriate label(s), cell references, and formulas; then print the report.
e. Save the completed spreadsheet with a file name of XXX7–M.

Word Processing:
a. Start up your word processor software and create a new document.
b. Copy and paste the spreadsheet summary report into the new document.
c. Format and enhance the report's appearance; then print the document.
d. Save the document as XXX7–M.

STEP 12:   **End the *Automated Accounting* session.**

Applying Your Technology Skills 7–M

Directions: Using Mastery Problem 7–M, write the answers to the following questions in the *Working Papers*.

Journals:
1. What is the amount of debit memorandum no. 37 for Dillon Lighting, Inc.?

2. What is the amount of credit memorandum no. 57 for Blair Lighting Co.?

3. What is the amount of purchase invoice no. 312 for Wyler Electric Light Co.?

4. What are the total debits and total credits in the purchases journal report?

5. What is the amount of check no. 636 for Billingsley, Inc.?

6. What are the total debits and total credits in the cash payments journal?

7. What is the amount of sales invoice no. 463 for Webster Lite Shoppe?

8. What are the total debits and total credits in the cash receipts journal?

Trial Balance:

9. What is the balance in the Cash account?

10. What is the balance in the Accounts Payable account?

Schedules of Accounts Payable and Accounts Receivable:

11. What is the current balance due to the vendor Foster Manufacturing?

12. What is the total amount owed to all vendors?

13. What is the amount due from the customer Milan Lighting Outlet?

14. What is the total amount due from all customers?

Loan Planner:

15. What are the number of payments based on Bank 1's data?

16. What are the number of payments based on Bank 2's data?

Virtual Reality Modeling Language (VRML) is a set of computer commands for use on the World Wide Web. With VRML, programmers can create 3D or virtual reality effects.

8
Plant Assets

LEARNING OBJECTIVES

Upon completion of this chapter, you will be able to:

1. Record additions, changes, and deletions on the plant assets input form.

2. Enter and correct plant asset data.

3. Display plant assets reports.

4. Generate and post monthly depreciation adjusting entries.

8

INTRODUCTION

Plant assets are assets used for a number of years in the operation of a business. A computerized plant asset system may be used to maintain records for all plant assets. The information provided by the plant asset system is used by the business in several ways. Accounting uses plant asset information to show costs, to show an asset's reduction in value due to usage, and to show asset disposition. An asset's reduction in value due to usage is called **depreciation. Asset disposition** means removing an asset from use in the business.

When an asset is purchased, it must be added to the plant asset file. When adding a plant asset, the useful life, original cost, salvage value, and depreciation method must be obtained. The **useful life** of an asset is the estimated amount of time an asset can be used in the business. The **original cost** of a plant asset is all costs paid to make the asset usable to a business. The amount an owner expects to receive when a plant asset is removed from use is known as an asset's **salvage value.** (Another name for salvage value is trade-in value.) There are several ways or methods to depreciate an asset. This chapter will use the straight-line method of depreciation. At the end of the accounting cycle, the plant asset depreciation

ETHICS

A new dilemma brought on us by the ever-increasing speed and capability of computers, and their decreasing price per unit of performance, involves the revival of deceased movie stars. Computers now have the ability to reconstruct the stars' images and voices through simulations. This means that Clark Gable could come back to star in the sequel to *Gone With the Wind,* or Marilyn Monroe could extend her career by "appearing" in completely new films for a new generation of fans.

To date, the expense of ultra-high-resolution computer animation, which is required to produce "human-quality" output, has prevented its use for anything other than brief scenarios. (Perhaps you have seen commercials or short movie scenes in which contemporary stars have "interacted" with departed actors.) With the cost of the computer hardware required to accomplish this task continually going down, the possibility of making entire movies using

"reconstructed" screen stars is becoming technologically and financially feasible.

a. Who do you think owns the likeness of the departed? Is it the person's estate or the movie studio to which the person was under contract?

b. Who has the right to decide, years after a celebrity's death, whether he or she would have any interest in doing a particular movie? Could a simulated performance trash the reputation of a star long after his or her demise?

c. Do you think this issue is something that today's living legends and their agents should consider now, or otherwise risk being haunted forever by the consequences of emerging computer technology?

adjusting entries are generated and posted to the general ledger. Changes, corrections, and deletions are made to the assets as needed.

Plant asset information is used beyond the accounting area. For example, plant assets reports are used for insurance purposes to ensure adequate coverage. In the case of an insurance claim, these reports are often used to determine the amount of the settlement. The information can also be used to estimate the worth of an asset for trade-in value. Trade-in value is considered as payment or partial payment toward another asset.

PLANT ASSETS INPUT FORM

Additions, changes, and deletions to plant assets may be recorded on the **plant assets input form,** as illustrated in Figure 8.1. The first entry reflects an addition. All data fields must be completed, including the appropriate accumulated depreciation and depreciation expense account numbers from the chart of accounts. The second entry demonstrates a change. Therefore, only the asset number and the fields that have changed need to be completed. The last entry shows a deletion. The asset number and (Delete) are recorded.

Mar. 01 1997	Purchased a Computer (P–133) for $3,250.77; salvage value, $300.00; useful life, 5 years; depreciation method, SL; assign asset no. 115.
June 10	Change the name of asset no. 210 to Computer Organizer.
July 21	Delete asset no. 105, Computer (486–33).

PLANT ASSETS INPUT FORM

Run Date 12/31/97   Problem No. Example

Asset No.	Asset Name	Date Acquired	Useful Life	Original Cost	Salvage Value	Accum. Deprec.	Deprec. Exp.	Deprec. Method
115	Computer (P–133)	03/01/97	5	3250.77	300.00	1540	6130	SL
210	Computer Organizer							
105	(Delete)							

Figure 8.1
Plant Assets Input Form

Each line is used to maintain one asset. Each column on the input form matches one of the columns in the plant assets Account Maintenance window in which the data will be keyed. The field names and a description of each column are illustrated in the plant assets Account Maintenance shown in Figure 8.2.

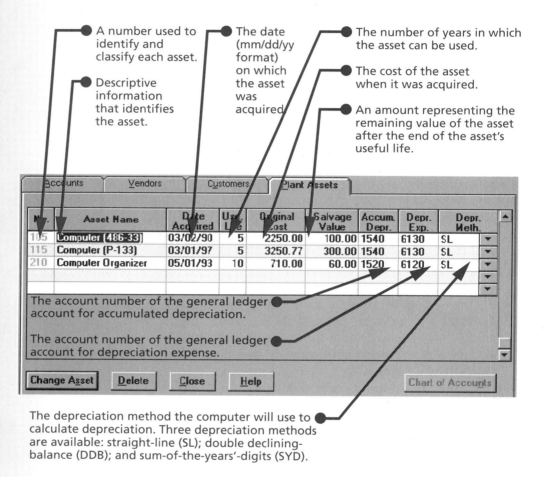

- A number used to identify and classify each asset.
- Descriptive information that identifies the asset.
- The date (mm/dd/yy format) on which the asset was acquired
- The number of years in which the asset can be used.
- The cost of the asset when it was acquired.
- An amount representing the remaining value of the asset after the end of the asset's useful life.

Nr.	Asset Name	Date Acquired	Use. Life	Original Cost	Salvage Value	Accum. Depr.	Depr. Exp.	Depr. Meth.
105	Computer (486-33)	03/02/90	5	2250.00	100.00	1540	6130	SL
115	Computer (P-133)	03/01/97	5	3250.77	300.00	1540	6130	SL
210	Computer Organizer	05/01/93	10	710.00	60.00	1520	6120	SL

The account number of the general ledger account for accumulated depreciation.

The account number of the general ledger account for depreciation expense.

[Change Asset] [Delete] [Close] [Help]   [Chart of Accounts]

The depreciation method the computer will use to calculate depreciation. Three depreciation methods are available: straight-line (SL); double declining-balance (DDB); and sum-of-the-years'-digits (SYD).

Figure 8.2
Plant Asset
Maintenance

MAINTAIN PLANT ASSET DATA

The process of adding, changing, and deleting assets is referred to as **plant asset maintenance.** When *Maintain Accounts* is chosen from the Data menu or the *Accts.* toolbar button is clicked, the Account Maintenance window will appear. Click the *Plant Assets* tab and enter the maintenance data. Figure 8.2 shows the maintenance data already entered from the plant assets input form in Figure 8.1. Asset number 105 is shown selected and about to be deleted.

Adding a New Asset

1: **Enter the asset number.**

2: **Enter the asset name, date acquired, useful life, original cost, and salvage value in the grid cell boxes.**

3: **Enter the appropriate accumulated depreciation and depreciation expense account numbers.**
With the focus on the desired text box, click *Chart of Accounts* to display the chart of accounts selection list. Select the desired account.

4: **Select the desired depreciation method from the drop-down list or use the default straight-line (SL) method.**

5: **Click *Add Asset.***

Changing Plant Asset Data

1: **Select the asset by clicking on the grid cell containing the data you wish to change.**

2: **Enter the correct data for the asset.**

3: **Click the *Change Asset* button.**
The Add Asset button will change to Change Asset when an existing asset is selected.

Deleting a Plant Asset

1: **Click the asset to be deleted.**

2: **Click the *Delete* button.**

A person who wants to buy or sell an item can probably find someone on the Internet who is either offering it or looking for it. Used items in good condition are sometimes offered at far less than retail prices.

DISPLAYING PLANT ASSETS REPORTS

Once the asset data has been entered, the plant assets reports can be generated.

1: **Click the *Reports* toolbar button.**

2: **Choose the *Plant Assets* option button from the Select a Report Group list.**
A list showing the Plant Assets List and Depreciation Schedules will appear, as shown in Figure 8.3.

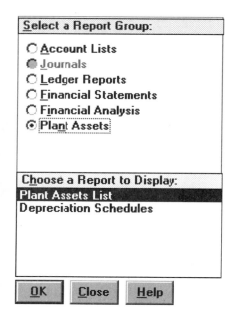

Figure 8.3
Report Selection
(Plant Assets
Reports)

3: **Select the plant assets report you would like to display from the Choose a Report to Display list.**
When the *Depreciation Schedules* are selected, the Depreciation Schedules window shown in Figure 8.4 appears, allowing you to select the range of assets for which depreciation schedules are to be generated. Figure 8.4 illustrates asset number 115 that was added earlier in this chapter.

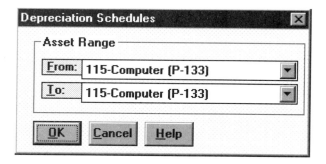

Figure 8.4
Depreciation
Schedule Range
Selection

4: **Click *OK*.**

Plant Assets List Report

The plant assets report that provides a complete detailed list of all plant assets owned is called a **plant assets list report.** The report provides information concerning the date acquired, depreciation method chosen, useful life, original cost, estimated salvage value, and depreciation accounts for each plant asset. The report is useful in detecting keying errors and verifying the accuracy of your input. An example of a plant assets list report is shown in Figure 8.5.

Gonzalez Jewelers
Plant Assets List
12/31/97

Asset	Date Acquired	Depr. Method	Useful Life	Original Cost	Salvage Value	Depr. Accts
110 Computer (Pentium)	06/10/94	SL	5	2928.00	200.00	1540 6130
115 Computer (P–133)	03/01/97	SL	5	3250.77	300.00	1540 6130
120 Dot Matrix Printer	03/01/93	SL	5	320.00	50.00	1540 6130
130 File Server (598-32)	07/31/96	SL	5	1295.50	200.00	1540 6130
135 Hard Disk Drive	04/30/97	SL	5	628.95	40.00	1540 6130
140 Ink Jet Printer	07/20/96	SL	5	435.95	45.00	1540 6130
150 Notebook Computer	03/01/95	SL	5	1550.00	135.00	1540 6130
160 Copy Machine	02/20/95	SL	5	3875.00	425.00	1540 6130
170 Facsimile Machine	02/20/95	SL	5	549.00	25.00	1540 6130
180 Electronic Calculator	09/30/97	SL	5	135.50	20.00	1540 6130
210 Computer Organizer	05/01/93	SL	10	710.00	60.00	1520 6120
220 Display Case	05/01/93	SL	10	1800.00	150.00	1520 6120
230 Storage Credenza	05/01/93	SL	10	295.75	30.00	1520 6120
240 File Cabinet (6 Drawer)	09/02/94	SL	10	339.00	25.00	1520 6120
250 Book Case (5 Shelf)	10/03/93	SL	10	289.00	35.00	1520 6120
260 Copy Machine Stand	11/10/96	SL	10	169.90	20.00	1520 6120
270 File Cabinet (4 Drawer)	10/31/97	SL	10	475.00	50.00	1520 6120
Total Plant Assets				19047.32		

Figure 8.5
Plant Assets List Report

Depreciation Schedules

The plant assets report that provides annual depreciation for each year for the life of the asset is called a **depreciation schedule.** Depreciation schedules can be generated for any range of assets. Depreciation is calculated based on the date acquired, original cost, salvage value, and depreciation method. An asset purchased in any month other than January has first-year and last-year amounts that are prorated from the month the asset was purchased. Using the straight-line method of depreciation results in an equal amount of depreciation expense being charged in each year of the asset's useful life. In the example shown in Figure 8.6, which utilizes the straight-line method, the asset was purchased on March 1. Therefore, the first year's depreciation is for the period March through December, which is ten months or 10/12ths of the annual depreciation of $590.15, or $491.80. The last two months are depreciated in the last year, for 2/12ths of the annual depreciation of $590.15, or $98.37.

Gonzalez Jewelers
Depreciation Schedules
12/31/97

	Year	Annual Deprec.	Accum. Deprec.	Book Value
(115) Computer (P–133)	1997	491.80	491.80	2758.97
Acquired on 03/01/97	1998	590.15	1081.95	2168.82
Straight-Line	1999	590.15	1672.10	1578.67
Useful Life = 5	2000	590.15	2262.25	988.52
Original Cost = 3250.77	2001	590.15	2852.40	398.37
Salvage Value = 300.00	2002	98.37	2950.77	300.00

Figure 8.6
Depreciation Schedule

GENERATING AND POSTING DEPRECIATION ADJUSTING ENTRIES

Depreciation adjusting entries are the journal entries recorded to update the Depreciation Expense and Accumulated Depreciation accounts at the end of the fiscal period. When *Depreciation Adjusting Entries* is selected from the Options menu, the software will analyze the plant assets records, determine the depreciation for the period, and generate the depreciation adjusting entries. A dialog box containing the adjusting entries will appear.

The depreciation adjusting entries can be generated for either a monthly or a yearly period, depending on how the Income Statement option button is set. This is usually selected during system setup and will be covered in Chapter 13. For the problems in this text, the software will generate monthly adjusting entries.

1:   Choose *Depreciation Adjusting Entries* **from the Options menu.** The confirmation dialog shown in Figure 8.7 will appear.

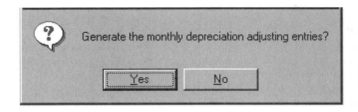

Figure 8.7
Confirmation
Dialog

2:   Click *Yes* **to generate the depreciation adjusting entries.** The dialog box shown in Figure 8.8 will appear. Rather than reducing the Asset account directly when depreciation expense is recorded, an Accumulated Depreciation account is used. This prevents the loss of important plant asset data.

Acct. #	Account Title	Debit	Credit
6120	Depr. Exp.--Ofc. Furn.	30.91	
6130	Depr. Exp.--Ofc. Eqpt.	225.49	
1520	Accum. Depr.--Ofc. Furn.		30.91
1540	Accum. Depr.--Ofc. Eqpt.		225.49

Post   Cancel   Help

Figure 8.8
Depreciation
Adjusting Entries
Dialog Box

3:   Click the *Post* **button.**

4:   The general journal will appear, containing the posted adjusting entry. Verify the accuracy of the entry and click *Close.* The adjusting entries will appear in the general journal as illustrated in Figure 8.9. If the adjusting entry is incorrect, return to the plant assets Account Maintenance window and make the necessary corrections. Then select the *General Journal* tab, delete the incorrect depreciation adjusting entry, and generate new adjusting entries.

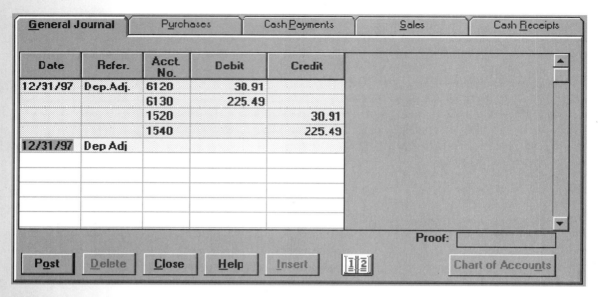

Figure 8.9
General Journal (Depreciation Adjusting Entries)

Chapter Review

1. Assets used for a number of years in the operation of a business are called plant assets. A computerized plant asset system is used to maintain records for all plant assets for a business. A plant assets input form is used to record all additions, changes, and deletions to plant assets.

2. Plant asset maintenance is the process of adding, changing, and deleting assets. Plant asset maintenance is performed by entering data in the Plant Assets tab within the Account Maintenance window.

3. The plant assets list report provides information concerning the costs of assets and is useful in detecting keying errors and verifying the accuracy of input. Depreciation schedules provide annual depreciation for each year for the life of the asset.

4. The software generates the depreciation adjusting entries by analyzing the plant asset records and determining the depreciation for the period.

T U T O R I A L   P R O B L E M   8 – T

In this tutorial problem, you will add, change, and delete plant assets. In addition, you will generate the plant assets list report and depreciation schedules.

STEP 1: **Start up *Automated Accounting 7.0.***

STEP 2: **Load the opening balances file, AA08–T.**
Click the *Open* toolbar button. Choose file AA08–T from the File list box.

STEP 3: **Enter your name in the User Name text box and click *OK*.**

STEP 4: **Save the file as XXX8–T.**
Click the *Save As* toolbar button, and save the file as XXX8–T.

STEP 5: **Enter the plant asset data.**
Click the *Accts.* toolbar button. When the Account Maintenance window appears, click the *Plant Assets* tab and enter the plant asset data listed below. Figure 8.10 shows how the assets appear on the plant assets input form. Asset number 105, Computer (486–33) has been deleted. Only the name of asset number 210 was changed.

PLANT ASSETS
INPUT FORM

Run Date 12/31/97   Problem No. 8–T

Asset No.	Asset Name	Date Acquired	Useful Life	Original Cost	Salvage Value	Accum. Deprec.	Deprec. Exp.	Deprec. Method
115	Computer (P–133)	03/01/97	5	3250.77	300.00	1540	6130	SL
135	Hard Disk Drive	04/30/97	5	628.95	40.00	1540	6130	SL
210	Computer Organizer							
105	(Delete)							
180	Electronic Calculator	09/30/97	5	135.50	20.00	1540	6130	SL
270	File Cabinet (4 Drawer)	10/31/97	10	475.00	50.00	1520	6120	SL

Figure 8.10
Completed Plant Assets Input Form

T U T O R I A L   P R O B L E M   8 – T

It is very important that you enter the correct date acquired for each plant asset. Many of the calculated depreciation amounts are date sensitive and will display incorrectly if the dates are entered incorrectly.

Note: Asset numbers 100–199 are assigned to Office Equipment. Account number 1540 (Accum. Depr.—Ofc. Eqpt.) is used to accumulate office equipment depreciation, and account number 6130 (Depr. Exp.— Ofc. Eqpt.) is used to record the depreciation expense. Asset numbers 200–299 are assigned to Office Furniture. Account number 1520 (Accum. Depr.—Ofc. Furn.) is used to accumulate office furniture depreciation, and account number 6120 (Depr. Exp.—Ofc. Furn.) is used to record the depreciation expense.

Mar. 01 1997	Purchased a Computer (P–133) for $3,250.77; salvage value, $300.00; useful life, 5 years; depreciation method, SL; assign asset no. 115.
Apr. 30	Purchased a Hard Disk Drive for $628.95; salvage value, $40.00; useful life, 5 years; depreciation method, SL; assign asset no. 135.
June 10	Change the name of asset no. 210 to Computer Organizer.
July 21	Delete asset no. 105, Computer (486–33).
Sept. 30	Purchased an Electronic Calculator for $135.50; salvage value, $20.00; useful life, 5 years; depreciation method, SL; assign asset no. 180.
Oct. 31	Purchased a File Cabinet (4 Drawer) for $475.00; salvage value, $50.00; useful life, 10 years; depreciation method, SL; assign asset no. 270.

STEP 6: **Display a plant assets list report.**
Click the *Reports* toolbar button. Choose *Plant Assets* and select the *Plant Assets List* report. Make sure the date on the Report Selection menu is set to 12/31/97. Click *OK.* The report is shown in Figure 8.11.

TUTORIAL PROBLEM 8 – T

Gonzalez Jewelers
Plant Assets List
12/31/97

Asset	Date Acquired	Depr. Method	Useful Life	Original Cost	Salvage Value	Depr. Accts
110 Computer (Pentium)	06/10/94	SL	5	2928.00	200.00	1540 6130
115 Computer (P–133)	03/01/97	SL	5	3250.77	300.00	1540 6130
120 Dot Matrix Printer	03/01/93	SL	5	320.00	50.00	1540 6130
130 File Server (598-32)	07/31/96	SL	5	1295.50	200.00	1540 6130
135 Hard Disk Drive	04/30/97	SL	5	628.95	40.00	1540 6130
140 Ink Jet Printer	07/20/96	SL	5	435.95	45.00	1540 6130
150 Notebook Computer	03/01/95	SL	5	1550.00	135.00	1540 6130
160 Copy Machine	02/20/95	SL	5	3875.00	425.00	1540 6130
170 Facsimile Machine	02/20/95	SL	5	549.00	25.00	1540 6130
180 Electronic Calculator	09/30/97	SL	5	135.50	20.00	1540 6130
210 Computer Organizer	05/01/93	SL	10	710.00	60.00	1520 6120
220 Display Case	05/01/93	SL	10	1800.00	150.00	1520 6120
230 Storage Credenza	05/01/93	SL	10	295.75	30.00	1520 6120
240 File Cabinet (6 Drawer)	09/02/94	SL	10	339.00	25.00	1520 6120
250 Book Case (5 Shelf)	10/03/93	SL	10	289.00	35.00	1520 6120
260 Copy Machine Stand	11/10/96	SL	10	169.90	20.00	1520 6120
270 File Cabinet (4 Drawer)	10/31/97	SL	10	475.00	50.00	1520 6120
Total Plant Assets				19047.32		

Figure 8.11
Plant Assets List Report

T U T O R I A L   P R O B L E M   8 - T

STEP 7:   **Display depreciation schedules for the new assets: 115, 135, 180, and 270.**

Choose the *Depreciation Schedules* option button from the Choose a Report to Display list, then click the *OK* command button. When the Depreciation Schedules window shown in Figure 8.12 appears, select an asset range of 115–Computer (P–133) to 115–Computer (P–133), the first asset, then click the *OK* command button. Repeat this process for each of the assets for which depreciation schedules are to be generated. The first depreciation schedule is illustrated in Figure 8.13.

Depreciation Schedules   ☒

┌─ Asset Range ─────────────────────────────┐
│ **From:** | 115-Computer (P-133)   ▼ | │
│   │
│ **To:** | 115-Computer (P-133)   ▼ | │
└──┘

[**OK**]   [**Cancel**]   [**Help**]

Figure 8.12
Selection Options
(Depreciation
Schedules)

Gonzalez Jewelers
Depreciation Schedules
12/31/97

	Year	Annual Deprec.	Accum. Deprec.	Book Value
(115) Computer (P–133)	1997	491.80	491.80	2758.97
Acquired on 03/01/97	1998	590.15	1081.95	2168.82
Straight-Line	1999	590.15	1672.10	1578.67
Useful Life = 5	2000	590.15	2262.25	988.52
Original Cost = 3250.77	2001	590.15	2852.40	398.37
Salvage Value = 300.00	2002	98.37	2950.77	300.00

Figure 8.13
Depreciation
Schedule

STEP 8:   **Generate the depreciation adjusting entries.**

Choose *Depreciation Adjusting Entries* from the Options menu. Click *Yes* when asked if you want to generate the depreciation adjusting entry. When the Depreciation Adjusting Entries appear, as shown in Figure 8.14, click the *Post* command button. The journal entry will reappear, posted, in the general journal. Click *Close*.

TUTORIAL PROBLEM 8 - T

Note: If your adjusting entry does not match Figure 8.14, check your plant assets list report for keying errors and make the necessary corrections. Return to the general journal window, delete the incorrect depreciation adjusting entry, and generate new adjusting entries.

Acct. #	Account Title	Debit	Credit
6120	Depr. Exp.--Ofc. Furn.	30.91	
6130	Depr. Exp.--Ofc. Eqpt.	225.49	
1520	Accum. Depr.--Ofc. Furn.		30.91
1540	Accum. Depr.--Ofc. Eqpt.		225.49

Figure 8.14
Depreciation Adjusting Entries

STEP 9:   **Display the adjusting entries.**
Click the *Reports* toolbar button. Choose the *Journals* option button, then select the *General Journal* report and click *OK.* When the Journal Report Selection window appears, choose *Customize Journal Report,* select a date range of December 31, 1997 through December 31, 1997, and enter a Reference restriction of Dep.Adj. Click *OK.* The report appears in Figure 8.15.

```
                        Gonzalez Jewelers
                         General Journal
                           12/31/97

-----------------------------------------------------------
Date    Refer.    Acct.   Title              Debit    Credit
-----------------------------------------------------------

12/31   Dep.Adj.  6120    Depr. Exp.—Ofc. Furn.   30.91
12/31   Dep.Adj.  6130    Depr. Exp.—Ofc. Eqpt.  225.49
12/31   Dep.Adj.  1520    Accum. Depr.—Ofc. Furn.           30.91
12/31   Dep.Adj.  1540    Accum. Depr.—Ofc. Eqpt.          225.49
                                              -----    -----
                          Totals             256.40   256.40
                                              =====    =====
```

Figure 8.15
General Journal Report (Adjusting Entries)

T U T O R I A L   P R O B L E M   8 – T

STEP 10: Display a trial balance.
Choose the *Ledger Reports* option button from the Report Selection window, select the *Trial Balance* report, then click the *OK* command button. The trial balance is shown in Figure 8.16.

Gonzalez Jewelers
Trial Balance
12/31/97

Acct. Number	Account Title	Debit	Credit
1110	Cash	37709.17	
1120	Accounts Receivable	23984.30	
1130	Merchandise Inventory	163825.00	
1140	Prepaid Insurance	460.00	
1150	Supplies	875.00	
1510	Office Furniture	8590.39	
1520	Accum. Depr.—Ofc. Furn.		3430.70
1530	Office Equipment	13910.00	
1540	Accum. Depr.—Ofc. Eqpt.		2844.72
2110	Accounts Payable		10656.74
2120	Sales Tax Payable		370.77
3110	Carlota Gonzalez, Capital		225947.93
3120	Carlota Gonzalez, Drawing	9200.00	
4110	Sales		294195.57
4120	Sales Discounts	2630.65	
4130	Sales Returns & Allow.	14720.87	
5110	Purchases	171261.90	
5120	Purchases Discounts		1384.85
5130	Purch. Returns & Allow.		7331.21
6110	Advertising Expense	1064.32	
6120	Depr. Exp.—Ofc. Furn.	30.91	
6130	Depr. Exp.—Ofc. Eqpt.	225.49	
6140	Insurance Expense	2955.05	
6150	Miscellaneous Expense	891.41	
6160	Office Salaries Expense	49358.03	
6170	Rent Expense	7720.00	
6180	Sales Salaries Expense	25032.42	
6190	Supplies Expense	6960.21	
6200	Telephone Expense	2995.70	
6210	Utilities Expense	1761.67	
	Totals	546162.49	546162.49

Figure 8.16
Trial Balance

STEP 11: Save your data.
Click the *Save* toolbar button.

T U T O R I A L   P R O B L E M   8 – T

STEP 12:   **Optional spreadsheet integration activity:**
Since not all assets depreciate the same amount each
year, the manager of the accounting department wants
you to use a spreadsheet template to answer "what if"
questions regarding the use of the declining-balance
method of depreciation. Assets such as computers and
other electronic equipment typically depreciate more in
the early years of useful life than in later years. The
declining-balance method results in a larger portion of
an asset being depreciated in the early years. Therefore,
you are to generate declining-balance schedules for
each of the new assets. The manager will use this
information to decide which asset should use this
method of depreciation.

a.   Display and copy the plant assets list report to the
clipboard in spreadsheet format.

b.   Start up your spreadsheet software and load
template file SS08–T.

c.   Select cell A1 as the current cell and paste the plant
assets list report into the spreadsheet.

d.   Enter the cell references and purchase month and
year of the first asset added to the file:
115–Computer (P–133) in cells D51 and D53–D57.
For example, in cell D51 enter +B12; in cell D53
enter 3; in cell D54 enter 1997; and so on.
Note: Compare the declining-balance spreadsheet
schedule to the straight-line schedule in Figure 8.13.
Notice that although the annual depreciation
amounts differ, the total amount of accumulated
depreciation at the end of the asset's useful life is
the same.

e.   Print the declining-balance schedule (cells A49–E67).
The completed schedule is shown in Figure 8.17.

f.   Save the spreadsheet data with a file name of
XXX8–T.

g.   What if the useful life is changed to 4 or 6 years? (It
is not necessary to save this what if data.) You have
now created a template file that you can use for the
remaining new assets (asset numbers 135, 180, and
270), if desired.

TUTORIAL   PROBLEM   8 - T

```
                    DECLINING-BALANCE METHOD

Description              =     Computer (P-133)
Date Purchased:
  Month                  =                3
  Year                   =             1997
Useful Life              =                5
Original Cost            =        $3,250.77
Salvage Value            =          $300.00
Declining Bal. Rate      =           40.00%


------------------------------------------------------------
                         Annual     Accum.     Book
Year   Description       Deprec.    Deprec.    Value
------------------------------------------------------------

1997   Computer (P-133)  $1,083.59  $1,083.59  $2,167.18
1998                       $866.87  $1,950.46  $1,300.31
1999                       $520.12  $2,470.59    $780.18
2000                       $312.07  $2,782.66    $468.11
2001                       $168.11  $2,950.77    $300.00
```

Figure 8.17
Declining-Balance Comparison (Computer P–133)

STEP 13:   **Optional word processing integration activity:**
            You have been asked to prepare a memo addressed to
            the manager of the accounting department. The memo
            is to show a comparison of asset number 115, Computer
            (P–133) *Automated Accounting*-generated straight-line
            schedule and the spreadsheet declining-balance
            schedule.
            a.   Start up your word processing software and create a
                 new document. If your software has templates, load
                 a memo format.
            b.   Enter the memo heading information as shown in
                 Figure 8.18. Copy and paste asset number 115,
                 Computer (P–133) *Automated Accounting*-
                 generated straight-line schedule and the
                 spreadsheet declining-balance schedule you saved in
                 the optional spreadsheet activity in Step 12 into the
                 body of the memo. As an alternative, you may place
                 the schedules vertically instead of horizontally as
                 shown in Figure 8.18 (placing the schedules
                 horizontally requires a great deal of formatting).
            c.   Print the memo.
            d.   Save the memo with a file name of XXX8–T.
            e.   End your word processing and spreadsheet sessions.

TUTORIAL PROBLEM 8-T

Memorandum

To: Manager, Accounting Department

From: Student Name

Date: (Current Date)

Re: Depreciation Schedule Comparison

As per your request, the following table depicts a comparison of the straight-line and declining-balance methods of depreciation for asset number 115, Computer (P-133).

		---- Declining-Balance ----			---- Straight-Line ----		
Year	Description	Annual Deprec.	Accum. Deprec.	Book Value	Annual Deprec.	Accum. Deprec.	Book Value
1997	Computer (P-133)	$1,083.59	$1,083.59	$2,167.18	$491.80	$491.80	$2,758.97
1998		866.87	1,950.46	1,300.31	590.15	1,081.95	2,168.82
1999		520.12	2,470.59	780.18	590.15	1,672.10	1,578.67
2000		312.07	2,782.66	468.11	590.15	2,262.25	988.52
2001		168.11	2,950.77	300.00	590.15	2,852.40	398.37
2002					98.37	2,950.77	300.00

Figure 8.18
Depreciation Comparison Memo

STEP 14:   **End the *Automated Accounting* session.**
Click the *Exit/Quit* toolbar button.

Although the Internet can be a valuable research tool, any in-depth inquiry takes time. Your message might even get lost the first time it is sent. So for any important research, plan to spend a while.

Applying Your Information Skills

I. MATCHING

Directions: In the *Working Papers,* write the letter of the appropriate term next to each definition.

    a. plant assets
    b. depreciation
    c. asset disposition
    d. useful life
    e. original cost
    f. salvage value
    g. plant assets input form
    h. plant asset maintenance
    i. plant assets list report
    j. depreciation schedule
    k. depreciation adjusting entries

1. The report that provides annual depreciation for each year for the life of an asset.

2. The process of adding, changing, and deleting assets.

3. An asset's reduction in value due to usage.

4. The amount an owner expects to receive when a plant asset is removed from use.

5. The estimated amount of time an asset can be used in the business.

6. Removing an asset from use in the business.

7. Assets used for a number of years in the operation of a business.

8. All costs paid to make an asset usable to a business.

9. A report that provides a complete detailed list of all plant assets owned.

10. The journal entries recorded to update the depreciation expense and accumulated depreciation accounts at the end of the fiscal period.

11. A form on which additions, changes, and deletions to plant assets may be recorded.

II. TRUE/FALSE

Directions: In the *Working Papers*, write T or F next to each statement.

1. When recording changes on the plant assets input form, all data fields must be recorded.

2. The report most useful in verifying the accuracy of your input is the depreciation schedule report.

3. Depreciation schedules can be generated for any range of assets.

4. Depreciation adjusting entries must be generated after the general journal is displayed on the screen.

5. Depreciation adjusting entries do not need to be posted.

III. QUESTIONS

Directions: Write the answers to each of the following questions in the *Working Papers*.

1. List three uses of the information provided by the plant asset system.

2. Briefly describe the procedure to generate the depreciation adjusting entries.

3. What report must be selected in order to obtain a listing of the depreciation adjusting entries?

Independent Practice Problem 8–P

In this problem, you will add, change, and delete plant assets. In addition, you will generate the plant assets list report, depreciation schedules, and depreciation adjusting entries.

Asset numbers 110–199 are assigned to Office Furniture, and asset numbers 210–299 are assigned to Office Equipment. Consult the chart of accounts stored with file AA08–P for the appropriate Accumulated Depreciation and Depreciation Expense account numbers.

STEP 1: **Start up *Automated Accounting 7.0.***

STEP 2: **Load the opening balances template file, AA08–P.**

STEP 3: **Enter your name in the User Name text box.**

STEP 4: **Save the file as XXX8–P.**

STEP 5: **Enter the plant asset data.**

Jan. 03 1997   Purchased a Book Shelf for $895.00; salvage value, $80.00; useful life, 10 years; depreciation method, SL; assign asset no. 180.

Note: When recording the year acquired, be sure to use a year of 1997.

Jan. 03   Purchased an Office Chair (Gray) for $425.00; salvage value, $45.00; useful life, 10 years, depreciation method, SL; assign asset no. 145.

Mar. 01   Delete the Typewriter (asset no. 200).

June 03   Purchased a Notebook Computer for $2,635.00; salvage value, $250.00; useful life, 5 years; depreciation method, SL; assign asset no. 260.

Aug. 06   Change the asset description of Laser Printer (asset no. 250) to Laser Printer NT.

Oct. 28   Purchased a CD-ROM Drive for $450.00; salvage value, $35.00; useful life, 5 years; depreciation method, SL; assign asset no. 270.

Dec. 02   Purchased a Telephone System, $3,468.85; salvage value, $300.00; useful life, 8 years; depreciation method, SL; assign asset no. 280.

STEP 6: **Display a plant assets list report. Use 12/31/97 as the run date for all reports.**

STEP 7: **Display depreciation schedules for the new assets.**

STEP 8: **Generate the depreciation adjusting entries.**

CHECK FIGURE:
Trial balance debit and credit totals = $559,977.55

STEP 9: **Display the adjusting entries.**

STEP 10: **Display a trial balance.**

STEP 11: **Save your data.**

STEP 12: **Optional spreadsheet integration activity:**
Generate declining-balance schedules for each of the new assets.
a. Display and copy the plant assets list report to the clipboard in spreadsheet format.
b. Start up your spreadsheet software and load template file SS08–T.
c. Select cell A1 as the current cell and paste the plant assets list report into the spreadsheet.
d. Enter the cell references and purchase month and year of asset number 280, Telephone System in cells D51–D57.
e. Print the declining-balance schedule.
f. Save the spreadsheet data with a file name of XXX8–P.
g. What if the useful life is changed to 7 or 10 years? (It is not necessary to save this what if data.) You may use this newly created template file for the remaining new assets, if desired.

STEP 13:   Optional word processing integration activity:
Prepare a memo addressed to the manager of the accounting department, showing a comparison of the *Automated Accounting*-generated straight-line schedule and the spreadsheet declining-balance schedule for asset number 280, Telephone System. Use Figure 8.18 as a guide.

a. Start up your word processing software and create a new document. If your software has templates, load a memo format.

b. Enter the memo heading information and copy and paste the *Automated Accounting*-generated straight-line schedule and the spreadsheet declining-balance schedule into the body of the memo. Paste the schedules vertically or horizontally with appropriate headings, and format as necessary.

c. Print the memo.

d. Save the memo with a file name of XXX8–P.

e. End your word processing and spreadsheet sessions.

STEP 14:   End the *Automated Accounting* session.

Applying Your Technology Skills 8–P

P

Directions: Using Independent Practice Problem 8–P, write the answers to the following questions in the *Working Papers*.

1. What is the total value of all plant assets based on original costs?

2. On what date was the Laser Printer NT acquired?

3. For asset number 180, Book Shelf, what will the accumulated depreciation be as of the end of 2000?

4. For asset number 145, Office Chair (Gray), what will the book value be as of the end of 2001?

5. For asset number 260, Notebook Computer, what is the annual depreciation for 1997?

6. For asset number 270, CD-ROM Drive, what will the book value be at the end of 2001?

7. For asset number 280, Telephone System, what will the annual depreciation be for the year 2005?

8. From the general journal report, what is the amount debited to Depreciation Expense—Office Equipment?

9. From the general journal report, what is the amount debited to Depreciation Expense—Office Furniture?

10. From the general journal report, what is the total amount of the debit column?

M   Mastery Problem 8–M

In this problem, you will add, change, and delete plant assets. In addition, you will generate the plant assets list report, depreciation schedules, and depreciation adjusting entries.

Asset numbers 100–199 are assigned to Vehicles, asset numbers 200–299 are assigned to Office Equipment, and asset numbers 300–399 are assigned to Store Equipment. Consult the chart of accounts stored with file AA08–M for the appropriate Accumulated Depreciation and Depreciation Expense account numbers.

STEP 1: Load the opening balances template file, AA08–M.

STEP 2: Enter your name in the User Name text box.

STEP 3: Save the data as XXX8–M.

STEP 4: Enter the additions, changes, and deletions to plant assets.

Apr. 06 1997   Purchased a Pentium Computer for $2,159.00; salvage value, $120.00; useful life, 5 years; depreciation method, SL; assign asset no. 270.

Apr. 06   Purchased an Ink Jet Printer for $599.00; salvage value, $50.00; useful life, 5 years; depreciation method, SL; assign asset no. 280.

Apr. 10   Purchased a Copy Machine for $3,417.85; salvage value, $200.00; useful life, 8 years; depreciation method, SL; assign asset no. 260.

June 10   Delete the Word Processer (asset no. 220).

Oct. 02   Purchased a Cash Register for $1,925.00; salvage value, $180.00; useful life, 8 years; depreciation method, SL; assign asset no. 350.

Nov. 01   Purchased a Security Display Case for $2,900.00; salvage value, $120.00; useful life, 12 years; depreciation method, SL; assign asset no. 360.

STEP 5: Display a plant assets list report and depreciation schedules for each of the new assets. Use 12/31/97 as the run date for all reports.

STEP 6: Generate the depreciation adjusting entries.

STEP 7: Display the adjusting entries.

STEP 8: Display a trial balance.

STEP 9: Save your data.

CHECK FIGURE:
Trial balance debit and credit totals = $574,729.82

STEP 10:   **Optional spreadsheet integration activity:**
Generate declining-balance schedules for each of the new assets.
a.   Copy and paste the plant assets list report into the spreadsheet template file SS08–T.
b.   Enter the cell references and purchase month and year of asset number 270, Pentium Computer in cells D51–D57.
c.   Print the declining-balance schedule.
d.   Save the spreadsheet data with a file name of XXX8–M.
e.   What if the useful life is changed to 4 or 6 years? (It is not necessary to save this what if data.) You may use this spreadsheet template file for the remaining new assets, if desired.

STEP 11:   **Optional word processing integration activity:**
Prepare a memo addressed to the manager of the accounting department, showing a comparison of the *Automated Accounting*-generated straight-line schedule and the spreadsheet declining-balance schedule for asset number 270, Pentium Computer.
a.   Create a new memorandum document. If your software has templates, load a memo format.
b.   Enter the memo heading information, and copy and paste the *Automated Accounting*-generated straight-line schedule and the spreadsheet declining-balance schedule into the body of the memo. Format the memo as necessary.
c.   Print the memo.
d.   Save the memo with a file name of XXX8–M.
e.   End your word processing and spreadsheet sessions.

STEP 12:   **End the *Automated Accounting* session.**

Applying Your Technology Skills 8–M

Directions: Using Mastery Problem 8–M, write the answers to the following questions in the *Working Papers*.

1.   What is the total value of all plant assets based on original costs?

2.   On what date was the Delivery Van (F100) acquired?

3.   For asset number 260, Copy Machine, what will the accumulated depreciation be as of the end of 2000?

4.   For asset number 270, Pentium Computer, what will the book value be as of the end of 2001?

5. For asset number 280, Ink Jet Printer, what is the annual depreciation for 1997?

6. For asset number 350, Cash Register, what will the book value be at the end of 2001?

7. For asset number 360, Security Display Case, what is the accumulated depreciation for the year 2004?

8. From the general journal report, what is the amount debited to Depreciation Expense—Vehicles?

9. From the general journal report, what is the amount debited to Depreciation Expense—Office Equipment?

10. From the general journal report, what is the amount credited to Accumulated Depreciation—Store Equipment?

ACCOUNTING CAREERS IN DEPTH

Budget Accountant

A budget accountant applies principles of accounting to analyze past and present financial operations, and estimates future revenues and expenditures in order to prepare budgets. A budget accountant performs the following duties:

- Analyzing records of present and past operations, trends and costs, estimated and realized revenues, administrative commitments, and obligations incurred in order to project future revenues and expenses, using a computer.
- Maintaining budgeting systems which provide control of expenditures made to carry out activities, such as advertising and marketing, production, maintenance, or to project activities such as the construction of buildings.

The educational requirements for a budget accountant include a college degree in accounting and preferably some work experience while in school. When students have acquired such work experience, they often have a competitive edge. Also, the internship or co-op experience may lead to the first job a student is offered when the college degree requirements have been met.

Analytical skills are very important in this career. It is necessary to be able to look at the "big picture" in order to accurately analyze reports or specific financial figures. Accountants must have the skills to create the financial reports and then analyze the figures used to prepare financial statements.

Choosing a career as a budget accountant can be as simple as balancing your checkbook and analyzing the trends of how you spend money; determining when you spend more for certain purchases; learning how much interest has accrued on your account; and then researching the possibility of transferring a portion of those funds in order to accrue a higher rate of return. Of course, doing this type of analysis for a corporation would involve many more factors and elements to consider.

Budget accountants are needed in all types of industries due to the nature of the work. You can choose the industry that interests you, and then assist a company in maintaining its budget while also being instrumental in keeping the company successful.

Corporations

LEARNING OBJECTIVES

Upon completion of this chapter, you will be able to:

1. Identify the appropriate journals and use the proper procedures to enter and post transactions for a business organized as a corporation.

2. Generate checks.

3. Generate the monthly financial statements.

INTRODUCTION

This chapter will identify the appropriate journals and proper procedures to enter and post transactions for a corporation. You will learn how to have the software generate checks for cash payments on account and direct payments. In addition, generating monthly financial statements will be covered.

A **corporation** is an organization that has many of the legal rights of an individual; however, it is typically owned by many people. Corporations exist separately from their owners. The ownership of a corporation is divided into units called **shares of stock.** The total shares of ownership in a corporation are called **capital stock.** Owners of the stock are called **shareholders.** A **board of directors** is elected by the shareholders to manage the corporation.

In a sole proprietorship or partnership, assets withdrawn from the business are recorded in the owner's drawing account. Shareholders may not withdraw assets from the corporation. However, earnings (called **dividends**) are distributed to shareholders. Earnings not yet distributed to shareholders are referred to as **retained earnings.**

For sole proprietorships and partnerships, the income tax liability for net income rests with the owners. Corporations must also pay income tax on their earnings.

JOURNAL ENTRIES

Several journal entries related to corporations are introduced in this chapter. The cash payments journal entries are slightly different than in previous chapters as the software will generate the vendor checks. A chart of accounts for Abbott Cosmetic Corp. is shown in Figure 9.1.

E T H I C S

A self-employed programmer was hired by a small company to develop the software for a payroll/personnel system the company had designed. After completing the project, the programmer sold the software, with minor modification, to other companies.

a. Who do you think owns the right to the programmer's code (program)?

b. Do you think that what the programmer did was ethical, unethical, or an act that could be considered computer crime? Justify your choice.

Abbott Cosmetic Corp.
Chart of Accounts
04/01/--

Assets

1110	Cash
1120	Petty Cash
1130	Accounts Receivable
1140	Merchandise Inventory
1150	Supplies—Office
1160	Supplies—Store
1170	Prepaid Insurance
1510	Office Equipment
1520	Accum. Depr.—Ofc. Eqpt.
1530	Store Equipment
1540	Accum. Depr.—Store Eqpt.

Liabilities

2110	Accounts Payable
2120	Sales Tax Payable
2130	Employee Income Tax Pay.
2140	Federal Income Tax Pay.
2150	FICA Tax Payable
2160	Medicare Tax Payable
2170	Unemploy. Tax Pay.—Fed.
2180	Unemploy. Tax Pay.—State
2190	Health Ins. Premium Pay.
2200	Disability Insurance Pay.
2210	Dividends Payable

Stockholders' Equity

3110	Capital Stock
3120	Retained Earnings
3130	Dividends
3140	Income Summary

Revenue

4110	Sales
4120	Sales Discount
4130	Sales Returns & Allow.

Cost

5110	Purchases
5120	Purchases Discount
5130	Purch. Returns & Allow.

Expenses

6110	Advertising Expense
6120	Credit Card Fee Expense
6130	Depr. Exp.—Office Eqpt.
6140	Depr. Exp.—Store Eqpt.
6150	Insurance Expense
6160	Miscellaneous Expense
6170	Payroll Taxes Expense
6180	Rent Expense
6190	Salaries Expense
6200	Supplies Expense—Office
6210	Supplies Expense—Store
6220	Utilities Expense

Corporate Income Tax

9110	Federal Income Tax Exp.

Figure 9.1
Chart of Accounts

INTERNET

Although ListServs are a popular way for people to communicate, ListServs make membership lists available to anyone. You can avoid some unsolicited advertising by removing your name and e-mail address from the membership list, using the *set listname conceal* command.

Making Cash Payments

This corporation does not write checks manually as all checks are generated by the computer. Each cash payment for which the computer is to generate a check must include the name of the vendor to whom the check is to be written. If the Vendor Name is left blank, a check will not be generated. Two transactions are entered and posted in the cash payments journal shown in Figure 9.2. The first transaction is an example of a cash payment on account with a discount. The second transaction is an example of a direct payment of an expense to a vendor. As an alternative, you may record the transactions on input forms before entering and posting the transactions at the computer.

Apr. 06   Paid cash on account to Anello Supply Depot, $878.80, covering M35 for $896.73, less 2% discount, $17.93. C1212.

   06   Paid cash to Eastern Utilities Co. for electric bill, $523.58. C1213.

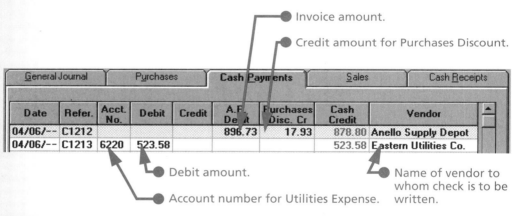

Figure 9.2
Cash Payments Journal

Declaring a Dividend

The decision by the board of directors to distribute earnings to the shareholders is called **declaring a dividend.** The dividend does not have to be distributed at the time it is declared. However, the declaration creates a liability to the corporation and requires a journal entry.

Apr. 10   Abbott Cosmetic Corp.'s board of directors declared a dividend, $3,100.00. M31.

The transaction is entered and posted in the general journal as illustrated in Figure 9.3.

To record this entry, debit the Dividends account (3130) and credit the Dividends Payable account (2210).

Figure 9.3
General Journal (Declaring a Dividend)

Paying a Dividend

When the dividends are paid, a check is written and the transaction is recorded as a cash payment to the account Shareholders Bank Account. The check is then deposited in a special bank account upon which the individual checks to the shareholders are drawn. The cash payments journal entry to record the payment of dividends is illustrated in Figure 9.4.

> Apr. 12   Paid cash to Shareholders Bank Account for first quarter dividends declared in April, $3,100.00. C1219.

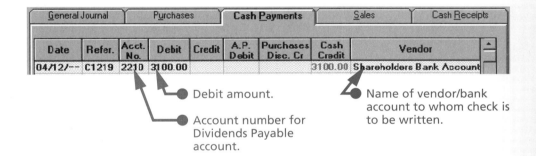

Debit amount.

Account number for Dividends Payable account.

Name of vendor/bank account to whom check is to be written.

Figure 9.4
Cash Payments (Paying a Dividend)

Recording Corporate Income Tax

Corporate income tax is the tax that corporations are required to pay on actual earnings. The corporation pays the tax each quarter, based on an estimated tax liability. The estimated taxes are based on estimated net income. At the end of the year, the corporation must file a tax return with the Internal Revenue Service based on actual earnings. If additional tax is owed beyond the estimate, the additional tax must be paid when the return is filed. If the estimate exceeds the actual taxes, the corporation may request a refund of the difference or apply the excess to the estimated tax for the following year.

Because Abbott Cosmetic Corp. completes the accounting cycle each month, an income tax adjustment is made each month. The corporation pays the estimated tax to the Internal Revenue Service on a quarterly basis. The payment of the quarterly estimated income tax is shown in Figure 9.5, and the monthly federal income tax adjustment is shown in Figure 9.6.

> Apr. 13   Paid cash to Internal Revenue Service for quarterly estimated federal income tax, $1,020.00. C1222.
>   30   Adjustment for estimated federal income tax, $350.00.

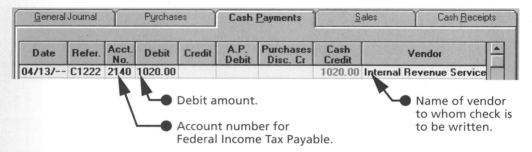

Debit amount.

Name of vendor to whom check is to be written.

Account number for Federal Income Tax Payable.

Figure 9.5
Cash Payments Journal (Payment of Quarterly Estimated Income Tax)

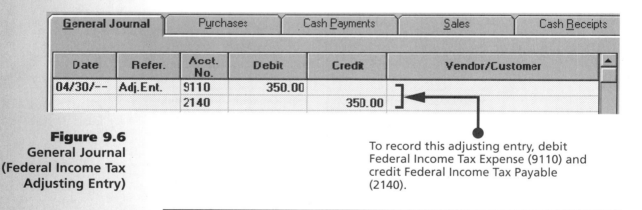

Figure 9.6
**General Journal
(Federal Income Tax
Adjusting Entry)**

To record this adjusting entry, debit Federal Income Tax Expense (9110) and credit Federal Income Tax Payable (2140).

CHECKS

If the Computer Checks option button is set to ON (this will be covered later in Chapter 13), a check will be generated each time a cash payment transaction involving a vendor is entered and posted. When the check appears on the display screen, it can be printed.

1:   Enter the cash payment on account or direct payment transaction, including a vendor, and click the *Post* command button.

A computer-generated check, similar to the example shown in Figure 9.7, will appear.

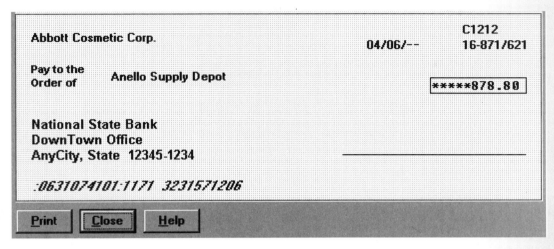

Figure 9.7
Check

2: **Click the *Print* command button to print the current check or click *Close* to dismiss the check and continue.**

INCOME STATEMENT BY MONTH AND YEAR

If the Income Statement option for Month and Year is set to ON (this will be covered in Chapter 13), the format of the income statement will be as shown in Figure 9.8. The report includes columns for the month and for the year. Also included for each column is a component percentage, indicating each amount's percentage of total operating revenue. When this format of the income statement is used, adjusting entries are entered and posted and financial statements are generated at the end of each month. The adjusting entries must be entered each month in order for the monthly column to be up-to-date and correct. Closing entries are not generated and posted until the end of the fiscal year.

Chapter Review

1. An organization that has many of the legal rights of a person, is owned by many people, and exists separately from its owners is called a corporation. Earnings that are distributed to shareholders

Abbott Cosmetic Corp.
Income Statement
For Period Ended 04/30/--

	Monthly Amount	Monthly Percent	Yearly Amount	Yearly Percent
Operating Revenue				
Sales	54211.11	100.45	210502.24	102.20
Sales Discount	−171.74	−0.32	−1783.98	−0.87
Sales Returns & Allow.	−68.42	−0.13	−2753.27	−1.34
Total Operating Revenue	53970.95	100.00	205964.99	100.00
Cost of Merchandise Sold				
Beginning Inventory	62064.00	115.00	62984.65	30.58
Purchases	37480.40	69.45	134675.35	65.39
Purchases Discount	−253.86	−0.47	−1792.76	−0.87
Purch. Returns & Allow.	−229.34	−0.42	−2554.12	−1.24
Merchandise Available for Sale	99061.20	183.55	193313.12	93.86
Less Ending Inventory	−64100.00	−118.77	−64100.00	−31.12
Cost of Merchandise Sold	34961.20	64.78	129213.12	62.74
Gross Profit	19009.75	35.22	76751.87	37.26
Operating Expenses				
Advertising Expense	480.95	0.89	2877.68	1.40
Credit Card Fee Expense	230.53	0.43	957.31	0.46
Depr. Exp.—Office Eqpt.	198.86	0.37	795.42	0.39
Depr. Exp.—Store Eqpt.	155.00	0.29	621.88	0.30
Insurance Expense	174.11	0.32	670.19	0.33
Miscellaneous Expense	124.60	0.23	421.47	0.20
Payroll Taxes Expense	782.75	1.45	3119.72	1.51
Rent Expense	2000.00	3.71	8000.00	3.88
Salaries Expense	9723.62	18.02	38754.43	18.82
Supplies Expense—Office	593.49	1.10	822.95	0.40
Supplies Expense—Store	343.95	0.64	547.89	0.27
Utilities Expense	523.58	0.97	2890.81	1.40
Total Operating Expenses	15331.44	28.41	60479.75	29.36
Net Income from Operations	3678.31	6.82	16272.12	7.90
Net Income before Income Tax	3678.31	6.82	16272.12	7.90
Income Tax				
Federal Income Tax Exp.	350.00	0.65	1377.12	0.67
Net Income after Income Tax	3328.31	6.17	14895.00	7.23

Figure 9.8
Income Statement

are called dividends. The decision by the board of directors to distribute earnings to the shareholders is called declaring a dividend. Paying a dividend involves recording a cash payment transaction for the amount of the dividends payable, then depositing the check generated in a special bank account on which the individual checks to the shareholders are drawn. Corporate income tax is a tax that the corporation pays each quarter, based on estimated tax liability. The estimated taxes are based on estimated net income.

2. Checks will be generated each time a cash payment transaction involving a vendor is entered and posted. Checks may be displayed and printed, if desired.

3. Companies may choose to prepare financial statements monthly. In this case, an income statement with monthly and yearly figures would be generated.

A C C O U N T I N G   C A R E E R S   I N   D E P T H

Audit Clerk

Audit clerks verify the accuracy of figures, calculations, and postings pertaining to business transactions recorded by other workers. An audit clerk performs the following duties:

- Examining expense accounts, commissions paid to employees, loans made on insurance policies, interest and account payments, cash receipts, sales tickets, bank records, inventory and stock-record sheets, and similar items to verify the accuracy of recorded data.
- Correcting errors or listing discrepancies for adjustment.
- Computing percentages and totals, using adding or calculating machines, and comparing results of recorded entries.

Audit clerks are also known by other titles, depending on the type of records to be audited. Some examples are: Cash-Sales Audit Clerk; Charge-Account Audit Clerk; C.O.D. Audit Clerk; Commission Auditor (insurance); Expense Clerk; Inventory-Audit Clerk; Journal-Entry Audit Clerk; and Medical-Records Auditor. As you can see, there are many opportunities to work as an audit clerk. The positions can be found in a variety of industries such as the medical, insurance, and retail fields.

A position as an audit clerk can be very detail-oriented because the work requires that the clerk check every detail of a transaction. In such a position, there are opportunities to learn many details of the organization in which you work. This will give you knowledge about different aspects of a company which could give you a competitive advantage when seeking opportunities for advancement.

There is always the chance that if you enjoy being an audit clerk, you may choose to further your education and become an auditor. If not, job satisfaction is still possible, especially if you choose to become an audit clerk in an area in which you are interested.

TUTORIAL PROBLEM 9-T

In this tutorial problem, you will process the monthly transactions, generate checks, generate monthly statements of account, and complete the end-of-month processing for a corporation.

Note: The following transactions are illustrated in the appropriate journals shown in Figures 9.9 through 9.14. Source documents are abbreviated as follows: Purchase Invoice No., P; Check No., C; Sales Invoice No., S; Cash Receipt No., R; Cash Register Tape, T; Memorandums, M; Debit Memorandums, DM; Credit Memorandums, CM.

Apr. 02   Granted credit to Noble's Beauty Shop for merchandise returned, $68.42, against S730. CM28.

02   Purchased merchandise on account from Haskins Chemical Co., $4,156.97. P501.

03   Sold merchandise on account to Tina's Fashion Salon. $6,931.70. S733.

04   Bought advertising on account from Caplan Marketing, $480.95. M36.

05   Received cash on account from Burgess Salon, $3,650.90, covering S726 for $3,687.78, less 1% discount, $36.88. R653.

05   Received cash on account from Polly's Hair Styles, $5,024.00, covering S731 for $5,074.75, less 1% discount, $50.75. R654.

06   Paid cash on account to Anello Supply Depot, $878.80, covering M35 for $896.73, less 2% discount, $17.93. C1212.

06   Paid cash to Eastern Utilities Co. for electric bill, $523.58. C1213.

07   Received cash on account from Nail & Hair Care, $4,116.93, covering S732 for $4,158.52, less 1% discount, $41.59. R655.

07   Purchased merchandise on account from Perry Salon Supplies, $5,885.95. P502.

07   Bought office supplies on account from Anello Supply Depot, $330.60. M37.

09   Paid cash on account to Huber Manufacturing Co., $1,519.05, covering P495 for $1,534.39, less 1% discount, $15.34. C1214.

09   Returned merchandise to Perry Salon Supplies, $229.34, against P500. DM39.

09   Paid cash to Parsons Cosmetic Supplies for miscellaneous expense, $107.52. C1215.

10   Paid cash on account to Tilton & Ruffin Corp., $1,035.99, covering P494 for $1,046.45, less 1% discount, $10.46. C1216.

10   Purchased merchandise on account from Huber Manufacturing Co., $4,939.65. P503.

11   Sold merchandise on account to Debbie's Hair Design, $7,149.65. S734.

12   Paid cash to Commissioner of Revenue for quarterly sales tax, $1,250.27. C1217.

12   Paid cash to Armor Insurance Assoc. for liability for first quarter insurance premiums: health insurance, $2,975.98; disability insurance, $869.45; total, $3,845.43. C1218.

12   Paid cash to Shareholders Bank Account for first quarter dividends declared in March, $3,100.00. C1219.

13   Paid cash on account to Caplan Marketing, $476.14, covering M36 for $480.95, less 1% discount, $4.81. C1220.

13   Paid cash to Internal Revenue Service for payroll taxes: employee income tax, $6,386.26; FICA tax, $1,799.91; and Medicare tax, $420.94; total, $8,607.11. C1221.

13   Paid cash to Internal Revenue Service for quarterly estimated federal income tax, $1,020.00. C1222.

14   Paid cash on account to Mcbride Beauty Supply, $2,593.27, covering P498 for $2,646.19, less 2% discount, $52.92. C1223.

14   Received cash on account from Dorsey Boutique, $4,209.75, covering S728 for $4,252.27, less 1% discount, $42.52. R656.

16   Bought store supplies on account from Anello Supply Depot, $531.30. M38.

16   Sold merchandise on account to Sunshine Tanning & Salon, $6,101.67. S735.

16   Paid cash on account to Kay & Harris Hair Products, $4,425.79, covering P496 for $4,470.50, less 1% discount, $44.71. C1224.

17   Purchased merchandise on account from Sterling Corporation, $5,136.05. P504.

TUTORIAL   PROBLEM   9 - T

17   Sold merchandise on account to Burgess Salon, $6,225.00. S736.

18   Paid cash to Hampton Leasing, Inc. for monthly rent, $2,000.00. C1225.

19   Sold merchandise on account to Anita Graham, $102.24, plus sales tax, $7.16; total, $109.40. S737.

19   Purchased merchandise on account from Mcbride Beauty Supply, $4,104.57. P505.

20   Received cash on account from Noble's Beauty Shop, $5,749.70, covering S730 less CM28, no discount. R657.

20   Paid cash on account to Anello Supply Depot, $844.66, covering M37 and M38 for $861.90, less 2% discount, $17.24. C1226.

21   Paid cash on account to Huber Manufacturing Co., $4,890.25, covering P503 for $4,939.65, less 1% discount, $49.40. C1227.

21   Recorded cash and credit card sales, $22,615.76, plus sales tax, $1,583.10; total, $24,198.86. T40.

23   Bought office supplies on account from Anello Supply Depot, $815.92. M39.

25   Sold merchandise on account to Nail & Hair Care, $5,085.09. S738.

26   Purchased merchandise on account from Huber Manufacturing Co., $5,197.98. P506.

26   Paid cash on account to Sterling Corporation, $2,186.34, covering P497, no discount. C1228.

26   Recorded credit card fee expense for March, $230.53. M40.

27   Paid cash on account to Mcbride Beauty Supply, $4,063.52, covering P505 for $4,104.57, less 1% discount, $41.05. C1229.

28   Purchased merchandise on account from Kay & Harris Hair Products, $3,596.63. P507.

28   Purchased merchandise on account from Tilton & Ruffin Corp., $4,462.60. P508.

30   Paid cash to Payroll Bank Account for monthly payroll, $5,569.33. Total payroll, $9,723.62, less deductions: employee income tax, $2,128.61;

TUTORIAL PROBLEM 9–T

FICA tax, $602.86; Medicare tax, $141.00; health insurance premium, $992.00; disability insurance premium, $289.82. C1230.
Note: The net payroll amount of $5,569.33 is derived by subtracting the deductions from the total gross payroll. The computer automatically makes the $5,569.33 credit to cash.

30 Recorded employer payroll taxes expense, $782.75 (FICA tax, $602.86; Medicare tax, $141.00; federal unemployment tax, $29.17; state unemployment tax, $9.72). M41. Record this transaction in the General Journal.

30 Paid cash to Petty Cash Custodian to replenish petty cash fund, $96.70: office supplies, $36.97; store supplies, $42.65; miscellaneous expense, $17.08. C1231.

STEP 1: **Start up *Automated Accounting 7.0.***

STEP 2: **Load the opening balance file AA09–T.**
Click the *Open* toolbar button, then choose file AA09–T from the File list box.

STEP 3: **Enter your name in the User Name text box and click *OK*.**

STEP 4: **Save the file with a file name of XXX9–T.**
Use Save As to save the file as XXX9–T, where XXX are your initials.

STEP 5: **Add Anita Graham to the customer list.**
Click the *Accts.* toolbar icon, then click the *Customers* tab. Enter Anita Graham as a new customer.

STEP 6: **Enter the April general journal transaction data shown in Figure 9.9.**
Click the *Journal* toolbar button. When the Journal Entries window appears, click the *General Journal* tab, then enter the journal entries.

TUTORIAL PROBLEM 9 – T

Date	Refer.	Acct. No.	Debit	Credit	Vendor/Customer
04/02/--	CM28	4130	68.42		
		1130		68.42	Noble's Beauty Shop
04/04/--	M36	6110	480.95		
		2110		480.95	Caplan Marketing
04/07/--	M37	1150	330.60		
		2110		330.60	Anello Supply Depot
04/09/--	DM39	2110	229.34		Perry Salon Supplies
		5130		229.34	
04/16/--	M38	1160	531.30		
		2110		531.30	Anello Supply Depot
04/23/--	M39	1150	815.92		
		2110		815.92	Anello Supply Depot
04/30/--	M41	6170	782.75		
		2150		602.86	
		2160		141.00	
		2170		29.17	
		2180		9.72	

Figure 9.9
General Journal

STEP 7:   Enter the April purchases journal transaction data shown in Figure 9.10.
Click the *Purchases* tab, then enter the journal entries.

Date	Refer.	Purch. Debit	A.P. Credit	Vendor
04/02/--	P501	4156.97	4156.97	Haskins Chemical Co.
04/07/--	P502	5885.95	5885.95	Perry Salon Supplies
04/10/--	P503	4939.65	4939.65	Huber Manufacturing Co.
04/17/--	P504	5136.05	5136.05	Sterling Corporation
04/19/--	P505	4104.57	4104.57	Mcbride Beauty Supply
04/26/--	P506	5197.98	5197.98	Huber Manufacturing Co.
04/28/--	P507	3596.63	3596.63	Kay & Harris Hair Products
04/28/--	P508	4462.60	4462.60	Tilton & Ruffin Corp.

Figure 9.10
Purchases Journal

T U T O R I A L   P R O B L E M   9 – T

STEP 8:   Enter the April cash payments journal transaction data shown in Figure 9.11 and generate the vendor checks. The first check is shown in Figure 9.12.
Click the *Cash Payments* tab, then enter the cash payments. The vendor checks will be displayed.

Date	Refer.	Acct. No.	Debit	Credit	A.P. Debit	Purchases Disc. Cr	Cash Credit	Vendor
04/06/--	C1212				896.73	17.93	878.80	Anello Supply Depot
04/06/--	C1213	6220	523.58				523.58	Eastern Utilities Co.
04/09/--	C1214				1534.39	15.34	1519.05	Huber Manufacturing Co.
04/09/--	C1215	6160	107.52				107.52	Parsons Cosmetic Supplies
04/10/--	C1216				1046.45	10.46	1035.99	Tilton & Ruffin Corp.
04/12/--	C1217	2120	1250.27				1250.27	Commissioner of Revenue
04/12/--	C1218	2190	2975.98				3845.43	Armor Insurance Assoc.
		2200	869.45					
04/12/--	C1219	2210	3100.00				3100.00	Shareholders Bank Account
04/13/--	C1220				480.95	4.81	476.14	Caplan Marketing
04/13/--	C1221	2130	6386.26				8607.11	Internal Revenue Service
		2150	1799.91					
		2160	420.94					
04/13/--	C1222	2140	1020.00				1020.00	Internal Revenue Service
04/14/--	C1223				2646.19	52.92	2593.27	Mcbride Beauty Supply
04/16/--	C1224				4470.50	44.71	4425.79	Kay & Harris Hair Products
04/18/--	C1225	6180	2000.00				2000.00	Hampton Leasing, Inc.
04/20/--	C1226				861.90	17.24	844.66	Anello Supply Depot
04/21/--	C1227				4939.65	49.40	4890.25	Huber Manufacturing Co.
04/26/--	C1228				2186.34		2186.34	Sterling Corporation
04/26/--	M40	6120	230.53				230.53	
04/27/--	C1229				4104.57	41.05	4063.52	Mcbride Beauty Supply
04/30/--	C1230	6190	9723.62				5569.33	Payroll Bank Account
		2130		2128.61				
		2150		602.86				
		2160		141.00				
		2190		992.00				
		2200		289.82				
04/30/--	C1231	1150	36.97				96.70	Petty Cash Custodian
		1160	42.65					
		6160	17.08					

Figure 9.11
Cash Payments Journal

TUTORIAL   PROBLEM   9 - T

Abbott Cosmetic Corp.   C1212
                                                                04/06/--   16-871/621

Pay to the
Order of   Anello Supply Depot

                                                                        |*****878.80|

National State Bank
DownTown Office
AnyCity, State 12345-1234

  :0631074101:1171 3231571206

Figure 9.12
First Check

STEP 9:   Enter the April sales journal transaction data shown in
          Figure 9.13.
          Click the *Sales* tab, then enter the journal entries.

Date	Refer.	Sales Credit	Sales Tax Credit	A.R. Debit	Customer
04/03/--	S733	6931.70		6931.70	Tina's Fashion Salon
04/11/--	S734	7149.65		7149.65	Debbie's Hair Design
04/16/--	S735	6101.67		6101.67	Sunshine Tanning & Salon
04/17/--	S736	6225.00		6225.00	Burgess Salon
04/19/--	S737	102.24	7.16	109.40	Anita Graham
04/25/--	S738	5085.09		5085.09	Nail & Hair Care

Figure 9.13
Sales Journal

STEP 10:   Enter the April cash receipts journal transaction data
           shown in Figure 9.14.
           Click the *Cash Receipts* tab, then enter the journal entries.

Date	Refer.	Acct. No.	Debit	Credit	A.R. Credit	Sales Credit	Sales Tax Pay. Cr	Sales Disc. Dr	Cash Debit	Custom
04/05/--	R653				3687.78			36.88	3650.90	Burgess Salo
04/05/--	R654				5074.75			50.75	5024.00	Polly's Hair S
04/07/--	R655				4158.52			41.59	4116.93	Nail & Hair C
04/14/--	R656				4252.27			42.52	4209.75	Dorsey Bouti
04/20/--	R657				5749.70				5749.70	Noble's Beau
04/21/--	T40					22615.76	1583.10		24198.86	

Figure 9.14
Cash Receipts Journal

T U T O R I A L   P R O B L E M   9 – T

STEP 11: **Display the journal reports.**
Click the *Reports* toolbar button. Choose the *Journals* option, then select and display each of the following journal reports: general journal, purchases journal, cash payments, sales journal, and cash receipts journal. When the Journal Report Selection window appears, enter a date range of April 1 to April 30 of the current year. The reports appear in Figures 9.15 through 9.19.

Abbott Cosmetic Corp.
General Journal
04/30/--

Date	Refer.	Acct.	Title	Debit	Credit
04/02	CM28	4130	Sales Returns & Allow.	68.42	
04/02	CM28	1130	AR/Noble's Beauty Shop		68.42
04/04	M36	6110	Advertising Expense	480.95	
04/04	M36	2110	AP/Caplan Marketing		480.95
04/07	M37	1150	Supplies—Office	330.60	
04/07	M37	2110	AP/Anello Supply Depot		330.60
04/09	DM39	2110	AP/Perry Salon Supplies	229.34	
04/09	DM39	5130	Purch. Returns & Allow.		229.34
04/16	M38	1160	Supplies—Store	531.30	
04/16	M38	2110	AP/Anello Supply Depot		531.30
04/23	M39	1150	Supplies—Office	815.92	
04/23	M39	2110	AP/Anello Supply Depot		815.92
04/30	M41	6170	Payroll Taxes Expense	782.75	
04/30	M41	2150	FICA Tax Payable		602.86
04/30	M41	2160	Medicare Tax Payable		141.00
04/30	M41	2170	Unemploy. Tax Pay.—Fed.		29.17
04/30	M41	2180	Unemploy. Tax Pay.—State		9.72
			Totals	3239.28	3239.28

Figure 9.15
General Journal Report

TUTORIAL PROBLEM 9-T

Abbott Cosmetic Corp.
Purchases Journal
04/30/--

Date	Inv. No.	Acct.	Title	Debit	Credit
04/02	P501	5110	Purchases	4156.97	
04/02	P501	2110	AP/Haskins Chemical Co.		4156.97
04/07	P502	5110	Purchases	5885.95	
04/07	P502	2110	AP/Perry Salon Supplies		5885.95
04/10	P503	5110	Purchases	4939.65	
04/10	P503	2110	AP/Huber Manufacturing Co.		4939.65
04/17	P504	5110	Purchases	5136.05	
04/17	P504	2110	AP/Sterling Corporation		5136.05
04/19	P505	5110	Purchases	4104.57	
04/19	P505	2110	AP/Mcbride Beauty Supply		4104.57
04/26	P506	5110	Purchases	5197.98	
04/26	P506	2110	AP/Huber Manufacturing Co.		5197.98
04/28	P507	5110	Purchases	3596.63	
04/28	P507	2110	AP/Kay & Harris Hair Product		3596.63
04/28	P508	5110	Purchases	4462.60	
04/28	P508	2110	AP/Tilton & Ruffin Corp.		4462.60
			Totals	37480.40	37480.40

Figure 9.16
Purchases Journal
Report

Abbott Cosmetic Corp.
Cash Payments Journal
04/30/--

Date	Ck. No.	Acct.	Title	Debit	Credit
04/06	C1212	2110	AP/Anello Supply Depot	896.73	
04/06	C1212	1110	Cash		878.80
04/06	C1212	5120	Purchases Discount		17.93
04/06	C1213	6220	Utilities Expense	523.58	
04/06	C1213	1110	Cash		523.58
04/09	C1214	2110	AP/Huber Manufacturing Co.	1534.39	
04/09	C1214	1110	Cash		1519.05
04/09	C1214	5120	Purchases Discount		15.34
04/09	C1215	6160	Miscellaneous Expense	107.52	
04/09	C1215	1110	Cash		107.52
04/10	C1216	2110	AP/Tilton & Ruffin Corp.	1046.45	
04/10	C1216	1110	Cash		1035.99
04/10	C1216	5120	Purchases Discount		10.46
04/12	C1217	2120	Sales Tax Payable	1250.27	
04/12	C1217	1110	Cash		1250.27

Figure 9.17
Cash Payments
Journal Report

Abbott Cosmetic Corp.
Cash Payments Journal
04/30/--

Date	Ck. No.	Acct.	Title	Debit	Credit
04/12	C1218	2190	Health Ins. Premium Pay.	2975.98	
04/12	C1218	2200	Disability Insurance Pay.	869.45	
04/12	C1218	1110	Cash		3845.43
04/12	C1219	2210	Dividends Payable	3100.00	
04/12	C1219	1110	Cash		3100.00
04/13	C1220	2110	AP/Caplan Marketing	480.95	
04/13	C1220	1110	Cash		476.14
04/13	C1220	5120	Purchases Discount		4.81
04/13	C1221	2130	Employee Income Tax Pay.	6386.26	
04/13	C1221	2150	FICA Tax Payable	1799.91	
04/13	C1221	2160	Medicare Tax Payable	420.94	
04/13	C1221	1110	Cash		8607.11
04/13	C1222	2140	Federal Income Tax Pay.	1020.00	
04/13	C1222	1110	Cash		1020.00
04/14	C1223	2110	AP/Mcbride Beauty Supply	2646.19	
04/14	C1223	1110	Cash		2593.27
04/14	C1223	5120	Purchases Discount		52.92
04/16	C1224	2110	AP/Kay & Harris Hair Product	4470.50	
04/16	C1224	1110	Cash		4425.79
04/16	C1224	5120	Purchases Discount		44.71
04/18	C1225	6180	Rent Expense	2000.00	
04/18	C1225	1110	Cash		2000.00
04/20	C1226	2110	AP/Anello Supply Depot	861.90	
04/20	C1226	1110	Cash		844.66
04/20	C1226	5120	Purchases Discount		17.24
04/21	C1227	2110	AP/Huber Manufacturing Co.	4939.65	
04/21	C1227	1110	Cash		4890.25
04/21	C1227	5120	Purchases Discount		49.40
04/26	C1228	2110	AP/Sterling Corporation	2186.34	
04/26	C1228	1110	Cash		2186.34
04/26	M40	6120	Credit Card Fee Expense	230.53	
04/26	M40	1110	Cash		230.53
04/27	C1229	2110	AP/Mcbride Beauty Supply	4104.57	
04/27	C1229	1110	Cash		4063.52
04/27	C1229	5120	Purchases Discount		41.05
04/30	C1230	6190	Salaries Expense	9723.62	
04/30	C1230	1110	Cash		5569.33
04/30	C1230	2130	Employee Income Tax Pay.		2128.61
04/30	C1230	2150	FICA Tax Payable		602.86
04/30	C1230	2160	Medicare Tax Payable		141.00
04/30	C1230	2190	Health Ins. Premium Pay.		992.00
04/30	C1230	2200	Disability Insurance Pay.		289.82
04/30	C1231	1150	Supplies—Office	36.97	
04/30	C1231	1160	Supplies—Store	42.65	
04/30	C1231	6160	Miscellaneous Expense	17.08	
04/30	C1231	1110	Cash		96.70
			Totals	53672.43	53672.43

Figure 9.17—Cont'd Cash Payments Journal Report ▶

TUTORIAL PROBLEM 9 - T

Abbott Cosmetic Corp.
Sales Journal
04/30/--

Date	Inv. No.	Acct.	Title	Debit	Credit
04/03	S733	1130	AR/Tina's Fashion Salon	6931.70	
04/03	S733	4110	Sales		6931.70
04/11	S734	1130	AR/Debbie's Hair Design	7149.65	
04/11	S734	4110	Sales		7149.65
04/16	S735	1130	AR/Sunshine Tanning & Salon	6101.67	
04/16	S735	4110	Sales		6101.67
04/17	S736	1130	AR/Burgess Salon	6225.00	
04/17	S736	4110	Sales		6225.00
04/19	S737	1130	AR/Anita Graham	109.40	
04/19	S737	4110	Sales		102.24
04/19	S737	2120	Sales Tax Payable		7.16
04/25	S738	1130	AR/Nail & Hair Care	5085.09	
04/25	S738	4110	Sales		5085.09
			Totals	31602.51	31602.51

Figure 9.18
Sales Journal Report

Abbott Cosmetic Corp.
Cash Receipts Journal
04/30/--

Date	Refer.	Acct.	Title	Debit	Credit
04/05	R653	1110	Cash	3650.90	
04/05	R653	4120	Sales Discount	36.88	
04/05	R653	1130	AR/Burgess Salon		3687.78
04/05	R654	1110	Cash	5024.00	
04/05	R654	4120	Sales Discount	50.75	
04/05	R654	1130	AR/Polly's Hair Styles		5074.75
04/07	R655	1110	Cash	4116.93	
04/07	R655	4120	Sales Discount	41.59	
04/07	R655	1130	AR/Nail & Hair Care		4158.52
04/14	R656	1110	Cash	4209.75	
04/14	R656	4120	Sales Discount	42.52	
04/14	R656	1130	AR/Dorsey Boutique		4252.27
04/20	R657	1110	Cash	5749.70	
04/20	R657	1130	AR/Noble's Beauty Shop		5749.70
04/21	T40	1110	Cash	24198.86	
04/21	T40	4110	Sales		22615.76
04/21	T40	2120	Sales Tax Payable		1583.10
			Totals	47121.88	47121.88

Figure 9.19
Cash Receipts Journal Report

TUTORIAL   PROBLEM   9 – T

STEP 12:   **Display a trial balance, a schedule of accounts payable, a schedule of accounts receivable, and the statements of account.**
Choose the *Ledger Reports* option and select and display each of the following reports: trial balance, schedule of accounts payable, schedule of accounts receivable, and statements of account. The reports are shown in Figures 9.20 through 9.22, and Figure 9.23 shows the first statement of account.

You may wish to print the trial balance report to use as the basis for recording the adjusting entries.

STEP 13:   **Enter the adjusting entries from the general journal shown in Figure 9.24.**
Click the *Journal* toolbar button. When the Journal Entries window appears, click the *General Journal* tab and enter the adjusting entries. The adjustment data for the month of April for Abbott Cosmetic Corp. is listed below.

Merchandise inventory $64,100.00
Office supplies inventory $1,600.00
Store supplies inventory $880.00
Value of insurance policies on April 30 . . . . . $975.89
Depreciation for the month:
    Office Equipment $198.86
    Store Equipment $155.00
Estimated federal income tax $350.00

TUTORIAL PROBLEM 9 - T

Abbott Cosmetic Corp.
Trial Balance
04/30/--

Acct. Number	Account Title	Debit	Credit
1110	Cash	11841.59	
1120	Petty Cash	100.00	
1130	Accounts Receivable	47577.78	
1140	Merchandise Inventory	62064.00	
1150	Supplies—Office	2193.49	
1160	Supplies—Store	1223.95	
1170	Prepaid Insurance	1150.00	
1510	Office Equipment	14084.06	
1520	Accum. Depr.—Ofc. Eqpt.		2386.25
1530	Store Equipment	9104.06	
1540	Accum. Depr.—Store Eqpt.		1867.50
2110	Accounts Payable		34087.35
2120	Sales Tax Payable		1590.26
2130	Employee Income Tax Pay.		2128.61
2150	FICA Tax Payable		1205.72
2160	Medicare Tax Payable		282.00
2170	Unemploy. Tax Pay.—Fed.		116.26
2180	Unemploy. Tax Pay.—State		38.75
2190	Health Ins. Premium Pay.		992.00
2200	Disability Insurance Pay.		289.82
3110	Capital Stock		73000.00
3120	Retained Earnings		19780.00
3130	Dividends	3100.00	
3140	Income Summary	920.65	
4110	Sales		210502.24
4120	Sales Discount	1783.98	
4130	Sales Returns & Allow.	2753.27	
5110	Purchases	134675.35	
5120	Purchases Discount		1792.76
5130	Purch. Returns & Allow.		2554.12
6110	Advertising Expense	2877.68	
6120	Credit Card Fee Expense	957.31	
6130	Depr. Exp.—Office Eqpt.	596.56	
6140	Depr. Exp.—Store Eqpt.	466.88	
6150	Insurance Expense	496.08	
6160	Miscellaneous Expense	421.47	
6170	Payroll Taxes Expense	3119.72	
6180	Rent Expense	8000.00	
6190	Salaries Expense	38754.43	
6200	Supplies Expense—Office	229.46	
6210	Supplies Expense—Store	203.94	
6220	Utilities Expense	2890.81	
9110	Federal Income Tax Exp.	1027.12	
	Totals	352613.64	352613.64

Figure 9.20
Trial Balance

Abbott Cosmetic Corp.
Schedule of Accounts Payable
04/30/--

Name	Balance
Anello Supply Depot	815.92
Haskins Chemical Co.	6100.43
Huber Manufacturing Co.	5197.98
Kay & Harris Hair Products	3596.63
Perry Salon Supplies	8777.74
Sterling Corporation	5136.05
Tilton & Ruffin Corp.	4462.60
Total	34087.35

Figure 9.21
Schedule of
Accounts Payable

Abbott Cosmetic Corp.
Schedule of Accounts Receivable
04/30/--

Name	Balance
Anita Graham	109.40
Burgess Salon	6225.00
Debbie's Hair Design	9952.71
Nail & Hair Care	5085.09
Studio 10 Styling Salon	3535.30
Sunshine Tanning & Salon	9423.07
Tina's Fashion Salon	13247.21
Total	47577.78

Figure 9.22
Schedule of
Accounts
Receivable

One widely used tool to ensure Internet security is the firewall. A firewall is software or a hardware/software combination that lets authorized users into or out of a system and keeps out everyone else.

TUTORIAL PROBLEM 9-T

STATEMENT OF ACCOUNT
Abbott Cosmetic Corp.

To: Anita Graham   Date 04/30/--

Date	Reference	Description	Charges	Credits	Balance
04/01/--		Balance Forward			.00
04/19/--	S737	Invoice	109.40		109.40

Figure 9.23
Statement of Account for Anita Graham

Date	Refer.	Acct. No.	Debit	Credit	Vendor/Customer
04/30/--	Adj.Ent.	1140	2036.00		
		3140		2036.00	
04/30/--	Adj.Ent.	6200	593.49		
		1150		593.49	
04/30/--	Adj.Ent.	6210	343.95		
		1160		343.95	
04/30/--	Adj.Ent.	6150	174.11		
		1170		174.11	
04/30/--	Adj.Ent.	6130	198.86		
		1520		198.86	
04/30/--	Adj.Ent.	6140	155.00		
		1540		155.00	
04/30/--	Adj.Ent.	9110	350.00		
		2140		350.00	

Figure 9.24
Adjusting Entries

T U T O R I A L   P R O B L E M   9 – T

STEP 14: **Display the adjusting entries.**
Click the *Reports* toolbar button. Choose the *Journals* option button, then select the *General Journal* report and click *OK*. When the Journal Report Selection window appears, choose the *Customize Journal Report* option and enter a Reference restriction of Adj.Ent. so that only the adjusting entries are reported. The report appears in Figure 9.25.

Abbott Cosmetic Corp.
General Journal
04/30/--

Date	Refer.	Acct.	Title	Debit	Credit
04/30	Adj.Ent.	1140	Merchandise Inventory	2036.00	
04/30	Adj.Ent.	3140	Income Summary		2036.00
04/30	Adj.Ent.	6200	Supplies Expense—Office	593.49	
04/30	Adj.Ent.	1150	Supplies—Office		593.49
04/30	Adj.Ent.	6210	Supplies Expense—Store	343.95	
04/30	Adj.Ent.	1160	Supplies—Store		343.95
04/30	Adj.Ent.	6150	Insurance Expense	174.11	
04/30	Adj.Ent.	1170	Prepaid Insurance		174.11
04/30	Adj.Ent.	6130	Depr. Exp.—Office Eqpt.	198.86	
04/30	Adj.Ent.	1520	Accum. Depr.—Ofc. Eqpt.		198.86
04/30	Adj.Ent.	6140	Depr. Exp.—Store Eqpt.	155.00	
04/30	Adj.Ent.	1540	Accum. Depr.—Store Eqpt.		155.00
04/30	Adj.Ent.	9110	Federal Income Tax Exp.	350.00	
04/30	Adj.Ent.	2140	Federal Income Tax Pay.		350.00
			Totals	3851.41	3851.41

Figure 9.25
General Journal Report (Adjusting Entries)

STEP 15: **Display a general ledger report for the Cash account.**
Choose the *Ledger Reports* option and select the *General Ledger* report. When the General Ledger Account Range window appears, select an account number range of 1110 to 1110, and click *OK*. The report is shown in Figure 9.26.

TUTORIAL PROBLEM 9 – T

Abbott Cosmetic Corp.
General Ledger
04/30/--

Account	Journal	Date	Refer.	Debit	Credit	Balance
1110-Cash						
	Balance Forward					14155.73Dr
	Cash Receipts	04/05	R653	3650.90		17806.63Dr
	Cash Receipts	04/05	R654	5024.00		22830.63Dr
	Cash Payments	04/06	C1212		878.80	21951.83Dr
	Cash Payments	04/06	C1213		523.58	21428.25Dr
	Cash Receipts	04/07	R655	4116.93		25545.18Dr
	Cash Payments	04/09	C1214		1519.05	24026.13Dr
	Cash Payments	04/09	C1215		107.52	23918.61Dr
	Cash Payments	04/10	C1216		1035.99	22882.62Dr
	Cash Payments	04/12	C1217		1250.27	21632.35Dr
	Cash Payments	04/12	C1218		3845.43	17786.92Dr
	Cash Payments	04/12	C1219		3100.00	14686.92Dr
	Cash Payments	04/13	C1220		476.14	14210.78Dr
	Cash Payments	04/13	C1221		8607.11	5603.67Dr
	Cash Payments	04/13	C1222		1020.00	4583.67Dr
	Cash Payments	04/14	C1223		2593.27	1990.40Dr
	Cash Receipts	04/14	R656	4209.75		6200.15Dr^
	Cash Payments	04/16	C1224		4425.79	1774.36Dr
	Cash Payments	04/18	C1225		2000.00	225.64Cr
	Cash Payments	04/20	C1226		844.66	1070.30Cr
	Cash Receipts	04/20	R657	5749.70		4679.40Dr
	Cash Payments	04/21	C1227		4890.25	210.85Cr
	Cash Receipts	04/21	T40	24198.86		23988.01Dr
	Cash Payments	04/26	C1228		2186.34	21801.67Dr
	Cash Payments	04/26	M40		230.53	21571.14Dr
	Cash Payments	04/27	C1229		4063.52	17507.62Dr
	Cash Payments	04/30	C1230		5569.33	11938.29Dr
	Cash Payments	04/30	C1231		96.70	11841.59Dr

Figure 9.26
General Ledger Report

STEP 16:   **Display the financial statements.**
Choose the *Financial Statements* option, then select and
display each of the following reports: income
statement, balance sheet, and retained earnings
statement. The reports are shown in Figure 9.27.

T U T O R I A L   P R O B L E M   9 – T

Abbott Cosmetic Corp.
Income Statement
For Period Ended 04/30/--

	Monthly Amount	Monthly Percent	Yearly Amount	Yearly Percent
Operating Revenue				
Sales	54211.11	100.45	210502.24	102.20
Sales Discount	−171.74	−0.32	−1783.98	−0.87
Sales Returns & Allow.	−68.42	−0.13	−2753.27	−1.34
Total Operating Revenue	53970.95	100.00	205964.99	100.00
Cost of Merchandise Sold				
Beginning Inventory	62064.00	115.00	62984.65	30.58
Purchases	37480.40	69.45	134675.35	65.39
Purchases Discount	−253.86	−0.47	−1792.76	−0.87
Purch. Returns & Allow.	−229.34	−0.42	−2554.12	−1.24
Merchandise Available for Sale	99061.20	183.55	193313.12	93.86
Less Ending Inventory	−64100.00	−118.77	−64100.00	−31.12
Cost of Merchandise Sold	34961.20	64.78	129213.12	62.74
Gross Profit	19009.75	35.22	76751.87	37.26
Operating Expenses				
Advertising Expense	480.95	0.89	2877.68	1.40
Credit Card Fee Expense	230.53	0.43	957.31	0.46
Depr. Exp.—Office Eqpt.	198.86	0.37	795.42	0.39
Depr. Exp.—Store Eqpt.	155.00	0.29	621.88	0.30
Insurance Expense	174.11	0.32	670.19	0.33
Miscellaneous Expense	124.60	0.23	421.47	0.20
Payroll Taxes Expense	782.75	1.45	3119.72	1.51
Rent Expense	2000.00	3.71	8000.00	3.88
Salaries Expense	9723.62	18.02	38754.43	18.82
Supplies Expense—Office	593.49	1.10	822.95	0.40
Supplies Expense—Store	343.95	0.64	547.89	0.27
Utilities Expense	523.58	0.97	2890.81	1.40
Total Operating Expenses	15331.44	28.41	60479.75	29.36
Net Income from Operations	3678.31	6.82	16272.12	7.90
Net Income before Income Tax	3678.31	6.82	16272.12	7.90
Income Tax				
Federal Income Tax Exp.	350.00	0.65	1377.12	0.67
Net Income after Income Tax	3328.31	6.17	14895.00	7.23

Figure 9.27
Financial
Statements
(cont'd on p. 296)

T U T O R I A L   P R O B L E M   9 – T

Abbott Cosmetic Corp.
Balance Sheet
04/30/--

Assets

Cash	11841.59
Petty Cash	100.00
Accounts Receivable	47577.78
Merchandise Inventory	64100.00
Supplies—Office	1600.00
Supplies—Store	880.00
Prepaid Insurance	975.89
Office Equipment	14084.06
Accum. Depr.—Ofc. Eqpt.	−2585.11
Store Equipment	9104.06
Accum. Depr.—Store Eqpt.	−2022.50

Total Assets   145655.77

Liabilities

Accounts Payable	34087.35
Sales Tax Payable	1590.26
Employee Income Tax Pay.	2128.61
Federal Income Tax Pay.	350.00
FICA Tax Payable	1205.72
Medicare Tax Payable	282.00
Unemploy. Tax Pay.—Fed.	116.26
Unemploy. Tax Pay.—State	38.75
Health Ins. Premium Pay.	992.00
Disability Insurance Pay.	289.82

Total Liabilities   41080.77

Stockholders' Equity

Capital Stock	73000.00
Retained Earnings	19780.00
Dividends	−3100.00
Net Income	14895.00

Total Stockholders' Equity   104575.00

Total Liabilities & Equity   145655.77

Abbott Cosmetic Corp.
Retained Earnings Statement
For Period Ended 04/30/--

Retained Earnings (Beg. of Period)	19780.00
Dividends	−3100.00
Net Income	14895.00
Retained Earnings (End of Period)	31575.00

**Figure 9.27
—Cont'd
Financial
Statements**

T U T O R I A L   P R O B L E M   9 – T

STEP 17:   **Generate an income statement and a balance sheet 3D bar graph.**
Click the *Graphs* toolbar button. Choose the *Income Statement* option, select the *3D Bar* option, then click *OK*. Repeat this procedure to generate the balance sheet bar graph. The bar graphs are shown in Figure 9.28.

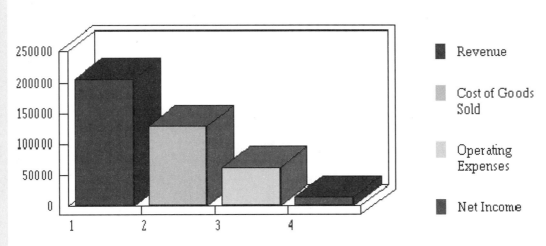

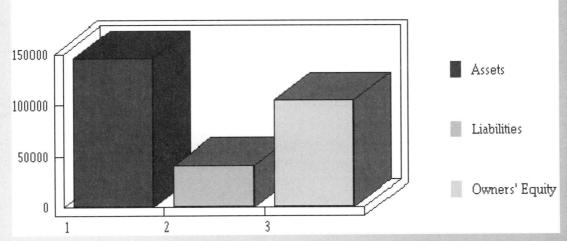

Figure 9.28
Income Statement and Balance Sheet Bar Graphs

TUTORIAL   PROBLEM   9 – T

STEP 18:   **Use the Save menu command to save your data.**
Click the *Save* toolbar button.

STEP 19:   **Calculate maturity dates and interest on notes.**
Use the Notes & Interest planner to calculate the
maturity date, interest, and maturity value for each of
the following notes. Use the current year for the date
of each note.
Choose the *Planning Tools* menu item from the Data
menu or click the *Tools* toolbar button. When the
Planning Tools window appears, click the *Notes &
Interest* tab, enter the data for note 1, and display a note
analysis report. Repeat the procedure for notes 2–5. The
note analysis report shown in Figure 9.29 is for note 1.

Note	Date of Note	Principal of Note	Interest Rate	Time of Note
1	Jan. 6	$5000.00	9.00	30 days (based on 360 days)
2	Mar. 15	6500.00	10.50	1 year (number of months)
3	May 1	2000.00	13.00	60 days (based on 365 days)
4	July 12	1800.00	11.75	6 months (number of months)
5	Sept. 21	4000.00	12.00	90 days (based on 360 days)

Abbott Cosmetic Corp.
Note Analysis
04/30/--

Date of the Note	01/06/--
Time of the Note	30 Days
Principal of the Note	5000.00
Interest Rate of the Note	9.00
Amount of Interest	37.50
Maturity Date of the Note	2/5/--
Maturity Value of the Note	5037.50

Figure 9.29
Note Analysis
(Note 1)

STEP 20:   **Optional spreadsheet and word processing activity:**
In addition to the income statement provided by the
automated accounting software, the manager of the
accounting department for Abbott Cosmetic Corp.
wants a condensed single-step income statement. This
income statement will be distributed to upper
management as a summary of the more detailed
Automated Accounting income statement.

T U T O R I A L   P R O B L E M   9 – T

Subsequent income statements may be pasted into this template file to produce an updated condensed income statement.

Spreadsheet:

a. Display and copy the income statement to the clipboard in spreadsheet format.

b. Start up your spreadsheet software and load template file SS09–T.

c. Select cell A1 and paste the income statement into the spreadsheet.

d. Enter the cell references and formulas to complete the condensed, single-step income statement in cells A61–D83. Note: Earnings per share is calculated by dividing the net income ($3,328.31) by the average number of shares of common stock outstanding (1350).

e. Print the income statement (cells A61–D83). The completed condensed, single-step income statement is shown in Figure 9.30.

f. Save the entire spreadsheet with a file name of XXX9–T.

```
                    Abbott Cosmetic Corp.
                      Income Statement
                  For Period Ended 04/30/--

REVENUE

Net Sales                                       $53,970.95

COSTS AND EXPENSES

Cost of Merchandise Sold    $34,961.20
Operating Expenses          $15,331.44

Total Costs and Expenses                        $50,292.64

INCOME BEFORE TAXES                              $3,678.31

Income Taxes                                       $350.00

NET INCOME                                       $3,328.31

Earnings Per Share                                   $2.47
```

Figure 9.30
Condensed, Single-Step Income Statement (Spreadsheet)

T U T O R I A L   P R O B L E M   9 – T

Word Processing:

a. Start up your word processing software and create a new document. Use a fixed font such as Courier.
b. Copy and paste the completed spreadsheet condensed, single-step income statement (cells A61–D83) into the new document.
c. Format and enhance the document's appearance.
d. Print the document. The completed income statement is shown in Figure 9.31.
e. Save the document with a file name of XXX9–T.
f. End your spreadsheet and word processing sessions.

```
                    Abbott Cosmetic Corp.
                      Income Statement
                   For Period Ended 04/30/--

REVENUE

Net Sales                                    $53,970.95

COSTS AND EXPENSES

Cost of Merchandise Sold     $34,961.20
Operating Expenses            15,331.44
                             ----------
Total Costs and Expenses                      50,292.64
                                             ----------
INCOME BEFORE TAXES                           $3,678.31
Income Taxes                                     350.00
                                             ----------
NET INCOME                                    $3,328.31
                                             ==========
Earnings Per Share                                $2.47
                                             ==========
```

Figure 9.31
Condensed, Single-Step Income Statement (Word Processed)

STEP 21:   End the *Automated Accounting* session.
Click the *Exit/Quit* toolbar button.

Applying Your Information Skills

I. MATCHING

Directions: In the *Working Papers,* write the letter of the appropriate term next to each definition.

> a. corporation
> b. shares of stock
> c. capital stock
> d. shareholders
> e. board of directors
> f. dividends
> g. retained earnings
> h. declaring a dividend
> i. corporate income tax

1. Owners of stock.

2. Units that represent the ownership of a corporation.

3. Earnings not yet distributed to shareholders.

4. The total shares of ownership in a corporation.

5. Earnings distributed to shareholders.

6. An organization that has many of the legal rights of an individual but is owned by many people.

7. A group elected by shareholders to manage a corporation.

8. The tax that corporations are required to pay on actual earnings.

9. The decision by the board of directors to distribute earnings to the shareholders.

II. QUESTIONS

Directions: Write the answers to each of the following questions in the *Working Papers.* Assume that the vendor checks and customer statements on account are being prepared by the computer.

1. What happens if you leave the Vendor field blank for a cash payment?

2. What is the decision by the board of directors of a corporation to distribute earnings to shareholders called?

3. Why is the check to pay dividends written to Shareholders Bank Account?

4. Which account is debited and which account is credited to record the adjusting entry for corporate income tax?

5. The income statement illustrated in this chapter has a percent column next to the monthly amount column and another percent column next to the yearly amount column. What do these percents represent?

P   Independent Practice Problem 9–P

In this problem, you will process the monthly transactions, generate vendor checks, generate customer statements of account, and complete the end-of-month processing for Abbott Cosmetic Corp. for the month of May of the current year. As you complete the problem, refer to the chart of accounts, vendor list, and customer list stored in problem AA09–P. Also, complete the Applying Your Technology Skills 9–P questions as you progress through the problem.

STEP 1:   Start up *Automated Accounting 7.0.*

STEP 2:   Load the opening balances file AA09–P.

STEP 3:   Enter your name in the User Name text box.

STEP 4:   Use the *Save As* command to save the opening balances file with a file name of XXX9–P.

STEP 5:   Enter the May transaction data.

May 01   Received cash on account from Nail & Hare Care, $5,034.24, covering S738 for $5,085.09, less 1% discount, $50.85. R658.

01   Purchased merchandise on account from Mcbride Beauty Supply, $5,291.04. P509.

02   Received cash on account from Anita Graham, $109.40, no discount. R659.

03   Paid cash on account to Huber Manufacturing Co., $5,146.00, covering P506 for $5,197.98, less 1% discount, $51.98. C1232.

03   Received cash on account from Sunshine Tanning & Salon, $9,423.07, covering S729 and S735, no discount. R660.

04   Purchased merchandise on account from Tilton & Ruffin Corp., $7,081.08. P510.

05   Paid cash on account to Kay & Harris Hair Products, $3,560.66, covering P507 for $3,596.63, less 1% discount, $35.97. C1233.

07 Purchased merchandise on account from Perry Salon Supplies, $259.25. P511.

08 Paid cash on account to Tilton & Ruffin Corp., $4,417.97, covering P508 for $4,462.60, less 1% discount, $44.63. C1234.

08 Paid cash to Eastern Utilities Co. for electric bill, $500.39. C1235.

09 Returned merchandise to Haskins Chemical Co., $1,625.14, against P501. DM40.

10 Paid cash on account to Mcbride Beauty Supply, $5,185.22, covering P509 for $5,291.04, less 2% discount, $105.82. C1236.

11 Purchased merchandise on account from Huber Manufacturing Co., $6,344.07. P512.

11 Received cash on account from Tina's Fashion Salon, $13,247.21, covering S724 and S733, no discount. R661.

12 Paid cash to Armor Insurance Assoc. for liability insurance, $494.78. C1237.

12 Paid cash on account to Tilton & Ruffin Corp., $7,010.27, covering P510 for $7,081.08, less 1% discount, $70.81. C1238.

14 Sold merchandise on account to Dorsey Boutique, $3,323.45. S739.

16 Granted credit to Burgess Salon for merchandise returned, $2,656.30, against S736. CM29.

17 Paid cash on account to Perry Salon Supplies, $2,891.79, covering P499 less DM39. C1239.

18 Purchased merchandise on account from Mcbride Beauty Supply, $5,009.12. P513.

19 Sold merchandise on account to Polly's Hair Styles, $2,195.74. S740.

19 Paid cash to Hampton Leasing, Inc. for monthly rent, $2,000.00. C1240.

21 Paid cash on account to Huber Manufacturing Co., $6,280.63, covering P511 for $6,344.07, less 1% discount, $63.44. C1241.

22 Bought office supplies on account from Anello Supply Depot, $95.20. M42.

23 Received cash on account from Dorsey Boutique, $3,290.22, covering S739 for $3,323.45, less 1% discount, $33.23. R662.

24 Bought store supplies on account from Anello Supply Depot, $214.45. M43.

25 Sold merchandise on account to Anita Graham, $74.92, plus sales tax, $5.24; total, $80.16. S741.

25   Received cash on account from Polly's Hair Styles, $2,173.78, covering S740 for $2,195.74, less 1% discount, $21.96. R663.

26   Paid cash on account to Mcbride Beauty Supply, $4,908.94, covering P513 for $5,009.12, less 2% discount, $100.18. C1242.

28   Sold merchandise on account to Noble's Beauty Shop, $8,953.45. S742.

28   Recorded credit card fee expense for April, $484.77. M44.

29   Sold merchandise on account to Sunshine Tanning & Salon, $6,454.39. S743.

29   Recorded cash and credit card sales, $22,709.90, plus sales tax, $1,589.69; total, $24,299.59. T41.

30   Paid cash on account to Haskins Chemical Co., $1,943.46, covering P491, no discount. C1243.

30   Purchased merchandise on account from Kay & Harris Hair Products, $8,975.75. P514.

31   Sold merchandise on account to Tina's Fashion Salon, $6,224.04. S744.

31   Paid cash to Payroll Bank Account for monthly payroll, $5,016.35. Total payroll, $8,952.62, less deductions: employee income tax, $1,969.58; FICA tax, $555.06; Medicare tax, $129.81; health insurance premium, $992.00; disability insurance premium, $289.82. C1244.

31   Recorded employee payroll taxes expense, $720.68 (FICA tax, $555.06; Medicare tax, $129.81; federal unemployment tax, $26.86; state unemployment tax, $8.95). M45. Record this transaction in the General Journal.

31   Paid cash to Petty Cash Custodian to replenish petty cash fund, $84.37: office supplies, $6.18; store supplies, $23.84; miscellaneous expense, $54.35. C1245.

STEP 6:   **Display the general, purchases, cash payments, sales, and cash receipts journal reports for the month of May. If errors are detected, make corrections using the respective journal data entry window.**

CHECK FIGURE:
Trial balance debit and
credit totals =
$402,545.64

STEP 7:   **Display a trial balance, schedule of accounts payable, schedule of accounts receivable, and statements of account.**

STEP 8:   Enter the adjusting entries. Use a reference of Adj.Ent. The adjustment data for the month of May for Abbott Cosmetic Corp. follows:

Merchandise inventory	$65,050.00
Office supplies inventory	$780.00
Store supplies inventory	$725.00
Value of insurance policies on May 31	$1,050.00
Depreciation for the month:	
Office Equipment	$198.86
Store Equipment	$155.00
Estimated federal income tax	$350.00

STEP 9:   Display the general journal report for the adjusting entries. Use a reference restriction of Adj.Ent. so that only adjusting entries will be included on the report.

STEP 10:   Display a general ledger report for the Cash account.

STEP 11:   Display the financial statements.

STEP 12:   Generate a sales line graph.

STEP 13:   Save your data.

CHECK FIGURE:
Income statement
monthly net income =
$2,109.20

STEP 14:   Calculate maturity dates and interest on notes. Use the Notes & Interest planner to calculate the maturity date, interest, and maturity value for each of the following notes. Use the current year for the date of each note.

Note	Date of Note	Principal of Note	Interest Rate	Time of Note
1	Jan. 15	$3000.00	10.50	60 days (based on 360 days)
2	Mar. 15	1500.00	9.00	30 days (based on 365 days)
3	June 1	2200.00	11.35	1 year (number of months)
4	Aug. 21	900.00	11.75	6 months (number of months)
5	Nov. 11	3500.00	12.25	120 days (based on 360 days)

STEP 15:   Optional spreadsheet and word processing activity: Create a condensed, single-step income statement that can be distributed to upper management as a summary of the more detailed *Automated Accounting* income statement.

Spreadsheet:

a. Display and copy the income statement to the clipboard in spreadsheet format.
b. Start up your spreadsheet software and load template file SS09–T. If you completed the optional spreadsheet activity in Tutorial Problem 9–T, load your spreadsheet solution file instead.
c. Select cell A1 and paste the *Automated Accounting* income statement into the spreadsheet.
d. Enter the cell references and formulas to complete the condensed, single-step income statement in cells A61–D83. Use Figure 9.30 as a guide.
    Note: Earnings per share is calculated by dividing the net income ($2,109.20) by the average number of shares of common stock outstanding (1350).
e. Print the completed income statement.
f. Save the entire spreadsheet with a file name of XXX9–P.

Word Processing:

a. Start up your word processing software and create a new document. Use a fixed font such as Courier.
b. Copy and paste the completed spreadsheet condensed, single-step income statement into the new document.
c. Format and enhance the document's appearance. Use Figure 9.31 as a guide.
d. Print the document.
e. Save the document with a file name of XXX9–P.
f. End your spreadsheet and word processing sessions.

STEP 16:   End the *Automated Accounting* session.

P Applying Your Technology Skills 9–P

Directions: Using Independent Practice Problem 9–P, write the answers to the following questions in the *Working Papers.*

Journals:

1. What is the amount of the debit to payroll taxes expense?

2. What is the amount of purchase invoice no. 509 to Mcbride Beauty Supply?

3. What is the total of the debit column on the cash payments journal?

4. What is the amount of sales invoice no. 743 to Sunshine Tanning & Salon?

5. What is the total of the credit column on the cash receipts journal?

Schedules of Accounts Payable and Receivable:

6. What is the amount owed to Haskins Chemical Co.?

7. What is the amount due from all customers?

Checks and Statements of Account:

8. What is the net amount paid to Haskins Chemical Co. with check no. 1243?

9. What is the amount due from Tina's Fashion Salon?

General Ledger Report:

10. What was the cash balance as of May 30?

11. What is the ending balance in the Cash account?

Financial Statements:

12. What are the sales for the year?

13. What are the sales for the month?

14. What are the purchases for the year as a percent of total operating revenue?

15. What are the total operating expenses for the month as a percent of total operating revenue?

16. What are the total assets?

17. What is the total stockholders' equity?

18. What is the amount of retained earnings at the end of the month?

Notes & Interest:

19. What is the maturity date, interest, and maturity value of note 1?

20. What is the maturity date, interest, and maturity value of note 2?

21. What is the maturity date, interest, and maturity value of note 3?

22. What is the maturity date, interest, and maturity value of note 4?

23. What is the maturity date, interest, and maturity value of note 5?

Mastery Problem 9–M

In this problem, you will process the monthly transactions, generate vendor checks, generate customer monthly statements of account, and

complete the end-of-month processing for Abbott Cosmetic Corp. for the month of June of the current year. As you complete this problem, refer to the chart of accounts, vendor list, and customer list stored with problem AA09–M when entering journal transactions. Also, complete the Applying Your Technology Skills 9–M questions as you progress through the problem.

STEP 1:   **Load the opening balances file AA09–M.**

STEP 2:   **Enter your name in the User Name text box.**

STEP 3:   **Save the opening balances file with a file name of XXX9–M.**

STEP 4:   **Enter the June transaction data.**

June 01   Received cash on account from Anita Graham, $80.16, no discount. R664.

02   Sold merchandise on account to Polly's Hair Styles, $7,914.12. S745.

04   Granted credit to Debbie's Hair Design for merchandise returned, $1,514.78, against S737. CM30.

06   Purchased merchandise on account from Huber Manufacturing Co., $7,986.78. P515.

06   Paid cash to Eastern Utilities Co. for electric bill, $548.02. C1246.

07   Paid cash to Armor Insurance Assoc. for insurance premium, $960.41. C1247.

08   Received cash on account from Noble's Beauty Shop, $8,863.92, covering S742 for $8,953.45, less 1% discount, $89.53. R665.

09   Received cash on account from Sunshine Tanning & Salon, $6,389.85, covering S743 for $6,454.39, less 1% discount, $64.54. R666.

09   Received cash on account from Tina's Fashion Salon, $6,161.80, covering S744 for $6,224.04, less 1% discount, $62.24. R667.

09   Paid cash on account to Kay & Harris Hair Products, $8,885.99, covering P514 for $8,975.75, less 1% discount, $89.76. C1248.

11   Purchased merchandise on account from Sterling Corporation, $7,072.67. P516.

12   Paid cash to Parsons Cosmetic Supplies for miscellaneous expense, $146.39. C1249.

13   Bought office supplies on account from Anello Supply Depot, $214.07. M46.

15   Paid cash on account to Huber Manufacturing Co., $7,906.91, covering P515 for $7,986.78, less 1% discount, $79.87. C1250.

16   Returned merchandise to Perry Salon Supplies, $1,142.91, against P503. DM41.

18   Sold merchandise on account to Studio 10 Styling Salon, $7,242.94. S746.

19   Paid cash to Hampton Leasing, Inc. for monthly rent, $2,000.00. C1251.

20   Recorded credit card fee expense for May, $514.69. M47.

21   Paid cash on account to Sterling Corporation, $7,001.94, covering P516 for $7,072.67, less 1% discount, $70.73. C1252.

21   Received cash on account from Debbie's Hair Design, $1,288.28, covering S727 less CM30, no discount. R668.

22   Sold merchandise on account to Nail & Hair Care, $7,277.19. S747.

23   Purchased merchandise on account from Tilton & Ruffin Corp., $8,172.00. P517.

25   Bought advertising on account from Caplan Marketing, $600.00. M48.

25   Sold merchandise on account to Anita Graham, $68.32, plus sales tax, $4.78; total, $73.10. S748.

26   Bought store equipment on account from Anello Supply Depot, $425.21. M49.

27   Paid cash on account to Haskins Chemical Co., $2,531.83, covering P501 less DM40, no discount. C1253.

28   Bought store supplies on account from Anello Supply Depot, $206.92. M50.

30   Paid cash to Payroll Bank Account for monthly payroll, $4,737.66. Total payroll, $8,379.06, less deductions: employee income tax, $1,843.39; FICA tax, $519.50; Medicare tax, $121.49; health insurance premium, $914.14; disability insurance premium, $242.88. C1254.

30   Recorded employee payroll taxes expense, $674.50 (FICA tax, $519.50; Medicare tax, $121.49; federal unemployment tax, $25.13; state unemployment tax, $8.38). M51.

30   Paid cash to Petty Cash Custodian to replenish petty cash fund, $93.40: office supplies, $76.13; store supplies, $17.27. C1255.

30   Recorded cash and credit card sales,
$18,753.22, plus sales tax, $1,312.73; total,
$20,065.95. T50.

STEP 5:   **Display the journal reports.**

STEP 6:   **Display the trial balance, schedule of accounts payable,
schedule of accounts receivable, and statements of account.**

STEP 7:   **Enter the adjusting entries. The adjustment data for the
month of June for Abbott Cosmetic Corp. follows:**

Merchandise inventory	$63,025.00
Office supplies inventory	$880.00
Store supplies inventory	$450.00
Value of insurance policies on June 30	$985.00
Depreciation for the month:	
Office Equipment	$198.86
Store Equipment	$160.00
Estimated federal income tax	$350.00

STEP 8:   **Display the adjusting entries.**

STEP 9:   **Display a general ledger report for the Cash account.**

STEP 10:   **Display the financial statements.**

STEP 11:   **Generate an income statement 3D bar graph and a sales
line graph.**

STEP 12:   **Save your data.**

STEP 13:   **Calculate maturity dates and interest on notes. Use the
Notes & Interest planner to calculate the maturity date,
interest, and maturity value for each of the following
notes. Use the current year for the date of each note.**

The income
statement bar
graph depicts the
yearly account
balances, not the
monthly balances.

Note	Date of Note	Principal of Note	Interest Rate	Time of Note
1	Feb. 1	$1800.00	11.00	30 days (based on 365 days)
2	Apr. 15	3600.00	8.75	60 days (based on 365 days)
3	Sept. 25	1950.00	13.00	120 days (based on 360 days)
4	Oct. 1	4200.00	12.75	1 year (number of months)

STEP 14:   **Optional spreadsheet and word processing activity:**
Create a condensed, single-step income statement. Then
use a word processor to format and enhance its
appearance for management.

Spreadsheet:

a. Start up your spreadsheet software and load template file SS09–T. If you completed the optional spreadsheet activity in Tutorial Problem 9–T or Independent Practice Problem 9–P, load your spreadsheet solution file instead.

b. Select cell A1 and copy and paste the *Automated Accounting* income statement into the spreadsheet.

c. Enter the cell references and formulas to complete the condensed, single-step income statement in cells A61–D83. Use Figure 9.30 as a guide.
Note: Calculate the earnings per share by dividing the net income by the number of shares of common stock outstanding (1350).

d. Print the completed income statement and save it with a file name of XXX9–M.

Word Processing:

a. Copy and paste the spreadsheet condensed income statement into a new document.

b. Format and enhance the document's appearance. Use Figure 9.31 as a guide.

c. Print the document and save it with a file name of XXX9–M.

d. End your spreadsheet and word processing sessions.

STEP 15: **End the *Automated Accounting* session.**

Applying Your Technology Skills 9–M

Directions: Using Mastery Problem 9–M, write the answers to the following questions in the *Working Papers*.

Journals:

1. What is the amount of the credit to FICA Tax Payable?

2. What is the amount of purchase invoice no. 515 to Huber Manufacturing Co.?

3. What is the total of the debit column on the cash payments journal?

4. What is the amount of sales invoice no. 746 to Studio 10 Styling Salon?

5. What is the total of the credit column on the cash receipts journal?

Schedules of Accounts Payable and Receivable:
6. What is the amount owed to Anello Supply Depot?

7. What is the amount due from all customers?

Checks and Statements of Account:
8. What is the net amount paid to Kay & Harris Products on check no. 1248?

9. What is the amount of credit memo no. 30 to Debbie's Hair Design?

General Ledger Report:
10. What is the ending balance in the Cash account?

Financial Statements:
11. What are the sales for the year?

12. What are the sales discounts for the month?

13. What is cost of goods sold for the year as a percent of total operating revenue?

14. What is the advertising expense for the month as a percent of total operating revenue?

15. What are the total assets?

16. What are the total liabilities?

17. What is the amount of retained earnings at the end of the month?

Notes & Interest:
18. What is the maturity date, interest, and maturity value of note 1?

19. What is the maturity date, interest, and maturity value of note 2?

20. What is the maturity date, interest, and maturity value of note 3?

21. What is the maturity date, interest, and maturity value of note 4?

E-mail is probably the most widely used feature of the Internet. Although this communication method is much faster than using postal service, it doesn't provide the same level of interaction as a telephone conversation does.

Reinforcement Activity R–3

In this problem, you will process the monthly transactions, generate vendor checks, generate monthly statements of account, and complete the end-of-month processing for Chateau Mfg. Corporation.

STEP 1: **Start up *Automated Accounting 7.0*.**

STEP 2: **Load the opening balances file AAR–3.**

STEP 3: **Enter your name in the User Name text box.**

STEP 4: **Use Save As to save the opening balances file with a file name of XXXR–3.**

STEP 5: **Add Bette Griffey to the customer list.**

STEP 6: **Enter the transaction data. Abbreviate the reference numbers as follows: Purchase Invoice No., P; Check No., C; Sales Invoice No., S; Cash Receipt No., R; Memorandums, M; Cash Receipts Tape, T. When entering the transactions, refer to the chart of accounts, vendor list, and customer list stored with template file AAR–3. Also, complete the Applying Your Technology Skills R–3 questions as you progress through the problem.**

Apr. 01 Paid cash on account to Reister Fireplace Co., $34,521.19, covering P2244 for $34,869.89, less 1% discount, $348.70. C4073.

01 Purchased merchandise on account from Rawls Corporation, $57,495.13. P2249.

02 Paid cash to Santos & Santos, Inc. for miscellaneous expense, $343.22. C4074.

02 Received cash on account from Lockwood Accessories, $50,687.44, covering S3811 for $51,199.43, less 1% discount, $511.99. R825.

03 Paid cash on account to Corbett, Inc., $52,294.81, covering P2245 for $52,823.04, less 1% discount, $528.23. C4075.

04 Received cash on account from Elder Fireplace Shop, $56,716.57, covering S3818 for $57,289.46, less 1% discount, $572.89. R826.

04 Paid cash on account to Rawls Corporation, $40,725.13, covering S2241 for $41,136.50 less 1% discount, $411.37. C4076.

06 Received cash on account from Vogel Fireplaces & Mantels $39,687.38, covering

S3820 for $40,088.26, less 1% discount, $400.88. R827.

07 Purchased merchandise on account from Wenzel Manufacturing, Inc., $53,341.79. P2250.

07 Paid cash on account to Bentson Office Products, $7,091.78, covering P2247, no discount. C4077.

08 Received cash on account from Valley View Fireplaces, $31,117.07, covering S3816 for $31,431.38, less 1% discount, $314.31. R828.

09 Sold merchandise on account to Fireplace Plus, Inc., $121,369.13. S3821.

09 Paid cash on account to Schooley Mfg., Inc., $66,899.80, covering P2246 for $68,265.10, less 2% discount, $1,365.30. C4078.

09 Returned merchandise to Tillman & Hubbell Co., $10,963.86, against P2240. DM225.

10 Paid cash on account to Rawls Corporation, $56,920.18, covering P2249 for $57,495.13, less 1% discount, $574.95. C4079.

10 Granted credit to Alsip Patio & Hearth for merchandise returned, $7,221.70, against S3812. CM211.

10 Bought office supplies on account from Bentson Office Products, $1,572.66. M266.

11 Purchased merchandise on account from Tillman & Hubbell Co., $42,247.28. P2251.

11 Sold merchandise on account to Valley View Fireplaces, $117,400.14. S3822.

13 Paid cash to Commissioner of Revenue for March sales tax, $4,882.69. C4080.

14 Purchased merchandise on account from Schooley Mfg., Inc., $61,251.60. P2252.

15 Granted credit to Fireplace Plus, Inc. for merchandise returned, $8,354.78, against S3814. CM212.

15 Paid cash to Poppel Insurance Agency for liability for March insurance premiums: health insurance, $13,454.05; disability insurance, $5,381.62; total, $18,835.67. C4081.

15 Paid cash to Internal Revenue Service for payroll taxes: employee income tax, $37,671.28; FICA tax, $11,122.00; and Medicare tax, $2,601.11; total, $51,394.39. C4082.

15 Paid cash to Internal Revenue Service for quarterly estimated federal income tax, $15,600. C4083.

16   Bought store supplies on account from Bentson Office Products, $1,886.26. M267.

16   Sold merchandise on account to Elder Fireplace Shop, $133,569.14. S3823.

17   Received cash on account from Alsip Patio & Hearth, $47,692.31, covering S3812 less CM211, no discount. R829.

17   Paid cash to Northeast Utilities Co. for electric bill, $1,516.27. C4084.

17   Paid cash on account to Wenzel Manufacturing, Inc., $52,808.37, covering P2250 for $53,341.79, less 1% discount, $533.42. C4085.

18   Received cash on account from Fireplace Plus, Inc., $120,155.44, covering S3821 for $121,369.13, less 1% discount, $1,213.69. R830.

18   Purchased merchandise on account from Corbett, Inc., $62,422.33. P2253.

18   Paid cash to Superior Leasing Co. for monthly rent, $5,000.00. C4086.

18   Returned merchandise to Wenzel Manufacturing, Inc., $5,333.99, against P2242. DM226.

20   Sold merchandise on account to Bette Griffey, $16,701.41, plus sales tax, $1,169.10; total, $17,870.51. S3824.

20   Paid cash on account to Tillman & Hubbell Co., $15,194.96, covering P2240 less DM225, no discount. C4087.

20   Purchased merchandise on account from Reister Fireplace Co., $41,855.84. P2254.

20   Bought advertising on account from Engel Marketing, Inc., $4,613.98. M268.

21   Received cash on account from Valley View Fireplaces, $116,226.14, covering S3822 for $117,400.14, less 1% discount, $1,174.00. R831.

21   Paid cash on account to Tillman & Hubbell Co., $41,824.81, covering P2251 for $42,247.28, less 1% discount, $422.47. C4088.

22   Paid cash to Shareholders Bank Account for first quarter dividends declared in March, $94,000.00. C4089.

22   Received cash on account from Berryhill Fireplace Co., $27,564.33, no discount. R832.

22   Granted credit to Western Hills Fireplaces for merchandise returned, $7,367.45, against S3813. CM213.

23   Bought store equipment on account from Bentson Office Products, $5,228.51. M269.

23 Sold merchandise on account to Vogel Fireplaces & Mantels, $130,054.95. S3825.

24 Paid cash on account to Schooley Mfg., Inc., $60,026.57, covering P2252 for $61,251.60, less 2% discount, $1,225.03. C4090.

24 Received cash on account from Fireplace Plus, Inc., $40,676.48, covering S3814 less CM212, no discount. R833.

25 Bought office equipment on account from Bentson Office Products, $6,327.69. M270.

25 Received cash on account from Elder Fireplace Shop, $132,233.45, covering S3823 for $133,569.14, less 1% discount, $1,335.69. R834.

25 Sold merchandise on account to Berryhill Fireplace Co., $125,792.15. S3826.

25 Purchased merchandise on account from Rawls Corporation, $79,128.25. P2255.

25 Recorded credit card fee expense for March, $631.14. M271.

27 Received cash on account from Bruce Duncan, $5,218.81, against S3819, no discount. R835.

27 Paid cash on account to Corbett, Inc., $61,798.11, covering P2253 for $62,422.33, less 1% discount, $624.22. C4091.

27 Paid cash on account to Wenzel Manufacturing, Inc., $34,520.40, covering P2242 less DM226, no discount. C4092.

27 Returned merchandise to Pucci Manufacturing, Co., $9,276.32, against P2248. DM227.

28 Purchased merchandise on account from Schooley Mfg., Inc., $70,980.84. P2256.

28 Purchased merchandise on account from Corbett, Inc., $87,475.99. P2257.

29 Paid cash on account to Reister Fireplace Co., $41,437.28, covering P2254 for $41,855.84, less 1% discount, $418.56. C4093.

29 Sold merchandise on account to Alsip Patio & Hearth, $63,234.07. S3827.

29 Sold merchandise on account to Bruce Duncan, $6,273.88, plus sales tax, $439.17; total, $6,713.05. S3828.

30 Paid cash to Payroll Bank Account for monthly payroll, $109,156.98. Total payroll, $179,387.04, less deductions: employee income tax, $37,671.28; FICA tax, $11,122.00; Medicare tax, $2,601.11; health insurance premium,

$13,454.05; disability insurance premium, $5,381.62. C4094.

30 Recorded employer payroll taxes expense, $19,284.11 (FICA tax, $11,122.00; Medicare tax, $2,601.11; federal unemployment tax, $717.55; state unemployment tax, $4,843.45). M272. Record this transaction in the General Journal.

30 Paid cash to Petty Cash Account to replenish petty cash fund, $187.05: office supplies, $109.16; store supplies, $60.54; miscellaneous expense, $17.35. C4095.

30 Received cash on account from Berryhill Fireplace Co., $124,534.23, covering S3826 for $125,792.15, less 1% discount, $1,257.92. R836.

30 Paid cash on account to Engel Marketing, Inc., $4,567.84, covering M268 for $4,613.98, less 1% discount, $46.14. C4096.

30 Recorded cash and credit card sales, $97,530.62, plus sales tax, $6,827.14; total, $104,357.76. T40.

STEP 7: Display the general, purchases, cash payments, sales, and cash receipts journal reports for the period April 1 to April 30 of the current year. If errors are detected, make corrections.

STEP 8: Display a trial balance, schedule of accounts payable, schedule of accounts receivable, and statements of accounts.

STEP 9: Enter the adjusting entries using the following adjustment data for the month of April. Use the trial balance generated in step 8 as the basis for making the adjusting entries. Use Adj.Ent. as the reference.

Merchandise inventory	$599,000.00
Office supplies inventory	$3,650.00
Store supplies inventory	$2,600.00
Value of insurance policies on April 30	$5,215.00
Depreciation for the period:	
Office Equipment	$2,093.96
Store Equipment	$1,565.25
Estimated federal income tax	$5,215.00

STEP 10: Display the general journal report for the adjusting entries. Use a reference restriction of Adj.Ent. so that only adjusting entries will be included on the report.

STEP 11: Display a general ledger report for the Cash account.

STEP 12:   **Display the income statement, balance sheet, and retained earnings statement.**

STEP 13:   **Generate a balance sheet 3D bar graph.**

STEP 14:   **Save your data.**

STEP 15:   **Optional spreadsheet and word processing activity:** Create a condensed multistep income statement from the detailed income statement provided by the *Automated Accounting* system.

Spreadsheet:
a.   Display and copy the income statement to the clipboard in spreadsheet format.
b.   Start up your spreadsheet software and load template file SSR–3.
c.   Select cell A1 and paste the income statement into the spreadsheet.
d.   Enter the cell references and formulas to complete the condensed, single-step income statement in cells A61–D79.
Note: Earnings per share is calculated by dividing the net income by the amount of capital stock as reported in the balance sheet.
e.   Print the completed income statement.
f.   Save the entire spreadsheet with a file name of XXXR–3.

Word Processing:
a.   Start up your word processing software and create a new document. Use a fixed font such as Courier.
b.   Copy and paste the completed spreadsheet condensed multistep income statement into the new document.
c.   Format and enhance the document's appearance.
d.   Print the document.
e.   Save the document with a file name of XXXR–3.
f.   End your spreadsheet and word processing sessions.

STEP 16:   **End the *Automated Accounting* session.**

Applying Your Technology Skills R–3

Directions: Using Reinforcement Activity R–3, write the answers to the following questions in the *Working Papers*.

Journals:

1. In the general journal, what is the amount of the debit to Payroll Taxes Expense?

2. What is the amount of purchase invoice no. 2251 for Tillman & Hubbell Co.?

3. What is the total of the debit column on the cash payments journal?

4. What is the amount of sales invoice no. 3823 for Elder Fireplace Shop?

5. What is the total of the credit column on the cash receipts journal?

Schedules of Accounts Payable and Receivable:

6. What is the amount owed to Corbett, Inc.?

7. What is the amount due from all customers?

Checks and Statements of Account:

8. What is the net amount of the check paid to Reister Fireplace Co. on April 1?

9. What is the amount of the credit memo to Alsip Patio & Hearth?

General Ledger Report:

10. What is the cash account balance as of April 29?

11. What is the ending balance in the Cash account?

Financial Statements:

12. What are the sales for the year?

13. What is the sales discount amount for the month?

14. What is the cost of merchandise sold for the year as a percent of total operating revenue?

15. What is the amount of advertising expense for the year as a percent of total operating revenue?

16. What are the total current assets?

17. What are the total liabilities?

18. What is the amount of retained earnings at the end of the month?

ACCOUNTING CAREERS IN DEPTH

Auditor

An auditor examines and analyzes accounting records to determine the financial status of a business and prepares financial reports related to operating procedures. An auditor performs the following duties:

- Reviewing records concerning assets, net worth, liabilities, capital stock, income, and expenditures.
- Inspecting accounting records to determine if accepted accounting procedure was followed in recording transactions.
- Counting cash on hand, and inspecting notes receivable and payable, securities, and canceled checks.
- Verifying journal and ledger entries of cash and check payments, purchases, expenses, and trial balances by examining and authenticating inventory items.
- Preparing reports for management concerning the scope of the audit and financial condition of the business.

Auditing is considered the bread-and-butter work of accounting. An auditor comes to really understand how money is being made in the company that is being audited.

The work of an auditor can be done in any type of organization such as a small business, corporation, or government agency. The educational requirement for an auditor is completion of a college degree. If possible, an internship or co-op with a company is ideal in order to get work experience while the student is still in college. There are usually many travel opportunities available to offices in various locations.

One of the main requirements of working as an auditor, as with other accounting careers, is the need to pay close attention to detail. It is one of the most important prerequisites in accounting, and especially in auditing, because you are checking and verifying the work of others.

Auditing in any environment can be a rewarding experience and can build a solid foundation and accounting background.

Some companies, particularly those that sell computer hardware and software, offer customer service on the Internet. Among the services offered on World Wide Web pages or on bulletin boards are free software upgrades and fixes.

10
Payroll

LEARNING OBJECTIVES

Upon completion of this chapter, you will be able to:

1. Complete employee input forms.

2. Perform employee maintenance.

3. Complete payroll transactions input forms.

4. Enter and correct payroll transactions.

5. Generate and post payroll journal entries.

6. Display payroll reports.

INTRODUCTION

In a computerized payroll system, the computer stores data such as an employee's name, address, Social Security number, marital status, number of withholding allowances, pay rate, and voluntary deductions. At the end of each pay period, all payroll transaction data, such as gross pay and deductions, are entered into the computer. The computer can calculate the withholding taxes and create the resulting journal entries.

After the employee data is entered, an employee list report can be displayed to verify the accuracy of input data. A payroll report can be displayed that provides earnings and withholdings for the month, quarter, and year at any time. *Automated Accounting 7.0* can generate the current payroll and employer's payroll tax expenses journal entries. At the end of the quarter, the quarterly report is generated, and at the end of the year, the W–2 statements of earnings and withholdings are also produced.

It is important to note that the program uses the payroll transaction dates that are entered to accumulate totals and process the end-of-quarter and end-of-year reports. Therefore, *it is very important that the correct payroll transaction dates be entered each pay period.*

EMPLOYEE INPUT FORM

In this payroll system, the additions, changes, and deletions to employee data may be recorded on an employee input form as illustrated in Figures 10.1 through 10.3. Figure 10.1 is an example of the addition of a new employee. Figure 10.2 shows a change in marital status and number of withholding allowances. Notice that only the employee number and the fields that have changed need to be completed. Figure 10.3 shows an employee deletion.

E T H I C S

Mary works for a local business that uses personal computers. Her brother, who is taking a computer course in high school, asks Mary if she would use one of the personal computers at her place of employment to complete a homework assignment for him. Her brother assures her that his homework will not take more than 20 minutes of computer time and suggests that she do this work after normal working hours.

a. Do you think that what Mary's brother is proposing is ethical or unethical?

b. What do you think Mary should do? Justify your answer.

```
                      EMPLOYEE
                      INPUT FORM

  Run Date 12/31/--                    Problem No. Example

  Employee Number    160

  Name               Wheatly, Frank       Salary Amount    2000.00
  Address            15 Jackson Pike      Hourly Rate
  City, State, and Zip  Biloxi, MS 39536-8011   Piece Rate
  Social Security No.  482-70-8945        Commission %
  Withholding Allow.  2
  Number Pay Periods  12                      MARITAL STATUS
  G.L. Account No.    545                   ○ Single
                                            ʋ Married
```

Figure 10.1
Employee Input Form (New Employee)

```
                      EMPLOYEE
                      INPUT FORM

  Run Date 12/31/--                    Problem No. Example

  Employee Number    110

  Name                                    Salary Amount
  Address                                 Hourly Rate
  City, State, and Zip                    Piece Rate
  Social Security No.                     Commission %
  Withholding Allow.  2
  Number Pay Periods                          MARITAL STATUS
  G.L. Account No.                          ○ Single
                                            ʋ Married
```

Figure 10.2
Employee Input Form (Changes to Employee)

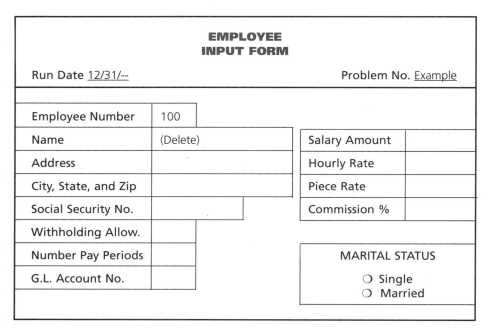

Figure 10.3
Employee Input
Form (Deletion)

Each field in the form corresponds to a grid cell in the Employees Account Maintenance window. The field names and a description of each column are illustrated in the Employees Account Maintenance window shown in Figure 10.4.

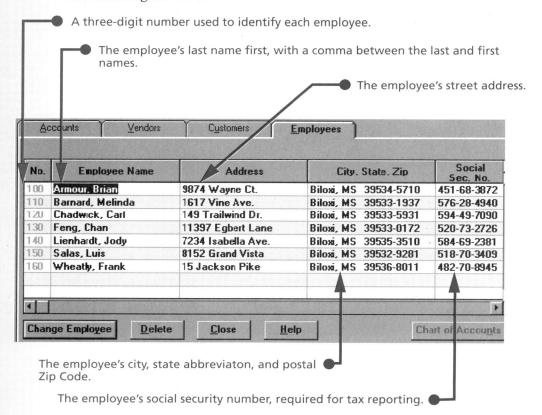

A three-digit number used to identify each employee.

The employee's last name first, with a comma between the last and first names.

The employee's street address.

Figure 10.4
Employee
Maintenance
(cont'd on
p. 325)

The employee's city, state abbreviaton, and postal Zip Code.

The employee's social security number, required for tax reporting.

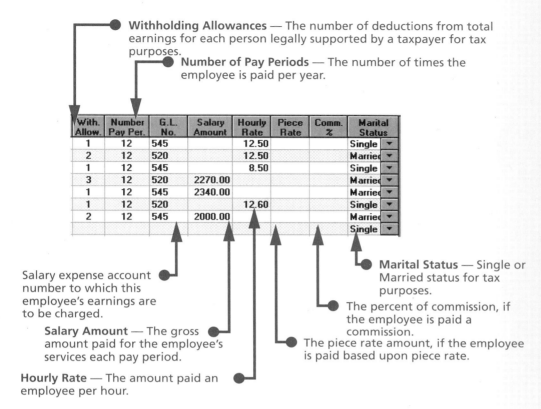

Withholding Allowances — The number of deductions from total earnings for each person legally supported by a taxpayer for tax purposes.

Number of Pay Periods — The number of times the employee is paid per year.

With. Allow.	Number Pay Per.	G.L. No.	Salary Amount	Hourly Rate	Piece Rate	Comm. %	Marital Status
1	12	545		12.50			Single ▼
2	12	520		12.50			Married ▼
1	12	545		8.50			Single ▼
3	12	520	2270.00				Married ▼
1	12	545	2340.00				Married ▼
1	12	520		12.60			Single ▼
2	12	545	2000.00				Married ▼
							Single ▼

Salary expense account number to which this employee's earnings are to be charged.

Salary Amount — The gross amount paid for the employee's services each pay period.

Hourly Rate — The amount paid an employee per hour.

Marital Status — Single or Married status for tax purposes.

The percent of commission, if the employee is paid a commission.

The piece rate amount, if the employee is paid based upon piece rate.

Figure 10.4—Cont'd
Employee Maintenance

EMPLOYEE MAINTENANCE

When *Maintain Accounts* is chosen from the Data menu or the *Accts.* toolbar button is clicked, the Account Maintenance window will appear. To enter payroll data, click the *Employees* tab. Figure 10.4 shows the maintenance data already entered from the Employee Input Forms in Figures 10.1 through 10.3. Employee no. 100 is shown selected, and about to be deleted.

Adding a New Employee

1: **Enter the employee number.**

2: **Enter the data fields in the grid cell boxes and choose the desired marital status.**
   When the focus moves to the marital status, choose *Single* or *Married* from the drop-down list, or key the first letter of the desired marital status (S or M).

3: **Press *Enter* or click *Add Employee*.**

Changing Employee Data

1: Select the employee by clicking the grid cell containing the data you wish to change.

2: Enter the correct data for the employee.

3: Click the *Change Employee* button.

Deleting an Employee

1: Click the employee to be deleted.

2: Click the *Delete* button.
Note: You will not be allowed to delete an employee with cumulative earnings for the current year until after the end of the calendar year.

PAYROLL TRANSACTIONS INPUT FORM

To facilitate data input, you may wish to record the payroll transaction data on the payroll transactions input form and then enter it into the computer. The input form illustrated in Figure 10.5 shows how the data for two employees are recorded. The first employee is paid hourly, and the second employee is salaried. Each has voluntary deductions. **Voluntary deductions** are employee-authorized withholdings from earnings for such options as health insurance, dental insurance, savings plans, and charitable contributions. The field names and a description of each column are illustrated in the Other Activities Payroll window shown in Figure 10.6.

PAYROLL TRANSACTIONS INPUT FORM

Run Date 12/31/--   Problem No. Example

Employee Name	Salary Amount	Reg. Hours	O.T. Hours	Pieces	Sales	Health Insurance	Dental Insurance	Credit Union
Barnard, Melinda		176	4.5			40.00	24.00	25.00
Feng, Chan						45.00	18.00	50.00

Figure 10.5
Payroll Transactions Input Form

Transaction date will also be the date printed on the payroll check.

The name of the employee to be paid.

The check number is automatically assigned.

The salary amount of an employee if the amount is different than the amount stored in the employee's record. This field may also be used to record extra pay that is to be received by an hourly employee.

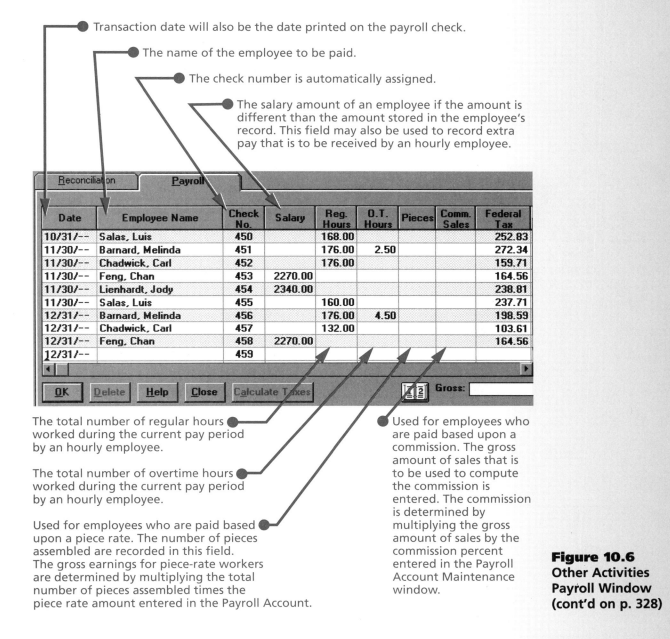

Date	Employee Name	Check No.	Salary	Reg. Hours	O.T. Hours	Pieces	Comm. Sales	Federal Tax
10/31/--	Salas, Luis	450		168.00				252.83
11/30/--	Barnard, Melinda	451		176.00	2.50			272.34
11/30/--	Chadwick, Carl	452		176.00				159.71
11/30/--	Feng, Chan	453	2270.00					164.56
11/30/--	Lienhardt, Jody	454	2340.00					238.81
11/30/--	Salas, Luis	455		160.00				237.71
12/31/--	Barnard, Melinda	456		176.00	4.50			198.59
12/31/--	Chadwick, Carl	457		132.00				103.61
12/31/--	Feng, Chan	458	2270.00					164.56
12/31/--		459						

OK   Delete   **Help**   **Close**   Calculate Taxes   Gross:

The total number of regular hours worked during the current pay period by an hourly employee.

The total number of overtime hours worked during the current pay period by an hourly employee.

Used for employees who are paid based upon a piece rate. The number of pieces assembled are recorded in this field. The gross earnings for piece-rate workers are determined by multiplying the total number of pieces assembled times the piece rate amount entered in the Payroll Account.

Used for employees who are paid based upon a commission. The gross amount of sales that is to be used to compute the commission is entered. The commission is determined by multiplying the gross amount of sales by the commission percent entered in the Payroll Account Maintenance window.

Figure 10.6
Other Activities
Payroll Window
(cont'd on p. 328)

A helper application is a program that runs alongside a Web browser and helps it handle data.

INTERNET

State Tax	City Tax	Social Security	Medicare	Health Insurance	Dental Insurance	Credit Union	Net Pay
59.56	21.17	131.24	30.69	40.00	24.00	30.00	1527.31
65.87	22.47	139.31	32.58	40.00	24.00	25.00	1625.31
31.30	14.96	92.75	21.69	40.00	24.00	35.00	1076.59
61.74	22.70	140.74	32.92	45.00	18.00	50.00	1734.34
70.38	23.40	145.08	33.93	45.00	28.00	75.00	1680.40
54.68	20.16	124.99	29.23	40.00	24.00	30.00	1455.23
65.06	22.84	141.63	33.12	40.00	24.00	25.00	1734.14
17.67	11.22	69.56	16.27	40.00	24.00	35.00	804.67
61.74	22.70	140.74	32.92	45.00	18.00	50.00	1734.34

These five fields contain the taxes withheld from an employee's pay. You may calculate and enter the amounts individually or have the program calculate the taxes.

These three fields contain voluntary deductions that are withheld from the employee's pay each period.

Figure 10.6—Cont'd
Other Activities
Payroll Window

PAYROLL TRANSACTIONS

Employee payroll transaction data for the pay period are entered into the Payroll tab in the Other Activities window. For each employee's payroll transaction, the payroll date, pay information, and employee deductions (if different from the previous pay period) are entered. The employee taxes can be either keyed or automatically calculated by the program. The payroll problems in this textbook have the program calculate employee taxes.

When the *Other* toolbar button is clicked, the Other Activities window will appear. Click the *Payroll* tab to display the payroll dialog shown in Figure 10.6. Note that the December 31st payroll transactions for Melinda Barnard and Chan Feng are those recorded on the Payroll Transactions Input Form shown in Figure 10.5.

Entering a Payroll Transaction

1: Enter the date of the check.

2: Select the employee from the Employee drop-down list or key the first letter of the last name until the correct employee name appears.

3: Verify that the check number displayed in the Check No. cell is correct. If not, key the correct check number.
The check number is automatically sequenced and generated. However, if the check number must be changed (i.e., for a special check), or the check numbering sequence needs to be

changed (i.e., switched banks or checking accounts), the desired check number may be keyed in this text box.

4: Strike the *Tab* key while the focus is on the Employee Name cell. If the employee is salaried, the salary amount will be displayed.
You may key a different salary amount that will override the amount shown. If a salaried employee is to be paid a one-time bonus, the amount entered would be the employee's normal salary plus the bonus amount. This text box may also be used to enter extra pay earned by hourly employees. The software will add the amount entered to the hourly employee's earnings.

5: If the employee is paid hourly, enter the regular hours worked in the Reg. Hours cell.

6: If the employee is paid hourly and has worked overtime, enter the overtime hours worked in the O.T. Hours cell.

7: Click the *Calculate Taxes* button to direct the software to calculate the employee taxes.
The taxes will be calculated and displayed in the employee taxes cells. Tax withholding amounts may also be keyed in the cells.

8: Enter the employee deductions.

9: Click *OK*.
A payroll check will be generated and displayed. A payroll check generated by the computer shows the net amount of pay (earnings after payroll taxes and other deductions) earned by the employee during the pay period. The payroll check shown in Figure 10.7 was generated for Melinda Barnard on 12/31/-- as recorded on the input form in Figure 10.5 and entered into the computer as shown in Figure 10.6.

The user must enter the employee deductions only the first time an employee is paid. After that, the software puts the deductions into the fields when the taxes are calculated.

Foltz Consulting Co.

456

12/31/--   16-871/621

Pay to the
Order of   Barnard, Melinda   ****1734.14

National State Bank
DownTown Office
AnyCity, State 12345-1234   _____

:063107410l:1171 3231571206

Figure 10.7
Payroll Check

10: Click the *Close* button to dismiss the check and continue, or click *Print* to print the check.

Correcting a Payroll Transaction

1: Select the payroll transaction you wish to correct.

2: Enter the corrections.

3: Click *OK*.
The software will update the employee's record, display a new check, and show the corrected data. The previously written check should be marked Void and filed as an audit trail document.

Deleting a Payroll Transaction

1: Select the payroll transaction you wish to delete.
Click any cell belonging to the employee to be deleted.

2: Click the *Delete* button to delete the selected payroll transaction.
The previously written check should be marked Void and filed as an audit trail document.

PAYROLL JOURNAL ENTRIES

Some companies will lump Social Security (also commonly referred to as FICA) and Medicare into one account and call it FICA Tax Payable. In this text, they will be kept separate.

Automated Accounting 7.0 can generate the current payroll journal entry (that includes salary expenses, employee federal tax payable, employee state tax payable, employee city tax payable, Social Security tax payable, Medicare tax payable, and voluntary deductions). It can also generate the employer's payroll taxes journal entry, which includes Social Security, Medicare, federal unemployment, and state unemployment taxes.

The journal entry to record the current payroll can be generated by choosing the *Current Payroll Journal Entry* menu item from the Options menu. The journal entry to record the employer's payroll taxes can be generated by choosing the *Employer's Payroll Taxes* menu item from the Options menu. The journal entry will appear in a dialog box for your verification. When it is posted to the general ledger, the general journal appears, showing the posted entry.

If you must make a change or correction to a payroll transaction after the journal entry has been generated and posted, you must first delete the old journal entry and then generate the corrected journal entry.

Generating the Current Payroll Journal Entries

1: Choose the *Current Payroll Journal Entry* menu item from the Options menu.

2: When the confirmation dialog shown in Figure 10.8 appears, click *Yes*.

The generated journal entries for the current payroll will appear in a dialog window as illustrated in Figure 10.9.

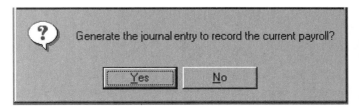

Figure 10.8
Current Payroll Journal Entry Confirmation Dialog

Acct. #	Account Title	Debit	Credit
520	Consultant Salaries Exp.	6828.68	
545	Office Salaries Exp.	5462.00	
265	Emp. Fed. Inc. Tax Pay.		1137.97
270	Emp. State Inc. Tax Pay.		333.32
275	Social Security Tax Pay.		762.02
280	Medicare Tax Payable		178.22
272	Emp. City Inc. Tax Pay.		122.90
297	Health Ins. Premiums Pay.		250.00
298	Dental Ins. Premiums Pay.		138.00
299	Credit Union Deduct. Pay.		265.00
285	Salaries Payable		9103.25

Post   Cancel   Help

Figure 10.9
Current Payroll Journal Entry

3: Click the *Post* button.

When the current payroll journal entry is posted, the general journal window will appear, showing that the entry has been automatically entered and posted. This entry is placed in the general journal in the event it must be changed or deleted at a later time.

Generating the Employer's Payroll Taxes Journal Entries

1: Choose *Employer's Payroll Taxes* from the Options menu.

2: When the confirmation dialog shown in Figure 10.10 appears, click *Yes*.

The generated journal entries for the employer's payroll taxes will appear in the general journal, as shown in Figure 10.11.

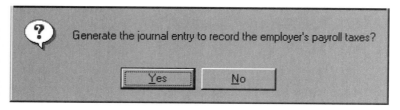

Figure 10.10
Employer's Payroll Taxes Confirmation Dialog

Acct. #	Account Title	Debit	Credit
550	Payroll Tax Expense	1064.23	
275	Social Security Tax Pay.		762.02
280	Medicare Tax Payable		178.21
290	State Unemp. Tax Payable		108.00
295	Federal Unemp. Tax Pay.		16.00

Post   Cancel   Help

Figure 10.11
Employer's Payroll Taxes Journal Entry

3: Click the *Post* button.

When the employer's payroll taxes journal entry is posted, it will reappear in the general journal window. The posted entry is placed in the general journal in the event it must be changed or deleted at a later time.

4: Click the *Close* button of the general journal.

PAYROLL REPORTS

After the payroll data for the period are recorded, the payroll reports are generated. There are four types of payroll reports available: Employee List Report, Payroll Report, Quarterly Report, and W–2 Statements.

After the payroll reports and other financial reports are generated, the period-end closing procedures may be completed. As you learned in earlier chapters, generating closing entries will prepare the temporary accounts for the next fiscal period. Likewise, generating closing entries will prepare the payroll system for the next fiscal period. Payroll transactions are purged and employee earnings and withholding accumulators are cleared.

Employee List Report

The **employee list report** provides a complete listing of the employee payroll information. The information appearing in the employee payroll list was entered into the computer via the Employees tab in the Account Maintenance window. This report is useful in verifying the accuracy of data entered into the Employees window.

1: **Click the *Reports* toolbar button.**

2: **Choose the *Payroll Reports* option from the Select a Report Group list.**
A list showing the Payroll reports will appear, as shown in Figure 10.12.

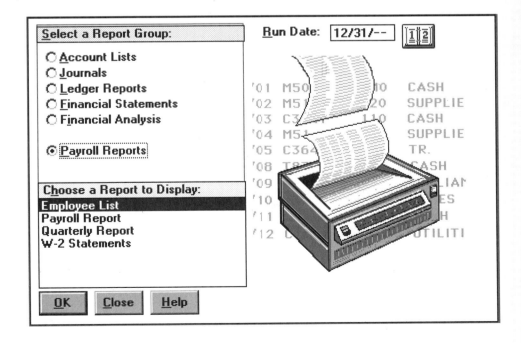

Figure 10.12
Report Selection (Payroll Reports)

```
                        Foltz Consulting Co.
                          Employee List
                             12/31/--

Emp.   Employee              Soc. Sec./    # Pay   G.L.   Salary/   Piece Rate/
No.    Name/Address          Mar. Stat.    Periods Acct.  Rate      Commission

110    Barnard, Melinda      576-28-4940   12      520
       1617 Vine Ave.        Married                               12.50
       Biloxi, MS 39533-1937 W/H 2

120    Chadwick, Carl        594-49-7090   12      545
       149 Trailwind Dr.     Single                                8.50
       Biloxi, MS 39533-5931 W/H 1

130    Feng, Chan            520-73-2726   12      520    2270.00
       11397 Egbert Lane     Married
       Biloxi, MS 39533-0172 W/H 3

140    Lienhardt, Jody       584-69-2381   12      545    2340.00
       7234 Isabella Ave.    Married
       Biloxi, MS 39535-3510 W/H 1

150    Salas, Luis           518-70-3409   12      520
       8152 Grand Vista      Single                               12.60
       Biloxi, MS 39532-9281 W/H 1

160    Wheatly, Frank        482-70-8945   12      545    2000.00
       15 Jackson Pike       Married
       Biloxi, MS 39536-8011 W/H 2
```

Figure 10.13
Employee List Report

3: **Choose *Employee List*, then click *OK*.**
An employee list report is shown in Figure 10.13.

Payroll Report

The **payroll report** provides employee earnings and withholding information for the month, quarter, and year. Earnings and withholding information for each employee appears at the beginning of the report. Summary information is included at the end of the report that provides information on earnings and withholdings for all employees. The payroll report should be generated each pay period.

1: **Click the *Reports* toolbar button. Choose the *Payroll Reports* option button from the Select a Report Group list.**

2: **Choose *Payroll Report*, then click *OK*.**
The first employee (Melinda Barnard) and the summary at the end of the payroll report are shown in Figure 10.14.

```
                          Foltz Consulting Co.
                             Payroll Report
                               12/31/--

-----------------------------------------------------------------
                                    Current   Quarterly   Yearly
-----------------------------------------------------------------

110-Barnard, Melinda   Gross Pay         2284.38   6531.26   26137.52
520-Consultant         Federal W/H        198.59    706.24    3064.98
Married Acct. 520       State W/H           65.06    184.83     747.78
W/H 2 576-28-4940      Soc. Sec. W/H      141.63    404.94    1620.53
Pay Periods 12         Medicare W/H        33.12     94.70     378.99
Salary                 City Tax W/H        22.84     65.31     261.38
Hourly Rate 12.50      Health Insurance    40.00    120.00     480.00
Piece Rate             Dental Insurance    24.00     72.00     288.00
Commission %           Credit Union        25.00     75.00     300.00
Check Number 456
Check Date 12/31/--    Net Pay           1734.14   4808.24   18995.86

/\/\/\/\/\/\/\/\/\/\/\/\/\/\/\/\/\/\/\/\/\/\/\/\/\/\/\/\/\/\/\/\/\/\/\/\/\/\

Payroll Summary        Gross Pay        12290.68  32882.36  127061.90
                       Federal W/H       1137.97   3262.32   13049.49
                       State W/H          333.32    894.17    3492.18
                       Soc. Sec. W/H      762.02   2038.70    7877.82
                       Medicare W/H       178.22    476.80    1842.46
                       City Tax W/H       122.90    328.82    1270.64
                       Health Insurance   250.00    670.00    2560.00
                       Dental Insurance   138.00    374.00    1436.00
                       Credit Union       265.00    695.00    2630.00

                       Net Pay           9103.25  24142.55   92903.31
```

Figure 10.14
Payroll Report

Quarterly Report

At the end of each quarter, the quarterly report must be generated. The **quarterly report** is used by the company to report Social Security and Medicare taxable wages to the Internal Revenue Service.

1: Click the *Reports* toolbar button. Choose the *Payroll Reports* option button from the Select a Report Group list.

2: Choose *Quarterly Report,* then click *OK.*
A quarterly report is shown in Figure 10.15.

Concerns about lost productivity are causing some companies to use devices that monitor employees' Internet use and restrict the availability of particular websites.

INTERNET

```
                              Foltz Consulting Co.
                               Quarterly Report
                                   12/31/--

  Soc. Sec.                                    Taxable        Taxable
  Number          Employee Name                Soc. Sec.      Medicare

  576-28-4940     Barnard, Melinda             6531.26        6531.26
  594-49-7090     Chadwick, Carl               4114.00        4114.00
  520-73-2726     Feng, Chan                   6810.00        6810.00
  584-69-2381     Lienhardt, Jody              7020.00        7020.00
  518-70-3409     Salas, Luis                  6407.10        6407.10
  482-70-8945     Wheatly, Frank               2000.00        2000.00

                  Totals                      32882.36       32882.36

                  Total Employees 6
```

Figure 10.15
Quarterly Report

W–2 Statements

A **W–2 statement** is a report that summarizes an employee's taxable wages and various withholdings. At the end of the year, the company must provide a W–2 statement to each employee paid during the past year, and must provide a copy to the Internal Revenue Service. The W–2 statement is used for individual tax reporting purposes.

1: Click the *Reports* toolbar button. Choose the *Payroll Reports* option button from the Select a Report Group list.

2: Choose *W–2 Statements,* then click *OK*.
A W–2 statement will appear, as illustrated in Figure 10.16.

3: Click the *Print* button to print the statement.

4: Click the >> button to advance to the next statement.

5: Click the << button to return to the previous statement.

6: Click the *Close* button to dismiss the statements window and continue.

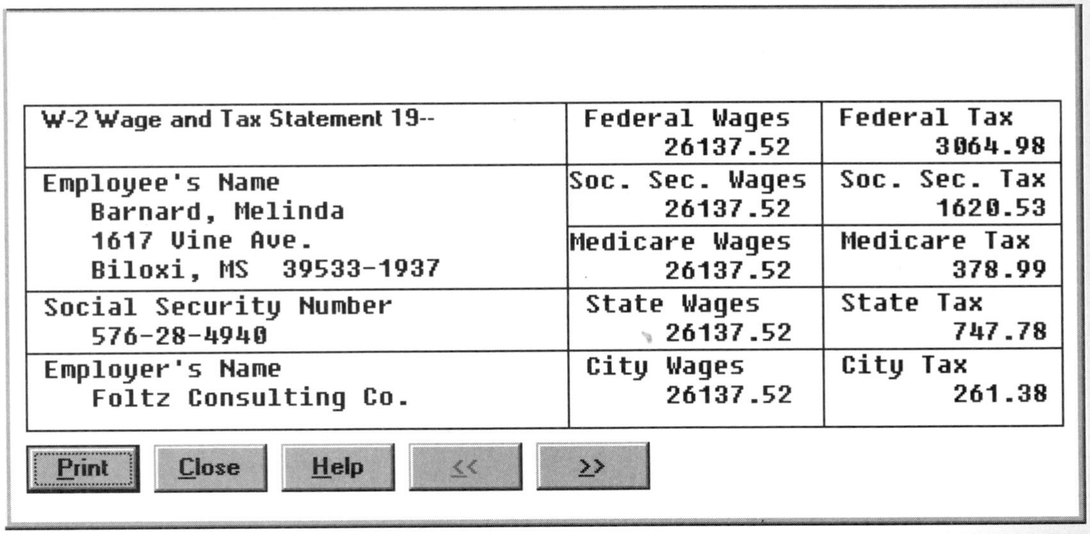

W-2 Wage and Tax Statement 19--	Federal Wages 26137.52	Federal Tax 3064.98
Employee's Name Barnard, Melinda 1617 Vine Ave. Biloxi, MS 39533-1937	Soc. Sec. Wages 26137.52	Soc. Sec. Tax 1620.53
	Medicare Wages 26137.52	Medicare Tax 378.99
Social Security Number 576-28-4940	State Wages 26137.52	State Tax 747.78
Employer's Name Foltz Consulting Co.	City Wages 26137.52	City Tax 261.38

[Print]   [Close]   [Help]   [<<]   [>>]

Figure 10.16
W–2 Statement

Chapter Review

1. A computerized payroll system stores data for each employee, permits pay-period transaction data to be entered, processes the data, and generates the required reports.

2. Employee input forms are completed when adding an employee to a payroll system, when making changes to employee information, or when deleting an employee from a payroll. To complete the input form, the following must be known: withholding allowances, number of pay periods, payroll general ledger account number, marital status, salary amount, and hourly rate.

3. To faciliate data input, a payroll transactions input form may be used to record the payroll transaction data.

4. Employee payroll transaction data are entered into the Payroll window. The purpose of entering the payroll transactions is to identify the employees to be paid for the current pay period, and to enter the employees' pay-period transaction data.

5. The current payroll journal entry (salary expenses, employee federal, state, and city tax payable, Social Security, Medicare, and voluntary deductions) and employer's payroll taxes journal entry

(Social Security, Medicare, federal unemployment, and state unemployment) can be generated by the *Automated Accounting* software after all payroll-related data have been entered.

6.   The employee list report is useful in verifying the accuracy of data keyed into the computer via the Employee Account Maintenance window. The payroll report provides earnings and withholding information for each employee for the month, quarter, and year. The quarterly report is created at the end of each quarter, and is used by the company to report Social Security and Medicare taxable wages to the Internal Revenue Service. W–2 statements are used for individual tax reporting purposes and are provided to each employee at the end of the year.

ACCOUNTING   CAREERS   IN   DEPTH

Cost Accountant

A cost accountant applies principles of cost accounting to conduct studies which provide detailed cost information not supplied by general accounting systems. A cost accountant's duties include:

- Planning, collecting, and studying data to determine costs of business activity, such as raw material purchases, inventory, and labor.
- Analyzing data obtained and recording results, using a computer.
- Analyzing changes in product design, raw materials, manufacturing methods, or services provided, to determine effects on costs.
- Analyzing actual manufacturing costs and preparing periodic reports comparing standard costs to actual production costs.
- Providing management with reports specifying and comparing factors affecting prices and profitability of products or services.

Preparation for a career as a cost accountant in most cases requires a four-year college degree in accounting. A cooperative education experience in an environment using cost accounting techniques would be helpful in landing the first job after completing college.

For a cost accountant, career opportunities can be found in manufacturing and other corporate environments because all businesses deal with controlling costs. Some students choose to work in a particular business environment in which they are interested, such as insurance, entertainment, or manufacturing.

The skills that can be helpful to a cost accountant include: the ability to install manual or computer-based cost accounting systems and to process information on these systems; a specialization in analyzing costs related to specific rate schedules; and a specialization in appraisal and evaluation of property or equipment.

If you enjoy analyzing costs and making decisions that assist you in providing alternatives which help to cut costs and increase profits in a business environment, this career could be a good choice for you.

TUTORIAL PROBLEM 10–T

In this tutorial problem, you will process the December payroll for Foltz Consulting Co. You will perform the operating procedures necessary to add new employees, make changes to employee data, and delete employees. In addition, you will process the monthly payroll and generate the payroll journal entries. Since this is the last payroll of the year, it will include the end-of-quarter and end-of-year reports. The following information is required to complete the December 31st payroll.

Addition of New Employee:

Wheatly, Frank
15 Jackson Pike
Biloxi, MS 39536-8011

Assign employee number 160; social security number, 482-70-8945; withholding allowances, 2; pay periods per year, 12; G.L. Account, 545 (Office Salaries Exp.); salaried, $2,000.00; married.

Changes to Current Employees:

Barnard, Melinda: Change the number of withholding allowances to 2 and the marital status to married.

Lienhardt, Jody: Change the street address to 7234 Isabella Ave.

Deletion of Employee:

Delete Employee No. 100 (Armour, Brian).

Employees to Be Paid This Pay Period:

Employee Number	Employee Name	Regular Hours	Overtime Hours	Health Insurance	Dental Insurance	Credit Union
110	Barnard, Melinda	176	4.5	40.00	24.00	25.00
120	Chadwick, Carl	132		40.00	24.00	35.00
130	Feng, Chan			45.00	18.00	50.00
140	Lienhardt, Jody			45.00	28.00	75.00
150	Salas, Luis	176	3.0	40.00	24.00	30.00
160	Wheatly, Frank			40.00	20.00	50.00

STEP 1:   **Start up _Automated Accounting 7.0._**

STEP 2:   **Load file AA10–T.**
Click the _Open_ toolbar button. Select file AA10–T from the File list box.

STEP 3:   **Enter your name in the User Name text box and click _OK_.**

STEP 4:   **Save the file as XXX10–T.**
Use Save As to save the file as XXX10–T (where XXX are your initials).

TUTORIAL PROBLEM 10-T

STEP 5: **Enter the employee maintenance data from the Employee Input Forms in Figure 10.17.**
Click the *Accts.* toolbar button. Click the *Employees* tab and enter the employee maintenance data.

EMPLOYEE INPUT FORM

Run Date <u>12/31/--</u>   Problem No. <u>Example</u>

Employee Number	160			
Name	Wheatly, Frank		Salary Amount	2000.00
Address	15 Jackson Pike		Hourly Rate	
City, State, and Zip	Biloxi, MS 39536-8011		Piece Rate	
Social Security No.	482-70-8945		Commission %	
Withholding Allow.	2			
Number Pay Periods	12			
G.L. Account No.	545			

MARITAL STATUS
○ Single
ʊ Married

EMPLOYEE INPUT FORM

Run Date <u>12/31/--</u>   Problem No. <u>Example</u>

Employee Number	110			
Name			Salary Amount	
Address			Hourly Rate	
City, State, and Zip			Piece Rate	
Social Security No.			Commission %	
Withholding Allow.	2			
Number Pay Periods				
G.L. Account No.				

MARITAL STATUS
○ Single
ʊ Married

Figure 10.17
Completed Employee Input Forms

T U T O R I A L   P R O B L E M   1 0 - T

EMPLOYEE INPUT FORM

Run Date <u>12/31/--</u>   Problem No. <u>Example</u>

Employee Number	140
Name	
Address	7234 Isabella Ave.
City, State, and Zip	
Social Security No.	
Withholding Allow.	
Number Pay Periods	
G.L. Account No.	

Salary Amount	
Hourly Rate	
Piece Rate	
Commission %	

MARITAL STATUS

○ Single
○ Married

EMPLOYEE INPUT FORM

Run Date <u>12/31/--</u>   Problem No. <u>Example</u>

Employee Number	100
Name	(Delete)
Address	
City, State, and Zip	
Social Security No.	
Withholding Allow.	
Number Pay Periods	
G.L. Account No.	

Salary Amount	
Hourly Rate	
Piece Rate	
Commission %	

MARITAL STATUS

○ Single
○ Married

Figure 10.17—Cont'd
Completed Employee Input Forms

T U T O R I A L   P R O B L E M   1 0 - T

Step 6:   **Enter the payroll transactions and generate payroll checks.**
Click the *Other* toolbar button. Click the *Payroll* tab and
enter the payroll transaction data provided in Figure
10.18. Have the program calculate taxes. The first
payroll check appears in Figure 10.19.
Note: It is very important that you enter the correct
date (December 31, 19--) when keying the payroll
transactions. Payroll processing is date sensitive and will
accumulate and display incorrectly if the dates are
entered incorrectly.

Date	Employee Name	Check No.	Salary	Reg. Hours	O.T. Hours	Pieces	Comm. Sales	Federal Tax
12/31/--	Barnard, Melinda	456		176.00	4.50			198.59
12/31/--	Chadwick, Carl	457		132.00				103.61
12/31/--	Feng, Chan	458	2270.00					164.56
12/31/--	Lienhardt, Jody	459	2340.00					238.81
12/31/--	Salas, Luis	460		176.00	3.00			276.46
12/31/--	Wheatly, Frank	461	2000.00					155.94

State Tax	City Tax	Social Security	Medicare	Health Insurance	Dental Insurance	Credit Union	Net Pay
65.06	22.84	141.63	33.12	40.00	24.00	25.00	1734.14
17.67	11.22	69.56	16.27	40.00	24.00	35.00	804.67
61.74	22.70	140.74	32.92	45.00	18.00	50.00	1734.34
70.38	23.40	145.08	33.93	45.00	28.00	75.00	1680.40
67.19	22.74	141.01	32.98	40.00	24.00	30.00	1639.92
51.28	20.00	124.00	29.00	40.00	20.00	50.00	1509.78

Figure 10.18
Completed Employee Transactions

```
Foltz Consulting Co.                                                   456
                                                    12/31/--       16-871/621

Pay to the
Order of       Barnard, Melinda

                                                    ****1734.14

National State Bank
DownTown Office
AnyCity, State  12345-1234                          _____

  :0631074101:1171  3231571206
```

Figure 10.19
First Payroll Check

T U T O R I A L   P R O B L E M   1 0 - T

STEP 7:   **Display the employee list report.**
Click the *Reports* toolbar button. Choose the *Payroll Reports* option. Select the *Employee List* report, then click *OK*. The report is shown in Figure 10.20. Verify the accuracy of the maintenance input, and make any corrections via the Employees tab in the Account Maintenance window.

Foltz Consulting Co.
Employee List
12/31/--

Emp. No.	Employee Name/Address	Soc. Sec./ Mar. Stat.	# Pay Periods	G.L. Acct.	Salary/ Rate	Piece Rate/ Commission
110	Barnard, Melinda 1617 Vine Ave. Biloxi, MS 39533-1937	576-28-4940 Married W/H 2	12	520	12.50	
120	Chadwick, Carl 149 Trailwind Dr. Biloxi, MS 39533-5931	594-49-7090 Single W/H 1	12	545	8.50	
130	Feng, Chan 11397 Egbert Lane Biloxi, MS 39533-0172	520-73-2726 Married W/H 3	12	520	2270.00	
140	Lienhardt, Jody 7234 Isabella Ave. Biloxi, MS 39535-3510	584-69-2381 Married W/H 1	12	545	2340.00	
150	Salas, Luis 8152 Grand Vista Biloxi, MS 39532-9281	518-70-3409 Single W/H 1	12	520	12.60	
160	Wheatly, Frank 15 Jackson Pike Biloxi, MS 39536-8011	482-70-8945 Married W/H 2	12	545	2000.00	

Figure 10.20
Employee List

STEP 8:   **Display the payroll report.**
Verify the Run Date as 12/31/--, then choose the *Payroll Report* option and click *OK*. The payroll report is shown in Figure 10.21. Verify the accuracy of the report and make any corrections via the Payroll tab in the Other Activities window.

344

CHAPTER 10 Payroll

TUTORIAL PROBLEM 10-T

Foltz Consulting Co.
Payroll Report
12/31/--

		Current	Quarterly	Yearly
110-Barnard, Melinda	Gross Pay	2284.38	6531.26	26137.52
520-Consultant	Federal W/H	198.59	706.24	3064.98
Married Acct. 520	State W/H	65.06	184.83	747.78
W/H 2 576-28-4940	Soc. Sec. W/H	141.63	404.94	1620.53
Pay Periods 12	Medicare W/H	33.12	94.70	378.99
Salary	City Tax W/H	22.84	65.31	261.38
Hourly Rate 12.50	Health Insurance	40.00	120.00	480.00
Piece Rate	Dental Insurance	24.00	72.00	288.00
Commission %	Credit Union	25.00	75.00	300.00
Check Number 456				
Check Date 12/31/--	Net Pay	1734.14	4808.24	18995.86
20-Chadwick, Carl	Gross Pay	1122.00	4114.00	17490.88
545-Office	Federal W/H	103.61	423.03	1847.37
Single Acct. 545	State W/H	17.67	80.27	358.44
W/H 1 594-49-7090	Soc. Sec. W/H	69.56	255.06	1084.42
Pay Periods 12	Medicare W/H	16.27	59.65	253.62
Salary	City Tax W/H	11.22	41.14	174.92
Hourly Rate 8.50	Health Insurance	40.00	120.00	480.00
Piece Rate	Dental Insurance	24.00	72.00	288.00
Commission %	Credit Union	35.00	105.00	420.00
Check Number 457				
Check Date 12/31/--	Net Pay	804.67	2957.85	12584.11
130-Feng, Chan	Gross Pay	2270.00	6810.00	27240.00
520-Consultant	Federal W/H	164.56	493.68	1974.72
Married Acct. 520	State W/H	61.74	185.22	740.88
W/H 3 520-73-2726	Soc. Sec. W/H	140.74	422.22	1688.88
Pay Periods 12	Medicare W/H	32.92	98.76	395.04
Salary 2270.00	City Tax W/H	22.70	68.10	272.40
Hourly Rate	Health Insurance	45.00	135.00	540.00
Piece Rate	Dental Insurance	18.00	54.00	216.00
Commission %	Credit Union	50.00	150.00	600.00
Check Number 458				
Check Date 12/31/--	Net Pay	1734.34	5203.02	20812.08
140-Lienhardt, Jody	Gross Pay	2340.00	7020.00	28080.00
545-Office	Federal W/H	238.81	716.43	2865.72
Married Acct. 545	State W/H	70.38	211.14	844.56
W/H 1 584-69-2381	Soc. Sec. W/H	145.08	435.24	1740.96
Pay Periods 12	Medicare W/H	33.93	101.79	407.16
Salary 2340.00	City Tax W/H	23.40	70.20	280.80
Hourly Rate	Health Insurance	45.00	135.00	540.00
Piece Rate	Dental Insurance	28.00	84.00	336.00
Commission %	Credit Union	75.00	225.00	900.00
Check Number 459				
Check Date 12/31/--	Net Pay	1680.40	5041.20	20164.80

Figure 10.21
Payroll Report

T U T O R I A L   P R O B L E M   1 0 - T

```
                              Foltz Consulting Co.
                              Payroll Report
                                  12/31/--

                                       Current     Quarterly    Yearly

150-Salas, Luis       Gross Pay        2274.30      6407.10     26113.50
520-Consultant        Federal W/H       276.46       767.00      3140.76
Single Acct. 520      State W/H          67.19       181.43       749.24
W/H 1 518-70-3409     Soc. Sec. W/H     141.01       397.24      1619.03
Pay Periods 12        Medicare W/H       32.98        92.90       378.65
Salary                City Tax W/H       22.74        64.07       261.14
Hourly Rate   12.60   Health Insurance   40.00       120.00       480.00
Piece Rate            Dental Insurance   24.00        72.00       288.00
Commission %          Credit Union       30.00        90.00       360.00
Check Number 460
Check Date 12/31/--   Net Pay          1639.92      4622.46     18836.68

160-Wheatly, Frank    Gross Pay        2000.00      2000.00      2000.00
545-Office            Federal W/H       155.94       155.94       155.94
Married Acct. 545     State W/H          51.28        51.28        51.28
W/H 2 482-70-8945     Soc. Sec. W/H     124.00       124.00       124.00
Pay Periods 12        Medicare W/H       29.00        29.00        29.00
Salary   2000.00      City Tax W/H       20.00        20.00        20.00
Hourly Rate           Health Insurance   40.00        40.00        40.00
Piece Rate            Dental Insurance   20.00        20.00        20.00
Commission %          Credit Union       50.00        50.00        50.00
Check Number 461
Check Date 12/31/--   Net Pay          1509.78      1509.78      1509.78

Payroll Summary       Gross Pay       12290.68     32882.36    127061.90
                      Federal W/H      1137.97      3262.32     13049.49
                      State W/H         333.32       894.17      3492.18
                      Soc. Sec. W/H     762.02      2038.70      7877.82
                      Medicare W/H      178.22       476.80      1842.46
                      City Tax W/H      122.90       328.82      1270.64
                      Health Insurance  250.00       670.00      2560.00
                      Dental Insurance  138.00       374.00      1436.00
                      Credit Union      265.00       695.00      2630.00

                      Net Pay          9103.25     24142.55     92903.31
```

**Figure 10.21—
Cont'd**
Payroll Report

STEP 9:   **Generate and post the journal entry for the current
payroll.**
Choose the *Current Payroll Journal Entry* menu item
from the Options menu. Click Yes when asked if you
want to generate the journal entries. When the entries
appear in the Current Payroll Journal Entries dialog box,
as shown in Figure 10.22, click *Post*. The journal entries
will reappear and will be posted in the general journal.

T U T O R I A L   P R O B L E M   1 0 - T

Acct. #	Account Title	Debit	Credit
520	Consultant Salaries Exp.	6828.68	
545	Office Salaries Exp.	5462.00	
265	Emp. Fed. Inc. Tax Pay.		1137.97
270	Emp. State Inc. Tax Pay.		333.32
275	Social Security Tax Pay.		762.02
280	Medicare Tax Payable		178.22
272	Emp. City Inc. Tax Pay.		122.90
297	Health Ins. Premiums Pay.		250.00
298	Dental Ins. Premiums Pay.		138.00
299	Credit Union Deduct. Pay.		265.00
285	Salaries Payable		9103.25

Figure 10.22
Current Payroll Journal Entry Dialog Box

If your journal entries do not match those shown in Figure 10.22, check your employee list and payroll report for keying errors, and make the necessary corrections. Return to the General Journal window, delete the incorrect entries, and generate new entries.

STEP 10: **Generate and post the employer's payroll taxes journal entry.**
With the General Journal window still displayed, choose *Employer's Payroll Taxes* from the Options menu. Click *Yes* when asked if you want to generate the journal entry. When the entries appear in the Payroll Taxes Journal Entries dialog box, as shown in Figure 10.23, click *Post*. The journal entries will reappear and will be posted in the general journal.

Acct. #	Account Title	Debit	Credit
550	Payroll Tax Expense	1064.23	
275	Social Security Tax Pay.		762.02
280	Medicare Tax Payable		178.21
290	State Unemp. Tax Payable		108.00
295	Federal Unemp. Tax Pay.		16.00

Figure 10.23
Employer's Payroll Taxes Journal Entry Dialog Box

T U T O R I A L   P R O B L E M   1 0 - T

STEP 11:   **Display the payroll journal entries.**
Click the *Reports* toolbar button. Choose the *Journals* option. Select the *General Journal* report, then click *OK*. When the Journal Report Selection window appears, choose the *Customize Journal Report* option and click *OK*. If necessary, set the date range to 12/31/-- through 12/31/--. The report appears in Figure 10.24.

```
                           Foltz Consulting Co.
                             General Journal
                                12/31/--

    -----------------------------------------------------------------
    Date    Refer.    Acct.   Title                  Debit     Credit
    -----------------------------------------------------------------

    12/31   Payroll    520    Consultant Salaries Exp.  6828.68
    12/31   Payroll    545    Office Salaries Exp.       5462.00
    12/31   Payroll    265    Emp. Fed. Inc. Tax Pay.             1137.97
    12/31   Payroll    270    Emp. State Inc. Tax Pay.             333.32
    12/31   Payroll    275    Social Security Tax Pay.            762.02
    12/31   Payroll    280    Medicare Tax Payable                178.22
    12/31   Payroll    272    Emp. City Inc. Tax Pay.             122.90
    12/31   Payroll    297    Health Ins. Premiums Pay.           250.00
    12/31   Payroll    298    Dental Ins. Premiums Pay.           138.00
    12/31   Payroll    299    Credit Union Deduct. Pay.           265.00
    12/31   Payroll    285    Salaries Payable                   9103.25

    12/31   Pay. Tax   550    Payroll Tax Expense       1064.23
    12/31   Pay. Tax   275    Social Security Tax Pay.            762.02
    12/31   Pay. Tax   280    Medicare Tax Payable                178.21
    12/31   Pay. Tax   290    State Unemp. Tax Payable            108.00
    12/31   Pay. Tax   295    Federal Unemp. Tax Pay.              16.00
                                                      --------   --------
                              Totals                  13354.91   13354.91
                                                      ========   ========
```

Figure 10.24
General Journal Report (Payroll Journal Entries)

STEP 12:   **Display the quarterly report.**
Choose the *Payroll Reports* option. Select the *Quarterly Report,* then click *OK*. The quarterly report appears in Figure 10.25.

TUTORIAL   PROBLEM   10 - T

Foltz Consulting Co.
Quarterly Report
12/31/--

Soc. Sec. Number	Employee Name	Taxable Soc. Sec.	Taxable Medicare
576-28-4940	Barnard, Melinda	6531.26	6531.26
594-49-7090	Chadwick, Carl	4114.00	4114.00
520-73-2726	Feng, Chan	6810.00	6810.00
584-69-2381	Lienhardt, Jody	7020.00	7020.00
518-70-3409	Salas, Luis	6407.10	6407.10
482-70-8945	Wheatly, Frank	2000.00	2000.00
	Totals	32882.36	32882.36
	Total Employees 6		

Figure 10.25
Quarterly Report

STEP 13:   **Display the W–2 statements.**

Select *W–2 Statements,* then click *OK*. The first statement is shown in Figure 10.26.

W-2 Wage and Tax Statement 19--	Federal Wages 26137.52	Federal Tax 3064.98
Employee's Name Barnard Melinda 1617 Vine Ave. Biloxi, MS 39533-1937	Soc. Sec. Wages 26137.52	Soc. Sec. Tax 1620.53
	Medicare Wages 26137.52	Medicare Tax 378.99
Social Security Number 576-28-4940	State Wages 26137.52	State Tax 747.78
Employer's Name Foltz Consulting Co.	City Wages 26137.52	City Tax 261.38

Figure 10.26
W-2 Statement

STEP 14:   **Save your data.**
Click the *Save* toolbar button.

STEP 15:   **Optional spreadsheet integration activity:**
Foltz Consulting Co. has asked you to use a spreadsheet to provide them with an estimate of how much it would cost the company to give each employee a 3% raise next year.

a. Copy the payroll report to the clipboard in spreadsheet format.
b. Start up your spreadsheet software and load the template file SS10–T.
c. Select cell A1 as the current cell and paste the report copied in step 15a into the spreadsheet.
d. Enter 3% in cell C94 (percent of increase in gross pay).
    Enter 6.2% in cell C95 (Social Security withholding rate).
    Enter 1.45% in cell C96 (Medicare withholding rate).
    Enter in cell C99 the formula to calculate the 3% increase amount of gross pay (+E81+(E81*C94)).
    Enter in cell C100 the formula to calculate the amount of Social Security (+C99*C95).
    Enter in cell C101 the formula to calculate the amount of Medicare (+C99*C96).
    Enter in cell D99 the formula to calculate the difference between last year's gross pay and the 3% increased gross pay amount (+C99–E81).
    Enter in cell D100 the formula to calculate the difference between last year's Social Security and the projected Social Security amount (+C100–E84).
    Enter in cell D101 the formula to calculate the difference between last year's Medicare and the projected Medicare amount (+C101–E85).
    Enter in cell D103 the formula to sum the total effect of a 3% increase in gross pay (+D99+D100+D101).
e. The completed spreadsheet is shown in Figure 10.27. Format your spreadsheet to match Figure 10.27. Print the results of a 3% increase in gross pay.
f. Save the spreadsheet with a file name of XXX10–T.
g. What would be the estimated cost to Foltz Consulting Co. for a 4% raise? What if the Social Security rate increases to 6.5% or the Medicare rate increases to 1.75%? Adjust the spreadsheet to reflect these changes.
h. End your spreadsheet session without saving your changes from step 15g.

TUTORIAL PROBLEM 10–T

```
Pay Increase:        3.00%
Soc. Sec. Rate:      6.20%
Medicare Rate:       1.45%

----------------------------------------------------------
                     Projections       Difference
----------------------------------------------------------

Gross Pay            $130,873.76       $3,811.86
Soc. Sec. W/H        $8,114.17         $236.35
Medicare W/H         $1,897.67         $55.21

Total                                  $4,103.42
```

Figure 10.27
Estimated Cost of 3% Raise

STEP 16: Optional word processing activity:
Prepare an address list of the current, active employees for the personnel department.
a. Display and copy the employee list to the clipboard in word processing format.
b. Start up your word processing software and create a new document. Use a fixed type font such as Courier.
c. Paste the employee list report into the document.
d. Enter headings, delete unwanted data, etc., and format the document to match Figure 10.28.
e. Print the completed address list.
f. Save the document with a file name of XXX10–T.
g. End your word processing session.

```
                        Foltz Consulting Co.
                        Employee Address List
                             12/31/--

----------------------------------------------------------------------
Emp.
No.    Employee Name    Address            City,   State, & Zip
----------------------------------------------------------------------

110    Barnard, Melinda 1617 Vine Ave.     Biloxi, MS 39533-1937
120    Chadwick, Carl   149 Trailwind Dr.  Biloxi, MS 39533-5931
130    Feng, Chan       11397 Egbert Lane  Biloxi, MS 39533-0172
140    Lienhardt, Jody  7234 Isabella Ave. Biloxi, MS 39535-3510
150    Salas, Luis      8152 Grand Vista   Biloxi, MS 39532-9281
160    Wheatly, Frank   15 Jackson Pike    Biloxi, MS 39536-8011
```

Figure 10.28
Employee Address List

STEP 17: End the *Automated Accounting* session.
Click the *Exit/Quit* toolbar button.

Applying Your Information Skills

I. MATCHING

Directions: In the *Working Papers,* write the letter of the appropriate term next to each definition.

  a. withholding allowances
  b. number of pay periods
  c. marital status
  d. salary amount
  e. hourly rate
  f. voluntary deductions
  g. employee list report
  h. payroll report
  i. quarterly report
  j. W–2 statement

1. A report that provides employee earnings and withholding information for the month, quarter, and year.

2. The gross amount paid for the employee's services each pay period.

3. A report that summarizes an employee's taxable wages and various withholdings, and is used for individual tax reporting purposes.

4. Single or married status for tax purposes.

5. Employee-authorized withholdings from earnings for such options as health insurance, dental insurance, savings plans, and charitable contributions.

6. The amount paid an employee per hour.

7. The number of deductions from total earnings for each person legally supported by a taxpayer for tax purposes.

8. A report that provides a complete listing of the employee payroll information.

9. The number of times an employee is paid per year.

10. A report used by a company to disclose Social Security and Medicare taxable wages to the Internal Revenue Service.

II. QUESTIONS

Directions: Write the answers to each of the following questions in the *Working Papers*.

1. If an employee is paid biweekly (every two weeks), what would you record in the employee data field, Number of Pay Periods?

2. Explain the difference between the Current Payroll Journal Entry and the Employer's Payroll Taxes menu items.

3. Explain the process for deleting a payroll transaction already entered.

4. How does the computer know what check numbers to assign to current payroll checks?

5. What is the purpose of the quarterly report?

 # Independent Practice Problem 10–P

In this problem, you will process the September and October monthly payrolls for Metro Merchandising. You will perform the operating procedures necessary to add new employees, make changes to employee data, and delete employees. In addition, you will process the payroll for the months of September and October. Since September is the end of a quarter, the September payroll will include the end-of-quarter report.

September Payroll:

Employees to Be Paid This Pay Period:

Employee Number	Employee Name	Regular Hours	Overtime Hours	Health Insurance	Dental Insurance	Credit Union
210	Farris, Anna			75.00	35.00	350.00
220	Flanigan, Bruce	176		65.00	25.00	75.00
240	Messner, Paula	176	2.5	85.00	35.00	100.00
250	Mohan, Catherine	176	1.5	65.00	25.00	100.00
260	Sheridan, Daniel			80.00	30.00	300.00
270	Wilkins, Donna	176		65.00	25.00	50.00

STEP 1: Start up *Automated Accounting 7.0.*

STEP 2: Load file AA10–P.

STEP 3: Enter your name in the User Name text box.

STEP 4: Use Save As to save the data with a file name of XXX10–P1.

STEP 5:   Enter the September payroll transactions. Use 09/30/-- as the transaction date and have the computer calculate taxes.

STEP 6:   Display a payroll report.

STEP 7:   Generate and post the journal entry for the current payroll.

STEP 8:   Generate and post the employer's payroll taxes journal entry.

STEP 9:   Display the September payroll journal entries.

STEP 10:   Display a quarterly report.

STEP 11:   Save your data as XXX10–P1.

STEP 12:   Optional spreadsheet integration activity:
Metro Merchandising has asked you to use a spreadsheet to prepare a payroll distribution of gross earnings report for the quarter.
a.   Copy the payroll report to the clipboard in spreadsheet format.
b.   Start up your spreadsheet software and load the template file SS10–P.
c.   Select cell A1 as the current cell and paste the report copied in step 12a into the spreadsheet.
d.   Enter +A3 in cell A106.
Enter *Payroll Distribution (Quarterly Gross Earnings)* in cell A107.
Enter +A5 in cell A108.
Enter *Employee* in cell A110.
Enter *Gross Earnings* in cell B110.
Enter the cell references to each employee and their corresponding quarterly gross earnings in the columns under the respective headings.
Enter the formula to sum the gross earnings.
e.   Generate a pie chart:
Select the range of cells containing the employee number/name and corresponding gross earnings, then choose the Chart or Graph menu item from the spreadsheet program you are using. If the computer asks for a graph name, etc., enter *Payroll Distribution*. Choose Pie Chart from the toolbar if the graph that appears is not a pie chart. Finally, if the spreadsheet you are using permits copying and

> **CHECK FIGURE:**
> Payroll Report: Current
> Total Gross Pay =
> $17,322.74

pasting the chart into the worksheet, copy and paste the chart into blank cells.

  f. Print the payroll distribution report portion of the spreadsheet and pie chart.

  g. Save the spreadsheet data with a file name of XXX10–P.

  h. End your spreadsheet session.

STEP 13: **End the *Automated Accounting* session.**

October Payroll:
The step-by-step instructions for completing the October payroll for Metro Merchandising are as follows:

Addition of New Employee:
Yeager, Keith
301 Silver Grove
Portland, ME 04109–7110

Assign employee number 280; social security number, 487-55-3613; withholding allowances, 2; pay periods per year, 12; G.L. Account No., 6170 (Office Salary Expense); salaried; married; salary amount, $2,850.00.

Changes to Current Employees:
Farris, Anna (Employee No. 210): Change the address to 6920 Amber Valley.

Mohan, Catherine (Employee No. 250): Change the social security number to 675-28-8744.

Deletion of Employee:
Delete Kimbler, James (Employee No. 230).

Employees to Be Paid This Pay Period:

Employee Number	Employee Name	Regular Hours	Overtime Hours	Health Insurance	Dental Insurance	Credit Union
210	Farris, Anna			75.00	35.00	350.00
220	Flanigan, Bruce	168	3.25	65.00	25.00	75.00
240	Messner, Paula	168		85.00	35.00	100.00
250	Mohan, Catherine	168	2.5	65.00	25.00	100.00
260	Sheridan, Daniel			80.00	30.00	300.00
270	Wilkins, Donna	168		65.00	25.00	50.00
280	Yeager, Keith			70.00	28.00	50.00

STEP 1: **Start up *Automated Accounting 7.0.***

STEP 2: **Load the September payroll data file saved in Step 11 (XXX10–P1).**

STEP 3: **Use Save As to save the data with a file name of XXX10–P2.**

STEP 4:   **Enter the employee maintenance data.**

STEP 5:   **Enter the October payroll transactions. Use 10/31/-- as the transaction date and have the program calculate taxes.**

STEP 6:   **Display the employee list report.**

STEP 7:   **Display the payroll report.**

STEP 8:   **Generate and post the journal entry for the current payroll.**

STEP 9:   **Generate and post the employer's payroll taxes journal entry.**

STEP 10:   **Display the October payroll journal entries.**

STEP 11:   **Save your data.**

STEP 12:   **Optional word processing integration activity:**
            The personnel department has asked you to prepare an employee report showing each employee's employee number, name, general ledger salary expense account number, and salary/hourly rate.
            a. Display and copy the employee list to the clipboard in word processing format.
            b. Start up your word processing software and create a new document. Use a fixed type font such as Courier.
            c. Paste the employee list report into the document.
            d. Enter headings, delete unwanted data, etc., and format the report for the desired data.
            e. Print the completed report.
            f. Save the document with a file name of XXX10–P.
            g. End your word processing session.

STEP 13:   **End the *Automated Accounting* session.**

> **CHECK FIGURE:**
> Payroll Report: Current Total Gross Pay = $19,842.91

Applying Your Technology Skills 10–P   **P**

Directions: Using Independent Practice Problem 10–P, write the answers to the following questions in the *Working Papers*.

September Payroll:
Use the payroll file you saved under file name XXX10–P1 to answer the following questions for the September payroll.

Payroll Report:
1. What is the number of withholding allowances for Anna Farris?

2. What is the current gross pay for Daniel Sheridan?

3. What is the amount withheld for the quarter for Medicare for Donna Wilkins?

4. What is the check number for the check written to Donna Wilkins?

5. What is the total current net pay for all employees?

6. What is the total yearly gross pay for all employees?

Journal Entries Report:
7. What is the amount of the debit to Sales Salary Expense?

8. What is the amount of the debit to Payroll Taxes Expense?

9. What is the amount of the credit to Salaries Payable?

Quarterly Report:
10. What is the Taxable Social Security amount for Bruce Flanigan?

11. What is the total Taxable Medicare amount for all employees for the quarter?

October Payroll:
Use the payroll file you saved under file name XXX10–P2 to answer the following questions for the October payroll.

Employee List:
1. What is the number of withholding allowances for Bruce Flanigan?

2. What is Paula Messner's social security number?

Payroll Report:
3. What is the salary amount for Keith Yeager?

4. What is the current federal withholding amount for Catherine Mohan?

5. What is the Social Security amount withheld for the year for Anna Farris?

6. What is the check number for the check written to Daniel Sheridan?

7. What is the net amount of the check to Keith Yeager?

8. What is the total Credit Union amount withheld for the year for all employees?

9. What is the total yearly gross pay for all employees?

Journal Entries Report:
10. What is the amount of the debit to Office Salary Expense?

11. What is the amount of the debit to Payroll Taxes Expense?

12. What is the amount of the credit to Salaries Payable?

Mastery Problem 10–M

In this problem, you will process the November and December payrolls for Metro Merchandising. Since December 31st is the end of the year, you will also display the quarterly report and W–2 statements.

November Payroll:
The payroll data for the November payroll are as follows:

Addition of New Employee:
Groves, Barbara
6807 Sweetbriar Dr.
Portland, ME 04110–2410

Assign employee number 230; social security number, 583-67-1785; withholding allowances, 4; pay periods per year, 12; G.L. Account No., 6210 (Sales Salary Expense); salaried; married; salary, $2,850.00.

Change to Current Employee:
Yeager, Keith (Employee No. 280): Change number of withholding allowances to 3.

Employees to Be Paid This Pay Period:

Employee Number	Employee Name	Regular Hours	Overtime Hours	Health Insurance	Dental Insurance	Credit Union
210	Farris, Anna			75.00	35.00	350.00
220	Flanigan, Bruce	168		65.00	25.00	75.00
230	Groves, Barbara			80.00	30.00	125.00
240	Messner, Paula	168	5.0	85.00	35.00	100.00
250	Mohan, Catherine	168		65.00	25.00	100.00
260	Sheridan, Daniel			80.00	30.00	300.00
270	Wilkins, Donna	168		65.00	25.00	50.00
280	Yeager, Keith			70.00	28.00	50.00

December Payroll:
The payroll data for the December payroll are as follows:

Employees to Be Paid This Pay Period:

Employee Number	Employee Name	Regular Hours	Overtime Hours	Health Insurance	Dental Insurance	Credit Union
210	Farris, Anna			75.00	35.00	350.00
220	Flanigan, Bruce	176		65.00	25.00	75.00
230	Groves, Barbara			80.00	30.00	125.00
240	Messner, Paula	176		85.00	35.00	100.00
250	Mohan, Catherine	176		65.00	25.00	100.00
260	Sheridan, Daniel			80.00	30.00	300.00
270	Wilkins, Donna	176		65.00	25.00	50.00
280	Yeager, Keith			70.00	28.00	50.00

STEP 1:   **Start up *Automated Accounting 7.0.***

STEP 2:   **Load opening balances file AA10–M.**

STEP 3:   Enter your name in the User Name text box.

STEP 4:   Save the data with a name of XXX10–M1.

STEP 5:   Enter the November employee maintenance and payroll transactions. Use a transaction date of 11/30/-- and have the program calculate taxes.

STEP 6:   Display the employee list report.

STEP 7:   Display the November payroll report.

CHECK FIGURE:
Payroll Report: Current
Total Gross Pay =
$22,676.03

STEP 8:   Generate and post the journal entries for the current payroll and employer's payroll taxes for November.

STEP 9:   Display the November payroll journal entries.

STEP 10:   Save your data with a file name of XXX10–M1.

STEP 11:   Use Save As to save the data with a name of XXX10–M2.

STEP 12:   Enter the December payroll transactions. Use a transaction date of 12/31/-- and have the program calculate taxes.

CHECK FIGURE:
Payroll Report: Current
Total Gross Pay =
$22,952.80

STEP 13:   Display a payroll report.

STEP 14:   Generate and post the journal entries for the current payroll and employer's payroll taxes for December.

STEP 15:   Display the December payroll journal entries.

STEP 16:   Display the quarterly report and W–2 statements.

STEP 17:   Save your data (as XXX10–M2).

STEP 18:   Optional spreadsheet integration activity:
Use a spreadsheet to provide an estimate of how much it would cost the company to give each employee a 4% raise next year. Assume that the Social Security rate will be 6.20% and the Medicare rate will be 1.45%.
a. Copy the payroll report to the clipboard in spreadsheet format.
b. Start up your spreadsheet software and load the template file SS10–M.
c. Select cell A1 as the current cell and paste the report copied in step 18a into the spreadsheet.
d. Enter the percentages and formulas required to complete the spreadsheet cells B120 through D129. Format the spreadsheet. Refer to Figure 10.27 as a guide if necessary.
e. Print the results of a 4% increase in gross pay.
f. Save the spreadsheet with a file name of XXX10–M.

g. What would be the estimated cost if a 4.5% raise is given to the employees? What if the Social Security rate increases to 6.75% or the Medicare rate increases to 1.85%? Adjust the spreadsheet to reflect these changes.

h. End your spreadsheet session without saving your changes from step 18g.

STEP 19:   Optional word processing integration activity:
Prepare an address list of the current, active employees.

a. Display and copy the employee list to the clipboard in word processing format.

b. Start up your word processing software and create a new document. Use a fixed type font such as Courier.

c. Paste the employee list report into the document.

d. Enter headings, delete unwanted data, etc., and format the document as necessary. Use Figure 10.28 as a guide.

e. Print the completed address list.

f. Save the document with a file name of XXX10–M.

g. End your word processing session.

STEP 20:   End the *Automated Accounting* session.

Applying Your Technology Skills 10–M

Directions: Using Mastery Problem 10–M, write the answers to the following questions in the *Working Papers*.

November Payroll:
Use the payroll file you saved under file name XXX10–M1 to answer the following questions for the November payroll.

Employee List:

1. What is the number of withholding allowances for Catherine Mohan?

2. What is Anna Farris's street address?

Payroll Report:

3. What is Bruce Flanigan's hourly rate?

4. What is the current gross pay for Barbara Groves?

5. What is the Medicare amount withheld for the quarter for Catherine Mohan?

6. What is Keith Yeager's gross pay for the quarter?

7. What is Daniel Sheridan's current net pay?

8. What is the total current net pay for all employees?

9. What is the total yearly gross pay for all employees?

Journal Entries Report:

10. What is the amount of the credit to Employee Federal Income Tax Payable?

11. What is the amount of the credit to Health Insurance Premiums Payable?

12. What is the amount of the credit to Employee City Income Tax Payable?

December Payroll:

Use the payroll file you saved under file name XXX10–M2 to answer the following questions for the December payroll.

Payroll Report:

1. What is the current net pay for Barbara Groves?

2. What is the current federal withholding amount for Anna Farris?

3. What is the Medicare amount withheld for the year for Daniel Sheridan?

4. What is the check number for the check written to Donna Wilkins?

5. What is the total current Dental Insurance amount withheld for all employees?

6. What is the total yearly Social Security withheld for all employees?

Journal Entries Report:

7. What is the amount of the credit to Medicare Tax Payable?

8. What is the amount of the debit to Payroll Taxes Expense?

9. What is the amount of the credit to Salaries Payable?

Quarterly Report:

10. What is the Taxable Social Security amount for Catherine Mohan?

11. What is the total Taxable Medicare amount for all employees for the quarter?

W–2 Statements:

12. What is the amount of state tax shown for Anna Farris?

13. What is the Medicare tax shown for Bruce Flanigan?

LEARNING OBJECTIVES

Upon completion of this chapter, you will be able to:

1. Complete inventory stock items input forms.

2. Enter inventory stock item maintenance.

3. Complete inventory transactions input forms.

4. Enter inventory transactions.

5. Display inventory transactions and reports.

6. Purge inventory transactions.

11

INTRODUCTION

Merchandise inventory is often one of the most costly assets of a retail business. The degree of success a business has in controlling merchandise inventory costs has a direct relationship to profitability. A merchandise inventory can consist of thousands of different items. Keeping records on so many items can be very time-consuming and error-prone. In addition to the cost of purchasing inventory, the total cost of carrying inventory is increased by pilferage and theft, taxes, insurance premiums, and interest payments on purchases that are financed.

Since the costs associated with merchandise inventory may be high, a business must try to keep the stock levels as low as possible yet maintain sufficient inventory to meet customer demand. If the inventory is too low, out-of-stock conditions may occur which could result in lost sales, loss of customer confidence, and reduced profits. Therefore, the business must keep the inventory as low as possible while avoiding out-of-stock conditions.

The merchandising business is faced with other difficult decisions related to merchandise inventory. A business must decide when and how many items to reorder. A business must also know which items are selling well and which are not. Without this information, the inventory might contain items that are not selling well yet are very expensive to maintain.

Because of the large number of items and high volume of transactions involved in maintaining inventory, a computerized system is favored over a manual system. In a computerized inventory system, relevant data is stored for each stock item such as stock number, description of the item, unit of measure, reorder point, and retail price. Periodically (daily, weekly, etc.), this data is updated. New stock items may be added to the file, data in existing stock items may be changed as necessary, and inactive stock items may be deleted. Once the stock item file has been maintained, the inventory transactions for the period are entered. These transactions consist of sales, sales returns, purchase orders, receipts into inventory, and purchases returns. Finally, the inventory reports are generated.

E T H I C S

A journalist, knowledgeable in the use of computer graphics, uses a paint and draw program to retouch a photograph of a suspected criminal to make the suspect appear mean and angry. The journalist then submits the altered photo to the editor to be included on the front page of the local newspaper.

a. Do you think that what the journalist did was ethical, unethical, or even a computer crime? Justify your choice.

b. What actions, if any, do you think the editor of the newspaper should take toward the journalist?

INVENTORY STOCK ITEMS INPUT FORM

Additions, changes, and deletions to obsolete inventory items may be recorded on an inventory stock items input form, as illustrated in Figure 11.1. The first entry is an addition of a new stock item. When a new stock item is added, each of the columns on the input form must be completed. The second entry is a change to an existing stock item. The retail price of stock number 1030, Harris Power Plus 75, is being changed to $849.00. When recording changes to data fields for an inventory item, you must include the Stock Number field as well as the data field(s) to be changed. Any data fields that have not changed may be left blank. The third entry shows the deletion of a stock item, number 4040. To delete a stock item, record the Stock Number and the notation (*Delete*) in the description field.

INVENTORY STOCK ITEMS
INPUT FORM

Run Date 03/07/--   Problem No. Example

Stock Number	Description	Unit of Measure	Reorder Point	Retail Price
4025	Glazer 16 lb. Paper	CS	24	29.95
1030				849.00
4040	(Delete)			

Figure 11.1
Inventory Stock Items Input Form

Each field in the form corresponds to a grid cell in the Inventory Account Maintenance window. The field names and a description of each column are illustrated in the Inventory Account Maintenance window shown in Figure 11.2.

An incompatibility occurs when software on your client computer cannot communicate with software on an Internet host. Causes of incompatibilities include different versions of software, mismatched software settings, and different hardware platforms.

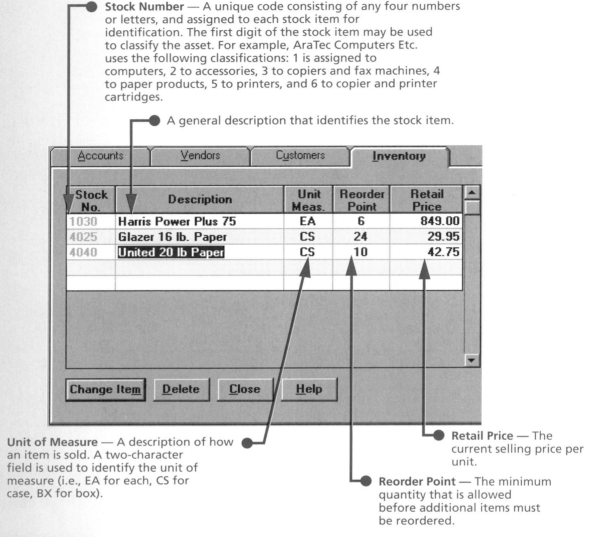

Stock Number — A unique code consisting of any four numbers or letters, and assigned to each stock item for identification. The first digit of the stock item may be used to classify the asset. For example, AraTec Computers Etc. uses the following classifications: 1 is assigned to computers, 2 to accessories, 3 to copiers and fax machines, 4 to paper products, 5 to printers, and 6 to copier and printer cartridges.

A general description that identifies the stock item.

Unit of Measure — A description of how an item is sold. A two-character field is used to identify the unit of measure (i.e., EA for each, CS for case, BX for box).

Retail Price — The current selling price per unit.

Reorder Point — The minimum quantity that is allowed before additional items must be reordered.

Figure 11.2
Stock Item Maintenance

INVENTORY STOCK ITEM MAINTENANCE

When *Maintain Accounts* is chosen from the Data menu or the *Accts.* toolbar button is clicked, the Account Maintenance window will appear. To perform inventory account maintenance, click the *Inventory* tab. Figure 11.2 shows the maintenance data already entered from the Inventory Stock Items Input Form shown in Figure 11.1. Note that stock number 4040 is shown selected and about to be deleted.

Table 11.1 contains a description of additional data that are stored with each inventory stock item record. These fields start with zero values. As transactions are entered, the data are updated. You will learn to enter inventory transactions later in this chapter.

FIELD NAME	DESCRIPTION
Quantity on Hand	The quantity of a stock item that is included in the merchandise inventory at the present time.
Quantity on Order	The quantity of a stock item that is currently on order but has not yet arrived.
Yearly Quantity Sold	An accumulation of the number of a stock item sold in the fiscal year.
Yearly Dollars Sold	An accumulation of the dollar value of a stock item sold in the fiscal year.
Last Cost Price	The price paid per unit for the most recent purchase of a stock item.
Average Cost	The weighted-average of the purchase prices for a stock item.

Table 11.1
Descriptions of Additional Inventory Data Stored by the Computer

Adding a New Inventory Stock Item

1:   Enter the stock number.

2:   Enter the data fields in the grid cell boxes.

3:   Click the *Add Item* button.

Changing Inventory Stock Item Data

1:   Select the stock item by clicking on the grid cell containing the data you wish to change. The *Add Item* button will change to *Change Item* when the insertion point is positioned in any grid cell box of an existing item.

2:   Enter the correct data for the stock item.

3:   Click the *Change Item* button.

Deleting an Inventory Stock Item

1:   Click the stock item to be deleted.

2:   Click the *Delete* button.
      You will not be allowed to delete a stock item that has current transaction data until after the transactions are deleted or purged, as discussed later in this chapter.

3:   When the delete confirmation dialog box appears, click *OK*.

INVENTORY TRANSACTIONS INPUT FORM

Transactions affecting inventory, such as sales, sales returns, purchase orders, receipts into inventory, and purchases returns, are recorded on an inventory transactions input form. The input form in Figure 11.3 shows a purchase order, a sale, a receipt into inventory, a sales return, and a purchases return.

INVENTORY TRANSACTIONS INPUT FORM

Run Date 03/07/--   Problem No. Example

Date mm/dd/yy	Inventory Item	Invoice No.	Quantity Sold	Selling Price	Quantity Ordered	Quantity Received	Cost Price
03/01/--	Copier Toner Cartridge	P431			36		
03/01/--	Neuman Pentium 150	S754	1	2879.00			
03/03/--	HL Personal Laser Printer	R817				2	285.00
03/05/--	MX10 Mouse	CM738	−1	49.00			
03/06/--	Neuman Pentium 150	DM417				−1	1735.00

Figure 11.3
Inventory Transactions Input Form

INVENTORY TRANSACTIONS

Transactions affecting inventory are entered into the Other Activities Inventory window. When the *Other* toolbar button is clicked, the Other Activities window will appear. Click the *Inventory* tab to display the Other Activities Inventory window, as shown in Figure 11.4. The transactions are those recorded on the Inventory Transactions Input Form in Figure 11.3.

Entering Inventory Transaction Data

1: Enter the date of the transaction.

2: Select the inventory item from the drop-down list or key the first letter of the stock item's description until the correct inventory item appears.

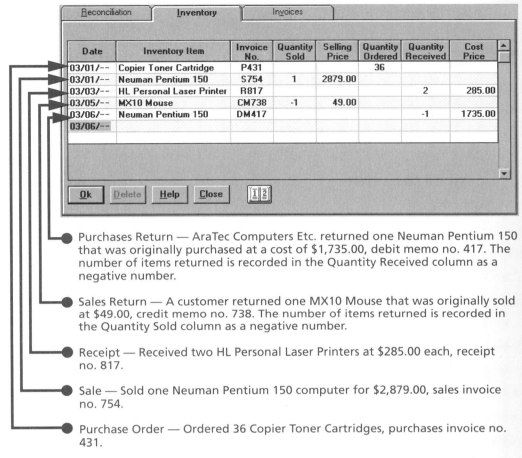

Purchases Return — AraTec Computers Etc. returned one Neuman Pentium 150 that was originally purchased at a cost of $1,735.00, debit memo no. 417. The number of items returned is recorded in the Quantity Received column as a negative number.

Sales Return — A customer returned one MX10 Mouse that was originally sold at $49.00, credit memo no. 738. The number of items returned is recorded in the Quantity Sold column as a negative number.

Receipt — Received two HL Personal Laser Printers at $285.00 each, receipt no. 817.

Sale — Sold one Neuman Pentium 150 computer for $2,879.00, sales invoice no. 754.

Purchase Order — Ordered 36 Copier Toner Cartridges, purchases invoice no. 431.

Figure 11.4
Inventory Transactions

3: Enter the transaction data in the appropriate grid cells.

4: Click *OK*.

Correcting an Inventory Transaction

1: Select the transaction by clicking the grid cell containing the data you wish to correct.

2: Enter the correction.

3: Click *OK*.

Deleting an Inventory Transaction

1: Select the transaction you wish to delete.
    Click any grid cell belonging to the transaction to be deleted.

2: Click the *Delete* button.

INVENTORY REPORTS

The procedure to display and print the inventory reports is identical to what you have used in previous chapters of this text. The inventory reports available provide management with valuable information regarding the current status of inventory items, the accuracy of inventory records, items at or below reorder point, inventory valuation, and yearly sales figures for each inventory item.

Inventory List

The purpose of the inventory list report is to provide the current status of each inventory item for reference. The report is also useful for verifying the accuracy of inventory maintenance.

1:   Click the *Reports* toolbar button.

2:   Choose the *Inventory Reports* option from the Select a Report Group list.
A list showing the inventory reports will appear, as shown in Figure 11.5.

3:   Choose the *Inventory List* report from the Choose a Report to Display list.

4:   Click *OK*.
An inventory list report is shown in Figure 11.6.

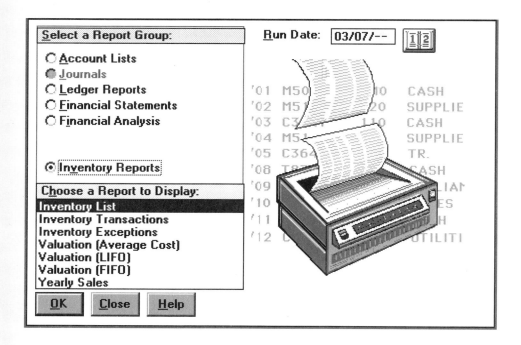

Figure 11.5
Report Selection
(Inventory
Reports)

Stock No.	Description	Unit Meas.	On Hand	On Order	Reorder Point	Average Cost	Last Cost	Retail Price
	AraTec Computers Etc. Inventory List 03/07/--							
1010	Apke ProLine XT	EA	11	0	8	899.00	899.00	1499.00
1020	AWM 133 MHz Micro	EA	5	3	5	1225.00	1225.00	2049.00
1030	Harris Power Plus 75	EA	7	0	6	520.71	535.00	849.00
1040	Iwasaki 90 MHz Notebook	EA	6	0	4	1500.00	1500.00	2499.00
1050	Neuman Pentium 150	EA	6	0	5	1759.37	1735.00	2879.00
1060	Preston Multimedia System	EA	7	0	6	800.00	800.00	1350.00
1070	Tanaka ThinkPad 701	EA	6	0	5	1025.00	1025.00	1699.00
1080	Yoshino Pentium 90	EA	7	0	6	764.48	775.00	1199.00
2010	Apke Color Scanner	EA	7	0	6	203.14	205.00	389.95
2020	DPG 28.8 External Modem	EA	13	0	12	145.00	145.00	249.00
2030	CXP 28.8 External Modem	EA	10	0	10	165.00	165.00	279.00
2040	MultiMedia Color Monitor	EA	8	0	6	477.16	410.00	749.00
2050	MX10 Mouse	EA	13	0	24	29.00	29.00	49.00
2060	Tanaka 4x CD-ROM	EA	12	0	10	210.00	210.00	349.00
2070	TC 2.0 GB Hard Drive	EA	13	0	10	217.73	210.00	399.00
2080	Yoshino Sound Blaster	EA	8	0	8	95.00	95.00	159.00
3010	Ellis Personal Copier	EA	8	0	6	235.00	235.00	396.95
3020	Ellis Commercial Copier	EA	2	0	3	1700.00	1700.00	2850.00
3030	Hayato Facsimile	EA	6	0	5	209.29	215.00	325.00
3040	Minnis Facsimile & Copier	EA	1	0	3	625.00	625.00	999.99
4010	A-1 Recycled Copy Paper	CS	7	36	24	11.35	11.35	18.95
4020	Facsimile Roll Paper	BX	12	0	12	27.50	27.50	45.75
4025	Glazer 16 lb. Paper	CS	0	36	24			29.95
4030	Glazer 20 lb. Paper	CS	22	12	24	23.95	23.95	39.95
5010	HL Personal Laser Print	EA	8	0	6	311.79	285.00	479.00
5020	Mori Color Laser Print	EA	2	0	3	1550.00	1550.00	2599.00
5030	Owen Ink Jet Printer	EA	9	0	8	200.00	200.00	339.00
5040	Tobis Bubble Jet Print	EA	9	0	8	225.00	225.00	379.00
6010	Huges X2 Laser Cartridge	EA	14	0	12	41.50	41.50	69.00
6020	Ink Jet Cartridge	EA	30	0	24	8.95	8.95	14.95
6030	Tobis Color Cartridge	EA	27	0	24	11.35	11.35	18.95
6040	Weldon Color Cartridge	EA	49	0	36	10.64	10.75	17.95
6050	Copier Toner Cartridge	EA	0	36	24			35.50

Figure 11.6
Inventory List Report

Inventory Transactions

The inventory transactions report lists selected groups of inventory transactions. You should display this report whenever you enter, correct, or delete inventory transactions. This will help verify that all data have been recorded and entered correctly. The printed report provides an audit trail for future reference.

1:   Click the *Reports* toolbar button. Choose the *Inventory Reports* option button from the Select a Report Group list.

2:   Choose the *Inventory Transactions* report and click *OK*.
     The Inventory Transactions Report Selection dialog box will
     appear, as shown in Figure 11.7.

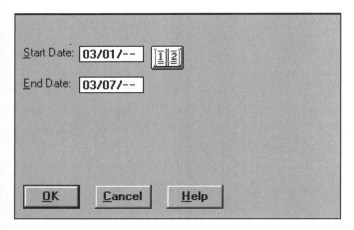

Figure 11.7
Inventory Transactions Report Selection Dialog Box

3:   Enter the range of dates to be included in the inventory
     transactions report, then click *OK*.
     An inventory transactions report is shown in Figure 11.8.

When the messages posted to a discussion group are first read and screened, the group is called a "moderated" group. Discussion groups without moderators are called "unmoderated."

```
                           AraTec Computers Etc.
                           Inventory Transactions
                                  03/07/--
```

Date	Stock No.	Description	Inv. No.	Quantity Sold	Selling Price	Quan. Ord.	Quan. Recd.	Cost Price
03/01	6050	Copier Toner Cartridge	P431			36		
03/01	4010	A-1 Recycled Copy Paper	P432			36		
03/01	1050	Neuman Pentium 150	S754	1	2879.00			
03/01	2010	Apke Color Scanner	S755	1	389.95			
03/01	2050	MX10 Mouse	S756	4	49.00			
03/02	1020	AWM 133 MHz Micro	P433			3		
03/02	4025	Glazer 16 lb. Paper	P434			36		
03/03	1050	Neuman Pentium 150	R816				6	1735.00
03/03	5010	HL Personal Laser Printer	R817				2	285.00
03/04	1010	Apke ProLine XT	S757	1	1499.00			
03/04	2030	CXP 28.8 External Modem	S758	1	279.00			
03/04	5030	Owen Ink Jet Printer	S759	1	339.00			
03/04	6020	Ink Jet Cartridge	S760	3	14.95			
03/04	4030	Glazer 20 lb. Paper	S760	3	39.95			
03/04	4020	Facsimile Roll Paper	S761	2	45.75			
03/05	2050	MX10 Mouse	S762	1	49.00			
03/05	2080	Yoshino Sound Blaster	S763	1	159.00			
03/05	2050	MX10 Mouse	CM738	−1	49.00			
03/06	1050	Neuman Pentium 150	DM417				−1	1735.00
03/07	3040	Minnis Facsimile & Copier	S764	1	999.99			
		Totals		19		111	7	

Figure 11.8
Inventory Transactions Report

Inventory Exceptions

The inventory exceptions report lists items in inventory that are out of stock, which occurs when quantity on hand is zero or less. It also lists items that are at or below the reorder point, which occurs when quantity on hand is less than or equal to the reorder point. This report alerts management to items in inventory that need attention.

1:   **Click the *Reports* toolbar button. Choose the *Inventory Reports* option button from the Select a Report Group list.**

2:   **Choose the *Inventory Exceptions* report and click *OK*.**
     An inventory exceptions report is shown in Figure 11.9.

```
                              AraTec Computers Etc.
                               Inventory Exceptions
                                    03/07/--

Stock                                Unit  On    On    Reorder
No.    Description                    Meas  Hand  Order Point   Exception

1020   AWM 133 MHz Micro             EA    5     3     5       At/below reorder point
2030   CXP 28.8 External Modem       EA    10          10      At/below reorder point
2050   MX10 Mouse                    EA    13          24      At/below reorder point
2080   Yoshino Sound Blaster         EA    8           8       At/below reorder point
3020   Ellis Commercial Copier       EA    2           3       At/below reorder point
3040   Minnis Facsimile & Copier     EA    1           3       At/below reorder point
4010   A-1 Recycled Copy Paper       CS    7     36    24      At/below reorder point
4020   Facsimile Roll Paper          BX    12          12      At/below reorder point
4025   Glazer 16 lb. Paper           CS    0     36    24      Out of stock
4030   Glazer 20 lb. Paper           CS    22    12    24      At/below reorder point
5020   Mori Color Laser Printer      EA    2           3       At/below reorder point
6050   Copier Toner Cartridge        EA    0     36    24      Out of stock
```

Figure 11.9
Inventory Exceptions Report

Inventory Valuation (Average Cost)

The **average cost inventory valuation method** calculates the ending inventory value by using the weighted-average of the purchase prices for all stock items on hand. The average cost report lists each item in inventory, showing the quantity currently on hand and the weighted average cost for each item. The software updates the average cost whenever inventory is received.

The following example shows how the software calculates the weighted average cost. Assume that there is 1 unit of stock number 1010 at $350.00, and 11 units at $380.00 each. The average cost would be calculated as follows:

Quantity	Cost	Total
1	× $350.00 =	$ 350.00
11	× 380.00 =	4180.00

12                                    $4530.00 ($4530.00 ÷ 12 = $377.50 average cost)

The quantity on hand and computed average cost are extended to determine the value of the inventory based on an average cost.

1: Click the *Reports* toolbar button. Choose the *Inventory Reports* option button from the Select a Report Group list.

2: Choose *Valuation (Average Cost)* and click *OK*.
An inventory valuation (average cost) report is shown in Figure 11.10.

```
                          AraTec Computers Etc.
                     Inventory Valuation (Average Cost)
                                03/07/--

Stock                      On            Value    Retail   Value
No.    Description         Hand   Cost   At Cost  Price    At Retail

1010   Apke ProLine XT      11   899.00   9889.00  1499.00  16489.00
1020   AWM 133 MHz Micro     5  1225.00   6125.00  2049.00  10245.00
1030   Harris Power Plus 75  7   520.71   3644.97   849.00   5943.00
1040   Iwasaki 90 MHz Notebook 6 1500.00  9000.00  2499.00  14994.00
1050   Neuman Pentium 150    6  1759.37  10556.22  2879.00  17274.00
1060   Preston Multimedia System 7 800.00 5600.00  1350.00   9450.00
1070   Tanaka ThinkPad 701   6  1025.00   6150.00  1699.00  10194.00
1080   Yoshino Pentium 90    7   764.48   5351.36  1199.00   8393.00
2010   Apke Color Scanner    7   203.14   1421.98   389.95   2729.65
2020   DPG 28.8 External Modem 13 145.00  1885.00   249.00   3237.00
2030   CXP 28.8 External Modem 10 165.00  1650.00   279.00   2790.00
2040   MultiMedia Color Monitor 8 477.16  3817.28   749.00   5992.00
2050   MX10 Mouse           13    29.00    377.00    49.00    637.00
2060   Tanaka 4x CD-ROM     12   210.00   2520.00   349.00   4188.00
2070   TC 2.0 GB Hard Drive 13   217.73   2830.49   399.00   5187.00
2080   Yoshino Sound Blaster 8    95.00    760.00   159.00   1272.00
3010   Ellis Personal Copier 8   235.00   1880.00   396.95   3175.60
3020   Ellis Commercial Copier 2 1700.00  3400.00  2850.00   5700.00
3030   Hayato Facsimile      6   209.29   1255.74   325.00   1950.00
3040   Minnis Facsimile & Copier 1 625.00  625.00   999.99    999.99
4010   A-1 Recycled Copy Paper 7  11.35     79.45    18.95    132.65
4020   Facsimile Roll Paper 12    27.50    330.00    45.75    549.00
4030   Glazer 20 lb. Paper  22    23.95    526.90    39.95    878.90
5010   HL Personal Laser Print 8 311.79   2494.32   479.00   3832.00
5020   Mori Color Laser Printer 2 1550.00 3100.00  2599.00   5198.00
5030   Owen Ink Jet Printer  9   200.00   1800.00   339.00   3051.00
5040   Tobis Bubble Jet Printer 9 225.00  2025.00   379.00   3411.00
6010   Huges X2 Laser Cartridge 14 41.50   581.00    69.00    966.00
6020   Ink Jet Cartridge    30     8.95    268.50    14.95    448.50
6030   Tobis Color Cartridge 27   11.35    306.45    18.95    511.65
6040   Weldon Color Cartridge 49  10.64    521.36    17.95    879.55

       Total Inventory Value             90772.02          150698.49
                                         ========          =========
```

Figure 11.10
Inventory Valuation (Average Cost) Report

Inventory Valuation (LIFO)

The **LIFO inventory valuation method** calculates the ending inventory value by using the price of merchandise purchased last for all stock items on hand. With the LIFO (last in, first out) method, the assumption is made that the last items received into inventory are the first to be sold. Therefore, any items remaining in inventory are the first items received. The software calculates LIFO on a perpetual basis, according to the order in which transactions are entered. The report lists the quantity in inventory for each different cost. The quantity and cost are extended to provide an inventory valuation based on the LIFO valuation method.

1:   Click the *Reports* toolbar button. Choose the *Inventory Reports* option button from the Select a Report Group list.

2:   Choose *Valuation (LIFO)* and click *OK*.
An inventory valuation (LIFO) report is shown in Figure 11.11.

Inventory Valuation (FIFO)

The **FIFO inventory valuation method** calculates the ending inventory value by using the price of merchandise purchased first for all stock items on hand. With the FIFO (first in, first out) method, the assumption is made that the first items received into inventory are the first sold. Therefore, any items remaining in inventory are the last items received. The report shows the quantity in inventory for each different cost. The quantity and cost are extended to provide an inventory valuation based on the FIFO valuation method.

1:   Click the *Reports* toolbar button. Choose the *Inventory Reports* option button from the Select a Report Group list.

2:   Choose *Valuation (FIFO)* and click *OK*.
An inventory valuation (FIFO) report is shown in Figure 11.12.

Yearly Sales

The yearly sales report provides management with unit and dollar sales for each item in inventory.

1:   Click the *Reports* toolbar button. Choose the *Inventory Reports* option button from the Select a Report Group list.

2:   Choose *Yearly Sales* and click *OK*.
A yearly sales report is shown in Figure 11.13.

```
                            AraTec Computers Etc.
                          Inventory Valuation (LIFO)
                                  03/07/--

--------------------------------------------------------------------------
Stock                           On            Value    Retail   Value
No.    Description              Hand   Cost   At Cost   Price    At Retail
--------------------------------------------------------------------------
1010   Apke ProLine XT          11    899.00   9889.00  1499.00   16489.00
1020   AWM 133 MHz Micro         5   1225.00   6125.00  2049.00   10245.00
1030   Harris Power Plus 75      2    485.00    970.00   849.00    1698.00
1030   Harris Power Plus 75      5    535.00   2675.00   849.00    4245.00
1040   Iwasaki 90 MHz Notebook   6   1500.00   9000.00  2499.00   14994.00
1050   Neuman Pentium 150        1   1850.00   1850.00  2879.00    2879.00
1050   Neuman Pentium 150        5   1735.00   8675.00  2879.00   14395.00
1060   Preston Multimedia System 7    800.00   5600.00  1350.00    9450.00
1070   Tanaka ThinkPad 701       6   1025.00   6150.00  1699.00   10194.00
1080   Yoshino Pentium 90        2    700.00   1400.00  1199.00    2398.00
1080   Yoshino Pentium 90        5    775.00   3875.00  1199.00    5995.00
2010   Apke Color Scanner        3    235.00    705.00   389.95    1169.85
2010   Apke Color Scanner        4    205.00    820.00   389.95    1559.80
2020   DPG 28.8 External Modem  13    145.00   1885.00   249.00    3237.00
2030   CXP 28.8 External Modem  10    165.00   1650.00   279.00    2790.00
2040   MultiMedia Color Monitor  3    460.00   1380.00   749.00    2247.00
2040   MultiMedia Color Monitor  5    410.00   2050.00   749.00    3745.00
2050   MX10 Mouse               13     29.00    377.00    49.00     637.00
2060   Tanaka 4x CD-ROM         12    210.00   2520.00   349.00    4188.00
2070   TC 2.0 GB Hard Drive      4    239.00    956.00   399.00    1596.00
2070   TC 2.0 GB Hard Drive      9    210.00   1890.00   399.00    3591.00
2080   Yoshino Sound Blaster     8     95.00    760.00   159.00    1272.00
3010   Ellis Personal Copier     8    235.00   1880.00   396.95    3175.60
3020   Ellis Commercial Copier   2   1700.00   3400.00  2850.00    5700.00
3030   Hayato Facsimile          2    195.00    390.00   325.00     650.00
3030   Hayato Facsimile          4    215.00    860.00   325.00    1300.00
3040   Minnis Facsimile & Copier 1    625.00    625.00   999.99     999.99
4010   A-1 Recycled Copy Paper   7     11.35     79.45    18.95     132.65
4020   Facsimile Roll Paper     12     27.50    330.00    45.75     549.00
4030   Glazer 20 lb. Paper      22     23.95    526.90    39.95     878.90
5010   HL Personal Laser Print   1    285.00    285.00   479.00     479.00
5010   HL Personal Laser Print   5    310.00   1550.00   479.00    2395.00
5010   HL Personal Laser Print   2    285.00    570.00   479.00     958.00
5020   Mori Color Laser Printer  2   1550.00   3100.00  2599.00    5198.00
5030   Owen Ink Jet Printer      9    200.00   1800.00   339.00    3051.00
5040   Tobis Bubble Jet Printer  9    225.00   2025.00   379.00    3411.00
6010   Huges X2 Laser Cartridge 14     41.50    581.00    69.00     966.00
6020   Ink Jet Cartridge        30      8.95    268.50    14.95     448.50
6030   Tobis Color Cartridge    27     11.35    306.45    18.95     511.65
6040   Weldon Color Cartridge   21     10.50    220.50    17.95     376.95
6040   Weldon Color Cartridge   28     10.75    301.00    17.95     502.60
                                                -------            ---------
       Total Inventory Value                   90300.80           150698.49
                                                ========           =========
```

Figure 11.11
Inventory Valuation (LIFO) Report

AraTec Computers Etc.
Inventory Valuation (FIFO)
03/07/--

Stock No.	Description	On Hand	Cost	Value At Cost	Retail Price	Value At Retail
1010	Apke ProLine XT	11	899.00	9889.00	1499.00	16489.00
1020	AWM 133 MHz Micro	5	1225.00	6125.00	2049.00	10245.00
1030	Harris Power Plus 75	2	485.00	970.00	849.00	1698.00
1030	Harris Power Plus 75	5	535.00	2675.00	849.00	4245.00
1040	Iwasaki 90 MHz Notebook	6	1500.00	9000.00	2499.00	14994.00
1050	Neuman Pentium 150	6	1735.00	10410.00	2879.00	17274.00
1060	Preston Multimedia System	7	800.00	5600.00	1350.00	9450.00
1070	Tanaka ThinkPad 701	6	1025.00	6150.00	1699.00	10194.00
1080	Yoshino Pentium 90	2	700.00	1400.00	1199.00	2398.00
1080	Yoshino Pentium 90	5	775.00	3875.00	1199.00	5995.00
2010	Apke Color Scanner	7	205.00	1435.00	389.95	2729.65
2020	DPG 28.8 External Modem	13	145.00	1885.00	249.00	3237.00
2030	CXP 28.8 External Modem	10	165.00	1650.00	279.00	2790.00
2040	MultiMedia Color Monitor	2	460.00	920.00	749.00	1498.00
2040	MultiMedia Color Monitor	6	410.00	2460.00	749.00	4494.00
2050	MX10 Mouse	13	29.00	377.00	49.00	637.00
2060	Tanaka 4x CD-ROM	12	210.00	2520.00	349.00	4188.00
2070	TC 2.0 GB Hard Drive	2	239.00	478.00	399.00	798.00
2070	TC 2.0 GB Hard Drive	11	210.00	2310.00	399.00	4389.00
2080	Yoshino Sound Blaster	8	95.00	760.00	159.00	1272.00
3010	Ellis Personal Copier	8	235.00	1880.00	396.95	3175.60
3020	Ellis Commercial Copier	2	1700.00	3400.00	2850.00	5700.00
3030	Hayato Facsimile	1	195.00	195.00	325.00	325.00
3030	Hayato Facsimile	5	215.00	1075.00	325.00	1625.00
3040	Minnis Facsimile & Copier	1	625.00	625.00	999.99	999.99
4010	A-1 Recycled Copy Paper	7	11.35	79.45	18.95	132.65
4020	Facsimile Roll Paper	12	27.50	330.00	45.75	549.00
4030	Glazer 20 lb. Paper	22	23.95	526.90	39.95	878.90
5010	HL Personal Laser Print	6	310.00	1860.00	479.00	2874.00
5010	HL Personal Laser Print	2	285.00	570.00	479.00	958.00
5020	Mori Color Laser Printer	2	1550.00	3100.00	2599.00	5198.00
5030	Owen Ink Jet Printer	9	200.00	1800.00	339.00	3051.00
5040	Tobis Bubble Jet Printer	9	225.00	2025.00	379.00	3411.00
6010	Huges X2 Laser Cartridge	14	41.50	581.00	69.00	966.00
6020	Ink Jet Cartridge	30	8.95	268.50	14.95	448.50
6030	Tobis Color Cartridge	27	11.35	306.45	18.95	511.65
6040	Weldon Color Cartridge	21	10.50	220.50	17.95	376.95
6040	Weldon Color Cartridge	28	10.75	301.00	17.95	502.60
	Total Inventory Value			90032.80		150698.49

Figure 11.12
Inventory Valuation (FIFO) Report

```
                        AraTec Computers Etc.
                           Yearly Sales
                             03/07/--

--------------------------------------------------------------
Stock                         Unit   Yearly    Yearly
No.    Description            Meas   Quantity  Amount
--------------------------------------------------------------

1010   Apke ProLine XT        EA      5        7495.00
1020   AWM 133 MHz Micro      EA      3        6147.00
1030   Harris Power Plus 75   EA      5        4495.00
1040   Iwasaki 90 MHz Notebook EA     2        4998.00
1050   Neuman Pentium 150     EA      3        8637.00
1060   Preston Multimedia System EA   1        1350.00
1070   Tanaka ThinkPad 701    EA      1        1699.00
1080   Yoshino Pentium 90     EA      2        2398.00
2010   Apke Color Scanner     EA      5        1949.75
2020   DPG 28.8 External Modem EA     4         996.00
2030   CXP 28.8 External Modem EA     2         558.00
2040   MultiMedia Color Monitor EA    4        2996.00
2050   MX10 Mouse             EA     11         539.00
2060   Tanaka 4x CD-ROM       EA      3        1047.00
2070   TC 2.0 GB Hard Drive   EA      5        1995.00
2080   Yoshino Sound Blaster  EA      2         318.00
3010   Ellis Personal Copier  EA      2         793.90
3020   Ellis Commercial Copier EA     1        2850.00
3030   Hayato Facsimile       EA      2         650.00
3040   Minnis Facsimile & Copier EA   2        2049.49
4010   A-1 Recycled Copy Paper CS     5          94.75
4020   Facsimile Roll Paper   BX      6         274.50
4025   Glazer 16 lb. Paper    CS
4030   Glazer 20 lb. Paper    CS     14         559.30
5010   HL Personal Laser Print EA     4        1916.00
5020   Mori Color Laser Printer EA    1        2599.00
5030   Owen Ink Jet Printer   EA      3        1017.00
5040   Tobis Bubble Jet Printer EA    1         379.00
6010   Huges X2 Laser Cartridge EA   10         690.00
6020   Ink Jet Cartridge      EA     18         269.10
6030   Tobis Color Cartridge  EA      5          94.75
6040   Weldon Color Cartridge EA     15         269.25
6050   Copier Toner Cartridge EA    ---      --------
                                    147       62123.79
                                    ===      ========
```

Figure 11.13
Yearly Sales Report

PURGE INVENTORY TRANSACTIONS

Automated Accounting 7.0 has a capacity of 400 inventory transactions. If this capacity is exceeded, an alert dialog box will appear, informing you of this condition. Before additional transactions can be entered, the previously entered transactions must be erased by choosing *Purge Inventory Transactions* from the Option menu. In the event you

accidentally choose this menu item, a dialog window will appear, asking you to confirm whether you indeed want to purge inventory transactions. Since stock items are updated when transactions are entered, purging inventory transactions will not cause any information to be lost. A backup file should be made, and a current transactions report should be printed before the inventory transactions are purged. This condition will not occur for any of the problems provided with this textbook since none exceed the system capacity.

Chapter Review

1. The degree of success a business has in controlling merchandise inventory has a direct relationship to profitability. Since the costs associated with merchandise inventory are high, a business must try to keep the stock levels as low as possible, yet maintain sufficient inventory to meet customer demand.

2. Additions, changes, and deletions to obsolete inventory items should be made prior to entering the inventory transactions for the current period. An inventory stock items input form is used to record the additions, changes, and deletions to inventory stock items.

3. After the inventory stock item additions, changes, and deletions are recorded on an inventory stock items input form, the stock item inventory maintenance is entered into the Account Maintenance Inventory window.

4. Transactions affecting inventory, such as sales, sales returns, purchase orders, receipts into inventory, and purchases returns are recorded on an inventory transactions input form.

5. After the transactions affecting inventory are recorded on the inventory transactions input form, the transactions are entered into the Other Activities Inventory window.

6. The inventory reports available provide management with valuable information regarding the current status of inventory items, the accuracy of inventory records, items at or below reorder point, inventory valuation, and yearly sales figures for each inventory item.

7. Purging inventory transactions is the process in which previously entered transactions are erased when system capacity is reached.

TUTORIAL PROBLEM 11-T

In this problem, you will process the inventory transactions for the week of March 1 through March 7 of the current year for AraTec Computers Etc. You will perform the operating procedures necessary to add new inventory stock items, make changes to existing inventory stock items, and delete an inventory stock item. Inventory maintenance is illustrated in Figure 11.14 and is shown as it would appear on the input form. In addition, you will process the orders, sales, receipts, sales returns, and purchases returns transactions that affect inventory. The transaction information is illustrated in Figure 11.15 as it would appear on the screen.

STEP 1: **Start up *Automated Accounting 7.0.***

STEP 2: **Load opening balances file AA11–T.**
Click the *Open* toolbar button and choose file AA11–T from the File list box.

STEP 3: **Enter your name in the User Name text box and click *OK*.**

STEP 4: **Save the file with a file name of XXX11–T.**
Click the *Save As* toolbar button and save the file as XXX11–T.

STEP 5: **Enter the following inventory maintenance data or use the information in the Inventory Stock Items Input Form shown in Figure 11.14.**
Click the *Accts.* toolbar icon. When the Account Maintenance window appears, click the *Inventory* tab, and enter the inventory stock item maintenance data.

New Inventory Items:
Stock No. 4025; Glazer 16 lb. Paper; unit of measure, CS; reorder point, 24; retail price, 29.95.

Stock No. 6050; Copier Toner Cartridge; unit of measure, EA; reorder point, 24; retail price, 35.50.

Changes to Inventory Items:
Retail price of Harris Power Plus 75 (Stock No. 1030), $849.00.
Retail price of Minnis Facsimile & Copier (Stock No. 3040), $999.99.
Reorder point of A–1 Recycled Copy Paper (Stock No. 4010), 24.

Delete:
United 20 lb Paper (Stock No. 4040)

▶

TUTORIAL PROBLEM 11-T

INVENTORY STOCK ITEMS
INPUT FORM

Run Date <u>03/07/--</u>   Problem No. <u>11-T</u>

Stock Number	Description	Unit of Measure	Reorder Point	Retail Price
4025	Glazer 16 lb. Paper	CS	24	29.95
6050	Copier Toner Cartridge	EA	24	35.50
1030				849.00
3040				999.99
4010			24	
4040	(Delete)			

Figure 11.14
Inventory Stock
Items Input Form

STEP 6:   **Enter the following inventory transactions, which are illustrated in Figure 11.15.**
Click the *Other* toolbar button. When the Other Activities window appears, click the *Inventory* tab and enter the inventory transaction data. The data already appearing in the window are the opening balances for this problem.

It is important that you enter the transactions in date sequence; otherwise, your reports will be incorrect because the computer calculates perpetual inventory according to the transactions' dates.

March 1–7 Weekly Transactions:
Mar. 01 Ordered the following merchandise:

Description	Invoice No.	Quantity Ordered
Copier Toner Cartridge	P431	36
A–1 Recycled Copy Paper	P432	36

TUTORIAL PROBLEM 11-T

Date	Inventory Item	Invoice No.	Quantity Sold	Selling Price	Quantity Ordered	Quantity Received	Cost Price
03/01/--	Copier Toner Cartridge	P431			36		
03/01/--	A-1 Recycled Copy Paper	P432			36		
03/01/--	Neuman Pentium 150	S754	1	2879.00			
03/01/--	Apke Color Scanner	S755	1	389.95			
03/01/--	MX10 Mouse	S756	4	49.00			
03/02/--	AWM 133 MHz Micro	P433			3		
03/02/--	Glazer 16 lb. Paper	P434			36		
03/03/--	Neuman Pentium 150	R816				6	1735.00
03/03/--	HL Personal Laser Printer	R817				3	285.00
03/04/--	Apke ProLine XT	S757	1	1499.00			
03/04/--	CXP 28.8 External Modem	S758	1	279.00			
03/04/--	Owen Ink Jet Printer	S759	1	339.00			
03/04/--	Ink Jet Cartridge	S760	3	14.95			
03/04/--	Glazer 20 lb. Paper	S760	3	39.95			
03/04/--	Facsimile Roll Paper	S761	2	45.75			
03/05/--	MX10 Mouse	S762	1	49.00			
03/05/--	Yoshino Sound Blaster	S763	1	159.00			
03/05/--	MX10 Mouse	CM738	-1	49.00			
03/06/--	Neuman Pentium 150	DM417				-1	1735.00
03/07/--	Minnis Facsimile & Copier	S764	1	999.99			

Figure 11.15
Inventory Transactions

Mar. 01 Sold the following merchandise:

Description	Invoice No.	Quantity Sold	Selling Price
Neuman Pentium 150	S754	1	2879.00
Apke Color Scanner	S755	1	389.95
MX10 Mouse	S756	4	49.00

Mar. 02 Ordered the following merchandise:

Description	Invoice No.	Quantity Ordered
AWM 133 MHz Micro	P433	3
Glazer 16 lb. Paper	P434	36

T U T O R I A L   P R O B L E M   1 1 – T

Mar. 03   Received the following merchandise:

Description	Invoice No.	Quantity Received	Cost Price
Neuman Pentium 150	R816	6	1735.00
HL Personal Laser Printer	R817	3	285.00

Mar. 04   Sold the following merchandise:

Description	Invoice No.	Quantity Sold	Selling Price
Apke ProLine XT	S757	1	1499.00
CXP 28.8 External Modem	S758	1	279.00
Owen Ink Jet Printer	S759	1	339.00
Ink Jet Cartridge	S760	3	14.95
Glazer 20 lb. Paper	S760	3	39.95
Facsimile Roll Paper	S761	2	45.75

Mar. 05   Sold the following merchandise:

Description	Invoice No.	Quantity Sold	Selling Price
MX10 Mouse	S762	1	49.00
Yoshino Sound Blaster	S763	1	159.00

Mar. 05   The following merchandise was returned to AraTec Computers Etc.:

Description	Invoice No.	Quantity Returned	Selling Price
MX10 Mouse	CM738	1	49.00

Mar. 06   AraTec Computers Etc. returned the following merchandise to a vendor:

Description	Invoice No.	Quantity Returned	Cost Price
Neuman Pentium 150	DM417	1	1735.00

Mar. 07   Sold the following merchandise:

Description	Invoice No.	Quantity Sold	Selling Price
Minnis Facsimile & Copier	S764	1	999.99

STEP 7:   **Make the following correction to one of the inventory transactions entered in step 6.**

T U T O R I A L   P R O B L E M   1 1 - T

The quantity received for stock number 5010, HL Personal Laser Printer, on March 3, should have been 2 instead of 3.

STEP 9: **Display an inventory list report.**
Click the *Reports* toolbar button. Choose the *Inventory Reports* option button, then select the *Inventory List* report. Click *OK*. The report appears in Figure 11.16.

AraTec Computers Etc.
Inventory List
03/07/--

Stock No.	Description	Unit Meas.	On Hand	On Order	Reorder Point	Average Cost	Last Cost	Retail Price
1010	Apke ProLine XT	EA	11	0	8	899.00	899.00	1499.00
1020	AWM 133 MHz Micro	EA	5	3	5	1225.00	1225.00	2049.00
1030	Harris Power Plus 75	EA	7	0	6	520.71	535.00	849.00
1040	Iwasaki 90 MHz Notebook	EA	6	0	4	1500.00	1500.00	2499.00
1050	Neuman Pentium 150	EA	6	0	5	1759.37	1735.00	2879.00
1060	Preston Multimedia System	EA	7	0	6	800.00	800.00	1350.00
1070	Tanaka ThinkPad 701	EA	6	0	5	1025.00	1025.00	1699.00
1080	Yoshino Pentium 90	EA	7	0	6	764.48	775.00	1199.00
2010	Apke Color Scanner	EA	7	0	6	203.14	205.00	389.95
2020	DPG 28.8 External Modem	EA	13	0	12	145.00	145.00	249.00
2030	CXP 28.8 External Modem	EA	10	0	10	165.00	165.00	279.00
2040	MultiMedia Color Monitor	EA	8	0	6	477.16	410.00	749.00
2050	MX10 Mouse	EA	13	0	24	29.00	29.00	49.00
2060	Tanaka 4x CD-ROM	EA	12	0	10	210.00	210.00	349.00
2070	TC 2.0 GB Hard Drive	EA	13	0	10	217.73	210.00	399.00
2080	Yoshino Sound Blaster	EA	8	0	8	95.00	95.00	159.00
3010	Ellis Personal Copier	EA	8	0	6	235.00	235.00	396.95
3020	Ellis Commercial Copier	EA	2	0	3	1700.00	1700.00	2850.00
3030	Hayato Facsimile	EA	6	0	5	209.29	215.00	325.00
3040	Minnis Facsimile & Copier	EA	1	0	3	625.00	625.00	999.99
4010	A-1 Recycled Copy Paper	CS	7	36	24	11.35	11.35	18.95
4020	Facsimile Roll Paper	BX	12	0	12	27.50	27.50	45.75
4025	Glazer 16 lb. Paper	CS	0	36	24			29.95
4030	Glazer 20 lb. Paper	CS	22	12	24	23.95	23.95	39.95
5010	HL Personal Laser Print	EA	8	0	6	311.79	285.00	479.00
5020	Mori Color Laser Print	EA	2	0	3 ·	1550.00	1550.00	2599.00
5030	Owen Ink Jet Printer	EA	9	0	8	200.00	200.00	339.00
5040	Tobis Bubble Jet Print	EA	9	0	8	225.00	225.00	379.00
6010	Huges X2 Laser Cartridge	EA	14	0	12	41.50	41.50	69.00
6020	Ink Jet Cartridge	EA	30	0	24	8.95	8.95	14.95
6030	Tobis Color Cartridge	EA	27	0	24	11.35	11.35	18.95
6040	Weldon Color Cartridge	EA	49	0	36	10.64	10.75	17.95
6050	Copier Toner Cartridge	EA	0	36	24			35.50

Figure 11.16
Inventory List Report

STEP 10: **Display the inventory transactions for the period March 1 through March 7.**
Select *Inventory Transactions* and click *OK*. When the Inventory Transactions dialog box appears, set the date range to March 1 through March 7 of the current year. The report appears in Figure 11.17.

AraTec Computers Etc.
Inventory Transactions
03/07/--

Date	Stock No.	Description	Inv. No.	Quantity Sold	Selling Price	Quan. Ord.	Quan. Recd.	Cost Price
03/01	6050	Copier Toner Cartridge	P431			36		
03/01	4010	A-1 Recycled Copy Paper	P432			36		
03/01	1050	Neuman Pentium 150	S754	1	2879.00			
03/01	2010	Apke Color Scanner	S755	1	389.95			
03/01	2050	MX10 Mouse	S756	4	49.00			
03/02	1020	AWM 133 MHz Micro	P433			3		
03/02	4025	Glazer 16 lb. Paper	P434			36		
03/03	1050	Neuman Pentium 150	R816				6	1735.00
03/03	5010	HL Personal Laser Printer	R817				2	285.00
03/04	1010	Apke ProLine XT	S757	1	1499.00			
03/04	2030	CXP 28.8 External Modem	S758	1	279.00			
03/04	5030	Owen Ink Jet Printer	S759	1	339.00			
03/04	6020	Ink Jet Cartridge	S760	3	14.95			
03/04	4030	Glazer 20 lb. Paper	S760	3	39.95			
03/04	4020	Facsimile Roll Paper	S761	2	45.75			
03/05	2050	MX10 Mouse	S762	1	49.00			
03/05	2080	Yoshino Sound Blaster	S763	1	159.00			
03/05	2050	MX10 Mouse	CM738	-1	49.00			
03/06	1050	Neuman Pentium 150	DM417				-1	1735.00
03/07	3040	Minnis Facsimile & Copier	S764	1	999.99			
		Totals		19		111	7	

Figure 11.17
Inventory Transactions Report

STEP 11: **Display the inventory exceptions report.**
Select *Inventory Exceptions* and click *OK*. The report appears in Figure 11.18.

T U T O R I A L   P R O B L E M   1 1 - T

AraTec Computers Etc.
Inventory Exceptions
03/07/--

Stock No.	Description	Unit Meas	On Hand	On Order	Reorder Point	Exception
1020	AWM 133 MHz Micro	EA	5	3	5	At/below reorder point
2030	CXP 28.8 External Modem	EA	10		10	At/below reorder point
2050	MX10 Mouse	EA	13		24	At/below reorder point
2080	Yoshino Sound Blaster	EA	8		8	At/below reorder point
3020	Ellis Commercial Copier	EA	2		3	At/below reorder point
3040	Minnis Facsimile & Copier	EA	1		3	At/below reorder point
4010	A-1 Recycled Copy Paper	CS	7	36	24	At/below reorder point
4020	Facsimile Roll Paper	BX	12		12	At/below reorder point
4025	Glazer 16 lb. Paper	CS	0	36	24	Out of stock
4030	Glazer 20 lb. Paper	CS	22	12	24	At/below reorder point
5020	Mori Color Laser Printer	EA	2		3	At/below reorder point
6050	Copier Toner Cartridge	EA	0	36	24	Out of stock

Figure 11.18
Inventory Exceptions Report

> **STEP 12:** **Display the average cost inventory valuation report.**
> Select *Valuation (Average Cost)* and click *OK*. The report
> appears in Figure 11.19.

A URL is an address or reference code that
makes it possible for a browser to find specific
hypertext documents. URLs must be keyed
exactly as they are written, which means that
every capital letter or lowercase letter must be
keyed correctly.

TUTORIAL PROBLEM 11-T

AraTec Computers Etc.
Inventory Valuation (Average Cost)
03/07/--

Stock No.	Description	On Hand	Cost	Value At Cost	Retail Price	Value At Retail
1010	Apke ProLine XT	11	899.00	9889.00	1499.00	16489.00
1020	AWM 133 MHz Micro	5	1225.00	6125.00	2049.00	10245.00
1030	Harris Power Plus 75	7	520.71	3644.97	849.00	5943.00
1040	Iwasaki 90 MHz Notebook	6	1500.00	9000.00	2499.00	14994.00
1050	Neuman Pentium 150	6	1759.37	10556.22	2879.00	17274.00
1060	Preston Multimedia System	7	800.00	5600.00	1350.00	9450.00
1070	Tanaka ThinkPad 701	6	1025.00	6150.00	1699.00	10194.00
1080	Yoshino Pentium 90	7	764.48	5351.36	1199.00	8393.00
2010	Apke Color Scanner	7	203.14	1421.98	389.95	2729.65
2020	DPG 28.8 External Modem	13	145.00	1885.00	249.00	3237.00
2030	CXP 28.8 External Modem	10	165.00	1650.00	279.00	2790.00
2040	MultiMedia Color Monitor	8	477.16	3817.28	749.00	5992.00
2050	MX10 Mouse	13	29.00	377.00	49.00	637.00
2060	Tanaka 4x CD-ROM	12	210.00	2520.00	349.00	4188.00
2070	TC 2.0 GB Hard Drive	13	217.73	2830.49	399.00	5187.00
2080	Yoshino Sound Blaster	8	95.00	760.00	159.00	1272.00
3010	Ellis Personal Copier	8	235.00	1880.00	396.95	3175.60
3020	Ellis Commercial Copier	2	1700.00	3400.00	2850.00	5700.00
3030	Hayato Facsimile	6	209.29	1255.74	325.00	1950.00
3040	Minnis Facsimile & Copier	1	625.00	625.00	999.99	999.99
4010	A-1 Recycled Copy Paper	7	11.35	79.45	18.95	132.65
4020	Facsimile Roll Paper	12	27.50	330.00	45.75	549.00
4030	Glazer 20 lb. Paper	22	23.95	526.90	39.95	878.90
5010	HL Personal Laser Printer	8	311.79	2494.32	479.00	3832.00
5020	Mori Color Laser Printer	2	1550.00	3100.00	2599.00	5198.00
5030	Owen Ink Jet Printer	9	200.00	1800.00	339.00	3051.00
5040	Tobis Bubble Jet Printer	9	225.00	2025.00	379.00	3411.00
6010	Huges X2 Laser Cartridge	14	41.50	581.00	69.00	966.00
6020	Ink Jet Cartridge	30	8.95	268.50	14.95	448.50
6030	Tobis Color Cartridge	27	11.35	306.45	18.95	511.65
6040	Weldon Color Cartridge	49	10.64	521.36	17.95	879.55
	Total Inventory Value			90772.02		150698.49

Figure 11.19
Inventory Valuation (Average Cost) Report

STEP 13:   **Display the LIFO inventory cost valuation report.**
Select *Valuation (LIFO)* and click *OK*. The report appears
in Figure 11.20.

TUTORIAL PROBLEM 11-T

AraTec Computers Etc.
Inventory Valuation (LIFO)
03/07/--

Stock No.	Description	On Hand	Cost	Value At Cost	Retail Price	Value At Retail
1010	Apke ProLine XT	11	899.00	9889.00	1499.00	16489.00
1020	AWM 133 MHz Micro	5	1225.00	6125.00	2049.00	10245.00
1030	Harris Power Plus 75	2	485.00	970.00	849.00	1698.00
1030	Harris Power Plus 75	5	535.00	2675.00	849.00	4245.00
1040	Iwasaki 90 MHz Notebook	6	1500.00	9000.00	2499.00	14994.00
1050	Neuman Pentium 150	1	1850.00	1850.00	2879.00	2879.00
1050	Neuman Pentium 150	5	1735.00	8675.00	2879.00	14395.00
1060	Preston Multimedia System	7	800.00	5600.00	1350.00	9450.00
1070	Tanaka ThinkPad 701	6	1025.00	6150.00	1699.00	10194.00
1080	Yoshino Pentium 90	2	700.00	1400.00	1199.00	2398.00
1080	Yoshino Pentium 90	5	775.00	3875.00	1199.00	5995.00
2010	Apke Color Scanner	3	235.00	705.00	389.95	1169.85
2010	Apke Color Scanner	4	205.00	820.00	389.95	1559.80
2020	DPG 28.8 External Modem	13	145.00	1885.00	249.00	3237.00
2030	CXP 28.8 External Modem	10	165.00	1650.00	279.00	2790.00
2040	MultiMedia Color Monitor	3	460.00	1380.00	749.00	2247.00
2040	MultiMedia Color Monitor	5	410.00	2050.00	749.00	3745.00
2050	MX10 Mouse	13	29.00	377.00	49.00	637.00
2060	Tanaka 4x CD-ROM	12	210.00	2520.00	349.00	4188.00
2070	TC 2.0 GB Hard Drive	4	239.00	956.00	399.00	1596.00
2070	TC 2.0 GB Hard Drive	9	210.00	1890.00	399.00	3591.00
2080	Yoshino Sound Blaster	8	95.00	760.00	159.00	1272.00
3010	Ellis Personal Copier	8	235.00	1880.00	396.95	3175.60
3020	Ellis Commercial Copier	2	1700.00	3400.00	2850.00	5700.00
3030	Hayato Facsimile	2	195.00	390.00	325.00	650.00
3030	Hayato Facsimile	4	215.00	860.00	325.00	1300.00
3040	Minnis Facsimile & Copier	1	625.00	625.00	999.99	999.99
4010	A-1 Recycled Copy Paper	7	11.35	79.45	18.95	132.65
4020	Facsimile Roll Paper	12	27.50	330.00	45.75	549.00
4030	Glazer 20 lb. Paper	22	23.95	526.90	39.95	878.90
5010	HL Personal Laser Printer	1	285.00	285.00	479.00	479.00
5010	HL Personal Laser Printer	5	310.00	1550.00	479.00	2395.00
5010	HL Personal Laser Printer	2	285.00	570.00	479.00	958.00
5020	Mori Color Laser Printer	2	1550.00	3100.00	2599.00	5198.00
5030	Owen Ink Jet Printer	9	200.00	1800.00	339.00	3051.00
5040	Tobis Bubble Jet Printer	9	225.00	2025.00	379.00	3411.00
6010	Huges X2 Laser Cartridge	14	41.50	581.00	69.00	966.00
6020	Ink Jet Cartridge	30	8.95	268.50	14.95	448.50
6030	Tobis Color Cartridge	27	11.35	306.45	18.95	511.65
6040	Weldon Color Cartridge	21	10.50	220.50	17.95	376.95
6040	Weldon Color Cartridge	28	10.75	301.00	17.95	502.60
	Total Inventory Value			90300.80		150698.49

Figure 11.20
Inventory Valuation (LIFO) Report

T U T O R I A L   P R O B L E M   1 1 – T

STEP 14:   **Display the FIFO inventory cost valuation report.**
Select *Valuation (FIFO)* and click *OK*. The report appears in Figure 11.21.

AraTec Computers Etc.
Inventory Valuation (FIFO)
03/07/--

Stock No.	Description	On Hand	Cost	Value At Cost	Retail Price	Value At Retail
1010	Apke ProLine XT	11	899.00	9889.00	1499.00	16489.00
1020	AWM 133 MHz Micro	5	1225.00	6125.00	2049.00	10245.00
1030	Harris Power Plus 75	2	485.00	970.00	849.00	1698.00
1030	Harris Power Plus 75	5	535.00	2675.00	849.00	4245.00
1040	Iwasaki 90 MHz Notebook	6	1500.00	9000.00	2499.00	14994.00
1050	Neuman Pentium 150	6	1735.00	10410.00	2879.00	17274.00
1060	Preston Multimedia System	7	800.00	5600.00	1350.00	9450.00
1070	Tanaka ThinkPad 701	6	1025.00	6150.00	1699.00	10194.00
1080	Yoshino Pentium 90	2	700.00	1400.00	1199.00	2398.00
1080	Yoshino Pentium 90	5	775.00	3875.00	1199.00	5995.00
2010	Apke Color Scanner	7	205.00	1435.00	389.95	2729.65
2020	DPG 28.8 External Modem	13	145.00	1885.00	249.00	3237.00
2030	CXP 28.8 External Modem	10	165.00	1650.00	279.00	2790.00
2040	MultiMedia Color Monitor	2	460.00	920.00	749.00	1498.00
2040	MultiMedia Color Monitor	6	410.00	2460.00	749.00	4494.00
2050	MX10 Mouse	13	29.00	377.00	49.00	637.00
2060	Tanaka 4x CD-ROM	12	210.00	2520.00	349.00	4188.00
2070	TC 2.0 GB Hard Drive	2	239.00	478.00	399.00	798.00
2070	TC 2.0 GB Hard Drive	11	210.00	2310.00	399.00	4389.00
2080	Yoshino Sound Blaster	8	95.00	760.00	159.00	1272.00
3010	Ellis Personal Copier	8	235.00	1880.00	396.95	3175.60
3020	Ellis Commercial Copier	2	1700.00	3400.00	2850.00	5700.00
3030	Hayato Facsimile	1	195.00	195.00	325.00	325.00
3030	Hayato Facsimile	5	215.00	1075.00	325.00	1625.00
3040	Minnis Facsimile & Copier	1	625.00	625.00	999.99	999.99
4010	A-1 Recycled Copy Paper	7	11.35	79.45	18.95	132.65
4020	Facsimile Roll Paper	12	27.50	330.00	45.75	549.00
4030	Glazer 20 lb. Paper	22	23.95	526.90	39.95	878.90
5010	HL Personal Laser Printer	6	310.00	1860.00	479.00	2874.00
5010	HL Personal Laser Printer	2	285.00	570.00	479.00	958.00
5020	Mori Color Laser Printer	2	1550.00	3100.00	2599.00	5198.00
5030	Owen Ink Jet Printer	9	200.00	1800.00	339.00	3051.00
5040	Tobis Bubble Jet Printer	9	225.00	2025.00	379.00	3411.00
6010	Huges X2 Laser Cartridge	14	41.50	581.00	69.00	966.00
6020	Ink Jet Cartridge	30	8.95	268.50	14.95	448.50
6030	Tobis Color Cartridge	27	11.35	306.45	18.95	511.65
6040	Weldon Color Cartridge	21	10.50	220.50	17.95	376.95
6040	Weldon Color Cartridge	28	10.75	301.00	17.95	502.60
	Total Inventory Value			90032.80		150698.49

Figure 11.21
Inventory Valuation (FIFO) Report

T U T O R I A L   P R O B L E M   1 1 – T

STEP 15: **Display the yearly sales report.**
Select *Yearly Sales* and click *OK*. The report appears in Figure 11.22.

AraTec Computers Etc.
Yearly Sales
03/07/--

Stock No.	Description	Unit Meas	Yearly Quantity	Yearly Amount
1010	Apke ProLine XT	EA	5	7495.00
1020	AWM 133 MHz Micro	EA	3	6147.00
1030	Harris Power Plus 75	EA	5	4495.00
1040	Iwasaki 90 MHz Notebook	EA	2	4998.00
1050	Neuman Pentium 150	EA	3	8637.00
1060	Preston Multimedia System	EA	1	1350.00
1070	Tanaka ThinkPad 701	EA	1	1699.00
1080	Yoshino Pentium 90	EA	2	2398.00
2010	Apke Color Scanner	EA	5	1949.75
2020	DPG 28.8 External Modem	EA	4	996.00
2030	CXP 28.8 External Modem	EA	2	558.00
2040	MultiMedia Color Monitor	EA	4	2996.00
2050	MX10 Mouse	EA	11	539.00
2060	Tanaka 4x CD-ROM	EA	3	1047.00
2070	TC 2.0 GB Hard Drive	EA	5	1995.00
2080	Yoshino Sound Blaster	EA	2	318.00
3010	Ellis Personal Copier	EA	2	793.90
3020	Ellis Commercial Copier	EA	1	2850.00
3030	Hayato Facsimile	EA	2	650.00
3040	Minnis Facsimile & Copier	EA	2	2049.49
4010	A-1 Recycled Copy Paper	CS	5	94.75
4020	Facsimile Roll Paper	BX	6	274.50
4025	Glazer 16 lb. Paper	CS		
4030	Glazer 20 lb. Paper	CS	14	559.30
5010	HL Personal Laser Printer	EA	4	1916.00
5020	Mori Color Laser Printer	EA	1	2599.00
5030	Owen Ink Jet Printer	EA	3	1017.00
5040	Tobis Bubble Jet Printer	EA	1	379.00
6010	Huges X2 Laser Cartridge	EA	10	690.00
6020	Ink Jet Cartridge	EA	18	269.10
6030	Tobis Color Cartridge	EA	5	94.75
6040	Weldon Color Cartridge	EA	15	269.25
6050	Copier Toner Cartridge	EA		
			147	62123.79

Figure 11.22
Yearly Sales Report

T U T O R I A L   P R O B L E M   1 1 – T

STEP 16: **Save your data.**
Click the *Save* toolbar button.

STEP 17: **Optional spreadsheet integration activity:**
AraTech Computers Etc. has asked you to use a spreadsheet to add additional information for gross profit and percent of gross profit to the yearly sales report.

a. Display and copy the inventory list report to the clipboard in spreadsheet format.

b. Start up your spreadsheet software, select cell A1 as the current cell, and paste the inventory list report from the clipboard into the spreadsheet.

c. Return to *Automated Accounting* and display and copy the yearly sales report to the clipboard in spreadsheet format.

d. Return to the spreadsheet, select a cell in column A that is three cells below the inventory list report pasted in step 17b (A45), and paste the yearly sales report from the clipboard.

e. Enter the words *Gross Profit* as a column header next to the Yearly Amount column heading.
Enter the words *% of Profit* as a column heading next to the Gross Profit column heading.
Enter the formula in cell F54 to calculate the gross profit, then copy it to cells F55–F86:

Yearly Amount – (Average Cost × Yearly Quantity)
+ E54 – (G10 * D54)

Enter the formula in cell G54 to calculate the percent of gross profit, then copy it to cells G55–G85:

Gross Profit ÷ Yearly Amount
+ F54/E54

Enter the formula to sum the Gross Profit Column (@SUM(F54..F86) in the total row at the end of the report.
Enter the formula to compute the total percent of profit (+F88/E88) in the total row at the end of the report.

▶

T U T O R I A L   P R O B L E M   1 1 – T

f. Format the yearly sales report by widening columns, formatting currency and percent, clearing division-by-zero error messages, etc.). The completed report is shown in Figure 11.23.

```
Student Name

AraTec Computers Etc.
Yearly Sales
As Of 03/07/--


--------------------------------------------------------------------------------
Stock                              Unit  Yearly    Yearly      Gross       % of
No.     Description                Meas  Quantity  Amount      Profit      Profit
--------------------------------------------------------------------------------

1010    Apke ProLine XT            EA    5         $7,495.00   $3,000.00   40.03%
1020    AWM 133 MHz Micro          EA    3         $6,147.00   $2,472.00   40.21%
1030    Harris Power Plus 75       EA    5         $4,495.00   $1,891.45   42.08%
1040    Iwasaki 90 MHz Notebook    EA    2         $4,998.00   $1,998.00   39.98%
1050    Neuman Pentium 150         EA    3         $8,637.00   $3,358.89   38.89%
1060    Preston Multimedia System  EA    1         $1,350.00     $550.00   40.74%
1070    Tanaka ThinkPad 701        EA    1         $1,699.00     $674.00   39.67%
1080    Yoshino Pentium 90         EA    2         $2,398.00     $869.04   36.24%
2010    Apke Color Scanner         EA    5         $1,949.75     $934.05   47.91%
2020    DPG 28.8 External Modem    EA    4           $996.00     $416.00   41.77%
2030    CXP 28.8 External Modem    EA    2           $558.00     $228.00   40.86%
2040    MultiMedia Color Monitor   EA    4         $2,996.00   $1,087.36   36.29%
2050    MX10 Mouse                 EA    11          $539.00     $220.00   40.82%
2060    Tanaka 4x CD-ROM           EA    3         $1,047.00     $417.00   39.83%
2070    TC 2.0 GB Hard Drive       EA    5         $1,995.00     $906.35   45.43%
2080    Yoshino Sound Blaster      EA    2           $318.00     $128.00   40.25%
3010    Ellis Personal Copier      EA    2           $793.90     $323.90   40.80%
3020    Ellis Commercial Copier    EA    1         $2,850.00   $1,150.00   40.35%
3030    Hayato Facsimile           EA    2           $650.00     $231.42   35.60%
3040    Minnis Facsimile & Copier  EA    2         $2,049.49     $799.49   39.01%
4010    A-1 Recycled Copy Paper    CS    5            $94.75      $38.00   40.11%
4020    Facsimile Roll Paper       BX    6           $274.50     $109.50   39.89%
4025    Glazer 16 lb. Paper        CS                             $0.00
4030    Glazer 20 lb. Paper        CS    14          $559.30     $224.00   40.05%
5010    HL Personal Laser Printer  EA    4         $1,916.00     $668.84   34.91%
5020    Mori Color Laser Printer   EA    1         $2,599.00   $1,049.00   40.36%
5030    Owen Ink Jet Printer       EA    3         $1,017.00     $417.00   41.00%
5040    Tobis Bubble Jet Printer   EA    1           $379.00     $154.00   40.63%
6010    Huges X2 Laser Cartridge   EA    10          $690.00     $275.00   39.86%
6020    Ink Jet Cartridge          EA    18          $269.10     $108.00   40.13%
6030    Tobis Color Cartridge      EA    5            $94.75      $38.00   40.11%
6040    Weldon Color Cartridge     EA    15          $269.25     $109.65   40.72%
6050    Copier Toner Cartridge     EA                             $0.00
                                         ---       ----------  ----------
                                         147       $62,123.79  $24,845.94  39.99%
                                         ===       ==========  ==========
```

Figure 11.23
Spreadsheet Yearly Sales Report

g. Print the yearly sales report.

h. Save your spreadsheet data with a file name of XXX11–T.

i. What would the gross profit and percent of gross profit be if *Last Cost* is used instead of the Average Cost to compute the Gross Profit?

j. End your spreadsheet session without saving your changes from step 17i.

STEP 18: **Optional word processing integration activity:**
The manager of the accounting department has asked you to provide a list of all inventory items currently on order. The list should include the average and last cost paid for each item on the list. A memorandum with space left for the inventory on-order information has already been prepared.

a. Display and copy the inventory list report to the clipboard in word processor format.

b. Start up your word processing software and load template file WP11–T as a text file.

c. Paste the contents of the clipboard into the memorandum at the location specified.

d. Remove the report heading and align the column headings. Remove all inventory items that do not have on-order quantities and format the information as necessary.

e. Enter your name and today's date where indicated.

f. Print the memorandum. The completed memorandum is shown in Figure 11.24.

g. Save the memorandum document with a file name of XXX11–T.

h. End your word processing session.

STEP 19: **End the *Automated Accounting* session.**
Click the *Exit/Quit* toolbar button.

T U T O R I A L   P R O B L E M   1 1 – T

```
                              MEMORANDUM

        TO:   Accounting Department Manager

      FROM:   Student Name

      DATE:   (Today's Date)

   SUBJECT:   Inventory items that are on order

As of the end of the current week, AraTec Computers Etc. inventory items that are
on order are listed below.  As per your request, I have included the average and
last costs of each item as well as additional information for your financial
planning.

-------------------------------------------------------------------------------------
Stock                         Unit   On     On      Reorder   Average   Last    Retail
No.    Description            Meas.  Hand   Order    Point     Cost      Cost    Price
-------------------------------------------------------------------------------------

1020   AWM 133 MHz Micro       EA     5      3        5        1225.00   1225.00  2049.00
4010   A-1 Recycled Copy Paper CS     7     36       24          11.35     11.35    18.95
4025   Glazer 16 lb. Paper     CS     0     36       24                            29.95
4030   Glazer 20 lb. Paper     CS    22     12       24          23.95     23.95    39.95
6050   Copier Toner Cartridge  EA     0     36       24                            35.50

Should you have any questions regarding the above information, or require
additional information, do not hesitate to give me a call.
```

Figure 11.24
Word Processing Memorandum

A robot is a program that automatically explores the World Wide Web by retrieving a document and then retrieving some or all of the documents that are linked to the original page. Robots are also called crawlers or spiders.

Applying Your Information Skills

I. MATCHING

Directions: In the *Working Papers*, write the letter of the appropriate term next to each definition.

a. stock number
b. unit of measure
c. reorder point
d. retail price
e. quantity on hand
f. quantity on order
g. yearly quantity sold
h. yearly dollars sold
i. last cost price
j. average cost
k. average cost inventory valuation method
l. LIFO inventory valuation method
m. FIFO inventory valuation method

1. A description of how an item is sold.

2. The quantity of a stock item that is included in the merchandise inventory at the present time.

3. The weighted-average of the purchase prices for a stock item.

4. The current selling price per unit.

5. The method of calculating ending inventory by using the price of merchandise purchased first for all stock items on hand.

6. The minimum quantity that is allowed before additional items must be reordered.

7. The method of calculating ending inventory by using the weighted-average of the purchase prices for all stock items on hand.

8. An accumulation of the dollar value of a stock item sold in the fiscal year.

9. The quantity of a stock item that is currently on order but has not yet arrived.

10. The method of calculating ending inventory value by using the price of merchandise purchased last for all stock items on hand.

11. A unique character code assigned to each stock item for identification.

12. An accumulation of the number of a stock item sold in the fiscal year.

13. The price paid per unit for the most recent purchase of a stock item.

II. QUESTIONS

Directions: Write the answers to each of the following questions in the *Working Papers*.

1. What problem may occur if the merchandise inventory is too low?

2. List five types of inventory transactions.

3. What is the purpose of the inventory list report?

4. What is the purpose of the inventory exceptions report?

5. What will happen if you attempt to delete an item that currently has inventory transaction data?

6. How does the computer determine the value of the inventory based on an average cost as shown in the valuation (average cost) report?

7. What assumption does the computer make to determine the value of the inventory based on the last-in, first-out method as shown in the valuation (LIFO) report?

8. What assumption does the computer make to determine the value of the inventory based on the first-in, first-out method as shown in the valuation (FIFO) report?

9. What information is provided in the yearly sales report?

Independent Practice Problem 11–P

In this problem, you will process the inventory transactions for the week of March 8 through March 14 for AraTec Computers Etc. You will perform the operating procedures necessary to add new inventory items and make changes to inventory data. In addition, you will process the weekly inventory transactions.

STEP 1:   Start up *Automated Accounting 7.0.*

STEP 2:   Load opening balances file AA11–P.

STEP 3:   Enter your name in the User Name text box and click *Ok.*

STEP 4:   Save the file with a file name of XXX11–P.

STEP 5:   Enter the following inventory maintenance data.

New Inventory Items:
Stock No. 3050; Office Color Copier; unit of measure, EA; reorder point, 4; retail price, $1,299.00.
Stock No. 2090; 3 1/2-Inch Disks; unit of measure, BX; reorder point, 36; retail price, $19.95.

Changes to Inventory Items:
Retail price of Mori Color Laser Printer (Stock No. 5020), $2450.00.

Reorder point of Weldon Color Cartridge (Stock No. 6040) to 32 and retail price to $18.25.

STEP 6:   Enter the following inventory transactions.

March 8–14 Weekly Transactions:

Mar. 08   Received the following merchandise:

Description	Invoice No.	Quantity Received	Cost Price
Copier Toner Cartridge	R818	36	21.00
A–1 Recycled Copy Paper	R819	24	11.50
Glazer 16 lb. Paper	R820	36	12.00
Glazer 20 lb. Paper	R821	12	23.95

Mar. 08   Sold the following merchandise:

Description	Invoice No.	Quantity Sold	Selling Price
Yoshino Pentium 90	S765	2	1199.00
Mori Color Laser Printer	S766	1	2450.00
Huges X2 Laser Cartridge	S766	3	69.00

Mar. 09   Ordered the following merchandise:

Description	Invoice No.	Quantity Ordered
Mori Color Laser Printer	P435	4
MX10 Mouse	P436	20
Office Color Copier	P437	6
3 1/2-Inch Disks	P438	48

Mar. 10   The following item was returned to AraTac Computers Etc.:

Description	Invoice No.	Quantity Returned	Selling Price
Ink Jet Cartridge	CM739	1	14.95

Mar. 11 Sold the following merchandise:

Description	Invoice No.	Quantity Sold	Selling Price
Glazer 16 lb. Paper	S767	2	29.95
AWM 133 MHz Micro	S768	1	2049.00

Mar. 12 Sold the following merchandise:

Description	Invoice No.	Quantity Sold	Selling Price
Hayato Facsimile	S769	1	325.00
MX10 Mouse	S770	3	49.00
TC 2.0 GB Hard Drive	S771	1	399.00

Mar. 13 AraTec Computers Etc. returned the following merchandise to a vendor:

Description	Invoice No.	Quantity Returned	Cost Price
Ellis Commercial Copier	DM418	2	1700.00

Mar. 14 Sold the following merchandise:

Description	Invoice No.	Quantity Sold	Selling Price
Tanaka ThinkPad 701	S772	1	1699.00
Tobis Bubble Jet Printer	S772	1	379.00
Glazer 16 lb. Paper	S772	2	29.95
Weldon Color Cartridge	S773	1	18.25

STEP 7: **Display an inventory list report.**

STEP 8: **Display the inventory transactions for the period March 8 through March 14.**

STEP 9: **Display the inventory exceptions report.**

STEP 10: **Display the average cost, LIFO, and FIFO inventory valuation reports.**

STEP 11: **Display the yearly sales report.**

STEP 12: **Save your data.**

STEP 13: **Optional spreadsheet integration activity:**
Use a spreadsheet to add gross profit and percent of gross profit to the yearly sales report. Refer to Figure 11.23 as a guide if necessary.
a. Display and copy the inventory list report to the clipboard in spreadsheet format.

CHECK FIGURE:
Valuation reports: inventory value based on retail = $137,829.49

b. Start up your spreadsheet software and paste the inventory list report from the clipboard into the spreadsheet.

c. Return to *Automated Accounting* and display and copy the yearly sales report to the clipboard in spreadsheet format.

d. Return to the spreadsheet, select a cell in column A that is three cells below the inventory list report pasted in step 13b, and paste the yearly sales report from the clipboard.

e. Enter the words *Gross Profit* as a column header next to the Yearly Amount column heading.
    Enter the words *% of Profit* as a column heading next to the Gross Profit column heading.
    Enter the formula to calculate the gross profit under the Gross Profit heading.
    Enter the formula to calculate the percent of gross profit under the % of Profit heading.
    Enter the formula to sum the Gross Profit Column.
    Enter the formula to compute the total percent of profit.

f. Format the yearly sales report by widening columns, formatting as currency and percent, clearing division-by-zero error messages, etc.).

g. Print the yearly sales report.

h. Save your spreadsheet data with a file name of XXX11–P.

i. What would the gross profit and percent of gross profit be if *Last Cost* is used instead of the Average Cost to compute the Gross Profit?

j. End your spreadsheet session without saving your changes from step 13i.

STEP 14:   Optional word processing integration activity:
You are to complete a memorandum to the manager of the accounting department that lists inventory items currently on order. The list should include the average and last cost paid for each item on the list. Refer to Figure 11.24 as a guide if necessary.

a. Display and copy the inventory list report to the clipboard in word processor format.

b. Start up your word processing software and load template file WP11–T as a text file.

c. Paste the contents of the clipboard into the memorandum at the location specified.

d. Remove the report heading and align the column headings. Remove all inventory items that do not have on-order quantities and format the information as necessary.
e. Enter your name and today's date where indicated.
f. Print the memorandum.
g. Save the memorandum document with a file name of XXX11–P.
h. End your word processing session.

STEP 15:   End the *Automated Accounting* session.

Applying Your Technology Skills 11–P

Directions: Using Independent Practice Problem 11–P, write the answers to the following questions in the *Working Papers*.

Inventory List Report:
1. What are the average and last cost prices for the Harris Power Plus 75 computer?

2. What is the retail price of the Hayato Facsimile?

3. What is the reorder point for the CXP 28.8 Internal Modem?

4. How many Ink Jet Cartridges are on hand?

Inventory Transactions Report:
5. What is the total quantity sold for all items?

6. What is the total quantity ordered?

7. What is the total quantity received?

Inventory Exceptions Report:
8. List the items that are out of stock.

9. List the items that are at or below the reorder point for which there are no items currently on order.

Inventory Valuation Reports:
10. What is the inventory value based on retail?

11. What is the inventory value based on average cost?

12. What is the inventory value based on LIFO?

13. What is the inventory value based on FIFO?

Yearly Sales Report:

14. Which item has the greatest sales volume based on the dollar amount?

15. Which item has the greatest sales volume based on quantity sold?

16. What is the total amount of yearly sales?

 # Mastery Problem 11–M

In Problem 11–M, you will process the inventory transactions for the week of March 15 through March 21 for AraTec Computers Etc. You will perform the operating procedures necessary to add new inventory items and make changes to inventory data. In addition, you will process the weekly inventory transactions.

STEP 1:   Load opening balances file AA11–M.

STEP 2:   Enter your name in the User Name text box.

STEP 3:   Save the data with a name of XXX11–M.

STEP 4:   Enter the inventory maintenance and transaction data for the period March 15 to March 21.

New Inventory Items:
Stock No. 1055; Pentium Pro 166; unit of measure, EA; reorder point, 3; retail price, $3,479.00.

Stock No. 2065; Tanaka 6x CD-ROM; unit of measure, EA; reorder point, 5; retail price, $399.00.

Changes to Inventory Items:
Retail price of Tanaka 4x CD-ROM (Stock No. 2060) to $289.00.

Retail price of Yoshino Pentium 90 (Stock No. 1080) to $1,095.00.

Retail reorder point of Facsimile Roll Paper (Stock No. 4020) to 8 and the retail price to $42.95.

Reorder point of Hayato Facsimile (Stock No. 3030) to 3.

Reorder point of Tobis Bubble Jet Printer (Stock No. 5040) to 4.

March 15–21 Weekly Transactions:

Mar. 16   Ordered the following merchandise:

Description	Invoice No.	Quantity Ordered
Minnis Facsimile & Copier	P439	6
Huges X2 Laser Cartridge	P440	24

Mar. 16   Received the following merchandise:

Description	Invoice No.	Quantity Received	Cost Price
AWM 133 MHz Micro	R822	3	1235.00
3 1/2-Inch Disks	R823	48	11.95
Office Color Copier	R824	6	775.00
Mori Color Laser Printer	R825	4	1550.00

Mar. 16   Sold the following merchandise:

Description	Invoice No.	Quantity Sold	Selling Price
Apke ProLine XT	S774	1	1499.00
A–1 Recycled Copy Paper	S775	2	18.95

Mar. 17   Ordered the following merchandise:

Description	Invoice No.	Quantity Ordered
Pentium Pro 166	P441	5
Tanaka 6x CD-ROM	P442	10

Mar. 17   Sold the following merchandise:

Description	Invoice No.	Quantity Sold	Selling Price
Iwasaki 90 MHz Notebook	S776	1	2499.00
Facsimile Roll Paper	S777	2	42.95

Mar. 18   The following item was returned to AraTec Computers Etc.:

Description	Invoice No.	Quantity Returned	Selling Price
MX10 Mouse	CM740	1	49.00

Mar. 18   Sold the following merchandise:

Description	Invoice No.	Quantity Sold	Selling Price
3 1/2-Inch Disks	S778	2	19.95
Office Color Copier	S779	1	1299.00
Copier Toner Cartridge	S779	2	35.50

Mar. 19   Sold the following merchandise:

Description	Invoice No.	Quantity Sold	Selling Price
Mori Color Laser Printer	S780	1	2450.00
Huges X2 Laser Cartridge	S780	3	69.00

Mar. 20   Sold the following merchandise:

Description	Invoice No.	Quantity Sold	Selling Price
Harris Power Plus 75	S781	1	849.00
Tobis Bubble Jet Printer	S781	1	379.00
Glazer 20 lb. Paper	S781	2	39.95
MX10 Mouse	S782	1	49.00

Mar. 21   AraTec Computers Etc. returned the following
           merchandise to a vendor:

Description	Invoice No.	Quantity Returned	Cost Price
Office Color Copier	DM419	1	775.00

STEP 5:   **Display an inventory list report.**

STEP 6:   **Display the inventory transactions for the period
                March 15 through March 21 of the current year.**

STEP 7:   **Display the inventory exceptions report.**

CHECK FIGURE:
Valuation reports:
inventory value based
on retail = $150,458.89

STEP 8:   **Display the inventory valuation reports.**

STEP 9:   **Display the yearly sales report.**

STEP 10:   **Save your data.**

STEP 11:   **Optional spreadsheet integration activity:**
                Use a spreadsheet to add gross profit and percent of
                gross profit to the yearly sales report based on *Last Cost.*
                Refer to Figure 11.23 as a guide if necessary.
                a. Display and copy the inventory list and yearly sales
                    reports into the spreadsheet.
                b. Enter the words *Gross Profit* and *% of Profit* as a
                    column headings in the Yearly Sales report.
                    Enter the formulas to calculate the gross profit
                    (using Last Cost) and the percent of gross profit.
                    Enter the formula to sum the Gross Profit Column
                    and compute the total percent of profit.
                c. Format the yearly sales report by widening columns,
                    formatting currency and percent, clearing division-
                    by-zero error messages, etc.).
                d. Print the yearly sales report.
                e. Save your spreadsheet data with a file name of
                    XXX11–M.
                f. What would the gross profit and percent of gross
                    profit be if *Average Cost* is used instead of the Last
                    Cost to compute the Gross Profit?

g. End your spreadsheet session without saving your changes from step 11f.

STEP 12: Optional word processing integration activity:
Complete the memorandum template that provides a list of inventory items currently on order. Refer to Figure 11.24 as a guide if necessary.
a. Display and copy the inventory list report to the clipboard in word processor format.
b. Start up your word processing software and load template file WP11–T as a text file.
c. Paste the contents of the clipboard into the memorandum at the location specified, then align column headings, remove all unnecessary data, and format the on-order information as necessary.
d. Enter your name and today's date where indicated.
e. Print the memorandum.
f. Save the memorandum document with a file name of XXX11–M.
g. End your word processing session.

STEP 13: End the *Automated Accounting* session.

Applying Your Technology Skills 11–M

Directions: Using Mastery Problem 11–M, write the answers to the following questions in the *Working Papers*.

Inventory List Report:
1. How many items are currently on hand for the Apke Color Scanner?
2. What is the last cost price for the MultiMedia Color Monitor?
3. What is the retail price of the Owen Ink Jet Printer?
4. What is the average cost of the TC 2.0 GB Hard Drive?
5. What is the reorder point for the Neuman Pentium 150 computer?

Inventory Transactions Report:
6. What is the total quantity sold for all items?
7. What is the total quantity ordered?
8. What is the total quantity received?

Inventory Exceptions Report:

9. List the items that are out of stock.

10. Of the items in question 9 that are out of stock, how many currently have items on order?

Inventory Valuation Reports:

11. What is the inventory value based on retail?

12. What is the inventory value based on average cost?

13. What is the inventory value based on LIFO?

14. What is the inventory value based on FIFO?

Yearly Sales Report:

15. What is the yearly amount of sales for the Iwasaki 90 MHz Notebook?

16. What is the total yearly amount of sales?

ACCOUNTING CAREERS IN DEPTH

Investment Analyst

An investment analyst analyzes financial information in order to forecast business, industry, and economic conditions and to make investment decisions. An investment analyst performs the following duties:

- Gathering and analyzing company financial statements; industry, regulatory and economic information; and financial periodicals and newspapers.
- Interpreting data concerning price, yield, stability, and future trends of investments.
- Summarizing data describing current and long-term trends in investments.
- Drawing charts and graphs to illustrate reports, using a computer.
- Recommending investment timing and buy-and-sell orders to companies or to the staff of investment establishments that advise clients.

The educational requirements for a position in investment analysis include a college degree in accounting or finance. This level of education is a particular advantage because of the preparation that accountants receive throughout a college career. In most cases, accountants must prepare financial statements and gather other information for financial reporting. So, it is necessary to also know how to analyze the reports that have been prepared.

As with other careers in accounting, it is most helpful if future investment analysts get the opportunity to work while in college. A cooperative work experience makes a student more marketable to potential employers. Ultimately, this experience helps accounting students understand the environment that they would work in if they later become investment analysts.

A career as an investment analyst can be practiced in many industries. This enables accounting students to choose an environment that interests them while being able to use the skills they've acquired. Also, accountants who have a personal interest in the industry in which they are working will obtain more enjoyment in their careers.

LEARNING OBJECTIVES

Upon completion of this chapter, you will be able to:

1. Complete the sales invoices input form.

2. Enter sales and sales return transactions and generate sales invoices.

3. Purge sales invoices.

INTRODUCTION

An organization's revenue depends upon its ability to sell its products or services to customers. To accomplish this task, a sales order processing system is used. **Sales order processing** comprises the procedures and controls involved in preparing invoices, updating accounting records, and shipping merchandise.

The complexity of sales order systems, and the procedures they use, vary greatly depending upon the size of the business and the products or services provided. Many businesses have turned to the computer to help their sales order processing due to the large volume of transactions and the complexities of maintaining accurate inventory and other accounting-related records. In general, a **computerized sales order processing system** comprises the procedures involved in preparing a sales invoice and automatically integrating the data it contains into the inventory and general ledger records. A **sales invoice** is a form used to describe the goods sold, the quantity, and the price. It is used as a source document for recording sales on account transactions.

Most computerized sales order processing systems enable businesses to prepare the invoice at the time of sale or at the time an order is received. As the sales invoice is prepared, the computer checks the inventory to make sure the goods are available. If any of the goods ordered are out of stock, the computer immediately notifies the user so action can be taken to replenish stock. When the computer finds stock on hand, it updates inventory and other accounting-related records and generates a sales invoice. Depending on the type of business and merchandise sold, the sales invoice may be given to the customer at the time of sale. Or, the sales invoice may be included with the merchandise when it is shipped to the customer. The sales invoice may be sent to the warehouse to be used to fill the order and prepare it for shipment.

When a sales invoice is included with the merchandise shipped to a customer, it is known as a packing slip.

E T H I C S

Many people believe that industry standards should be imposed to eliminate the incompatibility problems that exist among computer hardware manufacturers and software developers. For example, unless special hardware is added or special software is used, software that is written for an Apple Macintosh computer system will not run on an IBM personal computer. Other people believe that industry standards would inhibit creativity, restrict competition, and hamper product development.

a. Do you think the present incompatibility of hardware and software is an ethical issue? Explain.

b. Do you think industry standards should be imposed to make all computer hardware and software compatible? Defend your opinion.

A computerized sales order processing system should also be able to account for sales return transactions. A **sales return** is a credit allowed a customer for the sales price of returned merchandise, resulting in a decrease in the vendor's accounts receivable. In addition, the inventory records are updated to reflect the return of inventory.

In *Automated Accounting 7.0,* a complete invoice is prepared for each sale on account or each sales return. The sales invoice contains the customer name, credit terms, revenue account, invoice number, date, sales tax percent, as well as the quantity, description, and selling price of each item from inventory sold. As shown in Figure 12.1, when invoice data is entered, the inventory records are updated. Quantity on hand is reduced by the quantity sold or increased in the case of a sales return, and other sales information is stored for later reporting purposes. Journal entries resulting from the sale are created and entered into the sales journal and posted to the general ledger. The customer's account in the subsidiary ledger is updated to reflect the amount owed. Finally, a sales invoice is generated. A copy may be given to the customer at the time of the sale, packaged with the merchandise, or mailed after the merchandise is shipped. Sometime during the month, a statement of account that shows all account activity and current account balance is generated and sent to each customer who has an outstanding balance.

When a sales invoice is sent to the warehouse to be used to fill an order, it is known as a pick list or picking slip.

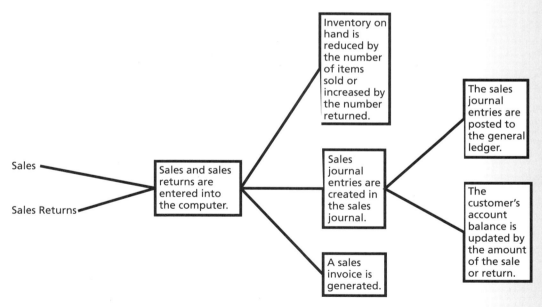

Figure 12.1
Computerized Sales Order Processing Integration

The examples used in this chapter are for VIP Copier & Fax Machines, a retailing business. The business sells copy machines, fax machines, and other related merchandise to local customers. Only information related to sales order processing and related reports will be discussed in this chapter.

SALES INVOICES INPUT FORM

The **sales invoices input form** is used to record sales and sales return transactions when a computerized sales order processing system is used. The sales invoices input form illustrated in Figure 12.2 shows how a sale to Klein & Associates and a sales return to Carol's Office Products are recorded.

SALES INVOICES INPUT FORM

Run Date 03/07/--   Problem No. Example

Customer	Terms	Revenue Account	Invoice Number	Date mm/dd/yy	Sales Tax %	Qty	Inventory Item	Price
Klein & Associates	2/10, n/30	Sales	S728	03/04/--	6	1	Desktop Facsimile	475.00
						2	CX10 Fax Cartridge	45.00
Carol's Office Products		Sales Ret	CM705	03/05/--	6	−1	Desktop Facsimile	475.00

● Sales Return—Customer returned one Desktop Facsimile machine that was originally sold at $475.00 with a 6% sales tax. The number of items returned is recorded in the Qty column as a <u>negative</u> number, and the Revenue Account column indicates that the transaction is a <u>Sales Return</u>.

● Sale—Sold one Desktop Facsimile for $475.00 and 2 CX10 Fax Cartridge at $45.00 each at 6% sales tax to Klein & Associates with terms of 2/10, n/30. If payment is made within 10 days, the customer can take a 2 percent discount off the sale price; if not, then payment in full is due in 30 days from the date of the invoice. The sales invoice number is recorded in the Invoice Number column, and the Revenue Account column indicates that the transaction is a <u>Sale</u>.

Figure 12.2
Sales Invoices Input Form (Examples)

Sales and sales return transactions are entered via the Other Activities Invoices window. Each field in the sales invoices input form corresponds to a text box or grid cell in this window. Therefore, the explanation provided in Figure 12.2 detailing how to record sales and sales return transactions on an input form are the same for entering them into the computer.

SALES AND SALES RETURN TRANSACTIONS

The Invoices screen is used to enter sales and sales return transactions and to generate sales invoices. Sales and sales return transactions entered in this window are automatically integrated into the general ledger and inventory records. A sales transaction automatically creates the respective journal entry in the sales journal and then posts the entry to the general ledger. A sales return transaction automatically creates the respective journal entry in the general journal and then posts the entry to the general ledger. Likewise, the transactions are automatically recorded in the Other Activities Inventory window to keep the inventory records up to date.

When the *Other* toolbar button is clicked or the *Other Activities* menu item is chosen from the Data menu, the Other Activities window will appear. Click the *Invoices* tab to activate it, as shown in Figure 12.3. The data shown in the example in Figure 12.3 comprise the first transaction recorded on the sales invoices input form in Figure 12.2.

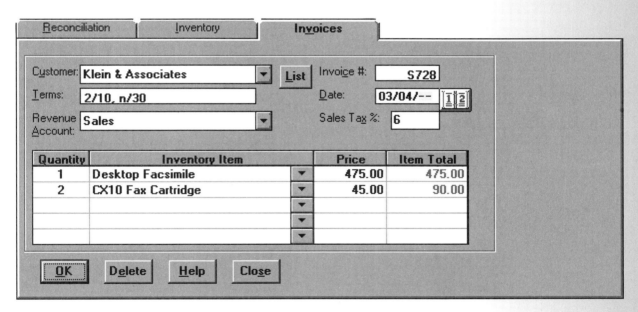

Figure 12.3
Invoices

Entering a Sale or Sales Return Transaction

1: Choose the Customer from the Customer drop-down list or key the first letter of the customer's name until the correct name appears.

2: **Enter the terms of the sale.**
The terms of the sale on the invoice shown in Figure 12.3 are 2/10, n/30 (read as "two ten, net thirty"). This means that the customer either can pay the invoice within ten days of the invoice date and take a 2 percent discount off the sale price, or can wait thirty days and then pay the full amount of the invoice. The Terms field will be left blank for sales return transactions.

3: **Choose the Sales, or Sales Returns and Allowances, account from the Revenue Account drop-down list.**

4: **Enter the sales invoice number, if not already displayed.**

5: **Enter the date of the transaction or use the calendar to set the desired date.**

6: **Enter the sales tax percent in the XX.X format.**
For example, a 6% sales tax is entered as 6 and a 6 1/2% sales tax is entered as 6.5.

7: **Enter the quantity in the Quantity field.**
If the item is a sales return, enter the quantity as a negative value (e.g., –3).

8: **Choose the inventory items from the Inventory Item drop-down list.**
You can also repetitively press the first letter of the item's description until the correct item appears in the text box.
Note: If the item chosen has an on-hand quantity at or below its reorder point, a warning message will appear within a red bar at the bottom of the window, indicating this condition.

9: **Enter the selling price in the Price field if it is not the same as that automatically displayed for the item.**
The Quantity times the Price will be extended and placed in the Item Total column.

10: **Repeat the previous three tasks for each item sold or returned by the customer.**

11: **Click *OK*.**
A computer-generated sales invoice, similar to the example shown in Figure 12.4, will appear.

12: **Click the *Print* button to print the invoice, or click the *Close* button to dismiss the invoice and continue.**
Note: At the bottom of the invoice, a Sub Total field displays the sum of the Item Total column, the sales tax has been calculated and displayed in the Sales Tax field, and the Total amount of the invoice is shown.

```
┌─────────────────────────────────────────────────────────┐
│              VIP Copier & Fax Machines                   │
│  Sold to: Klein & Associates      Number: S728           │
│  Terms: 2/10, n/30                Date:   03/04/--        │
│  ┌──────────┬─────────────────────┬─────────┬──────────┐ │
│  │ Quantity │     Description     │  Price  │Item Total│ │
│  │    1     │ Desktop Facsimile   │  475.00 │   475.00 │ │
│  │    2     │ CX10 Fax Cartridge  │   45.00 │    90.00 │ │
│  │          │                     │         │          │ │
│  │          │                     │Sub Total│   565.00 │ │
│  │          │                     │Sales Tax│    33.90 │ │
│  │          │                     │  Total  │   598.90 │ │
│  └──────────┴─────────────────────┴─────────┴──────────┘ │
│   [ Print ]    [ Help ]    [ Close ]                     │
└─────────────────────────────────────────────────────────┘
```

Figure 12.4
Sales Invoice

Changing a Sales Transaction

1: Click the *List* button to the right of the Customer drop-down list text box to display a list of invoices.
   An example list of invoices is shown in Figure 12.5.

```
┌─ Sales Invoices ─────────────────────────┐
│ CM705   Carol's Office Products          │
│ S725    J & M Construction Co.           │
│ S726    Baer Insurance Agency            │
│ S727    Morgan Home Center               │
│ S728    Klein & Associates               │
│ S729    Carol's Office Products          │
│ S730    Florence Carpets                 │
│ S731    Siegel Mortgage Co.              │
│                                          │
│   [ OK ]    [ Help ]    [ Close ]        │
└──────────────────────────────────────────┘
```

Figure 12.5
Sales Invoice List

2: Choose the Invoice to be changed from the Sales Invoices list and click *OK*.

3: Select the text box for the data you wish to change and enter the correction.

4: Choose *OK*.

Deleting a Sales Transaction

1: **Click the *List* button to the right of the Customer drop-down list text box to display a list of invoices.**

2: **Choose the invoice to be deleted from the list and click *OK*.**

3: **Click *Delete*.**
    When the delete confirmation dialog box appears, similar to Figure 12.6, click *OK*.

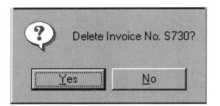

Figure 12.6
Delete
Confirmation
Dialog Box

PURGE SALES INVOICES

   Automated Accounting 7.0 has a capacity of 50 sales invoice transactions. If this capacity is exceeded, an alert dialog box will appear, informing you of this condition. Before additional invoices can be entered, the previously entered invoices must be erased by choosing the Purge Sales Invoices menu item from the Option menu. When this menu item is chosen, a dialog window will appear, asking you to confirm whether you want to purge sales invoice transactions. Since the sales invoices previously entered have been automatically integrated into the inventory and the general ledger, purging them will not cause any information to be lost. A backup file should be made before the sales invoices are purged. Exceeding sales invoice transaction capacity will not occur for any of the problems provided with this textbook since none surpass the system capacity.

Chapter Review

1. A computerized sales order processing system comprises the procedures involved in preparing a sales invoice and automatically integrating the data it contains into the inventory and general ledger. As sales invoice data are entered into the computer: (1) inventory records are updated, (2) journal entries resulting from the sale are created and entered into the sales journal and posted to

the general ledger, (3) the customer's account in the customer's file is updated, and (4) a sales invoice is generated.

2. The sales invoices input form may be used to record sales and sales return transactions.

3. Sales and sales return transactions are entered into the computer via the Other Activities Invoices window. A sales invoice is automatically generated by the computer for sales and sales return transactions entered into the computer.

4. Purging sales invoices is the process in which previously entered invoices are erased when capacity is reached.

ACCOUNTING   CAREERS   IN   DEPTH

Public Accounting Firms

Public accountants work in partnerships that provide accounting services to individuals, businesses, and governments. The largest high-profile firms are known as the Big Six and dominate the field of accounting. Those big six accounting firms are: Arthur Anderson, Deloitte & Touche, Ernst & Young, KPMG/Peat Marwick, Price Waterhouse, and Coopers & Lybrand. This field offers advancement potential to audit manager, tax manager, or partner—positions reached by only two to three percent of new hires.

A common entry-level strategy is to work for a public accounting firm to obtain broad experience before moving on to government or business. Most accountants at public accounting firms do not become partners, but the experience and training can be excellent.

Firms are implementing new electronic systems for submitting and preparing financial statements. Therefore, due to the likelihood that an entry-level accountant would use computers, it would be advantageous to have some computer coursework in addition to some on-the-job experience working with computers.

Most accountants spend several years at public accounting firms and then move on to different industries and put their experience to work. The skills gained in public accounting firms give the accountant a breadth and depth of knowledge and experience within different types of industries. Sometimes, accountants of public accounting firms are later hired by the clients of those firms because the accountants are familiar with the inner workings of the clients' businesses.

Public accounting firms are a great place to start, but they are also very competitive. The firms seek out the best and brightest college students to discuss future employment. Preparation for college-level accounting can begin as early as high school. Now is a good time to start planning to be ready for this kind of opportunity.

TUTORIAL PROBLEM 12-T

In this problem, you will process the sales and sales return transactions for the week of March 1st through March 7th of the current year for VIP Copier & Fax Machines. You will perform the operating procedures necessary to process sales and sales return transactions using the sales order processing features of *Automated Accounting*. The first sales transaction is illustrated in Figure 12.7 as it would appear on screen.

STEP 1: **Start up *Automated Accounting 7.0*.**

STEP 2: **Load opening balances file AA12–T.**
Click the *Open* toolbar button, then choose file AA12–T from the File list box.

STEP 3: **Enter your name in the User Name text box and click *OK*.**

STEP 4: **Save the file with a file name of XXX12–T.**
Click the *Save As* toolbar button and save the file as XXX12–T.

STEP 5: **Enter and display the sales invoice data. The March 2 sales invoice S725 is shown in Figure 12.7, and the accompanying invoice is shown in Figure 12.8 as a guide.**
From the Other Activities window, click the *Invoices* tab and enter the sales invoice data. If there is a price difference (i.e., March 7th sales invoice no. S731), make sure you key the data shown in the transaction statements.

March 1–7 Weekly Transactions:
Mar. 02   Sold the following merchandise to J & M Construction Co., terms 30 days, 6% sales tax, sales invoice no. S725:

Description	Quantity Sold	Selling Price
All-Pro Business Copier	1	899.00
M–10 Copier Cartridge	1	58.95
AMS 20 lb. Copy Paper	2	37.85

▶

Mar. 03 Sold the following merchandise to Baer Insurance Agency, terms 30 days, 6% sales tax, sales invoice no. S726:

Description	Quantity Sold	Selling Price
Phone Answer & Fax	1	329.95
Facsimile Roll Paper	1	24.95

Mar. 03 Sold the following merchandise to Morgan Home Center, terms 30 days, 6% sales tax, sales invoice no. S727:

Description	Quantity Sold	Selling Price
AMS 16 lb. Copy Paper	4	21.95
Laser Copier Cartridge	1	69.00

Mar. 04 Sold the following merchandise to Klein & Associates, terms 2/10, n/30, 6% sales tax, sales invoice no. S728:

Description	Quantity Sold	Selling Price
Desktop Facsimile	1	475.00
CX10 Fax Cartridge	2	45.00

Mar. 05 The following merchandise was returned to VIP Copier & Fax Machines by Carol's Office Products, 6% sales tax, sales return no. CM705:

Description	Quantity Returned	Price
Desktop Facsimile	1	475.00

Mar. 05 Sold the following merchandise to Carol's Office Products, terms 30 days, 6% sales tax, sales invoice no. S729:

Description	Quantity Sold	Selling Price
Professional Fax	1	999.00
CX10 Fax Cartridge	1	45.00

Mar. 06 Sold the following merchandise to Florence Carpets, terms 30 days, 6% sales tax, sales invoice no. S730:

Description	Quantity Sold	Selling Price
AMS 24 lb. Copy Paper	3	42.50
Copier 12 oz. Toner	2	12.95

Mar. 07 Sold the following merchandise to Siegel Mortgage Co., terms 30 days, 6% sales tax, sales invoice no. S731:

Description	Quantity Sold	Selling Price
Color Laser Copier	1	2837.10
Color Copier Cartridge	1	89.35

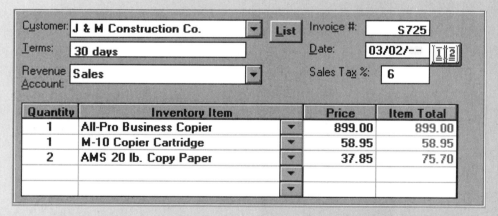

Figure 12.7
Data Entered for Sales Invoice S725

Lurkers are members of newsgroups or e-mail discussion lists who read the postings, but do not post messages of their own. Because you never know all the people who will be reading your messages, always use common sense and etiquette.

T U T O R I A L   P R O B L E M   1 2 – T

VIP Copier & Fax Machines

| **Sold to:** J & M Construction Co. | **Number:** S725 |
| **Terms:** 30 days | **Date:** 03/02/-- |

Quantity	Description	Price	Item Total
1	All-Pro Business Copier	899.00	899.00
1	M-10 Copier Cartridge	58.95	58.95
2	AMS 20 lb. Copy Paper	37.85	75.70
		Sub Total	1033.65
		Sales Tax	62.02
		Total	1095.67

Figure 12.8
Sales Invoice
S725

STEP 6:   **Display the inventory list report.**
Click the *Reports* toolbar button. Choose the *Inventory Reports* option button, then select *Inventory List*. Click *OK*. The report appears in Figure 12.9.

VIP Copier & Fax Machines
Inventory List
03/07/--

Stock No.	Description	Unit Meas.	On Hand	On Order	Reorder Point	Average Cost	Last Cost	Retail Price
1010	Z95 Desktop Copier	EA	12	0	10	192.06	196.00	349.00
1020	All-Pro Business Copier	EA	10	3	8	533.63	525.00	899.00
1030	Office Color Copier	EA	8	0	6	1005.63	1010.00	1685.00
1040	Color Laser Copier	EA	2	0	4	1699.00	1699.00	2895.00
1050	Superb Mini Copier	EA	13	0	6	135.00	135.00	225.00
2010	Phone Answer & Fax	EA	16	0	10	201.35	195.00	329.95
2020	Desktop Facsimile	EA	11	0	8	279.40	285.00	475.00
2030	Professional Fax	EA	8	0	6	626.11	598.00	999.00
2040	Office Fax & Copier	EA	9	0	5	775.00	775.00	1295.00
2050	Portable Facsimile	EA	12	0	6	165.00	165.00	279.95
3010	AMS 16 lb. Copy Paper	CS	31	0	24	13.00	13.00	21.95
3020	AMS 20 lb. Copy Paper	CS	79	0	36	22.69	22.65	37.85
3030	AMS 24 lb. Copy Paper	CS	41	0	24	25.00	25.00	42.50
3040	Facsimile Roll Paper	BX	23	0	12	14.95	14.95	24.95
3050	Recycled 20 lb. Paper	CS	34	0	24	16.46	16.75	27.95
4010	M-10 Copier Cartridge	EA	28	0	12	34.63	34.75	58.95
4020	Color Copier Cartridge	EA	26	6	10	51.83	52.00	89.35
4030	Laser Copier Cartridge	EA	7	0	10	41.25	41.25	69.00
4040	CX10 Fax Cartridge	EA	23	0	12	26.96	27.00	45.00
4050	Copier 12 oz. Toner	EA	16	0	12	7.50	7.50	12.95

Figure 12.9
Inventory List Report

T U T O R I A L   P R O B L E M   1 2 - T

STEP 7: **Display the inventory transactions for the period March 1 through March 7.**
Select *Inventory Transactions* and click *OK*. When the Inventory Transactions dialog box appears, set the date range to March 1 through March 7 of the current year. The report appears in Figure 12.10.

```
                        VIP Copier & Fax Machines
                          Inventory Transactions
                                03/07/--
```

Date	Stock No.	Description	Inv. No.	Quantity Sold	Selling Price	Quan. Ord.	Quan. Recd.	Cost Price
03/02	1020	All-Pro Business Copier	S725	1	899.00			
03/02	4010	M-10 Copier Cartridge	S725	1	58.95			
03/02	3020	AMS 20 lb. Copy Paper	S725	2	37.85			
03/03	2010	Phone Answer & Fax	S726	1	329.95			
03/03	3040	Facsimile Roll Paper	S726	1	24.95			
03/03	3010	AMS 16 lb. Copy Paper	S727	4	21.95			
03/03	4030	Laser Copier Cartridge	S727	1	69.00			
03/04	2020	Desktop Facsimile	S728	1	475.00			
03/04	4040	CX10 Fax Cartridge	S728	2	45.00			
03/05	2020	Desktop Facsimile	CM705	−1	475.00			
03/05	2030	Professional Fax	S729	1	999.00			
03/05	4040	CX10 Fax Cartridge	S729	1	45.00			
03/06	3030	AMS 24 lb. Copy Paper	S730	3	42.50			
03/06	4050	Copier 12 oz. Toner	S730	2	12.95			
03/07	1040	Color Laser Copier	S731	1	2837.10			
03/07	4020	Color Copier Cartridge	S731	1	89.35			
		Totals		22				

Figure 12.10
Inventory Transactions Report

STEP 8: **Display the yearly sales report.**
Select *Yearly Sales* and click *OK*. The report appears in Figure 12.11.

TUTORIAL PROBLEM 12-T

```
                    VIP Copier & Fax Machines
                          Yearly Sales
                           03/07/--

-------------------------------------------------------------
Stock                          Unit    Yearly      Yearly
No.    Description             Meas   Quantity     Amount
-------------------------------------------------------------

1010   Z95 Desktop Copier      EA       40       13960.00
1020   All-Pro Business Copier EA       35       31465.00
1030   Office Color Copier     EA        4        6740.00
1040   Color Laser Copier      EA        4       11522.10
1050   Superb Mini Copier      EA       15        3375.00
2010   Phone Answer & Fax      EA       49       16167.55
2020   Desktop Facsimile       EA       39       18525.00
2030   Professional Fax        EA        6        5994.00
2040   Office Fax & Copier     EA        6        7770.00
2050   Portable Facsimile      EA       12        3359.40
3010   AMS 16 lb. Copy Paper   CS       41         899.95
3020   AMS 20 lb. Copy Paper   CS       65        2460.25
3030   AMS 24 lb. Copy Paper   CS       31        1317.50
3040   Facsimile Roll Paper    BX       17         424.15
3050   Recycled 20 lb. Paper   CS       41        1145.95
4010   M-10 Copier Cartridge   EA       20        1179.00
4020   Color Copier Cartridge  EA       28        2501.80
4030   Laser Copier Cartridge  EA       31        2139.00
4040   CX10 Fax Cartridge      EA       25        1125.00
4050   Copier 12 oz. Toner     EA       20         259.00
                                       ---      ----------
                                       529      132329.65
                                       ===      ==========
```

Figure 12.11
Yearly Sales Report

STEP 9:   **Display a general journal report.**
Choose the *Journals* option, select *General Journal*, and click *OK*. When the Journal Report Selection window appears, select *Customize Journal Report* and enter a date range of March 1 to March 7 of the current year. The general journal report appears in Figure 12.12.

TUTORIAL PROBLEM 12-T

VIP Copier & Fax Machines
General Journal
03/07/--

Date	Refer.	Acct.	Title	Debit	Credit
03/05	CM705	4120	Sales Returns & Allow.	475.00	
03/05	CM705	2120	Sales Tax Payable	28.50	
03/05	CM705	1130	AR/Carol's Office Products		503.50
			Totals	503.50	503.50

Figure 12.12
General Journal Report

STEP 10:   **Display a sales journal report.**
Select *Sales Journal* and click *OK*. When the Journal Report
Selection window appears, select *Customize Journal
Report* and enter a date range of March 1 to March 7 of
the current year. The sales journal appears in Figure 12.13.

VIP Copier & Fax Machines
Sales Journal
03/07/--

Date	Inv. No.	Acct.	Title	Debit	Credit
03/02	S725	1130	AR/J & M Construction Co.	1095.67	
03/02	S725	4110	Sales		1033.65
03/02	S725	2120	Sales Tax Payable		62.02
03/03	S726	1130	AR/Baer Insurance Agency	376.19	
03/03	S726	4110	Sales		354.90
03/03	S726	2120	Sales Tax Payable		21.29
03/03	S727	1130	AR/Morgan Home Center	166.21	
03/03	S727	4110	Sales		156.80
03/03	S727	2120	Sales Tax Payable		9.41
03/04	S728	1130	AR/Klein & Associates	598.90	
03/04	S728	4110	Sales		565.00
03/04	S728	2120	Sales Tax Payable		33.90
03/05	S729	1130	AR/Carol's Office Products	1106.64	
03/05	S729	4110	Sales		1044.00
03/05	S729	2120	Sales Tax Payable		62.64
03/06	S730	1130	AR/Florence Carpets	162.60	
03/06	S730	4110	Sales		153.40
03/06	S730	2120	Sales Tax Payable		9.20
03/07	S731	1130	AR/Siegel Mortgage Co.	3102.04	
03/07	S731	4110	Sales		2926.45
03/07	S731	2120	Sales Tax Payable		175.59
			Totals	6608.25	6608.25

Figure 12.13
Sales Journal Report

TUTORIAL PROBLEM 12-T

STEP 11:   **Display a general ledger report for the Accounts Receivable, Sales, and Sales Returns & Allowances accounts.**

Choose *Ledger Reports,* select *General Ledger,* and then click *OK*. Enter the accounts receivable account (1130) in both the From and To drop-down text boxes in the account range dialog box. When displaying the Sales and Sales Return & Allowances Accounts, enter Sales (4110) in the From text box and Sales Returns & Allowances (4120) in the To text box. The reports appear in Figure 12.14 and 12.15 respectively.

```
                     VIP Copier & Fax Machines
                          General Ledger
                            03/07/--

-----------------------------------------------------------------
Account   Journal        Date    Refer.   Debit    Credit   Balance
-----------------------------------------------------------------

1130-Accounts Receivable
          Balance Forward                                   25569.98Dr
          Sales          03/02   S725     1095.67           26665.65Dr
          Sales          03/03   S726      376.19           27041.84Dr
          Sales          03/03   S727      166.21           27208.05Dr
          Sales          03/04   S728      598.90           27806.95Dr
          General        03/05   CM705              503.50  27303.45Dr
          Sales          03/05   S729     1106.64           28410.09Dr
          Sales          03/06   S730      162.60           28572.69Dr
          Sales          03/07   S731     3102.04           31674.73Dr
```

Figure 12.14 Accounts Receivable Account

```
                     VIP Copier & Fax Machines
                          General Ledger
                            03/07/--

-----------------------------------------------------------------
Account   Journal        Date    Refer.   Debit    Credit   Balance
-----------------------------------------------------------------

4110-Sales
          Balance Forward                                   126570.45Cr
          Sales          03/02   S725             1033.65   127604.10Cr
          Sales          03/03   S726              354.90   127959.00Cr
          Sales          03/03   S727              156.80   128115.80Cr
          Sales          03/04   S728              565.00   128680.80Cr
          Sales          03/05   S729             1044.00   129724.80Cr
          Sales          03/06   S730              153.40   129878.20Cr
          Sales          03/07   S731             2926.45   132804.65Cr

4120-Sales Returns & Allow.
          General        03/05   CM705   475.00             475.00Dr
```

Figure 12.15 Sales and Sales Returns & Allowances Accounts

T U T O R I A L   P R O B L E M   1 2 - T

STEP 12:   **Display a trial balance report.**
Choose the *Ledger Reports* option, select *Trial Balance,*
and click *OK*. The trial balance is shown in Figure 12.16.

VIP Copier & Fax Machines
Trial Balance
03/07/--

Acct. Number	Account Title	Debit	Credit
1110	Cash	4053.92	
1120	Petty Cash	150.00	
1130	Accounts Receivable	31674.73	
1140	Merchandise Inventory	52039.00	
1150	Supplies	2475.22	
1160	Prepaid Insurance	1555.23	
2110	Accounts Payable		5526.32
2120	Sales Tax Payable		345.55
3110	Susan Phelps, Capital		39693.42
3120	Susan Phelps, Drawing	5700.00	
4110	Sales		132804.65
4120	Sales Returns & Allow.	475.00	
5110	Purchases	71214.06	
6110	Advertising Expense	810.00	
6130	Miscellaneous Expense	440.25	
6150	Rent Expense	5000.00	
6170	Telephone Expense	1758.20	
6180	Utilities Expense	1024.33	
	Totals	178369.94	178369.94

Figure 12.16
Trial Balance

STEP 13:   **Display a schedule of accounts receivable.**
Select *Schedule of Accounts Receivable* and click *OK*.
The report is shown in Figure 12.17.

▶

T U T O R I A L   P R O B L E M   1 2 – T

```
                    VIP Copier & Fax Machines
                  Schedule of Accounts Receivable
                            03/07/--
    ----------------------------------------------------------------
    Name                                              Balance
    ----------------------------------------------------------------
    Baer Insurance Agency                             1979.59
    Carol's Office Products                           5461.42
    Florence Carpets                                  1176.24
    J & M Construction Co.                            2167.22
    Klein & Associates                                2044.15
    Malott Realty Co.                                12712.50
    Morgan Home Center                                1676.92
    Siegel Mortgage Co.                               4456.69
                                                      -------
    Total                                            31674.73
                                                     ========
```

Figure 12.17
Schedule of Accounts Receivable

STEP 14:   **Display an accounts receivable ledger.**
Select *Accounts Receivable Ledger* and click *OK*.
The report is shown in Figure 12.18.

```
                         VIP Copier & Fax Machines
                         Accounts Receivable Ledger
                                 03/07/--
  ----------------------------------------------------------------------------
  Account    Journal        Date   Refer.   Debit    Credit   Balance
  ----------------------------------------------------------------------------
  Baer Insurance Agency
           Balance Forward                                     1603.40Dr
           Sales          03/03  S726     376.19               1979.59Dr
  Carol's Office Products
           Balance Forward                                     4858.28Dr
           General        03/05  CM705              503.50     4354.78Dr
           Sales          03/05  S729     1106.64             5461.42Dr
  Florence Carpets
           Balance Forward                                     1013.64Dr
           Sales          03/06  S730     162.60               1176.24Dr
  J & M Construction Co.
           Balance Forward                                     1071.55Dr
           Sales          03/02  S725     1095.67             2167.22Dr
  Klein & Associates
           Balance Forward                                     1445.25Dr
           Sales          03/04  S728     598.90               2044.15Dr
  Malott Realty Co.
           Balance Forward                                    12712.50Dr
  Morgan Home Center
           Balance Forward                                     1510.71Dr
           Sales          03/03  S727     166.21               1676.92Dr
  Siegel Mortgage Co.
           Balance Forward                                     1354.65Dr
           Sales          03/07  S731     3102.04             4456.69Dr
```

Figure 12.18
Accounts Receivable Ledger

TUTORIAL PROBLEM 12 - T

STEP 15: **Display a statement of account for Carol's Office Products.**
Select *Statements of Account* and click *OK*. Advance through the statements by clicking on the >> button until Carol's Office Products appears as shown in Figure 12.19.

STATEMENT OF ACCOUNT
VIP Copier & Fax Machines

To:	Carol's Office Products				Date	03/07/--

Date	Reference	Description	Charges	Credits	Balance
03/01/--		Balance Forward			4858.28
03/05/--	CM705	Payment		503.50	4354.78
03/05/--	S729	Invoice	1106.64		5461.42

Figure 12.19
Carol's Office Products Statement of Account

STEP 16: **Save your data.**
Click the *Save* toolbar button.

STEP 17: **Optional spreadsheet and word processing integration activity:**
VIP Copier & Fax Machines has asked you to prepare a spreadsheet, based on current inventory information, that can be used to help analyze various percentages of retail price increases. You have been told that the inventory turnover ratio is currently 3.9 times. Inventory turnover ratio is the number of times the average amount of merchandise inventory is sold during a specific period of time. Management would like to see the effect of a 2% and 5% price increase on all items. You are to send Susan Phelps, the owner, a memo summarizing your findings and attach the spreadsheet

T U T O R I A L   P R O B L E M   1 2 - T

report. Susan Phelps and her managers will use this information, along with other data, to make their pricing decisions.

Spreadsheet:
a. Display and copy the Inventory Valuation (Average Cost) report to the clipboard in spreadsheet format.
b. Start up your spreadsheet software and load file SS12–T. Select cell A8 as the current cell, and paste the report from the clipboard into the spreadsheet.
c. To see the effect of the 2% increase, enter the number .02 in cell C2.
   Enter the number 3.9 in cell C3. Management has computed the inventory turnover ratio for you by dividing the cost of goods sold by the average inventory.
   Enter the following formula to calculate the percentage increase in cell H17: +F17+(F17*$C$2). Then copy the formula downward for each inventory item.
   Enter the following formula to calculate the new projected inventory value at retail in cell I17: +H17*C17. Then copy the formula downward for each inventory item and enter the formula to sum the column.
   Enter the following formula in cell C4 to find the increase in sales revenue assuming all the items in inventory are sold: +I38–G38.
   Enter the following formula in cell C5 to find the increase in sales based upon the inventory turnover ratio: +C4*C3.
   Enter the following formula in cell C6 to find the average number of days that inventory is on hand during the year: +365/C3.
d. Format the spreadsheet as necessary and print the report. The completed report is shown in Figure 12.20.
e. Enter the number .05 in cell C2 and print the report for a 5% increase.
f. Save your spreadsheet data with a file name of XXX12–T.

TUTORIAL PROBLEM 12-T

```
Percent of Increase:          2.00%
Inventory Turnover:           3.90
Current Increase:         $1,630.40
Yearly Increase:          $6,358.54
Avg. Days On Hand:            93.6

Student Name

VIP Copier & Fax Machines
Inventory Valuation (Average Cost)
As Of 03/07/--
```

Stock No.	Description	On Hand	Cost	Value At Cost	Retail Price	Value At Retail	Pojected Retail	Projected Value
1010	Z95 Desktop Copier	12	$192.06	$2,304.72	$349.00	$4,188.00	$355.98	$4,271.76
1020	All-Pro Business Copier	10	$533.63	$5,336.30	$899.00	$8,990.00	$916.98	$9,169.80
1030	Office Color Copier	8	$1,005.63	$8,045.04	$1,685.00	$13,480.00	$1,718.70	$13,749.60
1040	Color Laser Copier	2	$1,699.00	$3,398.00	$2,895.00	$5,790.00	$2,952.90	$5,905.80
1050	Superb Mini Copier	13	$135.00	$1,755.00	$225.00	$2,925.00	$229.50	$2,983.50
2010	Phone Answer & Fax	16	$201.35	$3,221.60	$329.95	$5,279.20	$336.55	$5,384.78
2020	Desktop Facsimile	11	$279.40	$3,073.40	$475.00	$5,225.00	$484.50	$5,329.50
2030	Professional Fax	8	$626.11	$5,008.88	$999.00	$7,992.00	$1,018.98	$8,151.84
2040	Office Fax & Copier	9	$775.00	$6,975.00	$1,295.00	$11,655.00	$1,320.90	$11,888.10
2050	Portable Facsimile	12	$165.00	$1,980.00	$279.95	$3,359.40	$285.55	$3,426.59
3010	AMS 16 lb. Copy Paper	31	$13.00	$403.00	$21.95	$680.45	$22.39	$694.06
3020	AMS 20 lb. Copy Paper	79	$22.69	$1,792.51	$37.85	$2,990.15	$38.61	$3,049.95
3030	AMS 24 lb. Copy Paper	41	$25.00	$1,025.00	$42.50	$1,742.50	$43.35	$1,777.35
3040	Facsimile Roll Paper	23	$14.95	$343.85	$24.95	$573.85	$25.45	$585.33
3050	Recycled 20 lb. Paper	34	$16.46	$559.64	$27.95	$950.30	$28.51	$969.31
4010	M-10 Copier Cartridge	28	$34.63	$969.64	$58.95	$1,650.60	$60.13	$1,683.61
4020	Color Copier Cartridge	26	$51.83	$1,347.58	$89.35	$2,323.10	$91.14	$2,369.56
4030	Laser Copier Cartridge	7	$41.25	$288.75	$69.00	$483.00	$70.38	$492.66
4040	CX10 Fax Cartridge	23	$26.96	$620.08	$45.00	$1,035.00	$45.90	$1,055.70
4050	Copier 12 oz. Toner	16	$7.50	$120.00	$12.95	$207.20	$13.21	$211.34
	Total Inventory Value			$48,567.99		$81,519.75		$83,150.15

Figure 12.20
Spreadsheet Price Increase Analysis (for 2% Increase)

g. Experiment: What would be the effect of a 3.5% price increase, or a 6.2 inventory turnover ratio? It is not required that you save this spreadsheet data.

Word Processing:
a. Start up your word processing software.
b. Create a new document in memorandum format to Susan Phelps, owner. A memorandum template may be used.
c. The completed memorandum is shown in Figure 12.21. Key and format the memo as necessary.
d. Copy and paste the results of the 2% and 5% analyses from the spreadsheet you saved to your disk (earlier in step 17) into the body of the memo. Format the spreadsheet information as necessary.

T U T O R I A L   P R O B L E M   1 2 - T

```
                        MEMORANDUM

        TO:   Susan Phelps, Owner

      FROM:   Student Name

      DATE:   (Today's Date)

   SUBJECT:   Retail Price Increase Analysis

   As per your request, below are the summarized
   projections of: (1) a 2% price increase with an
   inventory turnover ratio of 3.9, and (2) a 5%
   price increase with an inventory turnover ratio of
   3.9, based on the sale of the current inventory.
   The detailed spreadsheet reports are attached.
   Notice that I have used the inventory turnover
   ratio to calculate the yearly increase in projected
   revenue and the average number of days the
   inventory is on hand. I have also designed the
   spreadsheet analysis in such a way that information
   for other percentages and inventory turnover ratios
   can easily be obtained. Should you have any
   questions regarding the following information, do
   not hesitate to give me a call.

      Percent of Increase:        2.00%
      Inventory Turnover:         3.90
      Current Increase:       $1,630.40
      Yearly Increase:        $6,358.54
      Avg. Days On Hand:           93.6

      Percent of Increase:        5.00%
      Inventory Turnover:         3.90
      Current Increase:       $4,075.99
      Yearly Increase:       $15,896.35
      Avg. Days On Hand:           93.6
```

Figure 12.21
Price Increase Analysis Word Processing Memorandum

    e. Print the memorandum.
    f. Save the memorandum document with a file name of XXX12–T.
    g. End your spreadsheet and word processing sessions.

STEP 18: End the *Automated Accounting* session.
Click on the *Exit/Quit* toolbar button.

Applying Your Information Skills

I. MATCHING

Directions: In the *Working Papers,* write the letter of the appropriate term next to each definition.

a. sales order processing
b. computerized sales order processing system
c. sales invoice
d. sales return
e. sales invoices input form

1. A form used to describe the goods sold, the quantity, and price.

2. The procedures and controls involved in preparing invoices, updating accounting records, and shipping merchandise.

3. A credit allowed a customer for the sales price of returned merchandise, resulting in a decrease in the vendor's accounts receivable.

4. A system that comprises the procedures involved in preparing a sales invoice and automatically integrating the data it contains into the inventory and general ledger records.

5. A form used to record sales and sales return transactions when a computerized sales order processing system is used.

II. QUESTIONS

Directions: Write the answers to each of the following questions in the *Working Papers.*

1. Identify the tasks performed by the computer when sales and sales return data are entered.

2. How is the quantity recorded on the sales invoices input form for a sales return transaction?

3. Itemize the steps required to make a change to an existing sales invoice.

4. What do the terms 2/10, n/30 mean?

5. What totals are contained at the bottom of the computer-generated sales invoice?

6. Why are data not lost when sales invoices are purged?

Independent Practice Problem 12–P

In this problem, you will process the sales and sales return transactions for the week of March 8 through March 14 for VIP Copier & Fax Machines.

STEP 1:   Start up *Automated Accounting 7.0.*

STEP 2:   Load opening balances file AA12–P.

STEP 3:   Enter your name in the User Name text box and click *OK.*

STEP 4:   Save the file with a file name of XXX12–P.

STEP 5:   Enter the March 8 through March 14 sales and sales return transactions.

March 8–14 Weekly Transactions:

Mar. 08   Sold the following merchandise to Malott Realty Co., terms 2/10, n/30, 6% sales tax, sales invoice no. S732:

Description	Quantity Sold	Selling Price
AMS 24 lb. Paper	4	42.50
Laser Copier Cartridge	2	69.00

Mar. 09   Sold the following merchandise to Morgan Home Center, terms 30 days, 6% sales tax, sales invoice no. S733:

Description	Quantity Sold	Selling Price
Superb Mini Copier	1	225.00
M–10 Copier Cartridge	2	58.95
Recycled 20 lb. Paper	2	27.95

Mar. 10   Sold the following merchandise to Carol's Office Products, terms 30 days, 6% sales tax, sales invoice no. S734:

Description	Quantity Sold	Selling Price
Office Color Copier	1	1651.30
Color Copier Cartridge	1	89.35
AMS 16 lb. Copy Paper	3	21.95

Mar. 10   The following merchandise was returned to VIP Copier & Fax Machines by Florence Carpets, 6% sales tax, sales return no. CM706:

Description	Quantity Returned	Price
Copier 12 oz. Toner	1	12.95

Mar. 11   Sold the following merchandise to Siegel Mortgage Co., terms 30 days, 6% sales tax, sales invoice no. S735:

Description	Quantity Sold	Selling Price
Desktop Facsimile	1	475.00

Mar. 12   Sold the following merchandise to J & M Construction Co., terms 30 days, 6% sales tax, sales invoice no. S736:

Description	Quantity Sold	Selling Price
AMS 20 lb. Copy Paper	2	37.85
M–10 Copier Cartridge	2	58.95

Mar. 13   Sold the following merchandise to Klein & Associates, terms 2/10, n/30, 6% sales tax, sales invoice no. S737:

Description	Quantity Sold	Selling Price
Phone Answer & Fax	1	329.95
Facsimile Roll Paper	2	24.95
AMS 20 lb. Copy Paper	1	37.85

Mar. 14   Sold the following merchandise to Baer Insurance Agency, terms 30 days, 6% sales tax, sales invoice no. S738:

Description	Quantity Sold	Selling Price
AMS 20 lb. Copy Paper	2	37.85
Facsimile Roll Paper	2	24.95
Recycled 20 lb. Paper	1	27.95

STEP 6:   **Display the inventory list report.**

STEP 7:   **Display the inventory transactions for the period March 8 through March 14.**

CHECK FIGURE:
Inventory transactions
total quantity sold = 29

STEP 8:   **Display the yearly sales report.**

STEP 9:   Display the general journal report for the period March 8 through March 14.

STEP 10:   Display the sales journal report for the period March 8 through March 14.

STEP 11:   Display the Accounts Receivable, Sales, and Sales Returns & Allowances general ledger accounts.

STEP 12:   Display a trial balance.

STEP 13:   Display a schedule of accounts receivable.

STEP 14:   Display an accounts receivable ledger report.

STEP 15:   Display a statement of account for Florence Carpets.

STEP 16:   Save your data.

STEP 17:   Optional spreadsheet and word processing integration activity (you must complete the optional spreadsheet activity in step 17 of Tutorial Problem 12–T prior to solving this spreadsheet and word processing activity): Use the spreadsheet file you prepared in step 17 of Tutorial Problem 12–T as a template file to perform what-if analysis of projected price increases using various percentages and inventory turnover ratios. Send Susan Phelps a memo summarizing your findings and attach the spreadsheet reports.

> **CHECK FIGURE:**
> Trial balance total debits and credits = $182,347.50

Spreadsheet:
a. Display and copy the Inventory Valuation (Average Cost) report to the clipboard in spreadsheet format.
b. Start up your spreadsheet software, and load the file you saved in step 17 of Tutorial Problem 12–T (XXX12–T). Select cell A8 as the current cell, and paste the report from the clipboard into the spreadsheet. Make the appropriate adjustment to the total of the Projected Value column and change the formula in cell C4 to reflect this change, if necessary.
c. Perform the following two analyses:
    1. 2% price increase with an inventory turnover ratio of 6.2.
    2. 3.5% price increase with an inventory turnover ratio of 4.9.
d. Format the spreadsheet as necessary and print each report. Use Figure 12.20 as a guide.
e. Save your spreadsheet data with a file name of XXX12–P.

Word Processing:
a. Start up your word processing software.
b. Load the memorandum document you saved in Tutorial Problem 12–T.
c. Modify the document as necessary and paste the results of the two spreadsheet analyses from the spreadsheet into the body of the memo. Use Figure 12.21 as a guide.
d. Format the memo and spreadsheet information as necessary.
e. Print the memorandum.
f. Save the memorandum document with a file name of XXX12–P.
g. End your spreadsheet and word processing sessions.

STEP 18: End the *Automated Accounting* session.

Applying Your Technology Skills 12–P

Directions: Using Independent Practice Problem 12–P, write the answers to the following questions in the *Working Papers*.

Inventory List Report:
1. What is the average and last cost prices for the Phone Answer & Fax machine?

2. What is the retail price of the Office Color Copier?

3. How many cases of AMS 20 lb. Copy Paper are on hand?

Inventory Transactions Report:
4. What is the total quantity sold for all items?

5. What items were sold and listed on invoice number S736?

Yearly Sales Report:
6. Which item has the greatest sales volume based on the dollar amount?

7. What is the total amount of yearly sales?

General and Sales Journals:
8. In the general journal, what is the amount of sales return CM706 (including sales tax payable)?

9. What are the totals of the debit and credit columns in the sales journal?

General Ledger:

10. What was the Accounts Receivable account balance on March 11?

11. What was the Sales account balance on March 12?

12. What was the Sales Returns & Allowances account balance on March 10?

Trial Balance:

13. What is the current balance in Accounts Receivable?

14. What is the net amount of sales (Sales minus Sales Returns & Allowances)? Does it equal the total amount of yearly sales shown on the yearly sales report?

Schedule of Accounts Receivable, Accounts Receivable Ledger, and Statements of Account:

15. From the schedule of accounts receivable, what is the total due from all customers as of March 14? Does it equal the current balance in the Accounts Receivable account?

16. From the accounts receivable ledger, what is the amount owed by Klein & Associates?

17. Does the balance on Carol's Office Products' statement of account match the balance due in the schedule of accounts receivable and in the accounts receivable ledger? If yes, what is the amount?

Mastery Problem 12–M

In Problem 12–M, you will process the sales and sales return transactions for the week of March 15 through March 21 for VIP Copier & Fax Machines.

STEP 1:   Load opening balances file AA12–M.

STEP 2:   Enter your name in the User Name text box.

STEP 3:   Save the data with a name of XXX12–M.

STEP 4:   Enter the sales order transaction data for the period March 15 to March 21.

March 15–21 Weekly Transactions:

Mar. 16   Sold the following merchandise to Morgan Home Center, terms 30 days, 6% sales tax, sales invoice no. S739:

Description	Quantity Sold	Selling Price
Phone Answer & Fax	1	329.95
AMS 20 lb. Copy Paper	2	37.85
Facsimile Roll Paper	1	24.95

Mar. 17   Sold the following merchandise to J & M Construction Co., terms 30 days, 6% sales tax, sales invoice no. S740:

Description	Quantity Sold	Selling Price
Desktop Facsimile	1	465.50
M–10 Copier Cartridge	1	58.95
AMS 24 lb. Copy Paper	2	42.50

Mar. 18   The following merchandise was returned to VIP Copier & Fax Machines by Siegel Mortgage Co., 6% sales tax, sales return no. CM707:

Description	Quantity Returned	Price
Color Copier Cartridge	1	89.35

Mar. 18   Sold the following merchandise to Baer Insurance Agency, terms 30 days, 6% sales tax, sales invoice no. S741:

Description	Quantity Sold	Selling Price
Superb Mini Copier	2	225.00
CX10 Fax Cartridge	2	45.00

Mar. 19   Sold the following merchandise to Malott Realty Co., terms 2/10, n/30, 6% sales tax, sales invoice no. S742:

Description	Quantity Sold	Selling Price
Office Fax & Copier	1	1295.00

Mar. 20 Sold the following merchandise to Florence Carpets, terms 30 days, 6% sales tax, sales invoice no. S743:

Description	Quantity Sold	Selling Price
Superb Mini Copier	1	225.00
M–10 Copier Cartridge	2	58.95

Mar. 21 Sold the following merchandise to Malott Realty Co., terms 2/10, n/30, 6% sales tax, sales invoice no. S744:

Description	Quantity Sold	Selling Price
Phone Answer & Fax	1	329.95
Facsimile Roll Paper	1	24.95
AMS 16 lb. Copy Paper	2	21.95

Mar. 21 Sold the following merchandise to Klein & Associates, terms 2/10, n/30, 6% sales tax, sales invoice no. S745:

Description	Quantity Sold	Selling Price
Facsimile Roll Paper	1	24.95
Recycled 20 lb. Paper	2	27.95
AMS 20 lb. Copy Paper	3	37.85

STEP 5: Display the inventory list report.

STEP 6: Display the inventory transactions for the period March 15 through March 21 of the current year.

> **CHECK FIGURE:**
> Inventory transactions total quantity sold = 25

STEP 7: Display the yearly sales report.

STEP 8: Display the general journal for the period March 15 through March 21 of the current year.

STEP 9: Display the sales journal for the period March 15 through March 21 of the current year.

STEP 10: Display the Accounts Receivable, Sales, and Sales Returns & Allowances general ledger accounts.

STEP 11: Display a trial balance.

> **CHECK FIGURE:**
> Trial balance total debits and credits = $186,381.96

STEP 12: Display a schedule of accounts receivable.

STEP 13: Display an accounts receivable ledger report.

STEP 14: Display all the statements of account.

STEP 15:   Save your data.

STEP 16:   **Optional spreadsheet and word processing integration activity (you must complete the optional spreadsheet activity in step 17 of Tutorial Problem 12–T or Independent Practice Problem 12–P prior to solving this spreadsheet and word processing activity):**

Spreadsheet:
a.   Display and copy the Inventory Valuation (Average Cost) report to the clipboard in spreadsheet format.
b.   Start up your spreadsheet software, and load the file you saved in Tutorial Problem 12–T or Independent Practice Problem 12–P. Select cell A8 as the current cell, and paste the report from the clipboard into the spreadsheet. Make the appropriate adjustment to the total of the Projected Value column, and change the formula in cell C4 to reflect this change, if necessary.
c.   Perform the following two analyses:
   1.   5% price increase with an inventory turnover ratio of 4.7.
   2.   6% price increase with an inventory turnover ratio of 5.4.
d.   Format the spreadsheet as necessary and print each report. Use Figure 12.20 as a guide.
e.   Save your spreadsheet data with a file name of XXX12–M.

Word Processing:
a.   Start up your word processing software.
b.   Load the memorandum document you saved in Tutorial Problem 12–T or Independent Practice Problem 12–P.
c.   Modify the document as necessary and paste the results of the two spreadsheet analyses from the spreadsheet into the body of the memo. Use Figure 12.21 as a guide.
d.   Format the memo and spreadsheet information as necessary.
e.   Print the memorandum.
f.   Save the memorandum document with a file name of XXX12–M.
g.   End your spreadsheet and word processing sessions.

STEP 17:   **End the *Automated Accounting* session.**

Applying Your Technology Skills 12–M

Directions: Using Mastery Problem 12–M, write the answers to the following questions in the *Working Papers*.

Inventory List Report:
1. How many Professional Fax machines are on hand?

2. What is the retail price for the Color Laser Copier?

Inventory Transactions Report:
3. What is the total quantity sold for all items?

4. What items were sold and listed on invoice number S741?

Yearly Sales Report:
5. Which item has the greatest total quantity of items sold?

6. What is the total amount of yearly sales?

General and Sales Journals:
7. In the general journal, what is the amount of sales return CM707 (including sales tax payable)?

8. What are the totals of the debit and credit columns in the sales journal?

General Ledger:
9. What was the Accounts Receivable account balance on March 20?

10. What was the Sales account balance on March 20?

11. What was the Sales Returns & Allowances account balance on March 18?

Trial Balance:
12. What is the current balance in Accounts Receivable?

13. What is the net amount of sales (Sales minus Sales Returns & Allowances)? Does it equal the total amount of yearly sales shown on the yearly sales report?

Schedule of Accounts Receivable, Accounts Receivable Ledger, and Statements of Account:
14. From the schedule of accounts receivable, what is the total due from all customers as of March 21? Does it equal the current balance in the Accounts Receivable account?

15. From the accounts receivable ledger, what is the amount owed by Siegel Mortgage Co.?

16. From the customer statements, do the current account balances shown on each customer's statement of account match the balances shown in the schedule of accounts receivable and accounts receivable ledger?

ACCOUNTING CAREERS IN DEPTH

Financial Planner

A financial planner develops and implements financial plans for individuals, businesses, and organizations, utilizing a knowledge of tax and investment strategies, securities, insurance, pension plans, and real estate. A financial planner performs the following duties:

- Interviewing a client to determine the client's assets, liabilities, cash flow, insurance coverage, tax status, and financial objectives.
- Analyzing a client's financial status, developing a financial plan based on the analysis, and discussing financial options with the client.
- Preparing and submitting documents to implement the plan selected by the client.
- Maintaining contact with the client to revise the plan, based on modified needs of the client or on changes in the investment market.

A financial planner may also do the following:

- Referring a client to other establishments to obtain services outlined in the financial plan.
- Selling insurance to the client, recommending the amount and type of coverage.
- Buying and selling stocks and bonds for a client.
- Renting, buying, or selling property for a client.

As is apparent from the job duties listed above, a financial planner needs to be knowledgeable about a wide range of financial issues. As a result, the educational requirements for a financial planner include a college degree. In addition, a financial planner may be registered with professional self-regulatory associations and be designated as a Certified Financial Planner. In dealing with the public, a planner must be able to prove to potential clients that the planner has the skills and background necessary to wisely deal with the client's financial needs.

Financial planning is a career that can be very interesting to people who enjoy working with a wide variety of clients. It requires good human relations skills in addition to the ability to analyze information and develop a plan on the basis of the client's needs in light of the current and future economic environment.

LEARNING OBJECTIVES

Upon completion of this chapter, you will be able to:

1. Set up a computerized accounting system.

2. Enter the accounting system setup data.

INTRODUCTION

Many options are available that allow accounting system software to be tailored to a specific business. Because accounting software packages are written to handle a wide variety of business processing tasks, it is unlikely that a business user will use all of the capabilities and capacities of a given system. The problems that you have completed up to this point have been set up for you, including opening balances, type of business, etc.

In this chapter, you will learn how to set up a computerized accounting system and enter opening balance data for MCB Corporation, a merchandising wholesale business organized as a corporation. MCB Corporation wholesales power tools to retail stores.

Prior to setting up a computerized accounting system, you must carefully plan, design, and gather data. Account numbers must be assigned to each account to identify it as an asset, liability, equity, revenue, or expense account. Controlling account balances must match the totals of related subsidiary ledgers. Assets, liabilities, and equity account balances must be current. Total debit balances must equal total credit balances.

The menu items and windows that were used in earlier chapters for accounting system processing will not be covered in this chapter.

SYSTEM SETUP SPECIFICATIONS

The tasks necessary to set up a computerized accounting system are covered in this chapter. The order in which they must be performed is detailed in the problems at the end of the chapter.

E T H I C S

The use of automation in factories and computers in offices has led to the reduction and elimination of many jobs in the work force. Company management argues that the use of computers and automated systems improves efficiency, increases productivity, and helps the business stay competitive. Labor unions argue that companies that install these systems in their businesses have an obligation to the workers who are replaced.

a. What obligation, if any, do you think companies have toward their employees who are replaced?

b. What would you do, if anything, to help replaced workers?

c. What jobs can you think of that computers have created?

New

The **New command** in the File menu clears any existing data from memory in preparation for setting up a new accounting system. If you have data in memory, you should save it before you choose New. You will be asked to enter your name in the User Name text box so that your name can be associated with the newly created file.

Company Information

The Customize Accounting System window is used to provide setup information to *Automated Accounting 7.0*. It can be accessed by choosing *Customize Accounting System* from the Data menu or clicking the *Custom* toolbar button. Figure 13.1 shows the Company Info. tab in the Customize Accounting System window. The setup data for MCB Corporation is shown. The purpose and function of each text box, check box, and option button in the Company Info. tab is described in Table 13.1.

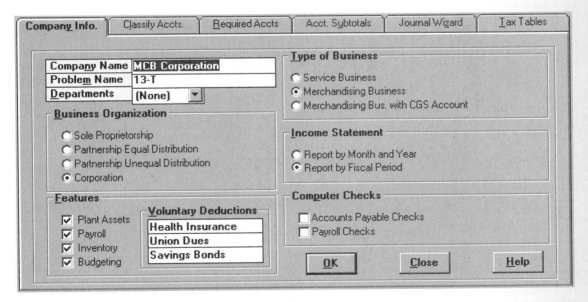

Figure 13.1
Company Information

OPTION	DESCRIPTION
Company Name	The company name is entered in this text box. The name of the company is displayed and printed as part of the heading for each report.
Problem Name	The problem name is entered in this text box. The problem name is printed at the top of the report along with the user name. The problem name also appears in the upper right corner of the *Automated Accounting 7.0* window as a reminder of the problem currently stored in memory.
Departments	This drop-down list allows you to select from three options: None, 2, or 3. Click the radio button of your choice.
Business Organization	The business organization option is used by the software during financial statement preparation and period-end closing. Click the radio button of your choice.
Features	A check box is provided for each type of accounting system to be included during setup. Appropriate windows, reports, data entry tabs, etc., are automatically activated, based upon the features selected. For example, when the Payroll check box is selected, an Employees tab appears in the Account Maintenance window to permit employee maintenance. A Payroll tab appears in the Other Activities window to permit entry of payroll transactions. A Payroll Reports option appears in the Report selection window that enables the user to display and print various payroll reports. When the Payroll feature is checked, a Voluntary Deductions group box will appear, permitting the user to enter the names of up to three different voluntary deductions that are to be withheld from the employee's pay. Click the check boxes of your choice.
Type of Business	The type of business option is used by the software to determine the format of the income statement. Click the radio button of your choice.
Income Statement	This option allows the income statement to be customized. If the option is set to Month & Year, the income statement will include a column for the current month and another column for the current year. Also included for each column is a percentage, indicating the percent each amount is of total operating revenue. If this option is set to Fiscal Period, only the amount column and percent of total operating revenue are included on the income statement representing the current fiscal period. Click the radio button of your choice.
Computer Checks	If the Accounts Payable Checks option is set On, checks will be generated each time a cash payment that involves a vendor is entered. If the Payroll Checks option is set On, pay checks will be generated each time a payroll transaction is entered for an employee. Click the check boxes of your choice.

Table 13.1
Company
Information Text
Boxes and
Option Settings

1:   **Enter the Company Name and Problem Name.**

2:   **Click the *Departments* drop-down list and select the number of departments.**

3:   **Select the appropriate type of business organization.**

4:   **Click each *Feature* check box to indicate the accounting system data that is to be included during setup.**
     If the Payroll feature is selected, the Voluntary Deductions group box will appear. Enter the names of up to three voluntary deductions that are to be withheld from employees' pay.

5:   **Select the appropriate type of business.**

6:   **Select the type of income statement desired.**

7:   **Click the appropriate *Computer Checks* check box to indicate if the computer is to generate Accounts Payable or Payroll Checks.**
     If neither of the check boxes is checked, the software assumes that checks are written manually.

8:   **Click *OK*.**

Classify Accounts

The Classify Accounts tab allows you to classify the general ledger accounts based on account number ranges. Figure 13.2 contains the account number ranges for MCB Corporation. In order to perform financial statement analysis, the range of account numbers for long-term assets and long-term liabilities must be established. This data is provided in the Extended Classification section of the window.

The account classification shown in Figure 13.2 is also the default classification used by the *Automated Accounting* system. Unless the account classification numbering scheme is different, it will not be necessary to change the account ranges as they appear. If they must be changed, do *not* key the actual range of account numbers, but enter the *potential* range. For example, if your chart of accounts currently has five assets ranging from account number 1110 to 1150, you should not specify the actual range, 1110 to 1150. Specify the potential range, such as 1000 to 1999, so that asset accounts added later will be included in the assets classification automatically. If your chart of accounts does not include a certain classification, key the anticipated account number range for that classification. For example, if your chart of accounts does not include Other Expenses, include a range of account numbers that are to be reserved for Other Expenses in the event they need to be added at a later date.

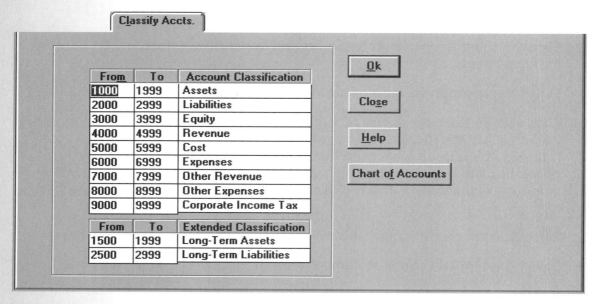

Figure 13.2
Classify Accounts

1: Click the *Classify Accts.* tab.

2: If different from the default settings, enter the account number range for each of the classes of accounts.
Click the *Chart of Accounts* button to select an account from the Chart of Accounts List window.

3: When all the account number ranges have been entered, click *OK*.

Required Accounts

Because you have a great deal of flexibility in assigning account numbers and titles, you must provide account numbers for certain key accounts. **Required accounts** are the accounts the software needs in order to prepare financial statements, to carry out integration among the systems (i.e., payroll, sales order processing), and to complete period-end closing tasks. The required accounts for MCB Corporation are shown in Figure 13.3.

Based upon the departmentalization, business organization, features, and type of business settings in the Company Info. tab, the computer will automatically determine and list the required accounts. For example, if the type of business is a service business, no merchandise inventory

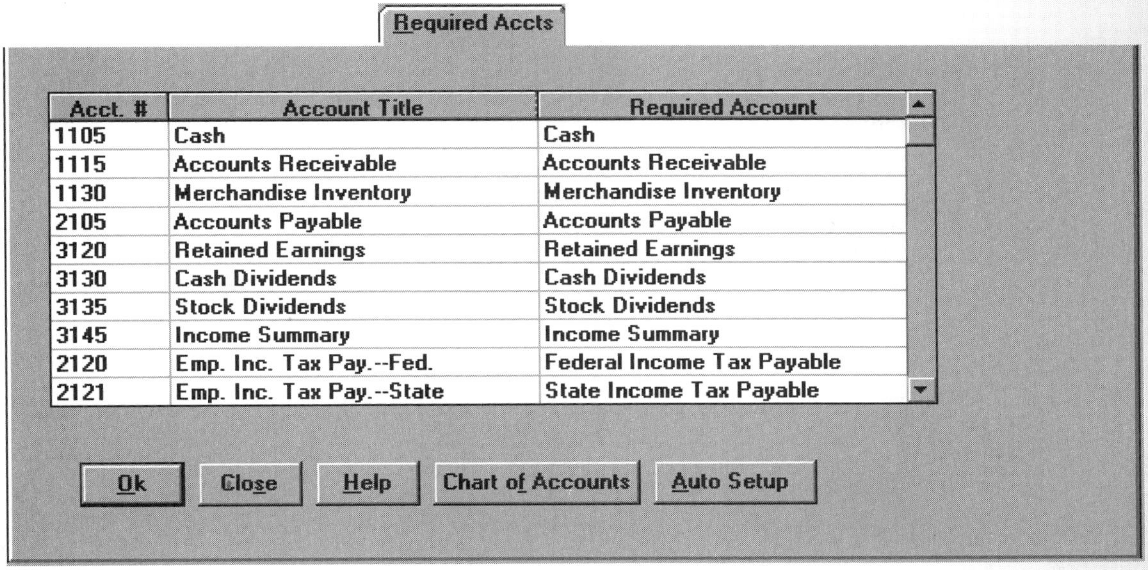

Required Accts

Acct. #	Account Title	Required Account
1105	Cash	Cash
1115	Accounts Receivable	Accounts Receivable
1130	Merchandise Inventory	Merchandise Inventory
2105	Accounts Payable	Accounts Payable
3120	Retained Earnings	Retained Earnings
3130	Cash Dividends	Cash Dividends
3135	Stock Dividends	Stock Dividends
3145	Income Summary	Income Summary
2120	Emp. Inc. Tax Pay.--Fed.	Federal Income Tax Payable
2121	Emp. Inc. Tax Pay.--State	State Income Tax Payable

Ok   Close   Help   Chart of Accounts   Auto Setup

Figure 13.3
Required Accounts

accounts are required. For a merchandising business, a Merchandise Inventory and an Income Summary account are required for each department. For a sole proprietorship and a partnership, capital account(s) are listed. For a corporation, a Stock Dividends account is required. If the corporation does not have stock dividends, the account number for the Cash Dividends account is entered.

1: **Click the *Required Accts.* tab.**

2: **Click the *Auto Setup* button.**
    The computer will search the newly entered chart of accounts and attempt to match the required accounts to the account titles. All matching accounts are displayed.

3: **Enter the account number for each of the unmatched accounts.**
    Click the *Chart of Accounts* button to select an account from the Chart of Accounts List window.

4: **When all the account numbers have been entered, click *OK*.**

Account Subtotals

The purpose of the Account Subtotals tab is to allow you to specify and select where subtotals are to be printed on the financial statements.

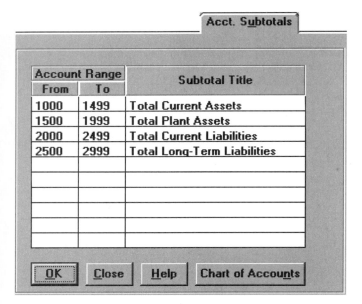

Figure 13.4
Account
Subtotals

For example, you may wish to tailor the balance sheet so that a subtotal prints after current assets and another after plant assets. To create subtotals, key the account number range of the accounts to be included in the subtotal and the title to be printed on the subtotal line. The account number ranges need not reference actual accounts. Instead, the potential range should be entered so that it will not be necessary to modify the account number range as accounts are added to the chart of accounts. The account subtotals for MCB Corporation are shown in Figure 13.4.

1:   **Click the *Acct. Subtotals* tab.**

2:   **Enter the account number range and title for each of the subtotals.**
     Click the *Chart of Accounts* button to view a chart of accounts list.

3:   **When all of the account number ranges and titles have been entered, click *OK*.**

Journal Wizard

Using special journals improves the efficiency of entering transaction data into the computer.

The **journal wizard,** shown in Figure 13.5, can be used to create special general, purchases, cash payments, sales, and cash receipts journals. Basic default journals are automatically provided when a new business is established. The journal wizard may be used to expand these default journals to better meet the needs of the business being

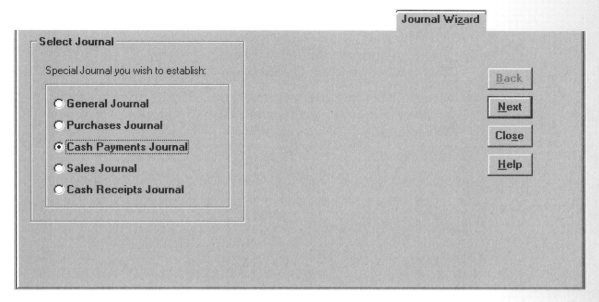

Figure 13.5
Journal Wizard

established. New journals will be saved along with your data and will be used when entering future transaction data. The journal wizard may also be used with an ongoing system to create special journals to more efficiently handle data entry activities. The example shown in Figures 13.5 through 13.8 was used to produce the cash payments journal for MCB Corporation shown in Figure 13.9.

1:   **Click the *Journal Wizard* tab.**

2:   **Select the journal to be created, Cash Payments.**

3:   **Click the *Next* button.**
     The dialog window shown in Figure 13.6 will appear.

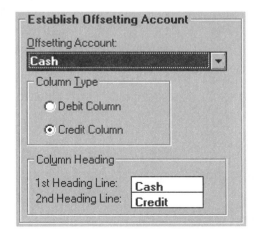

Figure 13.6
Establish
Offsetting
Account
Information

4:　Click the drop-down text box to select the offsetting account, Cash.

5:　Click the appropriate *Debit* or *Credit* column. The offsetting Cash account will be Credited.

6:　Enter a one- to two-line heading to identify the offsetting account column in the journal. Cash Credit was selected for this example.

7:　Click *Next*.
　　The dialog window shown in Figure 13.7 will appear.

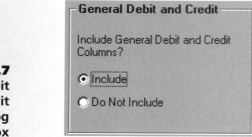

Figure 13.7
General Debit and Credit Column Dialog Box

8:　Click *Include* or *Do Not Include* to indicate if general debit and credit columns should be in the journal. Include was selected for this example.

9:　Click *Next*.
　　The dialog box shown in Figure 13.8 will appear.

Account	Header 1	Header 2	Debit	Credit
Accounts Payable	A.P.	Debit	☑	☐
Purchases Discount	Purchases	Disc. Cr	☐	☑

Special Journal Columns — Specify each additional special journal column:

Back　Finish　Close　Help

Figure 13.8
Special Journal Columns

10: Use the Account drop-down list to select the account to be included in the journal.

11: Enter the first and second header to identify the account column in the journal.

12: Click *Debit* or *Credit* to indicate if the account is to be treated as a debit or credit amount.

13: Repeat the above three steps for each column to be added to the journal.

14: Click *Finish*.
Click the appropriate tab in the Journal Entries window and verify that the newly created journal is correct (see Figure 13.9).

General Journal		Purchases		Cash Payments		Sales		Cash Receipts	

Date	Refer.	Acct. No.	Debit	Credit	A.P. Debit	Purchases Disc. Cr	Cash Credit	Vendor	
03/01/--									

Figure 13.9
Journal Wizard Created Cash Payments Journal

The Date and Reference column will also be included as the left-most columns in the journal. A Vendor or Customer column will also be added as the right-most column to the appropriate journal if the software detects that vendor or customer data exists.

Tax Tables

There are three sections in the Tax Tables tab, as shown in Figure 13.10. The first section, Federal Tax Brackets, contains the federal withholding rates. These rates may be updated at any time by keying in corrected rates in the appropriate column. Refer to the IRS Circular E (Employer's Tax Guide) for the most current rates. Section 2, State Tax Brackets, contains the state withholding rates used by the software for the problems in this textbook. Section 3, Rates and Limits, contains the various tax rates, upper limits, and allowance amounts required by the software to calculate employee and employer payroll taxes. Like the

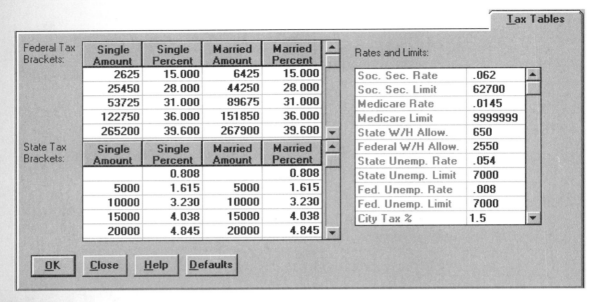

Figure 13.10
Tax Table

Federal Tax Brackets figures, the State Tax Brackets and Rates and Limits figures may be updated by keying corrected rates in the appropriate column. Refer to the appropriate state or local employer's tax guide for the most current rates.

It is recommended that you *not* change these rates, unless instructed to do so, when working with payroll problems in this textbook. If the brackets, rates, or percentages are changed, the calculated withholding amounts will no longer match the solutions provided to your instructor.

1: **Click the *Tax Tables* tab.**

2: **Click the appropriate field and enter the change(s) to the amounts and percentages.**
    Click the *Defaults* button to restore previously changed rates, limits, etc. to the withholding rates provided with the software.

3: **When the changes are complete, click *OK*.**

SYSTEM SETUP DATA

Once the Company Information has been entered, the chart of accounts, vendor, customer, opening balances, budget, plant assets, payroll, and inventory data can be entered.

Accounts Pick List

An **accounts pick list** is a preset master chart of accounts that may be used when adding to, creating, or updating a chart of accounts. As an alternative to keying the accounts, you can use the Pick List button located at the bottom of the Accounts Account Maintenance window as shown in Figure 13.11. You should use the Accounts Account Maintenance window to enter accounts that do not appear in the pick list, or to change the account titles as desired.

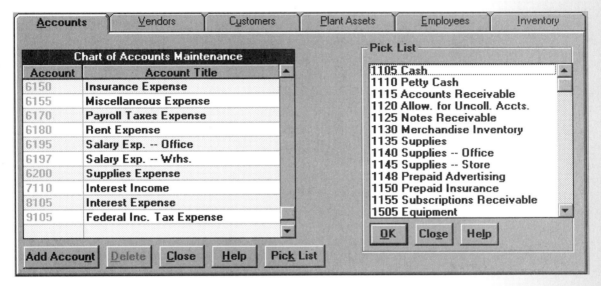

Figure 13.11
Chart of Accounts with Pick List

Adding an Account   An account can be added as follows:

1: Click the *Accts.* toolbar button, then click the *Accounts* tab.

2: Click the *Pick List* button.

3: **Select an account from the Pick List column and click *OK*.**
    The selected account will be placed in the Chart of Accounts Maintenance list.

4: **Click the *Add Account* button to add the selected account to the chart of accounts.**
    The selected account will be added to the chart of accounts and will appear in the Chart of Accounts Maintenance list.

Removing an Account   An account can be removed as follows:

1: **Select the account you wish to remove from the Chart of Accounts Maintenance list.**

2: **Click the *Delete* button.**

Opening Balances

Opening balances are the general and subsidiary ledger balances at the beginning of the fiscal period. The account balances must be recorded in the new accounting system before a company can begin recording accounting transactions. General ledger opening balance data is keyed into the general journal, and each opening balance is posted as a separate general journal entry. Likewise, each customer account balance must be keyed as a separate entry. The total of the balances for all the customers will be the balance of the Accounts Receivable general ledger account. Each vendor account balance must also be keyed as a separate entry. The total of the balances for all the vendors will be the balance of the Accounts Payable general ledger account.

As opening balance data is keyed, the debit and credit totals will not be equal until all transactions have been entered. However, you should post each transaction anyway. When the word BALANCE is keyed in the reference grid cells, the software will know that the entry is an opening balance and will not display the warning message that the entry is not in balance. After all data has been entered, you should verify the accuracy of the debit and credit totals shown on the trial balance.

Budgets

A **budget** is a financial plan for the future. Budgets are developed for a specific period of time, such as a month or year. While budgets can be developed for many aspects of a business, *Automated Accounting 7.0* uses budgets for income statement accounts only. Once budget data is entered, a performance report becomes available. The **performance report** compares actual revenues and expenses with budgeted revenues and expenses in income statement format.

The Budgets tab in the Other Activities window allows you to key the budgeted amounts—a task that is usually performed during accounting system setup if budgets are to be used. A budgeted amount is the estimated balance for that particular account at the end of the fiscal period. The account titles and current budget amounts (if any) are displayed in the window, as illustrated in Figure 13.12, so that you may either key new budget amounts or correct previously keyed budgeted amounts.

1: **Click the *Other* toolbar button, then click the *Budgets* tab.**

2: **Enter the budgeted amount for the first account.**

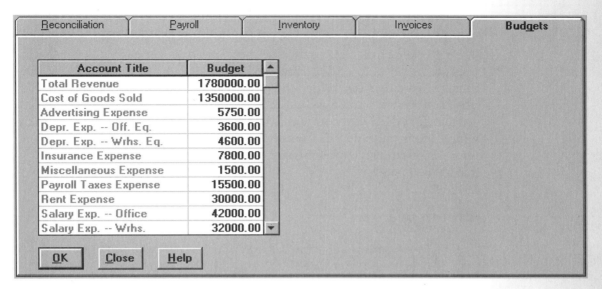

Figure 13.12
Budgets

3: Press the *Tab* key to move to the next account.
The accounts are scrollable. When you have entered the amount for the last account shown in the window, the accounts will scroll up so that you can enter the next budget amount. Similarly, if you press the Shift+Tab keys, the accounts will scroll down.

4: When all budget amounts have been entered, click *OK*.

Plant Assets

If plant assets are going to be part of the new accounting system, each of the plant assets must also be entered in the Plant Assets Account Maintenance window. If you need more information on adding plant assets, refer to Chapter 8.

Payroll

If payroll is going to be part of the new accounting system, each of the employees must be entered in the Employees Account Maintenance window. If you need more information on adding employees, refer to Chapter 10. If the accounting system is being established at a time other than the beginning of a new year, you must establish the quarterly and yearly earnings and withholdings for each employee. Quarterly and yearly

balances are established by either of two methods: (1) by running simulated payrolls for each pay period up to the desired date, or (2) by keying one payroll transaction for each employee for each quarter that represents the sum of that employee's earnings and withholdings for the quarter. In either case, since the payroll is date sensitive, be sure to use the appropriate pay-period or end-of-quarter dates. Since the accounting system for MCB Corporation is being established on March 1, and each employee is paid once each month, simulated payrolls can be run for the months of January and February to bring the quarterly and yearly balances up-to-date.

Inventory

Two tasks are required to set up an inventory system: (1) key the data for each stock item, and (2) enter opening balance historical data. The procedure to enter stock items was described in the Adding a New Inventory Stock Item section in Chapter 11. After the company's stock items have been entered, the historical data may be entered. The procedure to enter this data is the same as that described in the Entering Inventory Transaction Data section in Chapter 11.

Chapter Review

1. Prior to setting up a computerized accounting system, you must carefully plan, design, and gather data. The New command in the File menu clears any existing data from memory in preparation for setting up a new accounting system. The Customize Accounting System window is used to provide setup information to the *Automated Accounting* software.

2. The Classify Accounts tab allows you to classify the general ledger accounts based on account number ranges. Required accounts are needed by the software to prepare financial statements, to carry out integration among the systems (i.e., payroll, sales order processing), and to complete period-end closing tasks. Required accounts are entered in the Required Accts. tab. Account Subtotals may be used to specify and select where subtotals are to be printed on the financial statements. Subtotals are entered in the Acct. Subtotals tab.

3. The journal wizard can be used to create special general, purchases, cash payments, sales, and cash receipts journals to improve the efficiency of entering transaction data into the computer.

4. The federal tax brackets, state tax brackets, and rates and limits in the Tax Tables are required by the software to calculate employee and employer payroll taxes. Changes to the default settings may be made in the Tax Tables tab.

5. The Accounts Account Maintenance window allows you to create a chart of accounts, vendor list, and customer list. An accounts pick list from a master chart of accounts may be used to help create a chart of accounts.

6. Opening balances are entered in the general journal. If you key the word BALANCE in the general journal reference grid cells, the computer will know that the entry is an opening balance and will therefore not display the warning message that the entry is not in balance.

7. A budget is a financial plan for the future. Budget amounts are usually entered during accounting system setup if budgets are to be used in the new accounting system.

8. If payroll is going to be part of a new accounting system, each of the employees must be entered in the Employees Account Maintenance window. If a payroll system is being established at a time other than the beginning of a new year, you must establish the quarterly and yearly earnings and withholdings for each employee.

9. Two tasks are required to set up an inventory system: (1) key the data for each stock item, and (2) enter opening balance historical data.

INTERNET

In the days before graphical user interfaces, users could communicate only with text. Little pictures called "emoticons" were created that explained emotions better than using words. You may be familiar with the "smiley face" emoticon.

TUTORIAL PROBLEM 13-T

In this problem, you will set up a complete accounting system. You will complete the processing necessary to set up the general ledger, plant assets, payroll, inventory, and budget data for MCB Corporation as of March 1 of the current year.

STEP 1: **Start up *Automated Accounting 7.0*.**

STEP 2: **Use the New command to erase data in memory and prepare the computer for setup.**
Choose *New* from the File menu.

STEP 3: **Enter your name in the User Name text box and click *OK*.**

STEP 4: **Enter or set the data fields, check boxes, and option buttons in the Customized Accounting Systems' Company Info. window as follows:**
Click the *Custom* toolbar button.

Company Name	MCB Corporation
Problem Name	13–T
Departments	Non Departmentalized
Business Organization . .	Corporation
Features	Plant Assets
. . . .	Payroll
. . . .	Health Insurance
. . . .	Union Dues
. . . .	Savings Bonds
. . . .	Inventory
. . . .	Budgeting
Type of Business	Merchandising Business
Income Statement	Report by Fiscal Period
Computer Checks	None

STEP 5: **Save your data.**
Click the *Save As* toolbar button and save the data with a file name of XXX13–T.

STEP 6: **Enter the chart of accounts.**
Click the *Accts.* Toolbar button. When the Account Maintenance window appears, click the *Accounts* tab and click the *Pick List* button. When the Pick List window appears, select the desired account from the Pick List window, then click *OK* to place the selected account in the Chart of Accounts Maintenance window. Click *Add Account* to add the account to the chart of accounts.

Note: Several of the account titles chosen from the pick list should be changed to match MCB Corporation's chart of accounts.

As an alternative, key each of the accounts. The completed chart of accounts is shown in Figure 13.13.

Account	Account Title
1105	Cash
1115	Accounts Receivable
1130	Merchandise Inventory
1135	Supplies
1150	Prepaid Insurance
1520	Equipment -- Office
1530	Accum. Dep. -- Off. Eq.
1560	Warehouse Equipment
1565	Accum. Dep. -- Wrhs. Eq.
2105	Accounts Payable
2110	Salaries Payable
2120	Emp. Inc. Tax Pay.--Fed.
2121	Emp. Inc. Tax Pay.--State
2122	Emp. Inc. Tax Pay.--City
2125	Social Security Tax Pay.
2126	Medicare Tax Payable
2130	Sales Tax Payable
2135	Unemp. Tax Pay. -- Fed.
2140	Unemp. Tax Pay. -- State
2150	Health Ins. Prem. Pay.
2160	Union Dues Payable
2170	Savings Bonds Payable
2505	Notes Payable
3105	Capital Stock
3120	Retained Earnings
3130	Cash Dividends
3135	Stock Dividends
3145	Income Summary
4105	Sales
4110	Sales Discount
4115	Sales Ret. and Allow.
5105	Purchases
5110	Purchases Discount
5115	Purch. Ret. and Allow.
6105	Advertising Expense
6130	Depr. Exp. -- Off. Eq.
6140	Depr. Exp. -- Wrhs. Eq.
6150	Insurance Expense
6155	Miscellaneous Expense
6170	Payroll Taxes Expense
6180	Rent Expense
6195	Salary Exp. -- Office
6197	Salary Exp. -- Wrhs.
6200	Supplies Expense
7110	Interest Income
8105	Interest Expense
9105	Federal Inc. Tax Expense

Figure 13.13
Chart of Accounts

TUTORIAL PROBLEM 13-T

STEP 7: **Enter the vendors.**
Click the *Vendors* tab in the Accounts Maintenance window and enter each of the vendors as shown in Figure 13.14.

Vendor Name
Bruno Insurance Agency
Elam Development Co.
Ellis Power Tools, Inc.
Folz Manufacturing, Inc.
Long Shore Tool Supplies
Payroll Bank Account
Southern Utilities Co.
Talbot Advertising
West Coast Tool Corp.
Wilke Office Supplies

Figure 13.14
Vendors

STEP 8: **Enter the customers.**
Click the *Customers* tab in the Accounts Maintenance window and enter each of the customers shown in Figure 13.15.

Customer Name
Brockert Rentals
C B Industrial Tools
Deters Machinery
Merchant Power Tools
Scholz Hardware
Wilkens Power Machines
Wisdom Industries

Figure 13.15
Customers

STEP 9: **Verify account classification and extended account classification data. The software will automatically try to determine account classifications.**
Click the *Custom* toolbar button and choose the *Classify Accts.* tab. Verify the appropriate account number ranges as shown in Figure 13.16.

T U T O R I A L   P R O B L E M   1 3 - T

From	To	Account Classification
1000	1999	Assets
2000	2999	Liabilities
3000	3999	Equity
4000	4999	Revenue
5000	5999	Cost
6000	6999	Expenses
7000	7999	Other Revenue
8000	8999	Other Expenses
9000	9999	Corporate Income Tax

From	To	Extended Classification
1500	1999	Long-Term Assets
2500	2999	Long-Term Liabilities

Figure 13.16
Account
Classification

STEP 10:   Enter the required account data shown below.
Click the *Required Accts.* tab, then click *Auto Setup* to try to match as many required accounts to the chart of account titles as possible. Complete the unmatched required accounts by entering the appropriate account numbers, or using the Chart of Accounts list box to select the desired accounts. The completed required accounts are shown in Figure 13.17.

Acct. #	Account Title	Required Account
1105	Cash	Cash
1115	Accounts Receivable	Accounts Receivable
1130	Merchandise Inventory	Merchandise Inventory
2105	Accounts Payable	Accounts Payable
3120	Retained Earnings	Retained Earnings
3130	Cash Dividends	Cash Dividends
3135	Stock Dividends	Stock Dividends
3145	Income Summary	Income Summary
2120	Emp. Inc. Tax Pay.--Fed.	Federal Income Tax Payable
2121	Emp. Inc. Tax Pay.--State	State Income Tax Payable
2125	Social Security Tax Pay.	Social Security Tax Payable
2126	Medicare Tax Payable	Medicare Tax Payable
2150	Health Ins. Prem. Pay.	Health Insurance Payable
2160	Union Dues Payable	Union Dues Payable
2170	Savings Bonds Payable	Savings Bonds Payable
6170	Payroll Taxes Expense	Payroll Tax Expense
2140	Unemp. Tax Pay. -- State	Unemployment Tax Payable--State
2135	Unemp. Tax Pay. -- Fed.	Unemployment Tax Payable--Feder
2110	Salaries Payable	Salaries Payable
2122	Emp. Inc. Tax Pay.--City	City Income Tax Payable

Figure 13.17
Required Accounts

TUTORIAL PROBLEM 13 – T

STEP 11: **Enter the account subtotals.**
Click the *Acct. Subtotals* tab and enter the appropriate account number ranges and subtotal titles as shown in Figure 13.18.

Account Range		Subtotal Title
From	To	
1000	1499	Total Current Assets
1500	1999	Total Plant Assets
2000	2499	Total Current Liabilities
2500	2999	Total Long-Term Liabilities

Figure 13.18
Account
Subtotals

STEP 12: **Enter the general ledger opening balances.**
Click the *Journal* toolbar button, then click the General Journal tab and enter the data from the completed general journal shown in Figure 13.19.

Date	Refer.	Acct. No.	Debit	Credit	Vendor/Customer
03/01/--	Balance	1105	21993.03		
03/01/--	Balance	1115	2352.12		Merchant Power Tools
03/01/--	Balance	1115	1230.35		Wisdom Industries
03/01/--	Balance	1115	1911.11		C B Industrial Tools
03/01/--	Balance	1115	769.99		Brockert Rentals
03/01/--	Balance	1130	14492.40		
03/01/--	Balance	1135	1913.76		
03/01/--	Balance	1150	1300.00		
03/01/--	Balance	1520	14091.00		
03/01/--	Balance	1530		2912.91	
03/01/--	Balance	1560	30351.30		
03/01/--	Balance	1565		5978.60	
03/01/--	Balance	2105		8005.41	Long Shore Tool Supplies
03/01/--	Balance	2105		13138.65	West Coast Tool Corp.
03/01/--	Balance	2105		1851.63	Folz Manufacturing, Inc.
03/01/--	Balance	2105		6569.33	Ellis Power Tools, Inc.
03/01/--	Balance	2120		4094.93	
03/01/--	Balance	2121		1066.00	
03/01/--	Balance	2122		574.07	
03/01/--	Balance	2125		3559.26	
03/01/--	Balance	2126		832.42	
03/01/--	Balance	2130		1700.90	
03/01/--	Balance	2135		229.63	
03/01/--	Balance	2140		1550.00	
03/01/--	Balance	2505		6100.00	
03/01/--	Balance	3105		24500.00	
03/01/--	Balance	3120		7741.32	

Figure 13.19
General Ledger
Opening
Balances

TUTORIAL PROBLEM 13 – T

STEP 13:   **Enter budget amounts.**
Click the *Other* toolbar button and enter the budget amounts shown in Figure 13.20.

Account Title	Budget
Total Revenue	1780000.00
Cost of Goods Sold	1350000.00
Advertising Expense	5750.00
Depr. Exp. -- Off. Eq.	3600.00
Depr. Exp. -- Wrhs. Eq.	4600.00
Insurance Expense	7800.00
Miscellaneous Expense	1500.00
Payroll Taxes Expense	15500.00
Rent Expense	30000.00
Salary Exp. -- Office	42000.00
Salary Exp. -- Wrhs.	32000.00
Supplies Expense	3750.00
Interest Income	2000.00
Interest Expense	5000.00
Federal Inc. Tax Expense	40000.00

Figure 13.20
Budget Amounts

STEP 14:   **Display a chart of accounts, vendor list, and customer list.**
Click the *Reports* toolbar button. Select and display the Chart of Accounts, Vendor List, and Customer List. Set the Run Date to March 1 of the current year. Examine each report in Figure 13.21 and verify that the data you entered is correct.

STEP 15:   **Display a trial balance, schedule of accounts payable, and schedule of accounts receivable.**
Choose *Ledger Reports* in the Report Selection window, select and display the trial balance, schedule of accounts payable, and schedule of accounts receivable reports. The reports appear in Figure 13.22.
Note: Check the debit and credit totals of the trial balance report to make sure they equal. Also, make sure the account balances in the Accounts Receivable and Accounts Payable accounts are equal to the totals shown on the respective schedules. If the trial balance is out of balance, or the Accounts Receivable and Accounts Payable account balances are not correct, it can be assumed that a keying error has been made and that corrections are necessary.

T U T O R I A L   P R O B L E M   1 3 – T

MCB Corporation
Chart of Accounts
03/01/--

Assets

1105 Cash
1115 Accounts Receivable
1130 Merchandise Inventory
1135 Supplies
1150 Prepaid Insurance
1520 Equipment—Office
1530 Accum. Dep.—Off. Eq.
1560 Warehouse Equipment
1565 Accum. Dep.—Wrhs. Eq.

Liabilities

2105 Accounts Payable
2110 Salaries Payable
2120 Emp. Inc. Tax Pay.—Fed.
2121 Emp. Inc. Tax Pay.—State
2122 Emp. Inc. Tax Pay.—City
2125 Social Security Tax Pay.
2126 Medicare Tax Payable
2130 Sales Tax Payable
2135 Unemp. Tax Pay.—Fed.
2140 Unemp. Tax Pay.—State
2150 Health Ins. Prem. Pay.
2160 Union Dues Payable
2170 Savings Bonds Payable
2505 Notes Payable

Stockholders' Equity

3105 Capital Stock
3120 Retained Earnings
3130 Cash Dividends
3135 Stock Dividends
3145 Income Summary

Revenue

4105 Sales
4110 Sales Discount
4115 Sales Ret. and Allow.

Cost

5105 Purchases
5110 Purchases Discount
5115 Purch. Ret. and Allow.

Figure 13.21
Chart of Accounts, Vendor List and Customer List

MCB Corporation
Chart of Accounts
03/01/--

Expenses

6105 Advertising Expense
6130 Depr. Exp.—Off. Eq.
6140 Depr. Exp.—Wrhs. Eq.
6150 Insurance Expense
6155 Miscellaneous Expense
6170 Payroll Taxes Expense
6180 Rent Expense
6195 Salary Exp.—Office
6197 Salary Exp.—Wrhs.
6200 Supplies Expense

Other Revenue

7110 Interest Income

Other Expense

8105 Interest Expense

Corporate Income Tax

9105 Federal Inc. Tax Expense

MCB Corporation
Vendor List
03/01/--

Vendor Name

Bruno Insurance Agency
Elam Development Co.
Ellis Power Tools, Inc.
Folz Manufacturing, Inc.
Long Shore Tool Supplies
Payroll Bank Account
Southern Utilities Co.
Talbot Advertising
West Coast Tool Corp.
Wilke Office Supplies

MCB Corporation
Customer List
03/01/--

Customer Name

Brockert Rentals
C B Industrial Tools
Deters Machinery
Merchant Power Tools
Scholz Hardware
Wilkens Power Machines
Wisdom Industries

**Figure 13.21—
Cont'd
Chart of
Accounts, Vendor
List and
Customer List**

TUTORIAL PROBLEM 13-T

MCB Corporation
Trial Balance
03/01/--

Acct. Number	Account Title	Debit	Credit
1105	Cash	21993.03	
1115	Accounts Receivable	6263.57	
1130	Merchandise Inventory	14492.40	
1135	Supplies	1913.76	
1150	Prepaid Insurance	1300.00	
1520	Equipment—Office	14091.00	
1530	Accum. Dep.—Off. Eq.		2912.91
1560	Warehouse Equipment	30351.30	
1565	Accum. Dep.—Wrhs. Eq.		5978.60
2105	Accounts Payable		29565.02
2120	Emp. Inc. Tax Pay.—Fed.		4094.93
2121	Emp. Inc. Tax Pay.—State		1066.00
2122	Emp. Inc. Tax Pay.—City		574.07
2125	Social Security Tax Pay.		3559.26
2126	Medicare Tax Payable		832.42
2130	Sales Tax Payable		1700.90
2135	Unemp. Tax Pay.—Fed.		229.63
2140	Unemp. Tax Pay.—State		1550.00
2505	Notes Payable		6100.00
3105	Capital Stock		24500.00
3120	Retained Earnings		7741.32
	Totals	90405.06	90405.06

MCB Corporation
Schedule of Accounts Payable
03/01/--

Name	Balance
Ellis Power Tools, Inc.	6569.33
Folz Manufacturing, Inc.	1851.63
Long Shore Tool Supplies	8005.41
West Coast Tool Corp.	13138.65
Total	29565.02

MCB Corporation
Schedule of Accounts Receivable
03/01/--

Name	Balance
Brockert Rentals	769.99
C B Industrial Tools	1911.11
Merchant Power Tools	2352.12
Wisdom Industries	1230.35
Total	6263.57

Figure 13.22
Trial Balance, Schedule of Accounts Payable, and Schedule of Accounts Receivable

TUTORIAL   PROBLEM   13 - T

STEP 16:   **Create a special combination journal.**
MCB Corporation wants to use a combination journal to
enter all their transactions into the computer. (Note:
Some companies that do not have a large volume of
transactions prefer to journalize all transactions in a
single journal, called a combination or multi-column
journal.)
Click the *Custom* toolbar button. Click the *Journal
Wizard* tab, then select the *General Journal* option.
Click the *Next* button and create a sales credit column, a
cash debit column, and a cash credit column. The
completed journal is shown in Figure 13.23. Select the
General Journal from the Journal Entries window to
verify that your new combination journal is correct.
Notice that the opening balance data has been
automatically placed in the appropriate columns.

Date	Refer.	Acct. No.	Debit	Credit	Sales Credit	Cash Debit	Cash Credit	Vendor/Customer
03/01/--	Balance					21993.03		
03/01/--	Balance	1115	2352.12					Merchant Power Tools
03/01/--	Balance	1115	1230.35					Wisdom Industries
03/01/--	Balance	1115	1911.11					C B Industrial Tools
03/01/--	Balance	1115	769.99					Brockert Rentals
03/01/--	Balance	1130	14493.09					
03/01/--	Balance	1135	1913.76					

Figure 13.23
Journal Wizard Created Combination Column Journal

STEP 17:   **Enter the data to set up the plant assets.**
Click the *Accts.* toolbar button. Choose the *Plant Assets*
tab and enter the plant asset data shown in Figure
13.24.
Note: Asset numbers 100–199 are assigned to Office
Equipment, and asset numbers 200–299 are assigned to
Warehouse Equipment.

T U T O R I A L   P R O B L E M   1 3 – T

No.	Asset Name	Date Acquired	Use. Life	Original Cost	Salvage Value	Accum. Depr.	Depr. Exp.	Depr. Meth.	
110	Facsimile Machine	06/30/94	5	349.50	50.00	1530	6130	SL	▼
120	File Cabinet	11/30/95	10	625.00	75.00	1530	6130	SL	▼
130	Copy Machine	08/31/95	5	2695.00	250.00	1530	6130	SL	▼
140	Adeo Computer	05/31/94	5	9995.00	375.00	1530	6130	SL	▼
210	Delivery Van	10/01/94	10	8500.00	300.00	1565	6140	SL	▼
220	Yuki Computer	07/02/95	5	3895.00	200.00	1565	6140	SL	▼
230	Shelving	09/01/96	10	16995.00	1250.00	1565	6140	SL	▼

Figure 13.24
Plant Assets

STEP 18: **Display a plant assets report.**
Click the *Reports* toolbar button. Choose the *Plant Assets* option button from the Select a Report Group list and select the *Plant Assets List* report. Click *OK*. The report is shown in Figure 13.25.

```
                        MCB Corporation
                        Plant Assets List
                            03/01/--

---------------------------------------------------------------
                  Date      Depr.    Useful  Original  Salvage  Depr.
Asset             Acquired  Method   Life    Cost      Value    Accts
---------------------------------------------------------------
110 Facsimile Machine  06/30/94  SL      5       349.50    50.00    1530
                                                                    6130
120 File Cabinet       11/30/95  SL      10      625.00    75.00    1530
                                                                    6130
130 Copy Machine       08/31/95  SL      5       2695.00   250.00   1530
                                                                    6130
140 Adeo Computer      05/31/94  SL      5       9995.00   375.00   1530
                                                                    6130
210 Delivery Van       10/01/94  SL      10      8500.00   300.00   1565
                                                                    6140
220 Yuki Computer      07/02/95  SL      5       3895.00   200.00   1565
                                                                    6140
230 Shelving           09/01/96  SL      10      16995.00  1250.00  1565
                                                                    6140
                                                          -------
     Total Plant Assets                          43054.50
                                                          =======
```

Figure 13.25
Plant Assets Report

STEP 19: **Save the data.**
Click the *Save* toolbar button.

T U T O R I A L   P R O B L E M   1 3 - T

STEP 20:   **Set the City Tax rate to 2.0% in the payroll tax tables.**
Click the *Custom* toolbar button. Choose the *Tax Tables*
tab and enter 2.0 in the City Tax % text box. Click *OK*.
The completed tax table is shown in Figure 13.26.

Federal Tax Brackets:	Single Amount	Single Percent	Married Amount	Married Percent		Rates and Limits:	
	2625	15.000	6425	15.000		Soc. Sec. Rate	.062
	25450	28.000	44250	28.000		Soc. Sec. Limit	62700
	53725	31.000	89675	31.000		Medicare Rate	.0145
	122750	36.000	151850	36.000		Medicare Limit	9999999
	265200	39.600	267900	39.600		State W/H Allow.	650
State Tax Brackets:	Single Amount	Single Percent	Married Amount	Married Percent		Federal W/H Allow.	2550
		0.808		0.808		State Unemp. Rate	.054
	5000	1.615	5000	1.615		State Unemp. Limit	7000
	10000	3.230	10000	3.230		Fed. Unemp. Rate	.008
	15000	4.038	15000	4.038		Fed. Unemp. Limit	7000
	20000	4.845	20000	4.845		City Tax %	2

Figure 13.26
Tax Tables

STEP 21:   **Enter the employee data.**
Click the *Accts.* toolbar button. Choose the *Employees*
tab and enter the employee data shown in Figure 13.27.

No.	Employee Name	Address	City, State, Zip	Social Sec. No.	With. Allow.
110	Blades, Charles	3132 Shaw Dr.	Chicago, IL 60634-4030	576-89-3288	3
120	Mendez, Bella	8326 Highland Ave.	Chicago, IL 60636-7812	466-21-8976	1
130	Presnell, Maurice	59 Culver Ct.	Chicago, IL 60656-1916	645-89-1432	3
140	Trimble, Dennis	11682 Oakland Rd.	Chicago, IL 60639-5265	480-31-0415	1

Number Pay Per.	G.L. No.	Salary Amount	Hourly Rate	Piece Rate	Comm. %	Marital Status
12	6195	4575.00				Married ▼
12	6195	4800.00				Single ▼
12	6197		14.25			Married ▼
12	6197		14.25			Single ▼

Figure 13.27
Employees

TUTORIAL PROBLEM 13-T

STEP 22: **Enter and process the January payroll transactions.**
Click the *Other* toolbar button. Choose the *Payroll* tab and enter the January payroll transaction data shown in Figure 13.28. Have the computer calculate the withholding taxes.
Note: Be sure to enter the 01/31/-- payroll date when entering the payroll transactions, and start check numbering with check number 1235.

Date	Employee Name	Check No.	Salary	Reg. Hours	O.T. Hours	Pieces	Comm. Sales	Federal Tax
01/31/--	Blades, Charles	1235	4575.00					542.81
01/31/--	Mendez, Bella	1236	4800.00					979.29
01/31/--	Presnell, Maurice	1237		176.00	2.50			208.28
01/31/--	Trimble, Dennis	1238		176.00				334.22

State Tax	City Tax	Social Security	Medicare	Health Insurance	Union Dues	Savings Bonds	Net Pay
182.13	91.50	283.65	66.34	125.00		200.00	3083.57
200.98	96.00	297.60	69.60	85.00		100.00	2971.53
75.86	51.23	158.81	37.14	125.00	10.00	50.00	1845.12
78.52	50.16	155.50	36.37	85.00	10.00	75.00	1683.23

Figure 13.28
January Payroll Transactions

STEP 23: **Enter and process the February payroll transactions.**
Enter the February payroll transaction data shown in Figure 13.29. Have the computer calculate the withholding taxes.
Note: Be sure to enter the 02/28/-- payroll date when entering the payroll transactions.

STEP 24: **Display the employee list.**
Click the *Reports* toolbar button. Choose the *Payroll Reports* option and select the Employee List report. Click *OK*. The report is shown in Figure 13.30.

One reason for the tremendous popularity of the World Wide Web has been the ease with which people can construct their own Web pages.

T U T O R I A L   P R O B L E M   1 3 – T

Date	Employee Name	Check No.	Salary	Reg. Hours	O.T. Hours	Pieces	Comm. Sales	Federal Tax
02/28/--	Blades, Charles	1239	4575.00					542.81
02/28/--	Mendez, Bella	1240	4800.00					979.29
02/28/--	Presnell, Maurice	1241		168.00	1.50			187.97
02/28/--	Trimble, Dennis	1242		168.00	3.00			320.26

State Tax	City Tax	Social Security	Medicare	Health Insurance	Union Dues	Savings Bonds	Net Pay
182.13	91.50	283.65	66.34	125.00		200.00	3083.57
200.98	96.00	297.60	69.60	85.00		100.00	2971.53
69.30	48.52	150.42	35.18	125.00	10.00	50.00	1749.67
76.10	49.16	152.40	35.64	85.00	10.00	75.00	1654.57

Figure 13.29
February Payroll Transactions

```
                            MCB Corporation
                            Employee List
                               03/01/--
-----------------------------------------------------------------------
Emp.   Employee            Soc. Sec./      # Pay   G.L.   Salary/    Piece Rate/
No.    Name/Address        Mar. Stat.      Periods Acct.  Rate       Commission
-----------------------------------------------------------------------

110    Blades, Charles     576-89-3288     12      6195   4575.00
       3132 Shaw Dr.       Married
       Chicago, IL 60634-4030   W/H 3

120    Mendez, Bella       466-21-8976     12      6195   4800.00
       8326 Highland Ave.  Single
       Chicago, IL 60636-7812   W/H 1

130    Presnell, Maurice   645-89-1432     12      6197
       59 Culver Ct.       Married
       Chicago, IL 60656-1916   W/H 3               14.25

140    Trimble, Dennis     480-31-0415     12      6197
       11682 Oakland Rd.   Single
       Chicago, IL 60639-5265   W/H 1               14.25
```

Figure 13.30
Employee List

> **STEP 25: Display the payroll report.**
> Choose the *Payroll Report,* then click *OK.* The payroll report is shown in Figure 13.31.

T U T O R I A L   P R O B L E M   1 3 - T

MCB Corporation
Payroll Report
03/01/--

		Current	Quarterly	Yearly
110-Blades, Charles	Gross Pay	4575.00	9150.00	9150.00
6195-Salary	Federal W/H	542.81	1085.62	1085.62
Married Acct. 6195	State W/H	182.13	364.26	364.26
W/H 3 576-89-3288	Soc. Sec. W/H	283.65	567.30	567.30
Pay Periods 12	Medicare W/H	66.34	132.68	132.68
Salary 4575.00	City Tax W/H	91.50	183.00	183.00
Hourly Rate	Health Insurance	125.00	250.00	250.00
Piece Rate	Union Dues			
Commission %	Savings Bonds	200.00	400.00	400.00
Check Number 1239				
Check Date 02/28/96	Net Pay	3083.57	6167.14	6167.14
120-Mendez, Bella	Gross Pay	4800.00	9600.00	9600.00
6195-Salary	Federal W/H	979.29	1958.58	1958.58
Single Acct. 6195	State W/H	200.98	401.96	401.96
W/H 1 466-21-8976	Soc. Sec. W/H	297.60	595.20	595.20
Pay Periods 12	Medicare W/H	69.60	139.20	139.20
Salary 4800.00	City Tax W/H	96.00	192.00	192.00
Hourly Rate	Health Insurance	85.00	170.00	170.00
Piece Rate	Union Dues			
Commission %	Savings Bonds	100.00	200.00	200.00
Check Number 1240				
Check Date 02/28/96	Net Pay	2971.53	5943.06	5943.06
130-Presnell, Maurice	Gross Pay	2426.06	4987.50	4987.50
6197-Salary	Federal W/H	187.97	396.25	396.25
Married Acct. 6197	State W/H	69.30	145.16	145.16
W/H 3 645-89-1432	Soc. Sec. W/H	150.42	309.23	309.23
Pay Periods 12	Medicare W/H	35.18	72.32	72.32
Salary	City Tax W/H	48.52	99.75	99.75
Hourly Rate 14.25	Health Insurance	125.00	250.00	250.00
Piece Rate	Union Dues	10.00	20.00	20.00
Commission %	Savings Bonds	50.00	100.00	100.00
Check Number 1241				
Check Date 02/28/96	Net Pay	1749.67	3594.79	3594.79
140-Trimble, Dennis	Gross Pay	2458.13	4966.13	4966.13
6197-Salary	Federal W/H	320.26	654.48	654.48
Single Acct. 6197	State W/H	76.10	154.62	154.62
W/H 1 480-31-0415	Soc. Sec. W/H	152.40	307.90	307.90
Pay Periods 12	Medicare W/H	35.64	72.01	72.01
Salary	City Tax W/H	49.16	99.32	99.32
Hourly Rate 14.25	Health Insurance	85.00	170.00	170.00
Piece Rate	Union Dues	10.00	20.00	20.00
Commission %	Savings Bonds	75.00	150.00	150.00
Check Number 1242				
Check Date 02/28/96	Net Pay	1654.57	3337.80	3337.80
Payroll Summary	Gross Pay	14259.19	28703.63	28703.63
	Federal W/H	2030.33	4094.93	4094.93
	State W/H	528.51	1066.00	1066.00
	Soc. Sec. W/H	884.07	1779.63	1779.63
	Medicare W/H	206.76	416.21	416.21
	City Tax W/H	285.18	574.07	574.07
	Health Insurance	420.00	840.00	840.00
	Union Dues	20.00	40.00	40.00
	Savings Bonds	425.00	850.00	850.00
	Net Pay	9459.34	19042.79	19042.79

Figure 13.31
Payroll Report

T U T O R I A L   P R O B L E M   1 3 – T

STEP 26:   **Save the data.**
Click the *Save* toolbar button.

STEP 27:   **Enter the inventory stock item data.**
Click the *Accts.* toolbar icon. Choose the *Inventory* tab and
enter the inventory stock items shown in Figure 13.32.

Stock No.	Description	Unit Meas.	Reorder Point	Retail Price
110	Air Hammer	EA	3	895.00
120	Band Saw	EA	10	39.95
130	Circular Electric Saw	EA	12	45.65
140	Cordless Drill	EA	12	49.95
150	Industrial Stapler	EA	10	39.95
160	M-7 Electric Drill	EA	12	45.00
170	Nail Gun	EA	5	68.75
180	Power Band Saw	EA	4	489.00
190	Table Circular Saw	EA	5	735.00

Figure 13.32
Inventory Stock
Items

STEP 28:   **Enter the Inventory historical opening balance data.**
Click the *Other* toolbar button. Choose the *Inventory*
tab and enter the inventory historical opening balance
data shown in Figure 13.33.
Warning: The average cost is calculated as a running
total. That is, it is adjusted each time a transaction is
entered. Therefore, making corrections or changing the
sequence in which transactions are entered may distort
the average cost. If you must make a correction to
opening balance historical data, it is a good idea to
delete all occurrences of the inventory transaction first,
then rekey each occurrence in the order presented.

Internet hosts use a language called TCP/IP,
Transmission Control Protocol/Internet
Protocol. TCP keeps track of every part of a
transmitted message or file; IP is like an address
label that makes sure a message or file reaches
the correct user.

T U T O R I A L   P R O B L E M   1 3 – T

Date	Inventory Item	Invoice No.	Quantity Sold	Selling Price	Quantity Ordered	Quantity Received	Cost Price
03/01/--	Air Hammer	Bal.	8	895.00	20	6	523.00
03/01/--	Air Hammer	Bal.				12	535.00
03/01/--	Band Saw	Bal.	21	39.95	40	40	22.50
03/01/--	Circular Electric Saw	Bal.	33	45.65	50	25	27.25
03/01/--	Circular Electric Saw	Bal.				25	25.00
03/01/--	Cordless Drill	Bal.	38	49.95	65	30	28.75
03/01/--	Cordless Drill	Bal.				30	29.95
03/01/--	Industrial Stapler	Bal.	19	39.95	36	36	24.00
03/01/--	M-7 Electric Drill	Bal.	26	45.00	35	35	27.00
03/01/--	Nail Gun	Bal.	16	68.75	25	12	41.25
03/01/--	Nail Gun	Bal.				10	40.00
03/01/--	Power Band Saw	Bal.	9	489.00	16	8	290.00
03/01/--	Power Band Saw	Bal.				8	295.00
03/01/--	Table Circular Saw	Bal.	11	735.00	22	10	440.00
03/01/--	Table Circular Saw	Bal.				12	425.00

Figure 13.33
Inventory Historical Opening Balance Data

STEP 29:   **Display an inventory list report.**
Click the *Reports* toolbar button. Choose *Inventory Reports* from the Select a Report Group list and select the *Inventory List* report. Click *OK*. The report appears in Figure 13.34.

MCB Corporation
Inventory List
03/01/--

Stock No.	Description	Unit Meas.	On Hand	On Order	Reorder Point	Average Cost	Last Cost	Retail Price
110	Air Hammer	EA	10	2	3	535.00	535.00	895.00
120	Band Saw	EA	19	0	10	22.50	22.50	39.95
130	Circular Electric Saw	EA	17	0	12	25.00	25.00	45.65
140	Cordless Drill	EA	22	5	12	29.95	29.95	49.95
150	Industrial Stapler	EA	17	0	10	24.00	24.00	39.95
160	M-7 Electric Drill	EA	9	0	12	27.00	27.00	45.00
170	Nail Gun	EA	6	3	5	40.00	40.00	68.75
180	Power Band Saw	EA	7	0	4	295.00	295.00	489.00
190	Table Circular Saw	EA	11	0	5	425.00	425.00	735.00

Figure 13.34
Inventory List Report

STEP 30:   **Display the average cost valuation report.**
Select the *Valuation (Average Cost)* report from the
Choose a Report to Display list and click *OK*. The report
appears in Figure 13.35.

MCB Corporation
Inventory Valuation (Average Cost)
03/01/--

Stock No.	Description	On Hand	Cost	Value At Cost	Retail Price	Value At Retail
110	Air Hammer	10	535.00	5350.00	895.00	8950.00
120	Band Saw	19	22.50	427.50	39.95	759.05
130	Circular Electric Saw	17	25.00	425.00	45.65	776.05
140	Cordless Drill	22	29.95	658.90	49.95	1098.90
150	Industrial Stapler	17	24.00	408.00	39.95	679.15
160	M-7 Electric Drill	9	27.00	243.00	45.00	405.00
170	Nail Gun	6	40.00	240.00	68.75	412.50
180	Power Band Saw	7	295.00	2065.00	489.00	3423.00
190	Table Circular Saw	11	425.00	4675.00	735.00	8085.00
	Total Inventory Value			14492.40		24588.65

Figure 13.35
Inventory Valuation (Average Cost) Report

STEP 31:   **Save your data.**
Click the *Save* toolbar button.

STEP 32:   **Calculate the annual retirement income using the
Retirement Planner.**
Click the *Tools* toolbar button. When the Planning Tools
window appears, click the *Retirement Plan* tab. Click the
Annual Retirement Income option button. Enter the
following retirement data, and display the retirement
schedule reports. The retirement schedule reports are
shown in Figure 13.36.

Beginning Retirement Savings $5000.00
Annual Yield (Percent) 8.25
Current Age 26
Retirement Age 65
Withdraw Until Age 85
Annual Contribution $2500.00

TUTORIAL   PROBLEM   13 – T

Retirement Savings Plan
03/01/--

Schedule of Contributions

Age	Annual Contribution	Annual Yield	Retirement Savings
(Beginning Balance)			5000.00
26	2500.00	412.50	7912.50
27	2500.00	652.78	11065.28
28	2500.00	912.89	14478.17
29	2500.00	1194.45	18172.62
30	2500.00	1499.24	22171.86
61	2500.00	44192.03	582352.97
62	2500.00	48044.12	632897.09
63	2500.00	52214.01	687611.10
64	2500.00	56727.92	746839.02

Schedule of Retirement Income

Age	Annual Income	Annual Yield	Savings Balance
(Retirement Savings)			746839.02
65	71582.26	55708.68	730965.44
66	71582.26	54399.11	713782.29
67	71582.26	52981.50	695181.53
68	71582.26	51446.94	675046.21
69	71582.26	49785.78	653249.73
70	71582.26	47987.57	629655.04
82	71582.26	10495.20	137709.78
83	71582.26	5455.52	71583.04
84	71583.04	.00	.00

Figure 13.36
Retirement Planner Schedules

STEP 33:   **End the *Automated Accounting* session.**
              Click the *Exit/Quit* toolbar button.

Applying Your Information Skills

I. MATCHING

Directions: In the *Working Papers,* write the letter of the appropriate term next to each definition.

a. New command
b. required accounts
c. journal wizard
d. accounts pick list
e. opening balances
f. budget
g. performance report

1. Accounts the software needs in order to prepare financial statements, to carry out integration among the systems, and to complete period-end closing tasks.

2. The general and subsidiary ledger balances at the beginning of the fiscal period.

3. A report that compares actual revenues and expenses with budgeted revenues and expenses in income statement format.

4. A command in the File menu that clears any existing data from memory in preparation for setting up a new accounting system.

5. A software feature that can be used to create special general, purchases, cash payments, sales, and cash receipts journals.

6. A financial plan for the future.

7. A preset master chart of accounts that may be used when adding to, creating, or updating a chart of accounts.

II. QUESTIONS

Directions: Write the answers to the following questions in the *Working Papers.*

1. The Income Statement option in the Company Info. window allows two settings. List the two settings and explain the difference between them.

2. How is the data collected in the Required Accounts window used?

3. What is the purpose of the Account Subtotals window?

4. What is the purpose of the Classify Accounts window?

5. Briefly describe the two methods that can be used to create quarterly and yearly historical data for payroll setup.

6. What is the purpose of the journal wizard?

7. What is the purpose of the Tax Tables window?

P Independent Practice Problem 13–P

In this problem, you will perform the accounting system setup for Star Chimney Sweep, a chimney cleaning service owned and operated by Julie Boyd. Star Chimney Sweep is a service business that is organized as a sole proprietorship, is not departmentalized, prepares checks manually, and generates the income statement by fiscal period. The trial balance, schedule of accounts payable, and schedule of accounts receivable for Star Chimney Sweep as of February 1 of the current year are provided as follows:

General Ledger Account Titles and Balances:

Account Number	Account Title	Debit	Credit
Current Assets			
1105	Cash	2040.96	
1115	Accounts Receivable	6460.00	
1125	Notes Receivable	1200.00	
1135	Supplies	215.00	
1150	Prepaid Insurance	250.00	
Plant Assets			
1500	Equipment—Cleaning	2182.00	
1510	Accum. Dep.—Cln. Eq.		654.60
1520	Equipment—Office	5085.00	
1530	Accum. Dep.—Off. Eq.		1678.05
Current Liabilities			
2105	Accounts Payable		1051.82
2130	Sales Tax Payable		
Long-Term Liabilities			
2505	Notes Payable		4500.00
Capital			
3110	Julie Boyd, Capital		9548.49
3120	Julie Boyd, Drawing		
3135	Income Summary		

Revenue

4105	Sales
4110	Sales Discount

Expenses

6105	Advertising Expense
6120	Depr. Exp.—Cln. Eq.
6130	Depr. Exp.—Off. Eq.
6145	Insurance Expense
6165	Rent Expense
6190	Telephone Expense
6200	Utilities Expense
6210	Vehicle Expense

Other Revenue

7110	Interest Income

Other Expense

8105	Interest Expense

Schedule of Accounts Payable:

Name	Balance
Boone Hardware	135.00
Garcia Auto Center	265.45
Mega Office Supply	151.37
Selak Advertising	500.00
Total	1051.82

Schedule of Accounts Receivable:

Name	Balance
Belle Retirement Center	490.00
Highland Hills Apts.	1950.00
John Maddox	85.00
Ruth Steinfield	85.00
Taylor Condo Assoc.	3850.00
Total	6460.00

STEP 1:   Start up *Automated Accounting 7.0.*

STEP 2:   Use the New command from the File menu to prepare
the computer for setup.

STEP 3:   Enter your name in the User Name text box and click
OK.

STEP 4:   Enter the data fields and set the check boxes and option buttons in the Customize Accounting System's Company Info. window.

STEP 5:   Use Save As to save your data with a file name of XXX13–P.

STEP 6:   Enter the chart of accounts data.

STEP 7:   Enter the vendors data.

STEP 8:   Enter the customers data.

STEP 9:   Verify account classification and extended account classification account number ranges.

STEP 10:   Verify the required accounts data.

STEP 11:   Enter the following account subtotals:

Total Current Assets
Total Plant Assets
Total Current Liabilities
Total Long-Term Liabilities

STEP 12:   Enter the opening balances from the trial balance, schedule of accounts payable, and schedule of accounts receivable shown at the beginning of this problem.

STEP 13:   Display a chart of accounts, vendor list, and customer list. Be certain to set the run date to February 1 of the current year.

STEP 14:   Display a trial balance, schedule of accounts payable, and schedule of accounts receivable.

STEP 15:   Display a balance sheet.

STEP 16:   Calculate the annual contribution toward retirement using the Retirement Planner.
           Select the Annual Contribution option in the Calculate section of the window, and then enter the following information:

Beginning Retirement Savings $25000.00
Annual Yield (Percent) 8.50
Current Age   32
Retirement Age   65
Withdraw Until Age   85
Annual Retirement Income $75000.00

STEP 17:   Create a special cash receipts journal.

Expand the current cash receipts journal to include Sales, Sales Tax Payable, and Sales Discount (similar to what you used in Chapters 7 and 9). Use the Cash Receipts Journal option of the journal wizard to create the expanded journal.

STEP 18: Save your data.

STEP 19: End your *Automated Accounting* session.

Applying Your Technology Skills 13–P

Directions: Using Independent Practice Problem 13–P, write the answers to the following questions in the *Working Papers*.

1. What is the total of the Credit column in the trial balance?

2. What is the balance in the Accounts Receivable account in the trial balance?

3. What is the balance in the Accounts Payable account in the trial balance?

4. What is the amount owed to Selak Advertising?

5. What is the total owed to all vendors?

6. What is the amount due from Highland Hills Apts.?

7. What is the amount due from all customers?

8. From the balance sheet, what are the total current assets?

9. From the balance sheet, what are the total plant assets?

10. From the Retirement Savings Planner, what is the annual contribution required for an annual income of $75,000.00?

11. What is the retirement savings balance at the time of retirement at age 65?

Mastery Problem 13–M

In this problem, you will set up the general ledger, plant assets, payroll, and inventory data for Cahill's Fan City. Cahill's Fan City is a merchandising business organized as a sole proprietorship, is not departmentalized, prepares checks manually, and generates the income statement by fiscal period. The trial balance, schedule of accounts

payable, schedule of accounts receivable, budget amounts, plant assets, payroll, and inventory data required to set up the opening balances as of January 1 of the current year are provided as follows:

General Ledger Account Titles and Balances:

Account Number	Account Title	Debit	Credit
A s s e t s			
1105	Cash	10792.84	
1115	Accounts Receivable	40815.49	
1120	Allow. for Uncoll. Accts.		
1130	Merchandise Inventory	26492.40	
1140	Supplies—Office	2450.00	
1145	Supplies—Wrhs.	1928.50	
1150	Prepaid Insurance	3300.00	
1520	Equipment—Office	20996.38	
1530	Accum. Dep.—Off. Eq.		9900.48
1560	Equipment—Warehouse	13953.45	
1565	Accum. Dep.—Wrhs. Eq.		8601.97
L i a b i l i t i e s			
2105	Accounts Payable		30508.41
2110	Salaries Payable		
2120	Emp. Inc. Tax Pay.—Fed.		
2121	Emp. Inc. Tax Pay.—State		
2122	Emp. Inc. Tax Pay.—City		
2125	Social Security Tax Pay.		
2126	Medicare Tax Payable		
2130	Sales Tax Payable		
2135	Unemp. Tax Pay.—Fed.		
2140	Unemp. Tax Pay.—State		
2150	Health Insurance Payable		
2160	Dental Insurance Payable		
2170	Credit Union Deduct. Pay.		
O w n e r ' s E q u i t y			
3110	Matthew Cahill, Capital		71718.20
3120	Matthew Cahill, Drawing		
3135	Income Summary		
R e v e n u e			
4105	Sales		
4110	Sales Discount		
4115	Sales Ret. and Allow.		
C o s t			
5105	Purchases		
5110	Purchases Discount		
5115	Purch. Ret. and Allow.		

Expenses

6105	Advertising Expense
6130	Depr. Exp.—Off. Eq.
6140	Depr. Exp.—Wrhs. Eq.
6150	Insurance Expense
6155	Miscellaneous Expense
6170	Payroll Taxes Expense
6180	Rent Expense
6195	Salary Exp.—Office
6197	Salary Exp.—Wrhs.
6215	Telephone Expense
6225	Utilities Expense

Schedule of Accounts Payable:

Name	Balance
Abbot Exhaust Fan Co.	3345.77
Air Control Fan Corp.	12475.00
Decor Ceiling Fans	4939.73
RC Industrial Fans, Inc.	9747.91
Total	30508.41

Schedule of Accounts Receivable:

Name	Balance
Carmen Lopez	1275.00
David Gilliam	1015.00
General Hospital	12808.15
Marlar Construction Co.	2190.00
Sagel Valley Motel	8387.34
Winsor Treatment Center	15140.00
Total	40815.49

Links are specially highlighted words or graphics on World Wide Web (WWW) documents. Attached to links are instructions to jump automatically to another selection of text either in the same document or in a new document on a distant computer.

Budget Amounts:

Account Title	Budget Amount
Total Revenue	$1,265,000.00
Cost of Goods Sold	925,000.00
Advertising Expense	5,200.00
Depr. Exp.—Off. Eq.	4,050.00
Depr. Exp.—Wrhs. Eq.	5,750.00
Insurance Expense	12,500.00
Miscellaneous Expense	2,500.00
Payroll Taxes Expense	22,000.00
Rent Expense	36,000.00
Salary Exp.—Office	52,000.00
Salary Exp.—Wrhs.	42,000.00
Telephone Expense	6,000.00
Utilities Expense	15,500.00

Plant Assets:

Asset No.	Asset Name	Date Acquired	Useful Life	Original Cost	Salvage Value	Accum. Deprec.	Deprec. Exp.	Deprec. Method
Office Equipment								
110	Copy Machine	03/21/94	6	2895.00	225.00	1530	6130	SL
120	Facsimile Machine	01/28/95	5	875.00	75.00	1530	6130	SL
130	File Cabinet	04/20/95	10	760.00	50.00	1530	6130	SL
140	Computer System	02/24/96	5	2695.00	250.00	1530	6130	SL
Warehouse Equipment								
210	Fork Lift	10/31/96	8	3895.00	450.00	1565	6140	SL
220	Shelving	09/30/95	10	11985.00	850.00	1565	6140	SL
230	Hydraulic Hoist	02/20/95	10	2145.00	200.00	1565	6140	SL

Employees:

No. Name Address, City/State	SS No.	W/H Allow.	No. Pay Periods	G.L. Acct.	Salary/ Rate	Mar. Stat.
210 Apland, Velma 5573 Beverly Dr. Newark, NJ 07112-2100	435–24–5449	3	26	6195	2300.00	Mar.
220 Brantley, James 7718 Western Dr. Newark, NJ 07106-5618	767–33–8092	1	26	6197	2250.00	Single
230 Lenox, Timothy 749 East Sharon Ave. Newark, NJ 07108-7335	587–45–4204	1	26	6197	12.25	Single
240 Maddux, Joyce 95 Fox Chase Ct. Newark, NJ 07107-4550	495–30–9083	2	26	6195	11.85	Mar.

Note: Because the payroll system is being established on the first day of a new calendar year, it is not necessary to establish current, quarter-to-date, or year-to-date opening balance data.

Inventory:

Stock Items

Stock No.	Description	Unit of Measure	Reorder Point	Retail Price
1010	Abbot Exhaust Fan	EA	30	185.00
1020	DX–10 Exhaust Fan	EA	35	99.99
2010	Air Control Fan	EA	28	318.00
2020	RC Attic Fan	EA	25	145.00
3010	Decor Ceiling Fan	EA	25	395.00
3020	Remote Control Fan	EA	18	229.00
3030	TWD Ceiling Fan	EA	30	185.00

Historical Data

Date mm/dd	Description	Quantity Sold	Selling Price	Quantity Ordered	Quantity Received	Cost Price
01/01	Abbot Exhaust Fan	58	185.00	85	40	100.00
01/01	Abbot Exhaust Fan				40	110.00
01/01	DX–10 Exhaust Fan	67	99.99	110	110	58.95
01/01	Air Control Fan	46	318.00	70	35	190.00
01/01	Air Control Fan				35	184.50
01/01	RC Attic Fan	46	145.00	75	75	85.95
01/01	Decor Ceiling Fan	53	395.00	80	35	228.00
01/01	Decor Ceiling Fan				45	237.00
01/01	Remote Control Fan	29	229.00	60	60	135.00
01/01	TWD Ceiling Fan	63	185.00	100	100	109.00

STEP 1:   Start up *Automated Accounting 7.0.*

STEP 2:   Use the New command from the File menu to prepare the computer for setup.

STEP 3:   Enter your name in the User Name text box.

STEP 4:   Enter the data fields, and set the check boxes and option buttons in the Customize Accounting System's Company Info. window. The payroll voluntary deductions are Health Insurance, Dental Insurance, and Credit Union.

STEP 5:   Use Save As to save your data with a file name of XX13–M.

STEP 6:   Enter the chart of accounts data.

STEP 7:   Enter the vendors data.

STEP 8:   Enter the customers data.

STEP 9:   Verify account classification and extended account classification number ranges.

STEP 10: Verify the required accounts data.

STEP 11: **Enter the following account subtotals:**

> Total Current Assets
> Total Plant Assets
> Total Current Liabilities
> Total Long-Term Liabilities

STEP 12: **Enter the opening balances from the trial balance, schedule of accounts payable, and schedule of accounts receivable shown at the beginning of this problem.**

STEP 13: **Enter budget amounts.**

STEP 14: **Display a chart of accounts, vendor list, and customer list.**

STEP 15: **Display a trial balance, schedule of accounts payable, and schedule of accounts receivable.**

STEP 16: **Create a special cash payments journal.**
Expand the current cash payments journal to include Purchases Discount. Use the Cash Payments Journal option of the journal wizard to create the expanded journal.

STEP 17: **Enter the plant assets.**

STEP 18: **Display the plant assets list report.**

STEP 19: **Save your data.**

STEP 20: **Enter the employee data.**

STEP 21: **Display the employee list.**

STEP 22: **Enter a 1.5% city tax rate in the payroll tax tables.**

STEP 23: **Save your data.**

STEP 24: **Enter the inventory stock items.**

STEP 25: **Enter the inventory opening balance historical data.**

STEP 26: **Display an inventory list report.**

STEP 27: **Display the average cost inventory valuation report.**

STEP 28: **Save your data.**

STEP 29: **Use the following data to calculate annual retirement income:**

> Beginning Retirement Savings $3000.00
> Annual Yield (Percent) 7.50
> Current Age 22
> Retirement Age 65
> Withdraw Until Age 85
> Annual Contribution $2400.00

STEP 30: **End the *Automated Accounting* session.**

Applying Your Technology Skills 13–M

Directions: Using Mastery Problem 13–M, write the answers to the following questions in the *Working Papers*.

General Ledger:

1. What is the total of the Credit column in the trial balance?

2. What is the balance in the Accounts Receivable account in the trial balance?

3. What is the balance in the Accounts Payable account in the trial balance?

4. What is the amount owed to Air Control Fan Co.?

5. What is the total owed to all vendors?

6. What is the amount due from Marlar Construction Co.?

7. What is the amount due from all customers?

8. List the column headings in the new cash payments journal.

Plant Assets:

9. What is the salvage value of Asset Number 120 (Facsimile Machine)?

10. On what date was Asset Number 230 (Hydraulic Hoist) acquired?

11. What is the total original cost of all assets?

Payroll:

12. What is the salary amount for James Brantley?

13. What is Timothy Lenox's hourly pay rate?

14. What is Joyce Maddux's address?

Inventory:

15. What is the average cost of an Abbot Exhaust Fan?

16. What is the total inventory value at cost?

17. What is the total inventory value at retail?

Retirement Planner:

18. What is the amount of the annual retirement income?

19. What is the retirement savings balance at the time of retirement at age 65?

ACCOUNTING CAREERS IN DEPTH

Mortgage Clerk

A mortgage clerk performs any combination of the following duties to process payments and maintain records of mortgage loans:

- Typing letters, forms, checks, and other documents used for collecting, disbursing, and recording mortgage principal, interest, and escrow account payments, using a computer.
- Answering customer questions regarding mortgage accounts and correcting records, using a computer.
- Examining documents such as deeds, assignments, and mortgages, to ensure compliance with escrow instructions, institution policy, and legal requirements.
- Recording the disbursement of funds to pay insurance and tax.
- Typing notices to the government, specifying changes to loan documents, such as a discharge of mortgage.
- Ordering property insurance policies to ensure protection against loss on mortgaged property.
- Entering data in a computer to generate tax and insurance premium payment notices to customers.

- Reviewing printouts of allocations for interest, principal, insurance, or tax payments to locate errors.
- Correcting errors, using a computer.

A mortgage clerk may also be responsible for calling or writing loan applicants to obtain information for bank officials.

Experience with high-school accounting would provide a good background for a job applicant interested in a mortgage clerk position. In addition, attention to detail is an important requirement in this type of job. The ability to effectively deal with the public in answering questions and gathering information would also be necessary.

A mortgage clerk may be designated according to the type of work that has been assigned—for example, Escrow Clerk, Foreclosure Clerk, Insurance Clerk, or Tax Clerk. Because there are so many loan institutions, a job applicant would have a relatively large field in which to search for work. Once a position has been secured, the experience gained on the job would be helpful when looking toward advancement opportunities in the industry.

A

Access Key
An underlined letter within a menu item that may be keyed to choose that menu item.

Account Maintenance
The process of keeping a business's chart of accounts up to date by adding new accounts, changing titles of existing accounts, and deleting inactive accounts.

Accounts Payable Ledger Report
A report that shows detailed journal entry activity by vendor.

Accounts Pick List
A preset master chart of accounts that may be used when adding to, creating, or updating a chart of accounts.

Accounts Receivable Ledger Report
A report that shows detailed journal entry activity by customer.

Adjusting Entries
Journal entries recorded to update general ledger accounts at the end of a fiscal period.

Asset Disposition
Removing an asset from use in the business.

Average Cost
The weighted-average of the purchase prices for a stock item.

Average Cost Inventory Valuation Method
A method to calculate ending inventory value by using the weighted-average of the purchase prices for all stock items on hand.

B

Balance Sheet
A financial statement that reports assets, liabilities, and owner's equities on a specific date.

Bank Reconciliation
The process whereby the bank statement is reconciled to the checkbook balance every month.

Board of Directors
A group elected by shareholders to manage a corporation.

Budget
A financial plan for the future.

C

Capital Stock
The total shares of ownership in a corporation.

Cash Payment
Any type of transaction involving payment of cash.

Cash Payments Journal
The special journal used to record cash payments transactions.

Cash Payments Journal Input Form
A form on which all cash payments may be recorded.

Cash Payments on Account
Cash disbursements that *do* affect Accounts Payable.

Cash Receipt
Any type of transaction involving the receipt of cash.

Cash Receipt on Account
A receipt that involves cash from a customer on account and

that *does* affect Accounts Receivable.

Cash Receipts Journal
A journal used to enter all cash receipts transactions.

Cash Receipts Journal Input Form
A form on which cash receipts transactions may be recorded.

Chart
A pictorial representation of data that can be produced by a computer and depicted on the screen and printer.

Check Box
A box located to the left of each of several choices that contains either a blank or a check mark and permits the user to select or deselect the choices.

Choose
To direct computer software to take an appropriate action.

Click
Quickly pressing and releasing the mouse button.

Clipboard
A temporary storage area where a report may be copied, then pasted into another software application such as a spreadsheet or word processor.

Command Button
A rectangular shaped figure containing a label that specifies an immediate action or response that will be taken by the software when the command button is chosen.

Component Percentage
Shows the percentage relationship between one financial statement item and the total that includes that item.

Computerized Sales Order Processing System
A system that comprises the procedures involved in preparing a sales invoice and automatically integrating the data it contains into the inventory and general ledger records.

Corporate Income Tax
The tax that corporations are required to pay on actual earnings.

Corporation
An organization that has many of the legal rights of an individual; however, it is typically owned by many people.

Credit Memorandum
The form prepared by a vendor showing the amount deducted for returns and allowances.

Customer
A business or individual to whom merchandise or services are sold.

Debit Memorandum
The form prepared by a customer showing the price deduction for returns and allowances.

Declaring a Dividend
The decision by a board of directors to distribute earnings to the shareholders.

Depreciation
An asset's reduction in value due to usage.

Depreciation Adjusting Entries
Journal entries recorded to update the Depreciation Expense and Accumulated Depreciation accounts at the end of the fiscal period.

Depreciation Schedule
The plant assets report that provides annual depreciation for each year for the life of an asset.

Direct Payment
A cash disbursement that does *not* affect Accounts Payable.

Direct Receipt
A cash receipt that does *not* affect Accounts Receivable.

Discount Period
The time period during which a deduction of the invoice amount may be taken.

Dividends
Earnings by a corporation, distributed to shareholders.

Double Click
Pointing to an object on the screen and clicking on the mouse button twice very rapidly, once to select the item (highlight the item) and once to choose it.

Drag
Pressing and holding down the mouse button and moving the mouse.

Drop-Down Menu
A list of menu items that displays immediately below the selected menu title.

Employee List Report
A payroll report that provides a complete listing of the employee payroll information.

FIFO Inventory Valuation Method
A method that calculates the ending inventory value by using the price of merchandise purchased first for all stock items on hand.

Focus
The location within a window in which the software will receive the next piece of input.

General Journal Input Form
A journal with two amount columns in which all kinds of entries can be recorded.

General Journal Report
A display or printout of the general journal that is useful in detecting errors and verifying the equality of debits and credits.

General Journal Tab
The tab within the Journal Entries window that is used to enter and post general journal entries and to make corrections to or delete existing journal entries.

General Ledger Report
A report that shows detailed journal entry activity by account.

Graph
A pictorial representation of data that can be produced by the computer and depicted on the screen and printer.

Grid Cells
An arrangement of rows and columns that is used to enter, edit, or delete data and text.

Hourly Rate
The amount paid to an employee per hour.

Income Statement
A financial statement that provides information about the net income or net loss of a business over a specific period of time.

Income Summary Account
An account used to summarize the closing entries for the revenue and expense accounts.

Input Forms
Forms used to organize and record accounting transaction data for entry.

Journal
A record of the debit and credit parts of each transaction recorded in date sequence.

Journal Wizard
A software tool that can be used to create special general, purchases, cash payments, sales, and cash receipts journals.

Last Cost Price
The price paid per unit for the most recent purchase of a stock item.

LIFO Inventory Valuation Method
A method that calculates the ending inventory value by using the price of merchandise purchased last for all stock items on hand.

Marital Status
Single or Married status for tax purposes.

Menu Bar
An on-screen element that shows titles of menus available.

Menu Item
A command that directs the computer to execute a particular action.

Menu Title
The name of the drop-down menu.

Merchandise
Goods purchased by a business for resale.

Merchandise Inventory
An account that shows the value of goods on hand for sale to customers.

Merchandising Business
A business that purchases and resells goods.

New Command
The command in the File menu that clears any existing data from memory in preparation for setting up a new accounting system.

Number of Pay Periods
The number of times an employee is paid per year.

Opening Balances
The general and subsidiary ledger balances at the beginning of the fiscal period.

Option Button
A selection method that represents a single choice within a set of mutually exclusive choices; also called a radio button.

Original Cost
All costs paid to make a plant asset usable to a business.

Partnership
A business that is owned by two or more persons.

Payroll Report
A report that provides employee earnings and withholding information for the month, quarter, and year.

Performance Report
A report that compares actual revenues and expenses with budgeted revenues and expenses in income statement format.

Period-End Closing
The process of recording and posting closing entries to the general ledger to prepare temporary accounts for a new fiscal period.

Plant Asset Maintenance
The process of adding, changing, and deleting assets.

Plant Assets
Assets used for a number of years in the operation of a business.

Plant Assets Input Form
A form on which additions, changes, and deletions to plant assets may be recorded.

Plant Assets List Report
A report that provides a complete detailed list of all plant assets owned by a business.

Point
Moving the pointer to a specific location on the screen.

Point and Click
Pointing to an object on the screen and clicking on the mouse button.

Post Closing Trial Balance
A trial balance that verifies debits equal credits in the general ledger accounts after closing entries are posted.

Posting
The process of updating the ledger accounts with all debits and credits affecting each account.

Purchase on Account
A transaction in which merchandise that is purchased is paid for at a later date.

Purchases

The account where the cost of merchandise purchased for resale is recorded.

Purchases Discount

From the buyer's point of view, a deduction for early payment of an invoice.

Purchases Journal

The special journal used to record the purchase of merchandise on account.

Purchases Journal Input Form

A form on which purchases of merchandise on account may be recorded.

Quantity on Hand

The quantity of a stock item that is included in the merchandise inventory at the present time.

Quantity on Order

The quantity of a stock item that is currently on order but has not yet arrived.

Quarterly Report

A payroll report that is used by a company to report Social Security and Medicare taxable wages to the Internal Revenue Service.

Reorder Point

The minimum quantity that is allowed before additional items must be reordered.

Required Accounts

In a computerized accounting system, the accounts that the software needs in order to prepare financial statements, to carry out integration among the systems (i.e., payroll, sales order processing), and to complete period-end closing tasks.

Retail Price

The current selling price per unit.

Retained Earnings

Earnings of a corporation that have not yet been distributed to shareholders.

Salary Amount

The gross amount paid for the employee's services each pay period.

Sales Discount

From the seller's point of view, a deduction for early payment of an invoice.

Sales Invoice

A form that is used to describe goods sold, their quantity, and their price and which is used as the source document for recording sales on account transactions.

Sales Invoices Input Form

A form used to record sales and sales return transactions when a computerized sales order processing system is used.

Sales Journal

A journal used to enter sales on account transactions.

Sales Journal Input Form
A form on which sales on account transactions may be recorded.

Sales Order Processing
A system that comprises the procedures and controls involved in preparing invoices, updating accounting records, and shipping merchandise.

Sales Return
A credit allowed a customer for the sales price of returned merchandise, resulting in a decrease in the vendor's accounts receivable.

Sales Transaction
A transaction in which merchandise is sold in exchange for another asset, usually money.

Salvage Value
The amount an owner expects to receive when a plant asset is removed from use. Another name for salvage value is trade-in value.

Schedule of Accounts Payable Report
A report that lists each vendor account balance and total balance due all vendors.

Schedule of Accounts Receivable Report
A report that lists each customer account balance and total amount due from all customers.

Select
To highlight a menu title on the menu bar or a menu item.

Selection List Box
A list of choices associated with a text box from which the user may choose.

Shareholders
Owners of stock.

Shares of Stock
Units into which the ownership of a corporation is divided.

Shortcut Key
A key combination that allows a menu item to be selected directly without accessing the drop-down menu.

Sole Proprietorship
A business owned by one person.

Statement of Account
A report that shows a customer's name and date, description and amount of each sales invoice, payments on account, and total amount due for that customer.

Statement of Owner's Equity
A financial statement that shows the changes to owner's equity during a fiscal period.

Stock Number
A unique code consisting of any four numbers or letters, assigned to each stock item for identification.

Tab Sequence
The logical order in which a software program expects the user to proceed.

Temporary Accounts
Accounts that accumulate information until it is transferred to the owner's capital account.

Text Box
A field into which the user keys information.

Title Bar
An on-screen element that identifies the contents of the window.

Toolbar
Provides a shortcut method of accessing the most commonly used menu items by clicking a button.

Tooltip
An explanation of a toolbar icon that occurs when the mouse is dragged over an icon.

Unit of Measure
A two-character abbreviation that describes how an item is sold.

Useful Life
The estimated amount of time an asset can be used in a business.

Vendor
A business from which merchandise is purchased or supplies and other assets are bought.

Voluntary Deductions
Employee-authorized withholdings from earnings for such options as health insurance, dental insurance, savings plans, and charitable contributions.

W-2 Statement
A report that summarizes an employee's taxable wages and various withholdings.

Window
A rectangular area of the screen in which the software is communicating with the user.

Withholding Allowances
The number of deductions from total earnings for each person legally supported by a taxpayer for tax purposes.

Yearly Dollars Sold
An accumulation of the dollar value of a stock item sold in the fiscal year.

Yearly Quantity Sold
An accumulation of the number of a stock item sold in the fiscal year.

Index

P